Europe
on 84¢ a day

Creda
   Thanks for everything
You were a great teacher.
   Hope you will hit
this 84¢ a day price
when traveling across
the Europe.
   Best wish

Feb. 29/96

Hey, I'm back...

....Due to popular demand, Europe on 84¢ a Day is alive and well, after a 15 year hiatus. Although the book has not been in print since 1981, my travel methods continue to be well-received on the college lecture circuit, and it is due to your requests at my lectures that I have decided to update my book. The book has been completely revised to meet the needs of young travelers who wish to watch their pennies, yet bring home the best memories and experiences possible.

....And, no, the title has not been changed to "Europe on 86¢ or 99¢ a Day". My ideas and methods are inflation-proof!! Take my book on your travels and good luck, and "bon voyage".

Europe
on 84¢ a day

GIL WHITE

GIL WHITE

This Book is Dedicated To...

All restless spirits and itchy feet.

To Europeans who restored my faith in mankind.

A special dedication to my Mother and Father who prepared many lunches 'to go', kept me up to date with news while abroad and who worried about me, despite my reassurances.

Special thanks go to Anne Marie Montgomery for her professionalism as an editor and for her invaluable criticism.
And to Tim, Dan, Frank and John who lent me their ears every time I returned from abroad.

And last but not least my beautiful wife Laurie and our two children, Zachary and Mackenzie who constantly interrupted my train of thought as I wrote my book.

This edition is dedicated especially to my father, John Douglas White who honed my writing skills and who passed away on August 9, 1995 at the age of 78. My father was a prisoner of war for five years during WWII and his strength and courage taught me to never give up and always do the best you can at whatever you do.
We will all miss you, love from us all.

My Thanks To...

many people whose generosity and hospitality enabled me to see some fascinating places and have some unusual experiences.

A few highlights:

A visit to the dressing room of a Russian hockey team, trading my sweatsuit
  with a player and watching the game from the bench
A Finnish love affair
French cows - the longest in the world
Bodiam Castle
The Moroccan students who took me to a university class
Walking into a Finnish classroom, and taking a class picture to prove all
young Scandinavians do have blonde hair & blue eyes
The dance floors of Europe
Skiing in Austria
A lecture to English high-school students
The fjords of Norway
Suntanning on top of a pyramid in Cairo
Watching a seven year old boy conduct part of a synagogue service in
  Jerusalem
The Berlin Wall
Bartending in Geneva and Paris
The Hungarian student who sang religous songs for me on Christmas eve
The Acropolis
The Colosseum
The canals of Amsterdam
The French television host who invited me to stay with her family in Paris
A non-visit to a Turkish prison
The Cote d'Azur
The countryside in England and Scotland
Slivovitz toasts with a Croatian peasant family
An unexpected visit to a Greek country wedding
The Holy Sepulchre
The Jordanian who poured oil on top of his Mercedes-Benz engine
Darts in an Irish pub
The ancient city carved from rock at Petra, Jordan
Sweden's beautiful blondes
Floating on the Dead Sea
Portuguese prostitutes hitch-hiking the highway
A German driver traveling at 180 kmh
Rocks falling on our car in Bulgarian tunnels
The art of Florence
Copenhagen's thousands of cyclists
Belgium... and a house of my own
The wild horses of Spain

Eating dinner on a cold stone floor with Muhammed Ali and his family in Jordan

...and some not so happy memories...

Romanian immigration officials, who wasted my time
Standing in the cold driving sleet in Croatia
The Algerian border officials who turned me away
Luxembourg's fog
The death of the postman on the boat ride from Egypt to Greece
Getting the potent Dead Sea salt water in my eyes, cleansing but painful

Attending a university class, Rabat, Morocco.

Contents

Contents for Each Country: A Little History; General Information: Money, Visas; Peculiar Customs and Expressions, Best Festivals, Night Activities and More, Must See Tourist Sights, Best Scenery, Bus, Cycling, Hitch-Hiking, Train, Camping, Youth Hostel Town Locations & Their Telephone Numbers, Work, Babysitting, Useful Addresses and Tourist Offices, Foreign Embassy Addresses in Canada, the U.S. & the U.K., American, Canadian and British Embassies in each country, Driving Distances, Telephoning Abroad

1.

Foreword: "84 Cents" - What is this book really all about?

As a long time world traveler and lecturer on college campuses I've found that my topic "Europe on 84¢ a Day", never fails to evoke amusement, amazement or disbelief. People think that I must have slept in ditches and fields, stood in soup lines, picked through garbage cans, and waited all day for a ride. But using the creative cost-saving methods outlined in this book, I was able to sleep in a bed with a roof over my head 99% of the time, eat at least two good meals a day--eating like a king and wait no more than 15 to 20 minutes for most rides.

I first wrote "Europe on 84¢ a Day" in 1981, based on the costs of a four-month trip I made that year. Some days I spent $.84, some days $10 and some days $0.00. I simply plucked "84 Cents" out of the air to get across the point that you don't need thousands of dollars to go to Europe or Australia for three or four months. And the title is as valid now as it was then. One can still travel and have a great time on next to nothing. It doesn't matter if you take my book along next year or in the year 2020, the basic concept will remain the same. The "84 Cents" is meant to fire your imagination.

I spent just under $1,000 on my 1981 journey, seeing 30 countries in four months, and including return airfare. Since then, the price of a cup of coffee may have doubled, the charge at youth hostels has gone up and the value of the dollar has gone down. Students now have a tougher time finding jobs to finance their travels. But all these factors make the ideas in this book more relevant than ever.

To take inflation into account, I've costed out some price changes in the table on page 2 to demonstrate what my 1981 trip would cost in 1995. Keep in mind, if you don't keep to an "84 Cent" budget, you will be coming home a lot sooner than planned.

You could cut $900 from the 1995 trip by eliminating the Finnish bus tour, the boat from Egypt to Greece, and certain visa charges. But even with inflation, if I went to Europe tomorrow, I'm confident I could bring the total costs of this journey down to $1,400.

30 countries in 4 months including return airfare in 1981, 1995

	4 months	
	1981	1995
Airfare-standby, New York-London & return	$370.00	$400.00
Food	$100.00	$200.00
Accommodation	$2.75	$8.50
Transportation: by boat from Alexandria to Athens	$75.00	$400.00
Twice across the English Channel and from Scotland to Ireland and return	$85.00	$200.00
One short train trip in Spain	$20.00	$40.00
Visas	$20.00	$220.00
Gifts	$50.00	$100.00
Souvenirs	$15.00	$30.00
Beer & other drinks	$35.00	$65.00
Finnish bus tour to St.Petersburg, Russia (4 days)	$110.00	$450.00
Miscellaneous- postage; admission fees; local buses; film, batteries	$100.00	$200.00
	$982.75	$2313.50

It would be unrealistic to expect most travelers to keep within such a small budget*. No two travelers walk the same path or spend the same amount every day. Your actual budget, using my methods, is likely to be more than $1,400 but less than $3,000, including air fare, for three to four months. You certainly don't need $5,000 many students believe will buy them a reasonably exciting time away from home in 1995, or the $10,000 they believe would allow them to have an even better time. The best time I had in Europe was during a five-week period in which I spent precisely $0.00 on the three major expenses: transportation, accommodation and food.

I found out there is no correlation between dollars spent and the degree of fun or types of experiences you have traveling. This book will show you how to be creative and resourceful and to make your trip the best experience of your life. And you can't do that by staying in tourist hotels, taking trains or driving rental cars the whole time. The best way to really experience another country and another culture is by spending time with the people who live there, traveling with them in their cars, staying in their homes or their college dorms, and accepting the quite incredible friendliness and hospitality that is there if you look for it.

Even if you use only some of my cost-saving methods, you can certainly travel for three to four months through as many as 25 countries in Europe, North Africa and the Middle East for between $2,000 and $3,000, plus air fare. And the more of my methods you try, the longer

2

you'll be able to stay and the more countries you'll be able to visit. By keeping to my "84 Cents" a Day budget on my first trip to Europe, I was able to travel an extra four to six weeks and visit 10 more countries than I had planned...and to get involved in far more interesting situations than I would have encountered on a more conventional trip.

The methods I describe for getting free or cheap accommodation, food and transport are fun, creative and legal. And they can be adapted for nearly any country in the world. I concentrate on Europe because I have found most students and new graduates go there for their first major trip overseas. And many go back again and again.

There are two basic attitudes that will enable you to keep your costs down and at the same time feel that you are paying your way. First, you must have a genuine interest in meeting people. Seeing the mountains, ruins and statues is wonderful, but after a while they will blur in your memory, their names mostly forgotten. You will never forget the people you get to know and especially those who open their homes to you. Second, you must be willing to repay the people who offer you hospitality, either by performing a small chore or leaving a small gift. This book does not advocate free-loading, mooching, stealing, altering or forging train passes. you don't have to risk sacrificing your integrity or tarnishing your country's image to travel on the ultra-cheap...

* And here's the "84 Cent" Challenge! If you spend under $1,000 on a journey similar to mine, write me a letter. I'll publish it in my next edition or I'll buy you an "84 Cent" lunch...or maybe both.

Playing tennis near Wimbledon, England.

3

2.

Some Traveler's Tales - Encouraging Examples

My first exposure to the travel bug was in 1973. My destination was Sydney, Australia, where koala bears and kangaroos abound, and boomerangs that you thought would never come back, clunk you on the head. Or so I thought as I contemplated leaving home on my own for the first time, 16 years old and beset with a few fears and a full measure of naivete and ignorance.

The object of that first trip wasn't travel. It was tennis. I'd had some success in junior tennis in Ontario, Canada. Since there were no indoor tennis facilities in my area I found taking a bus to Toronto every weekend, to play with my buddy Danny Whittaker, was not improving my game rapidly enough and for two years had been trying to talk my parents into letting me go to a warmer climate with a year long outdoor tennis season. California was my first choice, but they felt I'd be able to continue my education more easily in a Commonwealth country where the school system was closer to Ontario's. Australia seemed a good compromise. My dream to be a tennis pro was intense. Most parents would never allow their son or daughter to leave home at such a young age and I will always be grateful to my parents who had the courage to let me pursue my dreams.

Attention high school students: If you want to study abroad, try to convince your parents to allow you to go, even if only for one semester. The cost of food, clothing and other incidentals may be less than the costs you incur at home. Based on the standard of living in many areas, lower costs will help offset the costs for airfare, long distance phone calls, and housing. This cost rationale was one of the main reasons my parents felt they could afford to let me pursue my tennis dreams.

Aside from my tennis ambitions, at 16, I'd already concluded that ' life was too short not to be as interesting as possible'. The rather structured and predictable years in high school, to be followed by another four years of study, seemed decidedly less attractive as a means of learning more about life and myself than did a tennis career and the variety of experiences it seemed to promise.

Not that I gave up school. In fact, while improving my game, I attended five high schools and three universities in three countries, so I didn't really escape the structured format of the educational system. But I certainly did, with that first trip to Australia, remove most of the predictability from my life.

Any apprehension I felt as the plane landed in Sydney, quickly dissipated, even though I was on the other side of the world with no one to meet me at the airport. I took a bus to downtown Sydney, stayed in a nice $3 hotel and called a number given to me by an Australian tennis player I had met in my home town. His parents told me to look for their other son, "a kid with red hair", at a tennis tournament the next day. After a few minutes of conversation, the red haired kid, Richard, took me completely by surprise by asking me to live with him and his parents. Their home sat on a cliff over-looking the Pacific Ocean a minute's walk from Sydney's famous Bondi Beach. While I was living with the family in Australia, their other son ended up living with my parents. This swap ended when their son returned home. I moved to a boarding house. The $27/week rent included three great meals a day. I settled into the new surroundings, made friends at school and on the tennis court, enjoyed learning to make my own decisions and found it all an invaluable learning experience. And although I saw little of Australia on that visit except for the Sydney area, and came home after a bout of homesickness after five months. Travel has been my passion ever since. And I learned several things, among them frugality. Before I left for Australia, I worked in a grocery store, raked leaves, and worked at the tennis club to earn as much money as possible. After an exciting 30 hour flight from Toronto to Sydney, and $800 later, I suddenly realized how fast one's hard earned money can disappear. At that precise moment, I learned the value of a dollar. In Australia, I supplemented my income by washing dishes four nights a week, I learned to manage my money, to be frugal and resourceful.

I also learned that traveling is a great education. Wanting to learn as much as I could about the world I live in, drove me to meet people and see as much as I could. Traveling convinced me, there are three basic educations in life - school, work and travel. At school or at work you have to work under certain conditions, rules or restrictions. You don't always have as much control or say over the situation as you might have as a traveler. While traveling, especially on your own, you learn much more about yourself in a short period than you could possibly learn during those years sitting behind a school or work desk. This is not to say you shouldn't travel with a friend, it's great to share the experiences, but you may find you become too dependent on

5

your friend. Every moment on your travels is an education in itself

Students who have traveled before going on to their careers tell me it was the best decision they ever made. After the first trip, whether it be a high school tour overseas or studying abroad, nearly every student will catch the 'travel bug' and will want to travel again at the next opportunity. You certainly mature faster and not only have a different appreciation of your own country, but understand, appreciate and respect the vast cultural differences that exist throughout the world. In North America, people sometimes have a narrow-minded, limited vision of the world around them. Travel bridges this gap, the world becomes a smaller place. I must admit I did pick up a disease on my travels which I will have for the rest of my life. Luckily, it is not life-threatening. I dub it the 'Peter Jennings' disease. Traveling has affected me in such a positive way I have to rush home every night to watch the world news. I have a greater interest in the events of the world and its people, especially those that occur in countries where I have traveled.

The Advantages of Traveling Solo

The next year in San Diego, California, where I went to continue my tennis and my schooling I discovered hitch-hiking as a practical, cheap and high-interest way to travel. I also quickly learned the lesson that hitching on my own was faster than traveling with a friend. My room-mate, Hans, and I set out one day for Bakersfield, California to play in a tennis tournament. By car the trip should take about three and a half hours, hitching no more than five or six, allowing two hours just to get through Los Angeles. We were hoping that our neat appearance and our tennis racquets would open car doors to us, but the rides came in spits and spurts and, it turned out, more spit than spurt. Eight hours later, in drenching rain, the lights of Los Angeles were finally in view. As in any city, hitch-hiking at night was slow and frustrating. Drivers are reluctant to stop for one silhouette in the dark, let alone two. Shortly before midnight, however, a driver finally lifted our soaked spirits and found us a shelter out of the rain at an all-night diner. We were finally out of L.A. But we could drink only so much coffee and if we were to play our first tennis match in nine hours time, we needed some sleep. Doing our best to be inconspicuous, we opened our books on our laps, pretended to read, and dozed sitting up.

What we had hoped would be a quick trip to Bakersfield turned out to be a 19-hour ordeal. We arrived at the tournament on time but minus sleep; both of us lost our first matches. The lesson I learned was hitch alone as much as possible and never in the dark.

The Over-Crowded Jail Cell

I returned home from California to

do my last year of high school and decided I'd like to follow the crowd to Fort Lauderdale during the Christmas holidays. I was all set to hitch-hike south but my parents gave me a one-way ticket for a Christmas present. I took $150 with me, determined to live as cheaply as possible and have the greatest time possible.

After one week in a hotel at a cost of $30 a night, I realized that I wouldn't last the three weeks unless I changed my spending pattern. Sleeping on the beach is illegal, but as I walked from the beach to my hotel each day I noticed a huge house with a sprawling backyard enclosed by a five-foot wall. There were no signs of life as the week passed, so I surmised the residents were spending their Christmas elsewhere. Why, I wondered, couldn't I sleep at the far end of the yard without disturbing the property or the neighbors? And so I did, arriving late each night and rising with the sun. It lasted ten days. I had been setting my alarm clock so I could leave early enough to avoid detection, but the ding-a-ling of the clock had evidently alerted a neighbor who complained to the gardener of the premises. The gardener seemed quite sympathetic to my situation, but told me it would be best if I found other sleeping arrangements.

That night, the drummer of a local band invited me to a party at his home and said I could crash there for the night. Somewhat timid about accepting hospitality from strangers at this point, I declined politely, got

a ride back to the beach, found a nearby hedge and, hoping the police who patrolled the beach wouldn't stray that far afield, slipped into my sleeping bag and went to sleep.

Unfortunately, a policewoman spotted my toes an hour before my alarm was to go off. Groggily, I found myself being led into a paddy wagon. I knew I hadn't committed any serious offence and wasn't too worried about the outcome, but after a few minutes in the wagon, I wasn't so sure. The other two men in the wagon had been picked up for the same offence as I had, but one of them was frantically trying to dispose of drugs. Fearing he would plant them on me, I tucked myself into a corner.

At the jail, I was shuttled into a cell with 26 others. There was an 80-year old man driving without insurance, a few junkies, six other people arrested for sleeping outdoors, some thieves, a teacher caught walking along the beach with a near-empty beer cup. An interesting bunch, but I was glad I wasn't staying long...I'd been told I would be going before the judge that afternoon.

In another hour, the cell was bursting at the seams with a continuing flow of customers. I was told I wouldn't get to see the judge until the following morning...30 hours, as it turned out, and not without incident. There were 16 bunks and if you were lucky enough to get one, or a foam mattress on the floor, you still weren't guaranteed much sleep. The inmates watched TV and played cards. One man, perhaps unhinged by his captivity, erupted in a rage and was put in solitary confinement across the hall. His screams prevented any further sleep. The next day another cellmate, unhappy with his meals, threw a tray of food at a guard and was ushered off to another solitary cell.

The arrival of a prisoner who was quickly nicknamed Pig Pen provided some diversion. His odor was so objectionable that some of the inmates forced him to sit in the corner on the open toilet. At shower time, he was thrown in to rinse off not once, but twice, but to little avail. The problem remained. In desperation he was sandwiched between two mattresses in the hope that the fabric would block the stench. It seemed to help and he uncomplainingly went off to sleep.

Finally I was taken to court, with 50 others. Ten of us were called before the judge for the offence known as "sleeping out in the open". I was $8 short of the $27 fine and my explanation failed to arouse any sympathy from the judge. On the way back to my cell I had the traditional single phone call. The only number I had belonged to a total stranger, given to me by a friend who was staying there for the holidays. My friend was out but when I explained my predicament, his host agreed to bring the necessary money. I was extremely grateful to him and relieved to be out. In retrospect it was another learning experience, an inside look at the American system of justice, but one I recommend you skip if you can.

The very next learning experience, later that day, taught me the importance of safe-guarding personal possessions while on the road. My wallet was stolen, or lost, on the beach.

I now had no choice but to start hitch-hiking home. My first ride took me from Fort Lauderdale all the way to Lansing, Michigan. My second one into Detroit at midnight... a somewhat daunting prospect. But the third ride was from two guys who were simply driving around the city with nothing to do . They said they would take me across the border to the highway on the Canadian side, then rather than drop me off in the dark of night they decided to take me to the first gas station along the highway which turned out to be 120 miles down the road outside London, Ontario. At the restaurant at 3 a.m. the two men said they would take me all the way home, another 100 miles . They took me right to my doorstep in St.Catharines, declined my invitation to sleep in our home and proceeded to drive to Niagara Falls to see the spectacular Niagara Falls for the first time. I arrived home as quickly as most people would have done driving all the way from Florida in their own cars.

Central America or Bust

By this time, my traveling experiences had been so rewarding and I was in such a funk about my tennis that I was encouraged to travel further and, only three weeks after returning from Florida, I decided to trade the rest of my final year at high school for a trip to Central America. I withdrew the last $600 from my bank account and set out in January, 1976.

The most difficult leg of the trip came early on. I was hoping to go south of the Great Lakes on my way west to Vancouver, British Columbia, but the U.S. immigration authorities at Fort Erie-Buffalo and Windsor-Detroit both turned me back. Hitch-hiking, they informed me, was illegal in the United States, which is not true. As long as you stand on the highway entrance ramps before you get to the signs that forbid pedestrians, horses and other non-motorized forms of transportation, then you are not breaking any laws. What the U.S. immigration officials were really trying to do, I believe, is keep one more illegal alien from entering their country and getting a job. When crossing borders, however, especially in North America, don't say you are going to hitch-hike. Cross borders with a friend in a car, by bus, train or by air.

In the second attempt, at Detroit, I tried to convince the border officials I was just going to see a basketball game but they searched my backpack more thoroughly than I'd expected and came up with my maps of Mexico and Central America. I was a little naive at the time to think I could fool the immigration officials. If I had had an onward ticket or return ticket on a bus or plane I wouldn't have been turned away. A backpack always

sets you apart from the typical tourist. So it was back to the Canadian route around the Great Lakes, a chilling prospect in midwinter.

Although the hike north of Lake Superior was cold. I experienced no serious problems. The worst was a night spent at a gas station trying to get a ride from scores of truck drivers, who are often forbidden by company policy to take on passengers, though many do break this rule. Just outside Winnipeg, Manitoba, two days later, I was stranded on a highway, shivering in the wind and wondering if the drivers who had warned me I would be committing suicide might be right after all. Then a moving van picked me up and took me right across the prairies to Calgary.

Another two nights sleeping in the cold in a schoolyard at Jasper, Alberta, provided another test of hardiness. I tried to flop on the firehouse floor but was turned down. The ground was frozen, of course, and I couldn't pound my tent pegs in, so I wrapped the tent around me and woke in the morning damp from condensation.

Next came the weirdest ride of the 2,000 or so I've had during my traveling days. Traveling through the Rocky Mountains, I was picked up by a group of some rather eccentric religious persuasion, who preached at the top of their lungs for two long hours hoping that God would see us safely through the mountains. When we stopped at a restaurant, the driver, upset that there were no religious tunes on the

9

juke box, formed a cross with two French fries, held it up in the air for everyone to see, poured ketchup over it, and chanted "This is from the blood of the Lamb," then doused them with coffee and put the fries in a bag to eat on the way to Vancouver. I felt a couple of 'coffeed French fries ' wouldn't harm me so I went along with his antics. Many young people who have never traveled much would have taken the first opportunity to thank these people for the ride and find another one. And understandably so. But you will find on your travels that you are constantly assessing the character of people who give you rides or offer you a place to stay. Of course, you do this for your own safety. You will learn to assess every encounter on an individual basis. In this case I felt these people were unusual but harmless.

Figuring a few offbeat sermons were a small price to pay for a warm spot in a car, I stuck it out. Just as I thought we were finally arriving in Vancouver, we made a sudden detour to see a friend of the driver and wound up having a midnight tour of his pig farm. I look back at this encounter as one of the most unusual experiences I have ever had on my travels.

After three days in Vancouver, it was time for a third attempt at crossing the American border. This time a friend agreed to drive me across. I emptied my backpack into his two empty suitcases to avoid questions about the purpose of my visit in the U.S. We crossed the border with no problems and stopped in Bellingham, Washington, where he bought some clothes to fill the suitcases and thus avoid any awkward questions about empty luggage on his return engagement with border officials. After many thanks, I was back on the road.

The trip down the west coast of the U.S. was rich in experiences. I took an interest in the drivers and in the people who put me up for the night, and kept my eyes and ears open for interesting things to see and do. I felt it was my responsibility to initiate conversations with the drivers, to put them at ease, to show an interest in people and in my surroundings. It was an attitude which made for interesting travel and brought many invitations into people's homes. The main goal of hitch-hiking is to save you transportation dollars and to get to your planned destination. Getting a ride is often the most you can hope to achieve. But if drivers are friendly enough to offer you food or a place to stay, it often results in experiences more rewarding than a visit to a pig farm with a religious fanatic.

In this spirit I got involved in such things as climbing Mount Rainer, walking 10 miles through a downpour and then running another eight through Olympic National Park to deliver mail for an archaeological expedition at an Indian excavation site, skiing Mount Hood; playing table tennis with one host and basketball with another; walking through the redwood forests; and playing the slot machines in Reno. Then there was the tour of the Hearst

10

castle; the spectacular drive along the California coast; attending two Johnny Carson shows and almost getting on the Hollywood Squares game show; borrowing a bicycle from a student at UCLA to cycle the canyons of Beverly Hills; attending university parties, sneaking my way onto the set of a western movie (deserted except for myself) and ... one of the most interesting experiences of my travels in the U.S.... a day at one of the most celebrated trials of the century.

I was staying with students at the University of California at Berkeley and when they told me it was possible to attend a session of the Patty Hearst trial if I was willing to stand in line, I set off at 1 a.m. to join the queue. People were stretched out on the sidewalk outside the Federal Building in sleeping bags. I was the 110th name on the roll call list which those waiting had to sign, and since only 30 people were allowed in for a session, it didn't look promising. I had to report back every three hours or be scratched off the list. The fellow ahead of me on the list had discovered a good place to sleep while we waited, though. It was a huge armoury housing supplies for earthquake victims in Guatemala.

Finally, the next day, after submitting to a body search for weapons, my turn came. Unfortunately, the lack of sleep over the few days took its toll...only sheer willpower kept my eyes open... and intermittently, at that....to see the kidnapped heiress on the stand with F. Lee Bailey questioning her about her involvement in her captors' bank robbery.

The next stop was San Diego where, with some old tennis and high school friends, I went to visit the famous zoo, and had an encounter of sorts with Dick Van Dyke, one of my favourite comedians. I spotted him strolling into the woods. As he saw me approach determined to get an autograph, he started to walk away. His walk then became a trot, so I decided to give chase. He speeded up again and I found myself running full tilt after him. "Mr. Van Dyke," I shouted, "may I have your autograph?" He stopped in his tracks three feet ahead of me, turned around and with a blunt "No," headed off through the woods.

After crossing into Mexico, I "yacht-hiked" my way from Cabo San Lucas, Baja, California to "mainland" Mexico and took a harrowing bus ride through the mountains to Mexico City. Just leaving Mexico City was a challenge in itself. I wanted to take the subway to the furthest outskirts to save some time. Twice I was prevented by the subway workers from getting onto the subway simply because I had a backpack. I slipped past on my third attempt. It took me four hours to hitch-hike my way out of Mexico City with its population of 10 million, but when I finally got to the outskirts I got another one of those "miracle" rides. Three young Mexicans out for a drive asked me where I was going. I said "Acapulco", and without any hesi-

11

tation they took me all the way to my destination.

Perhaps it was the tequila on the way, but later that night, camping on the beach, I realized I had that well-known Mexican phenomenon, Montezuma's Revenge. The Acapulco police, reputed to be corrupt, had said I could camp out on the beach at my own risk. I had first pitched my tent on a grassy area amongst some bushes between two hotels, but I had to abandon this spot when an employee decided not to just water the bushes, but my tent as well. After one of my several dashes during the night to nearby bushes, the police approached me. Their main question: Did I have a wife? seemed odd at the time, but the next day I was told that if the answer had been "yes", the police might have attempted to rape her. How true that story was I never knew, but I was wary of the police there after other travelers told me tales of being fined $70 for relieving them selves on the beach, and of having a van thoroughly searched for no apparent reason.

Some days later my driver and I were stopped at a bridge blocked by a dumpload of sand. The workers told us it would be at least three hours before work would resume to clear the bridge, unless we wanted to pay $10 to cross. I picked up the shovel and started to move the sand myself. The Mexican workers watched for a few minutes, extremely amused, then pitched in and in 10 minutes we were on our way, toll-free.

In general, I found Mexicans, including most of the police, helpful. Californians had warned me about Mexico. I would be robbed, they said; my throat would be slit. There have been some nasty incidents in Mexico but, as is the case elsewhere, if you pay too much attention to tales of caution, especially from people who have never traveled, you'll never leave home. Judging the worth of the warnings and advice you get before traveling can be difficult. If you have doubts about the safety of your itinerary, my advice is to talk to as many travelers as you can who have actually been that way recently, and discount rumors and second or third-hand information.

I traveled with the attitude that you'll never know what you don't try to find out and even if success seems dubious, almost anything is worth a try. I should have applied this attitude through the rest of Central America, but I'd heard hitch-hiking there was not easy and when two Panamanians picked me up near the Guatemalan border and offered to take me all the way through to Panama, I accepted. Looking back, that was one of the longest single rides and biggest mistakes of my hitch-hiking days. Although we had a great time together, I saw very little of the countries we traveled through, aside from the roadside scenery.

The whole trip from Canada took three months and cost $300, plus another $300 for airfare from Panama City to Miami.

12

Hitching On A Schedule

In September, 1976, I was back in high school in Ontario. During the ll-day school break, the following March I decided to attempt a 10-city tour of the U.S. Some hitch-hikers will claim you can't hitch on a schedule, I proved you could.

The first day took me from Toronto to New Orleans in 27 hours...starting out at 3 p.m. (although I usually always try to start my day at sunrise to maximize the amount of daylight for getting rides) I arrived at the University of New Orleans early enough the next evening to arrange a free night's sleep and still have time to accept a student's invitation for a motorcycle trip through the French Quarter and a bit of Mardi Gras adventure.

The next day it was a short trip to Houston where I spent four hours at the Rice University dance-a-thon and got permission to sleep on a wrestling mat in the gym.

San Antonio was next and then a ten-hour ride across the heart of Texas to New Mexico State University in Las Cruces. The first student I approached agreed to let me sleep in his room for the night.

My driver the following day stopped at a campsite at Yuma, Arizona, an hour short of my day's planned destination: San Diego. But it gave me a chance to get up before dawn to photograph the sunrise over the spectacular sand dunes there. The same driver took me on the next morning and went out of his way to drop me at the Mexican border.

I spent two hours souvenir shopping in Tijuana and still managed to hitch my way to San Diego, play two hours of tennis with an old friend, who drove me out to the highway and pointed me in the direction of Los Angeles. I was now four days out of Toronto and right on the schedule I had set for myself.

The first driver who picked me up invited me into her home for spaghetti and the night in San Bernadino. In the morning I set out for Death Valley which, in March at least, is not as ominous as it sounds. The heat was about the same as it is on the beach on a warm summer's day, but the rides were infrequent. Senior citizens in their campers were reluctant to pick up a hitchhiker, even one with a smile and a tennis racquet. My first ride took me half-way to my destination, Las Vegas, and this was one day I really wanted to remain on schedule, so I could arrive in Vegas when it was at its glittering night-time best. I'd never expected to have to get down on my knees and beg for a ride but after a two-hour wait, decided to try it. A young couple drove me right to the university in Las Vegas and, once again, the first student approached set me up for the night and another invited me to tour the Vegas strip for an evening that was worthwhile.

The Hoover Dam was next on the list of things to see and then came the Grand Canyon. I rode in with a student who parked in a campsite. We spent a pleasant evening toasting marshmallows, sipping wine and talking to fellow campers.

After a cramped sleep in the back seat of the car I got up early and set out for a jaunt which proved to be almost beyond my capabilities. I was told that to walk all the way down into the Grand Canyon and back up would take all day and that would put me behind schedule. So I didn't walk. I ran the nine miles down the path and a mile along the shore of the Colorado River, stopping only briefly to take pictures. I continued the pace as I started back up, but after four miles succumbed to dizziness, the result of effort and altitude. People offered me salt tablets and water which helped me to run and walk the remaining five miles and reach the top before noon. The next two rides were, happily, in vans where I was able to stretch out and rest my weary muscles.

I got to Salt Lake City at midnight just as the dormitory lights were going out at Brigham Young University. A dorm counsellor decided to bend the rules about visitors and let me sleep in a spare bed. In the morning I was treated to a university breakfast and set out for Denver. The scenery on the way to this mile-high city was spectacular and at this time of year, with lots of ski bums on the road, there was little trouble getting rides. I finished a full seven days on the road at a university fraternity party dancing to music of the fifties and the sixties.

It seemed to be party season at the universities. There was another the next night at the university in

Lawrence, Kansas, after a day of chilly winds as I travelled across the state.

Chicago was next...another campus, another student host. I was treated to pea soup by two overly - philosophical philosophy students and added a University of Chicago T-shirt to my collection. The whole trip cost me $90; $40 of that was spent on university T-shirts.

Detroit now loomed as the only obstacle on the home-stretch. I'd been lucky last time I went through that city at night, getting a ride all the way home to St.Catharines. And this time again I got a ride with a generous driver who went out of his way to drive me right to the Detroit-Windsor border. The rest of the trip was fast and uneventful; I got a drive to my door and was back in good time for the first day of classes.

Switching Roles With My Driver

It must have been a vintage year for hitch-hiking in 1977. When I finished high school that summer I set out for Pensacola Junior College, in Florida, to take up a tennis scholarship, and it was on this journey that I got the biggest bonus yet--a 10 year old Thunderbird for $25. I was picked up by a former marine who had just dropped off his ex-wife in Michigan and couldn't afford, he said, to drive his car the rest of the way back to California and was about to abandon it. Now I had become the driver and he, the passenger. I dropped him off in Nashville, and after confirming that the car was not stolen, I drove the tennis team for a year and took a holiday from hitch-hiking.

Aside from a quick trip to New York City to watch the U.S. Tennis Open, my thumb had become decidedly rusty when I decided in the Fall of 1980 to interrupt my university studies and go traveling again.

The "84 Cent" Budget

Three weeks of planning and I was off on the adventure outlined in this book. I originally planned to go around the world and this was the reason why I went so quickly through Europe, planning to get across the Sahara while it was still relatively cool and through West Africa before the rainy season in the Spring. The best way to go through the Sahara has been traditionally been to go to Algiers, pay a truck driver approximately, $20-$30 and join the truck caravan. It is the safest way to ensure that you are not stranded in the desert. Always go with a group of truckers, for if any truck breaks down there is another trucker to help repair the broken down vehicle.

I stuck to my schedule fairly well until I was stonewalled at the Algerian border. The Canadian Embassy in Morocco had told me that other hitch-hikers had been turned back at the Algerian border. I was told I had to take a boat or a plane to Algeria, but rather than spend $300 or more, I decided to give it a try. The Algerians were having no hitch-hikers; I must, they

told me, have my own vehicle if I wanted to travel by highway through their country. They stamped "annuler" in my passport and walked me back to the Moroccan border. It was time, I decided, to break my trip and come home to commit to paper some of the experiences I'd had and lessons I'd learned.

The information given by Embassies, by the way, while often helpful, usually errs on the side of caution, though not always. The British Embassy in Amman, Jordan told me, for instance, that I would need $400 to cross into Israel. I didn't have that much, but decided to try anyway and got into Israel without having to even declare how much money I had. The Egyptian Embassy in Amman assured me that there would be no problem at all getting an Egyptian visa at the Israeli-Egyptian border, but it turned out to be not the simple procedure they'd promised. While enroute to the Egyptian border, the driver who had to drop me off, told me the border closed on Thursdays at 4 p.m. until Sunday. Desperate to get to the border on time, I broke my $.84 budget and wasted $5 on a harrowing taxi ride to the border. Arriving at the border with a few minutes to spare, I was turned away by the Egyptian officials.

When I finally did enter Egypt, I was unhappy at having to change the mandatory $200 into Egyptian money, when I intended to spend no more than $30 or so. The only way to convert the money back into foreign currency is to present a bank teller with a plane or boat ticket to a destination outside the country. This presented me with a problem, since I intended to try and work on a ferry to take care of passage out of the country. I solved the problem, though, by putting on my best all-purpose clothes and visiting the casino in the Hilton Hotel in Cairo. After three hours of approaching Americans and Arabs in three-piece suits, I finally found a sympathetic Australian ear. We completed a fair exchange without any loss of commission or service charges from the banks.

And I certainly didn't need that $200 in Egypt. One of the greatest experiences, climbing the Pyramids, was absolutely free, though illegal (and, it should be added, it can be dangerous; there have been falls). I was with two Americans I had met on a local bus. As we started to climb the pyramid, a security guard chased us urging us to come down. After we threw him a few coins he left us alone to continue our climb to the top. The view of Cairo and the other pyramids make the 15 minute climb well worth the effort. The top has room for four or five intrepid souls to lie down a while and sunbathe.

It was one of many experiences I had during this trip because I was always on the lookout for something new to see or do. I accepted an invitation to a synagogue service in Tel Aviv and, despite holding the book upside down, enjoyed watching a Bar Mitzvah service for the seven year old boy who conducted part of the service, and found the whole experience rewarding.

There were many others - floating on the Dead Sea: attending a funeral in my best clothes--and backpack; visiting the casino in Monte Carlo (wear dress clothes - no jeans); helping an Englishman move furniture for an hour and a half for $25 plus a meal, drinks and a very comfortable nights sleep on a stack of blankets inside the moving van; pausing alone in frigid temperatures to watch the moon rise over the mountains and glisten on a Norwegian fjord, the Croatian woman I spent the evening with as the dictionary acted as our interpreter... all are pleasant memories. In Morocco I sat in on an English class, one of the most unusual classroom scenes I have ever witnessed. It seems when the university professor asks a question the students compete to give an answer by yelling as loud as they can. I also sat in on a class in Turkey, and in England I gave a brief lesson on Canadian geography as the class happened to be discussing the Welland Canal which is the very area of the world that I am from. In Istanbul, I tried to visit a prison. After watching the movie 'Midnight Express' I was curious to compare the prison conditions in the movie with the actual conditions in the country. Sometimes on your travels you will find yourself becoming an investigative reporter. With my camera, tape recorder in hand, and my local host, who called himself 'Casanova', we were refused, with much laughter. In Monte Carlo, when my pants needed pressing, rather than shell out a much needed five dollars to have them ironed, I knocked at a door. The woman who answered ironed them for me and sent me off with bread and cheese. Doing things like this may require a little nerve, but it's easy to be enterprising when you have to survive on your own, especially if you are really low on travel money that could be used for more important costs. I sometimes felt a little foolish, but you will find it really doen't hurt to ask.

Although I had some worries about traveling in certain countries, particularly in Eastern Europe and the Middle East, I found my fears were totally unfounded and that political tensions rarely affect the traveler. More importantly, I found that regardless of the color of our skin and the different languages we all speak, we are all the same. Approaching people in any country with that attitude will go a long way in making your travels more meaningful.

Turkey or Syria might not strike you as the best countries for a hitch-hiker, but people there were as friendly as any I met on my trip. I found the distorted ideas I had of Turkey from watching "Midnight Express" were just not true.

The Russian Rendezvous

Russia is another country people can be dubious about visiting. Since I couldn't hitch-hike in what was known as the USSR in 1980, I had to join a tour group. There were only ten Finns on the bus who were going to Leningrad one month before Christmas to buy vodka and party until they couldn't stand up any more. Perhaps I had watched too many spy movies but for my first few hours in Leningrad (now St.Petersburg) I was sure I was being followed. I'd breathed a sigh of relief when I got through customs without anyone even opening up my backpack and challenging my possession of a tape-recorder. But when I got it out in my hotel room, fearful that the room might be bugged, I started off by saying (feeling rather foolish), "I'm just taping as I have been in every other country I visited, commenting about my observations as I travel."

Taking a small tape-recorder with you on your travels will enable you to record conversations in peoples' homes or the sounds on the street corners of a particular city at Christmas time. When you play them twenty years from now, it will seem like your trip was just yesterday. Besides taking a 35 millimetre camera and a journal-diary, take a small transistor radio for it is really interesting to hear our songs interpreted in another language and sometimes very poorly.

The scene in my hotel room seemed all very melodramatic until an hour later in the hotel lobby, a young Russian couple approached me, asked questions about my country, then asked if I would help either of them defect from their country.

We exchanged a Canadian pin for a Lenin pin; they seemed sincere; we agreed to meet later in the evening in the Intourist Hotel bar. Just then a man wearing a Canadian pin and apparently trying to pass himself off as a Canadian tourist came up to us, speaking in a thick Russian accent. He tried to make us take our respective pins back, and escorted the young couple away. I heard that, back then, people were either fined or put in jail for a day or two for making contact with foreigners. And they didn't turn up for the rendez-vous. Not that I could help them defect in any way, but this was a golden opportunity to find out, first-hand, what was so wrong with their society that they would want to leave their own country and go to the extreme of breaking up their marriage.

After the first day with the tour group, I asked the Finnish tour guide if I could see the city on my own. I really felt I could only absorb so many paintings and museums in one day and felt I could learn more about the Russian way of life if I walked the streets by myself. I am glad the tour guide finally gave in to my request, as I was approached by many Russians. My mop of curly hair was definitely an oddity in Russia; one lady on an elevator touched it to see if it was real. Another man wanted to buy some of the clothes right off my back. In order to keep him happy and to avoid raising any suspicion, we sat on a park bench, and I sold him the socks off my feet for one ruble.

The same day I attended two third division hockey games. All I had to do was mention 'Canada' in the arena and the coach from Kiev took me into the dressing room to meet his players. All the players thinking I was a professional hockey player, stood up. I'm not, so I had to play the part a little bit. I had taken my track suit from my university for the sole purpose of trading it with one of the players. Three players argued as to who would receive mine. We finally made the trade and I received a beautiful red warm-up suit, a puck, and a goalie stick. I ended up hitch-hiking for ten days in Europe with my backpack, my huge Canadian flag and a goalie stick. This was a great souvenir and in order to guarantee its safe passage back to Canada, I mailed it from Germany. It came home one year later. As if this 'trade' was not enough, the coaches allowed me to sit on the bench to watch the game. The police tried to take me away, but the players stood up for me. At the end of the game, players at ice level tried to obtain more clothes from me.

The hockey was excellent and the crowds considerably livelier than the controlled Russians we saw on TV during the famous Canadian-USSR hockey series in 1972. They whistled, clapped, cheered and booed with great exuberance, with perhaps the loudest contribution from soldiers who berated the ref-eree. Not to be out-done, the referee would reply with a scowl and a fin-ger for the crowd.

On the down side, the food in

Russia was terrible and the beer tasted like barbed wire. In the Intourist Hotel our passports were unnecessarily checked on different room levels by elderly ladies, employees who had nothing else better to do. Twice in one evening I had to switch room-mates because they came back to their rooms so utterly drunk that their snoring prevented me from getting to sleep.

The most traumatic experience of my travels came on the return trip to Finland when we stopped in a small town to do some shopping. I used the time instead to wander through the town, and seeing through a school window some students playing basketball, hoped to join them. The kids reacted as if they had never seen or met a foreigner before. After playing in my hiking boots for half an hour, when I decided to find my way back to the tour bus, waiting for us at the railway station, I suddenly discovered I was lost. With visions of remaining in Russia forever and because of the total language barrier, I dashed about making train noises and imitating the motions of a train until I found a soldier who understood. I rejoined the group with minutes to spare. One thing I found out for sure, is that "choo-choo" is a universal word!

These experiences are just a sample of the exciting moments I shared with people in Europe and other countries. In the following chapters you will read other experiences to illustrate a particular method that allowed me to save on transportation, accommodation, food and other monetary matters. It's all there waiting. The opportunity to meet interesting people, see ancient ruins and the great sights you've always longed to see, the chance as well to do some things you probably never thought you had the nerve to do.

You can take a semester off from school or a leave of absence from work to do what you really want to but may have put off for the worst of reasons. For myself, the best of my education so far has come not from school or from work but from travel.

Remember, look both ways before you cross the street.

3.

Can You Use This Book - Are You a 'Viking' or a 'Book Worm'?

Have you been passing up the opportunity to see the world because you thought you couldn't afford to travel? Are you undecided about which is the best form of transportation to use while traveling through various countries - should I take the train, bus, cycle, rent a car or even hitch-hike? Should I join a tour group? Which airline can give me the best possible airfare? What about accommodation, food, and the foreign money exchange? How can I control these costs? Or perhaps you're an experienced traveler or hitch-hiker, itching to go on your next trip, but feel you don't have the necessary funds to cover the costs of food and accommodation on an extended trip. Besides finding the lowest airfare possible, deciding on which form of land transportation to use to get from city to city may greatly affect how much money you will be able to allot for accommodation and food. Conversely, if you spend very little on accommodation, you will have funds available to allow you to take the train or bus more often, rather than be really adventurous and hitch and cycle most of the time. You may find that you are more adept at saving in one area of travel than another.

If you have never traveled before it's hard to know which methods and ideas are best suited for your personality. To help you decide I have divided travelers into two groups. The extroverted person I will dub as the 'Viking'. This person is adventurous, free-spirited and definitely not shy. This person would tend to hitch-hike or cycle, be willing to stay with complete strangers and actively and consistently find ways to keep costs to a minimum. The 'Viking' is not afraid to rough it, i.e. pitch a tent in the middle of nowhere, walk many miles a day, and survive at least one day a week on a huge loaf of bread, if necessary. This traveler may have already been on a trip overseas, studied or worked abroad.

Then, we have the introverted person I will dub the 'Book Worm'. This person probably still lives at home, has never ventured out of his or her province or state, and is a TV junkie. He or she would prefer to take the train , rent a car, stay in good hotels, and eat at McDonalds in Rome. The 'Book Worm' sticks to the main tourist sites, loves to shop and takes a credit card along.

Whether you are a 'Viking or Book Worm', or somewhere in between, my goal in this chapter and in the rest of this book, is to convince you that sticking to one form of travel, i.e. taking only the train and staying only in hotels would be one of the biggest mistakes on your travels. I recommend that first time travelers or 'Book Worms' on a two-month trip, use trains and buses and stay in youth hostels for the first three weeks, and then gradually start using my methods as you overcome culture shock and gain confidence. As you feel more comfortable about being away from home, you can't help becoming more adventurous and you will decide to cycle, hitch-hike and stay with strangers. As you slowly work your way up to the status of a 'Viking' traveler, you will find that you will be better able to control your costs. The more 'Viking' you become, the more opportunities you will have to learn more about the people and their culture and save money at the same time.

Sometimes the best times happen without any pre-planning. Don't let your travels be too predictable and too structured. 'Winging it' or 'freestyle traveling' will provide the most excitement and adventure.

Some Questions to Answer

Is this sort of travel for you? Whether you find it satisfying or not will depend to a great extent on you. Before you buy a backpack, ask yourself these questions:
• Do I enjoy the company of others and get along easily with strangers?
• Am I personable enough to initiate and carry on a conversation with the drivers I meet or the people who welcome me into their homes?
• Am I willing to do something in return for people who help me on my travels; wash the dishes, change a tire, etc?
• Am I open-minded enough to cope with a highly flexible schedule and itinerary?
• Do I have the energy and stamina to walk a few kilometres each day?
• Am I thrifty and resourceful enough to make a little money stretch a long way?
• Am I open-minded enough to accept the varied lifestyles I'll encounter at close range and to find it a valuable experience?

If you can answer 'yes' to these questions, you can start shopping for that backpack and looking at airline schedules. With an open mind and some ingenuity, you will find adventure, excitement and an incredibly rich experience, all for a minimum financial outlay.

You'll succeed if you look at a day on the road as you'd look at a day in the office or classroom and put the same enthusiasm and effort into it. You clock in at 8 a.m., arriving fresh and eager for an eventful day on the road. A motorist picks you up and your "assignment" for the day has started: to learn from the motorist all you can about the people of his country, their lives and customs, his opinions on world matters and his pet peeves. Even discussions about why Europeans may like or dislike Americans or Canadians. You can use this opportunity to set the record straight and leave your driver or host with a favourable impression of you and your country. I must admit I was like a kid in a candy shop every time a car stopped to pick me up because I knew, even with the language barrier, we were both going to have a great interest in learning more about each other. The language barrier made the ride even more exciting and eventful. Meanwhile, the scenery unfolds around you and you make mental notes on the color and life so foreign to you. You clock out for the day after arriving at your destination. Perhaps you locate the address given to you by a motorist during the day and find yourself sitting down with your host, maybe in a hot tub having a cool one, telling yourself : Now that was a day well spent.

Knocked on a door in the countryside of Germany,
stayed one night with our hosts.

4.

A New Dimension in Traveling: The Art of Getting Free Transportation

What kind of trip will you get for "84 Cents" a day? Here's a fairly typical week the author spent in Europe:

lst Day: Ride to Dover; ferry to Calais, using the crossing to line up a ride to Paris; guest for candlelight dinner and overnight with French TV host; evening motorcycle tour of Paris.

2nd Day: French-style breakfast with a bowl of coffee; leisurely tour of the sights of Paris; lunch at a typical cafe; a lively university party in the evening; overnight at an Asian ambassador's home.

3rd Day: Some difficulty waking up; find a good hitch-hiking spot; five rides to Luxembourg and lunch courtesy of my last driver, a salesman; a ride all the way to Geneva; another university party, bartending chores; crash in the student dormitory.

4th Day: Local bus to highway; nurse gives me a ride to Zurich, also 10 addresses of her friends to stay with in West Africa, volunteers to call a man whose name was given to me by a motorist in Finland; man is flying out of town that night, but arranges for me to stay at a hotel, dinner and breakfast included; evening at local bar.

5th Day: Walk to highway; three quick rides to ski slopes near Innsbruck, recommended by drivers; free balloon ride; locate the owner of the ski hill, who allows me to work for five hours on the ski hill in return for a tow ticket and ski equipment; tour guide puts me up in his hotel room--no charge; evening with a South African ski group who know how to party.

6th Day: Skiing, late afternoon ride into Innsbruck, good sleep in a police cell.

7th Day: Wake-up call at 6:30; foot of snow has fallen overnight, changes to rain as I ride into Vienna with an artist; quiet evening and interesting conversation in his studio; good sleep.

This is faster than many people will want to travel, but it does illustrate that you can travel just as quickly hitch-hiking as many others do on fast-paced guided tours.

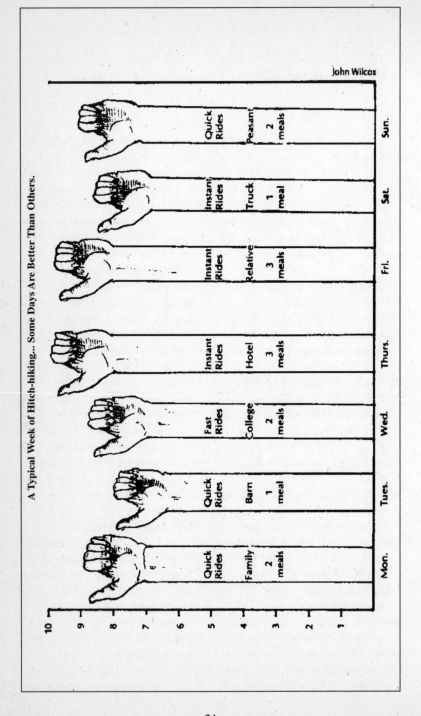

A Typical Week of Hitch-hiking... Some Days Are Better Than Others.

John Wilcox

	Mon.	Tues.	Wed.	Thurs.	Fri.	Sat.	Sun.
Rides	Quick Rides	Quick Rides	Fast Rides	Instant Rides	Instant Rides	Instant Rides	Quick Rides
Meals	Family 2 meals	Barn 1 meal	College 2 meals	Hotel 3 meals	Relative 3 meals	Truck 1 meal	Peasant 2 meals

24

So you can make the most of a short holiday if you want to, or travel at a more leisurely pace, spending time in places that particularly appeal to you. Whatever the rate at which you choose to travel, you will have little difficulty getting to your destinations.

Hitch-hiking is an increasingly popular form of travel for young people, more so in Europe than elsewhere in the world. Especially in the summer, the entrance ramps to the super-highways as well as the backroads of Europe are lined with backpackers and local young people. Hitch-hiking is even encouraged in many European countries. You can call 'ride' companies and have them arrange a ride to your destination for a small service fee. In Poland, drivers receive tickets from hitch-hikers; they turn these in at the end of the year to receive a gift from the govenment!! Given the fact that gasoline costs $3 to $7 a gallon, 75 cents a litre to $1.75 a litre (sold in litres) and the rising cost of all kinds of travel, the motorist who sees you along the entrance ramp will understand your reasons for seeking a ride. He realizes that you are a student and that it is very difficult to afford a car, pay for the gas, and pay for your tuition at the same time. Because of these high costs, students cycle and/or hitch-hike more than in North America. The driver has probably picked up hitch-hikers before and has also done it during his university days, wants to return the favor and is likely to be sympathetic.

Hitch-hiking has received unfair negative publicity because of misconceptions some Americans have, primarily linked to the crime rate in the U.S. It seems to be human nature to dwell on unfortunate incidents, but you never read about the person who had no problems on his travels - it doesn't sell newspapers. It is not as if every driver is thinking , "Well , the next student I see, I am going to kill him or mug him". Maybe a few people think that way in high crime areas, but people in general do not think that way, especially in Europe and other parts of the world. If you are ever in doubt about safety, common sense would suggest to you to take the bus or train. If you leave your troubles behind, guard your belongings a little more carefully, travel with an open-mind, you will have a wonderful trip.

I have had at least 2,000 rides throughout the world without one single incident where I was in any danger. Common sense prevailed each day as I learned how to handle people and cope with the situation at hand. I don't think luck had anything to do with my unblemished travel record. No offence intended, but people, especially guys who wear long hair past their shoulders with a touch of green, scruffy beards and with rings in their ears and noses, deal with drugs and look like they have the worst hangover are more apt to draw attention to themselves from the police. If that is your attitude, then you are more likely to be one of those people who wait all day for a single ride or the one we read about in the newspapers. Some of you may be muttering to yourself, ' I'll look the way and act the way I damn well please.' By looking presentable, you'll travel a lot faster by increasing the number and types of drivers that will pick you up, whether it be a salesman, campers, a nurse, or an elderly couple. With this image, you will get rides more quickly.

Keep in mind, securing rides in Europe, especially in high season (June-August) can be a challenge. The suggestions in this chapter aim to help you beat that competition.

First, give a little thought to why the motorist picks up hitch-hikers in general, and why he or she is likely to choose you in particular:

• He (or she) wants company to help him stay awake or to lessen the boredom of long hours of highway driving.
• He knows it's unpleasantly hot, cold or wet outside for the hitch-hiker.
• He's the Good Samaritan who feels an obligation to help anyone who needs assistance particularly the visitor to his country.
• He knows (presumably you don't) that hitch-hiking is forbidden on that particular highway, and wants to save you an encounter with the police.*
• He wants to add weight and stability to his car if the road is wet or icy.**

*As long as you are clean-cut, you don't carry any drugs, and your passport is in order, the worst the policeperson will do is tell you to go back to the entrance ramps of the highway to get rides where it is safer and within the law. Personally, I have never been hassled by police. They realize you probably don't know the hitch-hiking laws of the country, especially when the signs are in a foreign language. One great example of police hospitality was in Northern Ireland when the policeman actually flagged down a driver to give me a ride. Now you would never see that happening in North America! That's why I say people and even the police have different attitudes elsewhere in the world.

**An Austrian driver needed my weight to improve his ascent on the snowy mountain road. He made it clear he never picks up hitch-hikers but he was forced to make an exception.

He decides to pick you up, and not the other fellow because:

• You are well-groomed and neatly dressed. Many times I asked my driver, "Why did you pick me up and not the other person". Time and time again the reply was basically the same, "You look safe, clean, and you look like a student."
• You look like you want to go somewhere. Make eye contact with the driver to establish a sense of interest and trust. Don't wear sunglasses. Even though cars may be driving at 60 m.p.h. or 120 m.p.h. on the autobahn in Germany, eye contact will

be very helpful in getting a ride a lot sooner than later.

- You are carrying a national flag (approx. 4 feet by 6 feet), which arouses his interest.
- You're standing so that he can see you, not reading a newspaper or sitting on the grass soaking up the sun with your dog.
- And where he can conveniently stop. You have to think like the driver, asking yourself, 'Can he/ she pull over safely?'
- You are by yourself or half a male-female twosome. Two males with two big backpacks will have to wait longer for rides; cars are smaller in Europe. I recommend that you stand 100 yards apart. If a car stops for one of you, then ask the driver if he wouldn't mind taking along your friend as well.
- You have a minimum amount of luggage.
- Your driver wishes to practice his English. This is a great opportunity for the traveler to pick up words of the drivers language, picking up phonetics and accents for words helpful in your travels.
- You have a tennis racquet - this might suggest you need to get to a tennis tournament or at the very least, you are a sports minded person (can double as a weapon)

Not every day will be perfect, but if you follow these guidelines and some or all of the twenty-eight methods I will give you, you should plan on no more than 15-25 minutes between rides, which is shorter than waiting for a local city bus. Always allow an extra hour for every three hours of regular driving to compensate for any delays, especially if you are planning to reach your destination before the sun sets. Just realize the density of traffic varies from hour to hour and day to day. Hitching after dark, even if you stand under a light, can also mean a long wait. I don't recommend it and you will also miss the scenery.

Let's say you've been at an entrance ramp for five minutes and many cars are driving by and suddenly a car stops. Before you get in the car, ask the driver how far he or she is going.If it turns out the driver is only going five miles down the road, you should usually be patient and wait for a longer ride. You can only be this selective if there are many cars going by. But if you are at an entrance ramp with little traffic, you should take the five mile ride. Your driver may not be going all the way, but you may end up at a better hitch-hiking spot. Taking short rides will reduce frustration and boredom and you will meet more people and make more contacts on a daily basis.When you are trying to get a ride, you can use your map to indicate to your driver the destination or the direction in which you wish to go. If the driver mentions a destination that is not marked on the map, have him point out its location on the map to save any misunderstanding. This preliminary check also gives you time to size up the driver. I have never had to turn down a ride because of the way the driver looked or acted. Regardless of where your driver exits, there should be another entrance ramp where there might be more traffic than at the previous one.

It's perfectly possible, however, to observe all the above guidelines meticulously and still spend too many damp, chilly hours waiting for rides. Relieve the boredom or frustration by treating these as long walks, especially if you are on secondary roads. Hitch-hiking is a coined phrase , it means hitching rides and hiking (walking) along your route. Half the fun of hitch-hiking is exploring the countryside on foot. The greatest thing about hitch-hiking though, is undoubtedly the tremendous freedom you have. You can change your itinerary at a moment's notice. Or you can set yourself an itinerary and stick to it. Only four times during my trip through Europe did I fail to reach my intended destination for the day. I did trips London-Edinburgh, Copenhagen-Oslo, Oslo-Stockholm, Stockholm-Copenhagen, Florence-Monte Carlo, Vienna-Budapest, Istanbul-Ankara, Adana-Damascus, Paris-Barcelona (600 miles), each in a single day of hitch-hiking.

Your National, State or Provincial Flag

Every hitch-hiker has trademarks that identify him or her to the passing motorist. A smile or the color of your skin can affect the number of rides you get. But the greatest 'trademark' of all can be your national flag. Many hitch-hikers have small flags on their back-packs. These are only helpful on the city streets. Much more effective is a really good-sized flag, at least four feet by two-and-a-half feet, fluttering in the breeze, Attach one end of it to a sturdy stick and unfurl it every time you unfurl your thumb. When it's not in use, roll it up; it's a handy weapon for discouraging dogs from attacking your ankles.

The motorist will see the flag before he sees you. He may be well disposed to your country for any number of reasons: family or relatives there, visits he's made, good experiences picking up earlier hitch-hikers, wartime memories. He may be curious or he may simply think your outsize banner indicates a sense of humor. Once you get a ride, its a great way to 'break the ice' in the initial conversation.

I'd say my flag boosted the number of rides I got by 50 per cent. One Israeli by the Dead Sea said he always picked up Canadians. A remark that made me feel really proud to be from Canada.

Important Notice:

Many Americans ask me if they should tell people they are Canadian while traveling abroad. This is absolutely unnecessary, except perhaps in countries where the U.S. has severed diplomatic ties or had a significant military presence. I purposely did a test in many countries where I did not always show my big flag or tell people I was Canadian or American. I felt I was treated no differently than if I had identified my nationality. People generally cannot tell the difference between an American and a Canadian. Your success and how you are received by other people is much more dependent on your personality and how you come across. There will be occasions when you will find yourself having to defend your country in a bar or at a dinner table. This is an opportunity to rectify any misunderstandings and to set the record straight. But if you have told people you are from Canada, and you're not, then you will find it very difficult to answer questions about the country. Avoid placing yourself in an awkward position, be proud of your country and say where you are from. If you have reservations about this, you could take both American and Canadian flags with you, and see which one works best in each country. Better yet, take your state or provincial flag; drivers will definitely be curious to know where you are from.

Highway Hitch-Hiking - Location is Everything

Hitch-hiking on highways is just a way to get started. After your first ride of the day, you should use service centers and other methods outlined in this chapter as your preferred choices.

For long, fast rides the obvious place to be is on the entrance ramp to one of the multi-lane high-speed highways that crisscross Europe. To save yourself frustration, don't bother hitch-hiking in major cities; most people are just driving two or three miles to work and they will think it's not worth your while to pick you up. Spend three or four dollars for a bus or subway and take it to the outskirts of the city. You will find the expense to be money well spent. Once you are on the streets in the morning double or triple check your directions to the local bus or subway. Many European streets zig-zag in every direction. You may find yourself walking in the wrong direction, getting on the wrong bus, wasting time, money and energy. For the 'Book-Worm' traveler, verifying directions is a good way to get used to approaching strangers. Even with the language barrier, people will be very helpful. Try to avoid asking people your own age to verify your directions as they will often not be nearly as familiar as older people about the layout of the city. People in business suits usually have a better command of English than the ordinary citizen. This language disparity is particularly evident in Arab countries -so look for suits!

Timing is important. If you've spent the night in a city, ask your host the average driving time to your destination, the best bus or subway to take you as far out of the city as possible and how much time you should you allow to get from their home to the nearest highway entrance ramp. This will determine what time you should get up in the morning to get on your way. Personally, I wanted to make most of the day by arriving at the entrance ramp before sunrise. Having this information in advance will allow you to be more organized, make the most of the daylight hours and give you more confidence when you set out in the morning. By going over your map with your host you may also discover alternative routes to your destination that might be far more scenic and exciting than the major highway. Even though you're more likely to find a continuous flow of long-distance traffic on a major highway and travel faster, you won't have the opportunity to slow down or even walk through small towns, which will give you a special opportunity to get a better feel of the area and its people. You are more likely to discover tourist sites and other events taking place in the area.

If you are in a snowfall area, your motorist, signs and your map will indicate whether a particular mountain road or pass is closed for the winter. Be aware of weather conditions as certain mountain roads may be too hazardous to travel on. If you are uncertain about the conditions, check with the local police.

Position yourself on the entrance ramp, preferably on a straight stretch. If the entrance ramp is curved you will find motorists will be concentrating on the road and are not likely to see you soon enough. Cars tend to cut through the curve, so be sure to stand well over on the shoulder, well away from the path of the car and leaving room for the car to pull over safely. Also avoid standing just before a fork in the

road, where the motorist is deciding which way to go. Stand at least l00 yards beyond the fork. Also if the configuration of the roads is confusing, then walk further along the shoulder of the highway as far over as possible until you find the proper entrance ramp.

Also stand before the motorist gets to any signs that indicate hitch-hiking is illegal. As long as you stand before the sign and don't walk onto the shoulder of the highway, then you are within the law. In less populated parts of a country, you may find the traffic on the ramp is light and in this case I would walk along the shoulder of the highway to increase my chances of getting a ride, even if it is illegal. Police will probably ignore you. Police are human beings too; they realize you are a student traveling to see the world and as long as you don't look suspicious they will leave you alone. In Israel, one of the best countries for hitch-hiking, I found myself competing for a ride with the local soldiers and with my big Canadian flag, I was able to get a ride before they did. And I had only been there for three minutes.

Service Stations on the Highway

This is your best method of getting fast, frequent rides over long distances You can keep going all day, hopping from service station to service station. This method is especially important if you are heading towards a large city you want to bypass. Larger cities take more effort and time to get out of than smaller towns. You will save yourself a lot of time and aggravation, by asking your driver to drop you off at the last service center before his or her exit into the city. You will then be able to get rides from people who are going much further and can bypass the city.

Service stations are particularly suitable for female travelers because you can 'reverse the situation', you can approach people you would feel most comfortable traveling with, rather than always leaving it up to the drivers' discretion along the highway. You can approach motorists getting gas (it helps to get permission from the gas station attendant) or coming out of the restuarant. Both of you can get a close look at each other and the driver can decide whether you look like a safe and agreeable passenger. Simply tell them where you're from, where you're heading, be polite, and your chances will be very good. Service stations afford you shelter out of the rain, washroom facilities and even food, although at very inflated prices.

Using this method, I hitch-hiked from Paris to Barcelona in l0 hours. It took only four rides to cover l,000 kilometers (600 miles), scarcely longer than the motorist driving his own car non-stop. Twice when my drivers decided to take a 20 minute break, I was able to use the time to get other rides in less than five minutes. I always arranged to continue on with my original driver if I wasn't

able to get a ride by the time he finished his break.

Service Station Switch-Over

If you've developed good rapport with the motorist who is dropping you off at a service station, you can take the method above one step further. He will usually be quite willing to approach other drivers on your behalf to help you get your next ride. Since you've already proved to be a safe and pleasant company, the driver he approaches is more likely to take you on. This happened to me on a regular basis and often without any prompting. It goes to show you how friendly and trusting Europeans can be and it solves the language problem.

I started using this method after an Austrian truck driver, knowing I didn't speak German, voluntarily approached cars waiting in the lineup for petrol at a service station, and quickly got me a lift. It was the first of many such occasions.

Train Stop Switch-Over

Every once in a while, the car you're in will be delayed at a level crossing. If you know that the motorist you're with is not going much further, you should use the delay to find another driver in the lineup who can take you further. Tell your motorist what you're going to do and move quickly.

On a beautiful winter's day in Swe-

den, enroute to Denmark, I was engrossed in conversation with the driver when I noticed a car ahead with Danish licence plates. Shortly afterwards, waiting at a level crossing, I hopped out, spoke to the Danish driver, raced back for my backpack, said a quick thank you to my Swede, and was off to Denmark.

Accident Switch-Over

This is another opportunity to find a driver who's going further toward your destination than the one you're with.

In former Yugoslavia, which wasn't and still isn't a good hitch-hiking area and which also has a bad reputation for highway accidents, my driver and I came on a lineup of about 100 cars waiting to get by an accident. Even though my driver and I spoke not a word of each other's language, I managed to explain to him what I wanted to do. I took my backpack this time, and walked back along the line, asked about fifty motorists for a lift, while he approached the cars in front of us. When the traffic started to move, I was having no luck and wondering if this had been such a great idea after all, when a truck driver saw my predicament and signalled me to climb aboard.

"New Wave" Switch-Over

Ever picture yourself tooling down the highway at high speed carrying on a conversation, largely in sign language, with someone in another car beside you? That's the method I've dubbed "New Wave".

I was on a long run, hoping to get the ferry at Boulogne that day. We were in a comfortable French Citroen traveling at 120 k.p.h., enroute to Paris, a difficult city to get out of if you're hitch-hiking. Having been there previously, I did not want to get dropped off there. So when I saw a car with with a Great Britain sticker go by, I asked my driver if he would try to catch up, so I could find out if the British driver was heading around Paris for the ferry docks. My driver obliged, and soon the cars were speeding down the highway side by side at 150 k.p.h. I waved for the British driver to pull over, which he did; he followed right behind my driver into the rest area along the highway. No doubt he was confused, not sure if we were the police or something was wrong with his car. But he was happy to make the switch-over as he laughed about the motive and ingenuity of the method...and yes, he was going to Boulogne.

Toll Booths

Toll booths can be a hitch-hiker's best friend. Most countries will permit you to hitch at the entrance to toll roads (Italy being an exception). Since vehicles have to slow down to pay, the motorist and you have a good chance to look each other over and the driver can decide if he wants to pick you up. If the cars come to a standstill, you can tap on car windows and ask for a ride.

I had left Monte Carlo, planning to travel as far as Lyons that day, in a hurry to get to London for an appointment. But by mid-afternoon, progress had been slow. I found myself at a toll booth with light traffic and two other hitch-hikers. But the flag did it for me again. A Frenchman in a Cadillac (a decided rarity in Europe) picked me up and took me well beyond Lyons. He also invited me to stay at his home for the night. His resources having gone into his car rather than in his living space, I ended up in my sleeping bag on the bathroom floor, but reasonably comfortable and content.

Rest Areas

Highway rest areas, where drivers stop for a quick nap or a quick lunch, can be very good spots to get rides, for the same reasons that service stations are. The motorist is stopped, and he has a chance to size you up.

It was a foggy English morning in the Sussex countryside. I could hardly see my flag, let alone approaching cars. But after 15 minutes walking, I found a rest area and stopped to wait for a vehicle to pull in. Sure enough, one did, the driver waited for the fog to lift a bit, and off we went.

Prearranged Rides

Arranging a ride the night before is a great time-saver. Many drivers "camp" for the night, or part of it, at restaurants and highway service stations or at roadside campgrounds or rest areas. If you find yourself at one of these places in the evening, you should try to arrange to meet a driver at a predetermined time in the morning.

Somewhere north of Belgrade, my driver dropped me at a highway restaurant. I decided, since it was late, to look for a place to rest for the night, but before doing so, arranged with a truck driver, who said he was leaving at 8 a.m., to take me along. As it happened, I woke at about 6 a.m., decided to double check in case the driver decided to leave early. Sure enough, he was about to leave without me. Whether I'd misunderstood the time or he'd had an attack of insomnia I never learned. At any rate, he waited cheerfully while I ran to get my backpack and join him.

Notes on Car Windows

If you're at a highway service station, rest area or hotel and spot a vacant vehicle which looks like a good prospect, simply write a note describing yourself and your destination, and asking for a ride in the appropriate language, if possible. Then tuck the note under the windshield wiper. Always look at the licence plates; they will always tip you off as to what direction the car is likely headed.

It was a chilly, damp night at a rest area in France, the last day of my travels before returning to Canada. All the owners of the vehicles were staying at the hotels across the road. Rather than go and bother them I simply found a couple of likely-looking cars with English licence plates and wrote a note:

Hello: I am a university student from Canada. I am hitch-hiking to Calais. May I get a ride with you? I am sleeping, unfortunately, in the bushes directly ahead of your car. Could you please wake me up in the morning (in case my alarm didn't go off). I would appreciate your help. Thank you, Gil

At 8 a.m. , I was tapped on the shoulder by a young couple who turned out to be art dealers. Not only were they amused by my note, but, more important, they were going to my destination. During the ride, after only knowing them for 20 minutes, they asked if I would deliver one of the 20 paintings they had bought in Switzerland to a friend of theirs in Manhattan. They paid me $25 to do this; I ended up being a courier, and I probably saved them $200 or $300 for performing this service. In return, they paid for my boat ride to England and the train ride to London. I stayed for two nights in their beautiful mansion before heading home. The U.S. immigration officials at John F. Kennedy airport wanted to open the painting to look for drugs. They gave up after a while, but this was a lesson to be careful in transporting items for strangers. When I delivered the painting, it was to the home of the

vice-president of Sotheby's; the largest auctioneer in the world. I was invited to stay for the night. Everything in their home was antique, even the bed sheets! I wasn't invited to attend their party that night, I had to stay in my room. It didn't matter. I was tired from the time change and the long flight.

Quite a pay-off from placing a silly note on the windshield of a car. Experiences like this convinced me that it doesn't hurt to try new methods.

Stalled Vehicles

Once in a while you'll find yourself hiking along the road looking for a better spot for hitching. And sooner or later you're likely to find a stalled vehicle. Run, don't walk-and offer your services. The motorist can hardly refuse you a ride afterwards...well, that's how it *should* work.

I was 20 kilometres out of Madrid. Spain is not a good country for hitching and the way things were going, I felt I was in for a bad day. Cars kept passing and I kept trudging along. Then, about a kilometre ahead I saw a car stopped on the shoulder. I jogged up to it and offered the motorist my help. But the language barrier and negative vibes from the driver defeated me. I was about to move on when the tow truck arrived, got the car mobile and... you guessed it...gave me a ride.

34

Stoplights and Stop Signs

These are good places to try for a ride for obvious reasons. The driver has to stop and has a chance to look you over. If the weather is not the best or if he has an empty car, he may even feel guilty if he doesn't give you a ride. Eye contact and a friendly expression may be all you need.

Hungary is a good country for hitch-hiking in any case, but I found one of my more unusual rides I rode in while waiting at a stoplight which was conveniently jammed on red. I found myself waved into the backseat of what I fondly remember as the Hungarian Tin Box, a sort of customized old-fashioned home furnace on wheels. But the driver was friendly and he was going my way.

Ferries and Boats: Marine Hitching

Getting a free ferry ride will be a challenge to the most resourceful hitch- hiker, but it can be done. Your first step is to find the name of the shipping line that is going to your destination. Then you can:

- Hang around the dock next to the ship, or better yet, locate the crew's lunchroom in the dock area and see if a crewman will slip you onto the boat (perhaps for a few dollars) or ask an officer to let you on free.
- Ask an officer about the chances of working your passage on that voyage and the return voyage.

- Approach a truck driver, who may have a ticket for a second driver, but no second driver.
- Choose a ferry company that offers a flat rate for a car and up to four passengers, and approach cars lined up on the dock to see if they'll take you along at no extra cost to themselves.

This is a great test of your ingenuity and an opportunity to save a significant portion of your travel dollars.

Before you try to find a free ride, however, you should cover yourself in case you don't find one. Locate a travel office, either at the docks or in the town, and shop around for the least expensive ferry. Make sure you present your 'International Student Identity Card ' at every opportunity you have; I saved 50% on a boat trip from Alexandria, to Athens. The card is honored by most vendors. Compare shipping lines, times, and frequency of departures and fares. (Off-season you may be able to bargain a bit with travel agents, especially on the run from Italy to Greece and vice-versa.) Once you have all the information, give yourself at least an hour or two to get a free ride, but don't miss the boat!

I struck gold twice in one day. Before spending my precious dollars for the crossing from Sweden to Finland, I approached three musicians with a van, with the larcenous idea they might be willing to let me hide in it. As it turned out, they had an extra ticket as one of their band *members was sick, which saved me $25. Once at sea, I asked the captain about working my return passage later on. He explained that he couldn't hire foreigners and then proceeded to write me out a free return ticket. I was very grateful for the incredible hospitality.*

Ferries and Boats: Happy Hunting Grounds

You'll probably enjoy sea crossings, if the weather is decent or you've got a supply of seasickness pills. But you'll enjoy them even more if you have assured rides on the other side that will take you to your land destination.

One method is to ask an officer on board to make a request for you over the P.A. system. (This didn't work for me, but it's worth a try.)

Your best bet is to approach motorists lined up on the dock. They have to report as much as an hour or more before sailing, which gives you an excellent chance to go from driver to driver looking for a ride. This is a great method for women to try as you should have no problem finding someone with whom you will feel comfortable riding. Again, be sure to look at the licence plates. You will almost always find one going to your destination.

So good is this method that you may have an embarassment of choices. Crossing from Calais to Dover one day, I was undecided: Would I go straight to London or to some relatives in the country? I decided to go to whichever place I could most easily get a lift. To my surprise, I found drivers going to both places and ended up flipping a coin.

Bus Tours

I don't recommend bus tours as the best way to see the world for university students, but they can provide you with a bit of luxury hitch-hiking. They won't stop for you on the road, but if you happen to strike up an acquaintance with a member of a tour group on the street or at a tourist attraction, it can be a golden opportunity. The tour guide, if he has empty seats, may find it difficult to refuse your request for a ride, especially in front of his tour group.

On a sunny day, Venice is like no other city in the world, but the hitch-hiking opportunities are obviously limited. For once, I wasn't even thinking about my next ride as I toured the city on foot. The flag on my backpack led to chats with many other Canadians and tourists from other countries..among them a group of Australians on a six-week tour of Italy. One thing led to another and I soon had an invitation to travel on to Perugia with them the next day. After a particularly intensive week of hitch-hiking, the day in the bus with a group of uninhibited Aussies was a wonderful break.

Signs

It's helpful to have a sign with large letters indicating your destination, especially if you're on a road that is going to branch off shortly in several directions. Make sure you bring a few heavy duty magic markers. You can find pieces of cardboard at grocery stores and service stations. But if you don't have a sign, a very simple method is to stand by a road sign and simply point to the appropriate destination, you can even use a stick or tree branch.

I was heading for Badajoz in Spain and once again facing the general Spanish reluctance to pick up hitch-hikers, I had no cardboard sign, but found a sign on the roadside advising that a service station was 20 kilometers ahead. Using my rolled-up flag as a cuestick I pointed to the sign. The method caught someone's attention and I was plucked off the road and driven to the station. Not an exciting story, but at least it pays to be enterprising.

Vehicles That Have Already Passed You

If you happen to get a drive with someone who likes to travel at high speed, you may find yourself zipping past motorists who earlier passed you by on the highway. Later, as you try for another ride, they'll be surprised to see you again standing on the shoulder of the highway. This is your second chance to get their attention and if your "trademark" is visible enough, such as your big flag, they will realize they've seen you before. They may also decide that if someone else has picked you up, you can't be all that bad.

On the outskirts of a small town in former Yugoslavia, after a long wait, my smile or my flag finally did the trick and I found myself with a driver in a hurry. We sped by scores of cars that had earlier sped by me. When I found myself once again at the side of the road with my thumb out, I expected they'd all pass me by again. But one young woman, evidently reassured that my earlier driver hadn't come to a bad end, overcame her doubts and stopped for me.

Balloons

This would be one heck of a way to hitch-hike. I haven't tried it yet, unless you count one short trip 100 feet straight up and down again, at an Austrian ski resort.

It was a promotional gimmick and the locals were paying for the experience of a brief balloon ride. But a hitch-hiker never gives up and I managed to get a free ride. This ride afforded a beautiful view of the mountains around me.

Only slightly unusual, but perfectly practical, is the next method.

Yacht-Hiking

If you travel along the Mediterranean you'll pass acres of yachts, especially along the French and Italian Rivieras. You'll find the longest yachts and some of the richest people in the world at the docks of St.Tropez. Since people who own boats seem to spend a lot of time puttering about and working on them, it's possible to strike up a conversation with them, which could mean a very pleasant ride somewhere, or especially if you're at all experienced on boats, a chance to crew on an extended cruise. This is another great way for women to get a ride, but rather than swim in the harbor like I did, you can check the billboards in local hotels, bars or pubs where you might find an advertisement for extra help required on a yacht or boat. Also, avoid swimming because of potential sharks in some waters around the world. I should point out the Mediterranean is shark-free!!

My only venture into yacht-hiking was in 1975. The place was Cabo San Lucas in Baja California, a popular seaside spot with scores of tourist yachts. You might recognize this port from the old 'Love Boat Show', not that I would ever admit to watching it. I could have taken the ferry for only $10 to mainland Mexico, but I knew $10 would go a long way in Mexico so I thought it would be worth hitching a ride on a yacht. Since most of the yachts were moored rather than docked, I donned bathing suit and goggles and started swimming from yacht to yacht, eventually having to resort to dog-paddling. I yelled out 'Ahoy there, anyone aboard?' hoping to show a bit of humor. It took three days, but I found two men who were

delivering a yacht to its owner. They took me on as an extra hand and I was on my way to the resort of Puerto Vallarta. My only work was watching the navigation needle from 1 a.m. to 4 a.m. to make sure the yacht didn't stray off course. I am sure most people would have paid the $10 for the ferry, but this method gave me an excuse to remain in a beautiful area a couple of extra days.

Citizens Band Switch-Over

This is another method which I've tried only in North America. Where drivers use them however, to warn others of problems ahead or just to make conversation, they can provide a great service to hitch-hikers. The driver may agree, to radio other drivers looking for a car going to your destination, then plan a meeting at a service station, rest area or some other point further down the road.

I've made many 'C.B. Switch-Overs' in North America, but the most memorable was on a balmy day in Florida when I was riding in a sleek Datsun 280Z and managed to switch to another sleek Datsun 280Z driven by an equally sleek young woman.

Airplanes at Small Airports

I haven't had any experience with this exotic form of hitch-hiking, but met one traveler who managed it by hanging around the pilots' lunch room at an airport. Depending on the country you are in, this could pose problems in getting past security guards. Visit small airports only and you could bump into a pilot with a two or four seater who wouldn't mind some company. You could save yourself a bundle and some time, to say nothing of seeing the landscape from a different angle. Offering some money towards gas could increase your chances dramatically.

Two Rides, One Driver

If your driver is stopping in a city to do some business and then going on in your direction make arrangements with the driver to pick you up if he sees you again on the road still trying to get a ride.

Wrong-Sign-Right-Road Method

Here's a way to stop the most reluctant or timid motorist, if your flag and your smile are not doing the job. Let's say you're going from London to Edinburgh, and you have been standing on the entrance ramp for an hour or more. Catch the drivers' attention by changing the sign to Dover, even though the city is south of you, in the opposite direction. It's simple, a bit larcenous and ---I am told---extremely effective. Even though drivers will initially think you are a complete idiot, just make it clear that you weren't trying to be deceptive, but were just a little frustrated and trying to have a little fun. Don't forget, nobody knows you and this method can help get you back on schedule.

The enterprising hitch-hiker who
developed this method used it with great success on a trek across Canada, whenever he was having difficulty getting rides. Almost without exception, a motorist would stop to tell him he was standing on the wrong side of the road. When told that the hiker knew perfectly well where he was going and it was all a ruse to get a ride, the motorist tended to find the gambit very amusing and, having stopped, could hardly refuse to take the hitch-hiker along anyway.

'You're on the Air' Method

If you're ever stuck for a ride in a small town, ask the locals if the nearest radio station will air a request for a ride. You'll find Disc Jockeys will give details of your destination, where you are and what you look like. This service is available in a few European cities. (See Chapter 13, Countries in a Capsule).

It was a Sunday morning-family day, with cars full and the rest of the world asleep or at church. I was at a gas station in Arcata, California and it was a gas station attendant who suggested I try the local radio station. The DJ was happy to oblige and a few minutes later I heard: 'There's a college student all the way from Canada in need of a ride. He's at the Shell station on l0l South and he sounds like a nice chap...' When that didn't bring results I called back and changed my destination to Redding. I also gave him another record request... the first one, 'Love to Love You, Baby' by Donna Summer, was, in his words 'a little too risqué for our people' (I guess it would be, especially on a Sunday). Before long I was on my way to my second destination and listening to my second request, 'Ventura Highway', being played, chatting to the station fan who picked me up.

Ride Boards

Universities in North America and Europe often have ride boards in their student centres, where students looking for rides or drivers looking for passengers post notes. The snag here, for the traveler on a rock bottom budget, is that you may be required to pay a share of the gas. You may be asked to share some of the driving so be sure to bring your International Drivers License - they are easy to get. But it's worth it, especially for those women who would never want to try and get rides on the highway.This method is a great opportunity to seek out some adventure. If you're not in a hurry and your thumb is worn out, it can often mean a ride with congenial company.

You will find addresses and telephone numbers for 'Allo Stop' in a few countries in 'Countries in a Capsule'. These are hitch-hiking companies that arrange rides for a small fee; you are required to pay gas and possibly other costs.

Drive-Away Services

If you are not one to hitch-hike or just want to get behind the wheel yourself for a while, drive-away services can provide wheels for long distance trips. Check the classified section of the newspaper and the yellow pages of your telephone directory. You may get yourself a car to drive from Toronto to Miami or New York to Los Angeles. You only get one full tank of gas, limited time for sight-seeing on the way and you may or may not (more likely not) get some help with accommodation and food expenses. You must have a clean driving record, expect to stay on the prescribed driving route to the drop-off town or city. You won't necessarily find a car going exactly where you want to go , so expect to take a bus or train, or hitch-hike to your final destination. You are allowed only a certain number of miles over the prescribed route, any miles over and above that, you may have to pay a rate per mile. Expect to put down a security deposit, such as $300. If you damage the car or drive too many miles then the drive-away service will deduct this from your deposit. It is not as easy to drive a car as it used to be because of car thefts; expect to present your driving record. Make sure you read the fine print before you sign, and make sure you are properly covered by your own insurance company.

Not long ago on my lecture tour, I decided to fly from Buffalo to Los Angeles and then drive a car from L.A. back to the East Coast. The drop-off point happened to be near a college *where I was going to give a lecture. When I was driving the Fiero (same car I had back home!) on the way to Santa Barbara the car suddenly stopped on a busy bridge. The tank was empty even though the fuel guage read one-third full! With hardly any space to pull over, I spotted in my rearview mirror a car heading right for me at 60 m.p.h. With my flashers on, I frantically waved for the driver to avoid me. Luckily he only grazed the side of the car, but he somehow blew out my rear tire. I never did meet the driver, but at least other drivers stopped to help me. Now I had to spend the rest of the day at a repair shop, pay the $250 repair bill, and a $50 towing charge, and re-schedule my lecture. When I dropped the car off at the Pontiac dealership in Pennsylvania I was reimbursed for the repairs, but not for the blown tire. The driveaway service deducted $90 from my $300 deposit to pay the claims adjuster. If not for my persistence, I probably would have never received the remainder of my deposit. The whole debacle took over four months to settle. Again, read the fine print very carefully. Ask a lot of questions, especially about the deposit conditions. On the flip side, the two gentlemen who helped me on the bridge, took me to the service station, waited until the car was repaired, and followed me to the next town to make sure I got there in one piece.*

You may have gathered from reading the preceding methods that a sense of humour is very important in making my methods work. I hope you will agree that half the fun of traveling is getting to your destination and how you do it. Traveling is not just sight-seeing in the cities. Any of us can hop on a train, which is o.k. for some poeple, but your best memories will come from trying my more unusual methods for cutting travel costs.

Some Do's and Don'ts for the Hitch-Hiker

Don't fall asleep. The driver has picked you up for company and to do you a favour, so scintillate a bit. If there is a complete language barrier, you can at least be attentive to the driver and the scenery. Even if you doubt if the driver can understand you, speak a few words, slowly and distinctly; you may find out he/she understands more than you expect him to. Your efforts to communicate will put the driver at ease.

If there's another hitch-hiker in the car, be careful not to spend all your time talking to him or her, leaving out your host. Don't be rude to either the fellow who picks you up, or the one who doesn't. Rude gestures won't help the next would-be hitch-hiker. Try not to pay for rides. It defeats the purpose of hitch-hiking, though drivers in most Arab countries may ask for money; use your discretion. Rich Arabs driving expensive cars usually pick up the poor people who have to get to the next town to do their shopping and charge them for the ride; usually only 25 cents or so. Most of these drivers are more interested in meeting foreigners than in asking for money. I made it clear when cars did stop that I had no money to pay for rides and they were still happy to take me along. When Arabs hitchhike they wave their hands up and down. If you stand there with your thumb out the drivers won't understand what you are doing. Using the thumb is actually a rude gesture in their culture.

If a driver ignores you or hesitates to take you along, don't give up, especially at service stations. If the people have any doubt about you and your character, show your passport to convince them you are a foreigner. Don't forget you have a backpack which identifies you as a traveler and if you look like a college student, that will help you tremendously in getting rides. Maintain a cheerful smile and a pleasant manner. At the end of the ride, shake your driver's hand and express your appreciation.

If you follow this advice, you should get many rides and if you follow through as a good passenger, your driver is more likely to offer rides to others. No doubt getting a ride is your main objective, to get from A to B, but I have found most rides to be fascinating and an enriching mini-cultural experience for several reasons. Drivers can:

• Tell you about the countryside and the history of the area.
• Tell you about ruins that you should visit and about a festival in the next of couple of days that would be worth waiting for.

• Present you with a different point of view of world affairs.
• Tell you about his latest divorce or other personal problems.
• Allow you to get out of the car and take pictures without the fear he will drive off with your backpack. (Make sure you establish a sense of trust first, get to know the driver a little bit.)
• Give you the address of friends or relatives who would be willing to lodge you for the night.
• Invite you to a meal or stay at his home overnight.
• Offer you a job or tell you where you can find casual employment such as picking grapes, being a nanny or waiter, or shearing sheep on a farm.

There are certainly many possibilities. The motorist you travel with each day will at the very least be interesting as a person; he will also be a key factor in the success you have in keeping your food costs low and finding accommodation. Read on.

Rating the Countries for Hitch-Hiking

Each of the countries listed opposite is rated on a scale of one to ten, based on the author's personal experience and the experience of the many other hitch-hikers he has talked to. But how well you do in any country depends to a great extent on you: on your dress and grooming, on whether you have chosen a good spot on a major route. It can also depend on the time of year and weather.
(See chart opposite.)

5.

The Art of Finding Free Accommodation

"The perfect guest is the one who can make his host feel at home".
Gil White from his easy chair sipping a pina colada.

The most rewarding challenge on your travels will be your effort to secure over-night accommodation for "84 Cents" or less. And the reward will be far more than just financial. During four months of hitch-hiking in 1980 I spent a meagre $2.75 on accommodation. But the cost savings are almost irrelevant. The effort you put into finding a place to stay and the experiences you have as a result are bound to be highlights of your trip. Imagine yourself, for instance, lodging at an Arab, Swedish or Hungarian home. If you follow even some of the 25 cost-saving methods outlined in this chapter, you will find yourself getting a close-up look at the contrasting lifestyles of these people and many others. You'll discover there's no better way to gain insight into how the people live than by taking part in eye-opening discussions and tasting the local food

at its home-cooked best. You will acquire an appreciation of their culture not available to the ordinary traveler, hopping from hotel to hotel with a tour group.

If your goal is just to see the sights or to party five nights a week, you will miss out on the best part of traveling which is meeting the people. Ninety per cent of the stories I hear from other travelers concern the times they spent with local people. Not everyone is prepared to depend on other people for a place to stay. The line between accepting hospitality and abusing it is a fine one and opinions are bound to differ on where that line should be drawn. Depending on people is part and parcel of this whole book and the key to success in keeping your costs to "84 Cents" or less. Since I believe you can't get something for nothing, you should make an effort to repay your hosts by either doing a small chore or leaving a gift. If you don't feel like doing chores, then you may wish to give your host a token $5-$20 gift (giving money is a little tacky - especially if you are

44

staying with well-to-do people). Repaying people will allow you to stay a night or two with a clear conscience and earn your keep. All of us are unofficial ambassadors of our country; it is important to leave a good image and it will help the fellow traveler who might stay with the same people later.

Arabs are actually offended if you try to repay them, they tend to regard you not only as a guest of their home, but of their country. Since they won't let you work, hide the gift if they don't accept it, but make sure your host will be easily able to find it after you've said goodbye.

I didn't have as much money as many other travelers, but I didn't mind doing work to repay my hosts. This got me more involved with their way of life and made my stay much more interesting. I looked at it this way: either I could work for 6-12 months slaving away at a lousy job to help pay for my travels, or leave sooner taking sufficient funds to get by and satisfy custom officials, and do similar work in someone's home in another country. Jobs that may seem lousy back home may seem more interesting abroad and you will find other chores unique to the area.

There are Many Methods

Drivers
Motorists will often invite you in for the evening if you make a real effort to be sociable during the ride, explain to them that you are on a shoestring budget and that you would like to do some work or pay them for the stay, and make it clear you are not keen on sleeping outdoors. Be sincere, don't be sociable solely for the purpose of getting a place to stay. I found that it didn't occur to many drivers that I would be interested in staying with them; they presumed I wanted to keep traveling. In reversing the situation and initiating this request you don't have to be aggressive or forward. The end of the day when the sun is setting is the best time to try.

The idea of 'hitching' a bed as well as a ride first suggested itself to me when I was hitch-hiking to Central America through Washington. A doctor picked me up on a very dark, moonless evening, asked me where I was heading and then invited me to stay in his home. We had only known each other for three minutes, so I was reluctant to accept his invitation immediately. But when he told me he was married, had a farm with horses and five daughters - I accepted right away. Besides a warm bed for the night, plus dinner and breakfast, I gained the pleasure of getting to know him and his family and the knowledge -- since borne out in many other corners of the world - that there are many people willing to help a complete stranger. You definitely learn to trust people. I've stayed with a Scottish minister, Irish newlyweds, a Finnish teacher, among many others who were my drivers.

45

When the father brings home a total stranger from another land unexpectedly, I have always found a positive reaction from the wife and children.

Good Address Book: Friends...

Friends, and friends of friends, are invaluable when you're looking for a place to stay. Talk to every friend you have at school or in town, garner as many addresses as you can before you leave home and as you go along. Although the idea of arriving unannounced and surprising an old pal or your old pal's parents may be enticing, it's usually better to phone ahead when you arrive in town to make sure the person is at home. Even if you have many addresses you shouldn't go out of your way to stay with everybody. You might want to phone them for advice or assistance in an emergency. On the other hand, if you do arrive on the doorstep to find your friend isn't there, neighbors can be sympathetic. Even though you may not stay with the people you planned to, it doesn't matter, you probably don't know the people you were hoping to stay with in any case. You will often find your hosts will treat you like their son or daughter who might be going to school in the United States or Canada.

In Paris, I had difficulty finding the address of an apartment and wound up knocking on the wrong door. The woman who answered the door telephoned the person for me, but she turned out to be a 75 year old who did not want a stranger in her home. This was very understandable. The woman, without hesitation, invited me to stay with her family. It turned out she was a famous TV host - the equivalent to Diane Sawyer. Her husband was a radio producer and everyone in the family owned a motorcycle. I ended up having a high speed ride through Paris. I also went to a university party with their son near the Eiffel Tower, partying with the sons and daughters of some very affluent Parisians and diplomats. In order to have a few beers that night I offered to give out tickets at the door and help with a few chores in return for all I could drink. It was a great night to say the least! I also had a ' behind -the-screen' look at a live French TV production with my host, Madame Beauchamp, wearing my suit and tie.

...and Relatives

Before you leave home, it's a good idea to do a little shaking of the family tree. Most North Americans can find some relatives, close or distant, somewhere on the other side of the Atlantic. Some of my most pleasant evenings have been spent with relatives I had never met before, getting to know them and learning something about the areas my ancestors had come from. These relatives may, in turn, tell you about other distant members of your family whom you can visit, or they may suggest friends of theirs for you to put in your address book.

The advice about phoning ahead first is sound here too... though it's hard to resist the temptation to arrive on the doorstep of a member of your family you've never met, with no advance warning. But don't abuse the hospitality of your relatives, don't expect them to pay for everything. I stayed with my British relatives for only four days out of four months abroad and one day was spent at a relatives funeral. Great timing!

On a crisp and cool October evening I walked over a long bridge arriving in beautiful Kirkcaldy, Scotland. When I found a telephone booth I called my relatives whom I had never seen or heard from before and the conversation went something like this...

'Hello, Uncle George? It's Gil White from Canada, son of your brother, John White.'
'Who?'
'It's Gil White, the tennis player, I'm calling from a telephone booth in Kirkcaldy.'
'From where? Oh, Kirkcaldy!!
Our different accents made it very difficult to understand each other, especially with the antiquated phone. The conversation was quite comical and slightly embarassing, but I was quickly picked up and had a wonderful time going to bars and restaurants and getting to know my long-lost relatives.

Universities

A university campus can be a lifesaver for the young traveler looking for a place to stay. Ask any friendly-looking student coming out of a residence if he/she can put you up for the night. Possibly his roommate went away for a few days or you could mention that you wouldn't mind sleeping on the floor with your sleeping bag. If the person you approach can't accommodate you in a dormitory or an off-campus apartment, chances are he will be able to suggest someone else who can. Seeing that you are a foreigner with a backpack, young people react in an understanding manner. Since most of the dorm rooms are occupied during the school year or are only rented out in the summer, you will increase your chances by approaching students. If you ask the resident hall desk first - they are either going to say all the dorms are full or ask if you are the guest of a student and since you probably don't know anyone, you will be turned away, although in some situations I have been able to stay with resident hall directors. In essence, a student can easily get you in as long as they agree to act as your 'friend ' or 'sponsor'. If the student is hesitant in sponsoring you, you can show your passport to put his/her mind at ease.

During the summer, dormitories are available for people of all ages for $5-$20 per night. This is a great alternative to hotels and youth hostels. You can use the sport facilities on campus and eat in the cafeterias at reasonable prices. During school session it is obviously a lively place to stay with many opportunities to meet people at movies, dances or parties. I've gone to sporting events, saunas in Finland, fraternity parties Italian style, university classes in Morocco, Turkey and many other countries. I have had some of my best times at universities.

Whether you are with your driver or cycling into town, your driver and most people in town will know where the nearest university is located. On many occasion, my driver has dropped me off right at the university.

One of my most memorable stays was in Geneva. Arriving in the city early in the evening, I asked a young woman for directions to the university. It happened she was on her way there and she also knew a student with whom I could stay. I volunteered to bartend at a party in the dormitory. With my hosts' encouragement to help myself to as many drinks as I wanted, I soon became a dancing bartender.

In Venice, I found a college and a female student who was going into the residence. I asked her if she knew a male student with whom I could stay and without hesitating, she said I could stay in her room. She said she would 'sponsor' me to stay in the residence. I was taken aback by her invitation! We changed clothes separately, slept in different beds, she studied and I went about the streets of Venice on my own. This was a tremendous test of trust. I

don't think North American females would be as accommodating and trusting. Experiences like this illustrate the differences in cultures around the world.

I was lucky to stay at the university in Helsinki for six nights with some great Finnish students. At a university dance, I got some very outdated viewpoints about the North American way of life and how minorities are treated. Relish these conversations as an opportunity to dispel many myths.

Countryside Door to Door, Farmhouses and Barns

At night, you won't plan to be dropped off from your ride in open countryside or to be too tired to cycle to the next town, but it happens and when it does, try to get the driver to put you down where there are signs of life or cycle to the first lit farm house you see. I have found people living in the country are often more receptive than city-dwellers to young student travelers with backpacks who knock on their doors. City homeowners are wary of strangers because of crime; farmers around the world tend to be more trusting. So walk up to a farmhouse that looks occupied and you'll probably be amazed at the reception you get. I was apprehensive about doing this at first. But my options were to sleep outside in the cold, with nobody to talk to, or to stay with the locals, see how they live and do some work for a bed and two meals.

It will often happen that you and the farmer don't speak a common language. Use pantomime to get across that you would like to stay the night, that you have a sleeping bag and a bed is not necessary, and point to your watch indicating that you will leave early in the morning, to prove that you won't be an impostion. The pantomime in itself is often an ice-breaker. You can start by asking to sleep in the barn, but as often as not will be invited into the house. You would be surprised to discover how much you learn from each other even with a language barrier. Bring pictures of your family and postcards of your country to help overcome the lack of conversation.

If you don't feel sociable some nights or you are too tired from traveling, at least ask the farmer if you can pitch your tent on his property. There's nothing worse than being kicked off the property at 3 a.m. If you are in a remote area there is nothing to worry about, except for curious animals.

Try to avoid knocking on a farmer's door during supper hour; wait until at least 7p.m.

It was somewhere in what was then Yugoslavia, on a cold, dark evening. I had been dropped off in the countryside and walked until I came to a farm-house. I knocked on the door and there appeared seven curious peasants. I did my pantomime, which was almost immediately understood, and was invited in. We spent three hours at the dinner ta-ble communicating by hand language and facial expressions - for neither of us knew the other's language. There was only so much we could do with our hands and faces. After a while it becomes repetitive and tiring, but it was an incredible learning experience. The evening was filled with toasts with slivovitz (a very strong liqueur), and an exchange of souvenirs. With no words spoken, I gained an insight and understanding of the rural lifestyle in this part of the world that a packaged tour could never provide. And it was obvious my hosts enjoyed the evening immensely. Chances were they had never before entertained a foreign visitor and perhaps never would have the chance again. Due to the lack of beds, I ended up sleeping in the same bed with the daughter and the person who appeared to be her father- I wasn't too sure. I slept on the edge of the bed with my clothes on. In the morning, the peasant woman poured a slivovitz and motioned for me to drink it and this was before breakfast! Assuming this was one of their customs I didn't want to offend them, but I had to turn down the fourth before I became sick. Just when I thought I was recovering from the drinks, she cooked the eggs in half an inch of oil. I concluded these unhealthy cooking practices explained their heavy builds.

A Swedish farmer allowed me to sleep in his barn. With a roof over my head and a most comfortable bed of straw to sleep on I fell asleep to the grunts and squeals of the horses and pigs below. To say the least, the night air was aromatic with healthy nitrogen filling my lungs. I had a good night and was treated next morning to a Swedish country-style breakfast.

One day in West Germany I was picked up by a driver who already had another hitch-hiker from Salt Lake City as a passenger. We decided to travel together for a couple of days. The first day we volunteered to stay in a police cell and the second night we knocked on a farmers' door. We were invited in and spent the evening with the parents and daughter, drinking, eating and laughing the night away.

Deluxe Hotels (Free)

It's not too often you'll be able to stay free at a hotel. If it happens it's usually through the extreme generosity of another traveler who would put you up at his home if he could and since he can't, offers to pay for a hotel room. I spent eight nights of my four-month trip at hotels, all at no cost.

The outstanding one came about after a frustrating time trying to cross the border from Israel to Egypt. During one of my rides I learned the border would close at 4 p.m. until Sunday. In a bit of a panic, I gave up hitch-hiking and took a taxi. The driver sped me across the Sinai at 140 k.p.h., delivering me to the border with 15 minutes to spare. The Israelis processed my papers quickly and whisked me on to a bus to take me to the Egyptian border post. I was shocked when officials told me I had to get my visa in Israel. I had been informed the day before by an Egyptian ambassdor that there would be no problem getting the visa at the border!! As I stood there pleading with the Egyptians to let me through, an American tour group was crossing in the other direction. As I turned back to the Israeli side, upset and uncertain what to do next, one of the Americans invited me to ride with the group on its bus to the Dead Sea. This wasn't on my itinerary but, given a free ride, why not? After a couple of hours of storytelling, I remarked how wonderful it would be to pitch my tent by the Dead Sea. The American insisted that wouldn't be necessary; I must stay at their hotel as his guest. I made several polite refusals, but gave in gracefully when he insisted. The $39 hotel room provided the most expensive sleep I had during my trip.

Note: There are some events that you have no control over especially when other people want to show their hospitality whether it's the driver buying you a meal or someone you meet. Whether some people think young travelers eat insects or sleep in train stations, I cannot say, but this may help explain why some people feel it is necessary to offer their help. You can't seek out this type of hospitality, but should be very grateful if it happens to you and it happens to travelers all the time.

SERVAS

SERVAS is an excellent worldwide organization designed to help build world peace through international understanding. When you become a member for $55 per year, you have the wonderful opportunity to stay with a host family in another country and are provided with a list of addresses. It is preferred you prearrange your visit through letters so that the host is prepared for your arrrival. If you wait until you arrive in the country you may find your potential hosts already have someone else staying or may have gone away on their own holidays. It is best to initially advise your hosts the approximate date of your arrival and once you are close to your destination, let them know at least three days ahead of time the exact date. There is no work involved, cash is not accepted; a gift is the proper way to thank your host. Visits of one or two days are typical. Staying longer is at the discretion of your host; don't ask. There are some misconceptions that you can stay for a week or two, dump your luggage, and go off on your own.

Your hosts may become your tour guide and take you around town or they may just have time for conversation after work. All hosts want to do what they can to increase international understanding. Hosts are not expected to provide elaborate meals or luxurious accommodations; a sofa and pot luck supper with the family is fine. This method is particularly suitable for people who do not want to sleep in hostels, police stations or knock on doors in the countryside. You are not required to put your name on the list as a host family, but if you want to become a host, you must agree to accept travelers of any race, creed and nation and you must support the aims of SERVAS. When you apply, you will be asked to prepare a letter about yourself and your travel plans, and to supply two letters of reference, at least one of which must be from someone who knows you in a professional or educational capacity. You will also be asked to arrange an interview. Be sure to allow time to complete these arrangements well before you plan to start your trip. All SERVAS travelers carry a personal Letter of Introduction validated by a SERVAS representative. This is your guarantee that they have been interviewed and approved as SERVAS travelers. It also helps you get acquainted. **Contact:** 11 John St. Room 407, New York, NY 10038 tel: (212) 267-0252; in Canada, 229 Hillcrest Ave. Willowdale, Ontario M2N 3P3, telephone number requested to be unlisted.

Bed and Breakfast

One of the best ways to experience the culture of a country, albeit at a cost well beyond "84 Cents" a day is the bed and breakfast establishment.

These are popular in Great Britain and other European countries. Your host provides accommodation and a full breakfast to start off your day. Most times your host will sit with you at breakfast and at the very least, give you a brief insight into their life and customs. If you can afford to stay in these places, I highly recommend you do so. There are plenty of bed and breakfast guidebooks in your nearest bookstore. In Germany, Austria and Switzerland they are called 'zimmer frei or privat zimmer', in France-chambre d'hote, Greece and Slovenia-dhomatia and sobe, Spain-quartos, camas, casas particular, Italy-pensione, locanda or Albergo; in Scandinavia-rom, bus rum; Denmark-Vaerelser. Prices range from $10 to over $100. Depending on the country you are in, it would be wise to barter a little bit, especially during the low - season.

Hotels: Staff Rooms

A likely prospect for staying at hotels is to try for a vacant staff room. In any popular tourist area, during the off-season (usually Sept.-May) there will be reduced staff in the hotels and vacant rooms. Ask to speak to the manager. Explain that you'd like to wash dishes for no more that three or four hours in return for a night's rest, dinner and breakfast. Even if there's no work to do, the manager may allow you to stay anyway. Start with the five-star hotels and work your way down. You will have more success going

to the smaller, independent hotels where the manager is the owner and can make the decision himself, rather than the chain hotels where the manager may have to go through too much red tape just for one night's work.

In Scotland, I contemplated paying $3 for a youth hostel in Inverness, but was disappointed to see all these students from around the world sitting there watching TV. This didn't seem to be a fun way to spend an evening, so I decided it would be more interesting to bargain with the manager of a nearby luxury hotel. At first it seemed I would be turned away but the manager finally said he did have some vacant staff rooms. I had a lot of fun washing dishes, witnessed some entertaining Scottish folk dancing, savored my dinner, followed by a hot bath and great breakfast in the morning. All in return for a little initiative.

Youth Hostels
(listed country by country in Chapter 13)

More than 3,000 youth hostels in Europe provide a great opportunity to control your accommodation costs and are probably the best place to stay for the first time traveler. If you are planning to travel for three months, you might plan to stay in them for the first three weeks. Then once you've become accustomed to traveling, I strongly suggest that you branch off and find different types of places to stay. Hostels are cheap, today's prices ranging anywhere from $1 in Damascus to $15-$20 in London or Paris during the high season. You won't learn much about the culture, but you will meet fellow travelers who will provide a wealth of information. If someone has just come from a country you are going to visit, ask questions about the conditions. Is it stable?, What's the best way to travel there?, Should I cycle, hitch-hike or take the train? Both employees and other travelers at the youth hostel will also be able to tell you of the hottest night club to visit or the hippest and cheapest restaurant. In most cases you can leave your backpack and bicycle there without worry as you sight-see about the town. You can shower, wash your clothes, make new friends and find new traveling companions. Some hostels offer really cheap and nutritious meals. Be sure to get a youth hostel card which will allow you to get the best rate and even book ahead. These days, people of all ages can stay in most youth hostels and two to four people can stay in a small private room for a slightly higher charge. In fact, the international organization and many national ones have dropped "youth" from their titles.Bedding is provided but you do need to bring or rent your sheets and pillowcases or a sheet sleeping bag in some hostels. Hostels charge an extra $2-$5 for the linen. Beside bringing a sleeping bag, save some money by bringing your own linen.

Booking ahead through the International Booking Network

You will find youth hostels will fill up very early in the day in major cities and popular tourist areas during the high season. Hostelling International now has a computerized international booking network (IBN) that allows you book in advance. You can pay for reservations in the local currency where you make the booking, avoiding bank or exchange charges - and secure accommodation in advance. There is a booking charge of $5.00 for Canadians and $5 for Americans. Many hostels now accept credit cards which makes it easy to book ahead by telephone. You can also book ahead by letter enclosing an international postal reply coupon (available from most Post Offices) and a self-addressed envelope. If you book without paying a deposit, you need to arrive at the hostel and claim your reservation by 6 p.m., unless other arrangements are made. No doubt, you can arrive at the hostel doorstep without a reservation, but you will find hostels fill up very early in the day in popular tourist areas during the high season. There's nothing worse than waiting until eight o'clock in the evening, arriving at a youth hostel to find it full and being forced to find more expensive accommodation. In the chapter, Countries in a Capsule, you will find every youth hostel listed for each country; the hostels that are part of the **"IBN"** are highlighted in **bold lettering**. If you wish to get the complete book on youth hostels, Hostelling International Handbook, Volume 1, contact any one of the national youth hostel organizations and make sure you get your Hostelling International (HI) card.

I'll never forget staying in a youth hostel in Damascus, Syria for 50 cents. I slept on a mattress that felt 100 years old and washroom facilities were horrid. Needless to say I didn't have a great night's sleep. You will find, however that ALL youth hostels belonging to HOSTELLING INTERNATIONAL have high standards of cleanliness and hygiene.

For more information contact:

American Youth Hostels (AYH), 733, 15thSt. NW, suite 840, Washington, DC 20005 tel: (202) 783-6161. Membership cards cost $25, renewals-$20, under 18-$10, over 54-$15, family cards-$35.

Hostelling International-Canada, National Office, 400 - 205 Catherine St., Ottawa, Ontario, Canada K2P 1C3, tel: (613) 237-7884, fax (613) 237-7868. Membership cards cost $25 for those 18 and over (including those 54 and older) and $35 for a two year card, renewals cost the same, students under 18, the card costs $12.
For more information, refer to chapter 15 pages 290-291.

YHA (England & Wales), Trevelyan House, #8 St. Stephens Hill, St. Albans, Hertfordshire, AL1 2DY England, tel: 44 - (1727) 855 215. Membership cards cost £9.30 for those 18 and over and for those under 18, the cost is £3.20.

Bars, Discotheques, Parties, Dances

Meeting the locals wherever they gather can make for an enjoyable evening and it's also a good way to find a bed. Dance, buy a drink for a new friend, and then decide if you should explain your situation. Many 'Book Worm' travelers and most people, for that matter, would probably like to know early in the day where they are going to stay for the evening rather than leave it to chance as I often did. Finding a place to stay late at night was a test of my best traveling skills.

I was at an international student Christmas party in Paris, not far from the Eiffel Tower, without a place to stay for the night, but not much worried about it, given the large number of people at the party. The livelier the evening got, the less I worried about it. Finally at 3 a.m., hearing two students talking about leaving in a taxi, I asked if I could share the ride. During the ride I suddenly remembered that I had no destination. One of the students, it turned out, was the daughter of an Asian ambassador to France living in the very elegant Place Victor Hugo. I was invited home to Papa and the embassy.

Ferries

An overnight ferry ride can provide a bed as well - a berth if you want to splurge - a lounge chair (usually gratis), or, in warm weather, your sleeping bag on the deck, Unroll it early, though. On popular runs in high season, the deck will be rail-to-rail with other backpackers.

Daytime ferry crossings, on the other hand, give you time to meet other passengers and you may find yourself invited to travel on to someone's home.

The crossing from Stockholm, Sweden to Turku, Finland, takes ten hours. I did it in both directions and each time met a lovely young woman. Had I been from their native lands, I don't think it would have occurred to either of them to put me up. As it turned out, the Finn lived with her parents, who made me welcome. The Swede was on her way to a reunion with her husband after two months, but despite the obvious fact that he had hoped to greet her alone, he was a gracious host and we spent a pleasant evening talking over homemade hot drinks.

Unsolicited Invitations into Homes

The ultimate demonstration of human trust is an invitation from complete strangers into their home. Whether its the backpack or plaid pants, foreigners stand out in a crowd and local people, especially in developing or third world countries tend to gravitate to them. You will be minding your own business and suddenly you are approached by a person wanting to try out lingo picked up from American movies and TV.

Hitching through Bulgaria to the Turkish border with three Turkish students I arrived at the Turkish border to find that martial law had been implemented. This meant we had to endure lengthy security checks. After turning all our luggage and the car inside out, border officials allowed us through. (At any border crossing it is best to get out of the car and meet your driver on the other side in case he or she is smuggling contraband.) During the ride into Istanbul I saw people crossing the highway at will causing near accidents, ignoring stoplights and driving with mud-caked headlights. It was like stepping into another world. Minutes after I was deposited on the city streets, a man invited me to meet a friend of his. Somewhat dubious at first, I followed him. The Turkish man I met was an English teacher who invited me to stay in his apartment for two nights. The teacher, who calls himself 'Casanova', his friend and I sat in his apartment toasting from tiny glasses filled with sweet Turkish coffee. As beautiful Turkish music played in the background, I noticed his lack of material possessions. He had only a TV, a table, refrigerator, blankets for beds and a hole in the floor for the toilet. We spent the whole evening comparing our cultures. Here is part of the conversation I recorded.

Casanova: Hello Gil, welcome to Turkey, we are very glad to meet you.
Gil: Thank you.
Casanova: Between Turkey and Canada will be a good friendship. We meet and between Turkish government and Canada government and we try for peace in the world, you brought your flag, Canada flag and Turkish flag must be always up. And all my compliments to Canadian people and poor people.
Gil: Not the rich people.
Casanova: If rich people are honest, ok, if rich people exploits the poor people, workers, not compliments, I have hates.
Gil: Yes, you do not like rich people who exploit.
Casanova: I like honest people, I like workers, I like social democrats, no socialsim, no facism, no capitalism.
Alper: In past, at present and in the future, you and all the Canadian people, you are most welcome, welcome to Turkey!!
Gil: Thank you, I would like to visit a Turkish prison tomorrow, if possible, is it possible?
Casanova: Yes, of course.
Gil: I hope they don't put me in the prison, I hope!!

I wanted to visit the prison to see how accurately the movie 'Midnight Express' reflected the actual conditions in Turkey. I wasn't crazy enough to try this by myself, Casanova agreed to accompany me. Pretending to be a reporter, I walked to the gates with my camera and tape recorder in hand, but the guards just chuckled and turned us away.

After a couple of rides from Amman, Jordan, I arrived in a small town called Shobak, only 30 miles from the ruins of the magnificent ancient city of Petra. My goal was to sleep in the caves there the way the people used to. But as I reached the edge of the village, a voice called out to me in good English saying there would be no more cars going to Petra that day. I looked back to see a man, his wife and four children on a balcony surveying me. "Please come into my house for the night and meet my family," he shouted. I yelled back that I would try for another hour; but he was right, there were no more cars. When I knocked on his door, the first thing he said was, "My name is Mohammed Ali" and then proceeded to shadow box with me. Mohammed's children, he told me, had never met a foreigner. It was they who had noticed my flag fluttering, thought I was from France, and had begged their father to invite me in. Even though I was not from France, I was still allowed to stay. It was a wonderful evening. I learned more in one night with the family than if I had stayed in a youth hostel for six nights in the same town. They wanted to hear anything and everything about my country and my travels. Before dinner, one of their children came to me with a bucket of water. It is a custom to wash your hands, face and feet before eating (I'm not sure of the order). Sitting cross-legged on the cold stone floor for three hours became painful. These people managed the whole time without budging. His wife brought a plate of food that would have fed ten people. The wife and children watched us eat, smiled and listened to our conversation. The custom is for the wife and children to eat only after the husband and guest have finished. I also learned it is rude to point to anybody when you talk to them, show the soles of your feet, and that Mohammed is only allowed four wives! I slept in a bed with a heavy blanket at least three inches thick! - I couldn't turn over, but at least I stayed very warm. We also exchanged gifts - I gave them a Canadian sweatshirt and I received the typical headress they wear called a chech, chechia, or keffiyeh.

After I wrote him a thank you letter, he responded with a letter that I will always treasure:

"Hello, How are you, my good friend? Thank you for your letter which I received today. It gives me a great deal of pleasure for your reaching your home savely.

I hope you are very well now, I thank you for your impressions while you were in Jordan. I told my wife and my children about your letter and they feel pleasure. I could not describe how glad they became and they began to remember you.

I built a new house, it is a big and good house. I feel pleasure because it is mine. Thank you for your sentences which you told me while you in my house as: 'make yourself comfortable' instead of 'take your rest' and 'okay' instead of 'nevermind'.

I hope if you were in my house for a month, I could not speak and write everything because my English language is not so good, but surely I would like to be my friend forever. Our school is full with fruits and vegetables and I hope if you had been here in the summer instead of winter because winter in Jordan is very cold, especially Shobak.

Thank you again for your good letter and impressions and I hope you good health, please give my best wishes to your family,

So long   Yours,
*   Mohammed Ali*

If you can collect letters like this one, then you have accomplished the most any traveler could hope for.

One last example worth mentioning was my stay with the Moroccan students in the capital, Rabat. I was sitting on a park bench basking in the sun when a man my age introduced himself, wanting to try out his American lingo. He asked me to stay with him and his fellow students. I found myself in a maze of one story mud buildings with dirt floors and no plumbing. In this 'pad', I stayed with students who had to study by candle light! Seven of us ate dinner, eating from the same plate, using our fingers as utensils. I appreciated the small lesson of sharing food and never worried about getting sick. I was invited the next day to an English university class and witnessed what seemed like scenes from the floor of the New York stock ex-

change. When the teacher asked questions, everybody yelled out the answer as loud as they could. Even though I yelled out the answer, the teacher ignored me. At the very least it was an eye-opening look into the Moroccan educational system.

These experiences are just a sampling of my days on the road. I never felt I was ever imposing on my host's privacy. I could clearly see they were delighted to have a foreigner in their home.

Young People in City Centers

Every city has one or more sectors where the young congregate: pinball arcades, parks, shopping areas, etc. After you find it, approach someone who looks friendly, explain your predicament, and you should find it solved in short order.

I first tried this method at the suggestion of a young Hungarian couple who gave me a ride into Budapest and assured me that many of the young people strolling the streets would want to meet a foreigner and would be willing to put me up for the night. In fact, my driver acted as interpreter, writing down for me in his language that I needed a place to stay and another note asking for directions to get out of the city. I handed the note to a young man who, it turned out, shared an apartment with two other students. It was Christmas Eve and the only sign of holiday celebration was the singing of religious songs in Hungarian by

my new friends, which I tape-recorded for them.

You should make a point of celebrating Christmas in another country just to see how it compares with our traditions during the holiday season. In Australia, for example, many people eat their turkey dinner on the beach and let's hope it's not a windy day!

Police Cells

Traditionally touted as the last resort of a penniless traveler, police cells can be safe and clean accommodation. Especially in towns of fewer than 30,000 people, they are often vacant except for the chronic town drunk who is down the hall in his own cell. Obviously, they are not advertised, but anyone on the street can direct you to the police station, and the police often seem to feel obligated to take in strangers, especially young backpackers. Simply explain to the officer you are low on money, you can't afford to sleep in the $40 hotel. If the weather is horrible, this is not a bad place to be for the 'Viking' traveler. The police will want to see your passport, and you will increase your chances of being 'booked ' into a cell if you are clean cut and, of course, you don't carry any drugs. You are locked up for the evening - obviously you can't wander around the station and they will take your belt so you don't hang yourself. If you're lucky, you might be fed bread and water. Don't forget, not every town

58

has a youth hostel. If you spent just $40 one or two times a week just for seven hours sleep you will run out of money very quickly and find yourself coming home a lot sooner than planned.

I've stayed in only four police stations as a student traveler and every stay was unique. In Oregon, where I was the first occupant the jail had had in some time, I was fed bread and water for dinner and then, for security reasons, my hosts insisted on taking mug shots which I sent home to my parents. They were not amused. In Innsbruck, Austria, I stayed the night and check-out time was an early 6 a.m. I left to enjoy a pleasant snowfall on the deserted streets.

The student from Salt Lake City whom I met while hitch-hiking joined me for a fun night at the local police station in a small German town. Before we were locked up for the night, we had coffee with the police officers and chatted for an hour. We had a shower and then had our police officer friend take a picture of us in our cell, amused as we were about the situation.

My last time in the clinker was in Pretoria , South Africa. The officer who let me in went home at the end of his shift and forgot to let me out. I didn't mind spending a couple of extra hours, for I shared the cell with a white man who was against apartheid. His views made for an enlightening visit. Even though I stayed in this police cell in a major

city, I strongly recommend that you stick to the small town police stations where the atmosphere is likely to be friendlier and less intimidating.

Camping

Many campsites in Europe are reasonably priced, some as low as $5 for a night's stay. Most have good showers and washing facilities, sometimes a grocery store and restaurant. You can't have fires, and quiet time starts around 10 p.m. Theft is rarely a problem. Just leave your belongings inside your tent, but only if there is a gate keeper at the entrance. Staying at campsites can be better than sleeping in the woods. You could try to offer your services to save some money. Some owners might allow you to stay gratis for a night in the off-season, even if there is no work to be done. Contact tourist offices or national camping organizations for lists of European campgrounds or get 'Europa Camping and Caravanning' for $13. Some European campgrounds require the 'International Camping Carnet (membership card-it can usually be bought on site). You can get the card for $30 from the National Campers and Hikers Association, 4804 Transit Rd. Bldg #2, Depew, NY 14043, tel: (716) 668-6242. In Canada: contact: Ontario Private Campground Association (non-profit), 40 University Ave. suite 1116, Toronto, Ontario, M5J 1T1, tel: (416) 977-0454 or the Ministry of Culture, Tourism and Recreation at 1-800-668-2746 which runs the provincial parks and campgrounds. A national campers association in Canada is in process of being formed.

Average prices for campsites are in US dollars per person. Tents in some countries are extra. Here's a sampling:

Austria $3.50, Belgium $1.75, Denmark $5.50, Finland $10, France $10, Germany $14, Greece $3, Italy $5, Portugal $2, Spain $3, Switzerland $5

Puerto Escondido, Mexico , something of a tourist trap, has a picturesque campsite. I asked the owner if I could work in return for a place to pitch my tent. It turned out to be more work than I'd bargained for - three hours in in the hot sun, digging out sand for a latrine ditch! At least the tropical milkshakes provided by the owner cooled me down as did the luke-warm swim in the ocean.

Trucks, Vans and Cars

This is not the most desirable type of accommodation, but a roof over your head is a night out of the rain. If you're with a driver who intends to keep going all night you can often sleep in the back. Many trucks, in fact, are set up with bunks.

Just outside Belfast, I was picked up by an Irishman who lived in my country for 10 years. He introduced me to his friends in a Londonderry pub and after an extremely convivial evening of playing darts and drink-

ing, I ended up sleeping in the van, next to the stick-shift, while he slept with his girl for the evening!! At around 3 a.m. I had to relieve myself. I was approached by two police officers who wanted to be sure that the van didn't have any bombs in it. For the fun of it, I recorded our conversation, and replied, with a slurred tongue which was masked by my accent, that there was just me and the fruits and vegetables. And off they went as I went back to my stick-shift.

Trains

If you have to take a train somewhere, you can make it overnight so you get a free night's sleep. On the down side, you may miss some great scenery. And unless you can afford a berth (couchette) you will not get a comfortable rest sleeping upright in a seat. Some trains can be bumpy and noisy. Keep your most important belongings on you or inside your bed (not in your backpack), such as your passport, visas, money, and camera. Through Italy especially, you will find thieves wandering through the trains at night. Also a problem on overnight ferries! Having to sleep with one eye open most of the night will just make you feel tired for the next day. When you do take the train, make an effort to meet Europeans and look forward to using this as an opportunity to learn more about their culture.

Although it's a cardinal sin for a true

hitch-hiker I took a train from Madrid to Irun, Spain. I decided a few beers were warranted as an anaesthetic. I had the worst sleep of my life... either Spanish beer was weak or the Spanish roadbeds were too rough as the high braking squeals signalled many stops in small towns.

Fields

Where there are fields, there are apt to be hitch-hikers and cyclists, and other forms of wild life as well. But if all other methods fail, you can find a patch of grass on which to pitch your tent or, if it's a nice night, just to unroll your sleeping bag. There is no cost and not much reward either, unless you prefer to sleep outside in solitude and close to nature. It's nice to know that you can sleep nearly anywhere in Scandinavia,where the governments declare that the land is accessible to everybody. You must be at least 100 metres away from the nearest building.

One cold January night in southern Ontario, a driver who'd had too much to drink, dropped me in the middle of nowhere. The temperature was -8C (l0 degrees F) and while I didn't relish sleeping outdoors, there didn't seem to be much choice. A locked shed by the highway provided shelter from the wind, and I nervously unrolled my sleeping bag onto my ground-mat and slipped in, wearing about five layers of clothing. Fortunately neither brain nor alarm clock

froze. I woke after a sound sleep with cold feet and the solid conviction that I preferred a roof over my head, winter or summer.

Airports

Possible, but not recommended. The seating is usually not comfortable for stretching out and the lights are bright all night. If you are waiting stand-by for an early morning flight, then it is worth it. Take advantage of the airport lockers and set your alarm so you don't miss your flight.

Monasteries, Missionaries, Crisis Centres and Hotlines

Here, I speak from hearsay rather than personal experience. Monasteries are traditionally hospitable to travelers and in some parts of the world will still offer the wanderer a bed and a meal. Many of those on the regular traveler's trail, however, have had so many visitors stay without contributing anything to their costs that they can no longer afford to take people in. Missionaries and young workers in Peace Corps type projects are another source of lodging and help in third world countries. Crisis centres and hotlines, a North American phenomenon, would presumably be willing to help if you were really in a desperate situation, but they are set up to serve local people suffering real crises, not the penny-pinching traveler.

61

How to Repay Your Hosts for their Hospitality

- Use the methods outlined in this chapter to find a bed and then offer to pay. If you are in a home in England, Sweden or Italy I would suggest $10-$15, if you are in countries such as Hungary, Turkey and Morocco, $5-$10. Payments are dependent on how many meals they feed you.
- If your hosts refuse to take any money, use the money you've saved to return their hospitality by giving them or their children a gift, or an outing to a cafe. I recommend bringing gifts from your country for it may be difficult to find a gift shop when you really need one. Bring gifts that say something about your country, such as sweatshirts and T-shirts.Once I knew I wasn't going to be in the colder climates anymore, I gave my sweatshirts to my hosts. Take at least 20-25 cassette tapes - rock, pop, country, and classical; stamp packages from your post office valued from $5-$15. Each stamp is an excellent souvenir of your country - stamps depicting mountains, flowers, presidents or monarchs and even Elvis Presley and Marilyn Monroe. Some of these gifts may seen trivial to you, but a Hungarian peasant would find the gift a wonderful souvenir. Other small gifts which cost little or nothing, such as Canadian or American pins(available at embassies), posters, postcards from your home town, small foreign coins, all give pleasure out of all relation to their value.

- My favorite method of repayment was doing small chores. I don't think doing the dishes is a fair way to repay your hosts for accommodation and two or three meals. It is merely symbolic and too easy. Chores that I suggest - chopping wood, doing errands, shoveling the snow, cooking a meal American or Canadian style, helping with the children or even becoming a nanny for a day or two (which may develop into a week or month - you never know what may develop) - raking leaves, shearing sheep, painting, washing the car...
- The simplest return for hospitality is to be the best possible guest. You will usually find your host in interested in you, your lifestyle, your travels, your country. Conversation costs nothing. Entertain if you can. If you have a guitar on your back, the problem is solved. Polaroid cameras are still useful, though no longer the great novelty they used to be. I found my mini tape-recorder gave great pleasure to many people, who had never before heard themselves on tape. When you play the tapes back 10 or 20 years from now, it will to seem as if your travels were just yesterday. Other travelers develop expertise in card tricks, or magic stunts which are very effective in surmounting any language barrier.
- The bread-and-butter letter is as appropriate in these circumstances as it is at home, either in the form of a postcard sent further along in your trip or after you get home. Make sure you give them your address and invite them to stay in your home one day. The extent to which

you reimburse your host is a personal matter. But the experiences you have are bound to be unforgettable.

Even if you never make the effort to get accommodation, you are almost certain to be offered it from time to time. However, if you are determined to avoid hotel costs and limit your youth hostel stays, you will have to ask about 75 percent of the time, either by knocking on doors (farmers only) or staying at universities.

If you don't think you have the nerve, consider the alternatives you'll face. Sooner or later you will find yourself in unfamiliar territory with no affordable hotels. You can choose to sleep outdoors, uneasy, lonely and bored. If the alternative is a warm bed in a nearby house...well, it really *doesn't* hurt to ask.

What moves a perfect stranger to offer hospitality? Many reasons. Seeing your backpack, he realizes you haven't much money and are unfamiliar with the area. It gives many people real pleasure to show hospitality; in some cultures it is seen as a duty. If you knock on most Arabs' doors, they will not turn you away for it is an ancient Arab custom to allow all strangers into their homes. Some people feel really honored to have a foreign visitor and some may feel offended if you turn down the proferred kindness.

Try a little positive thinking. Ask yourself these questions:
• In the car: I wonder if this driver would mind putting me up for the night? After all, it's late and I'll be leaving early in the morning.
• In the country: Surely, this farmer wouldn't mind if I slept in his barn? If I offer to do some work for him, maybe he'll even invite me into the house.
• In the city: Where do young people congregate? Where are the universities, local bars and discotheques?

Grooming

As has probably occurred to you by now, this type of traveling presents some difficulties to the person who likes to shower twice a day. Sleeping in a barn and presenting a well-groomed appearance the next day when you are out on the road looking for a ride is not always easy.

If you are staying with a family or students, it's usually no problem to have a bath and do some laundry. You will find laundromats in some cities, but they are generally very expensive by North American standards. Youth hostels have laundry machines in many locations. Wait until your clothes have fully dried, there's nothing worse than traveling with a backpack of heavy damp clothes.

You can use washrooms in hotels, restaurants and airports for a light sponge bath, shaving and washing your hair, and sometimes for a little light laundry. Don't take your time and don't leave a mess. There are showers and bathing facilities in many big city train stations and at public baths, but these, of course, cost money.

Grooming is important in getting rides and hospitality; it also makes you feel better and eager to confront each day's traveling.

6

The Art of Finding Free Food

Travelers need a balanced diet just like everyone else. Skipping meals will result in fatigue, lower resistance to colds, and other ailments. An empty stomach can also result in headaches and a state of depression and anxiety, so be sure to eat at least two good meals a day. You'll find walking an extra 5-10 miles a day that you are not accustomed to will make you ravenous. I am pleased to report that I left for Europe weighing 160 pounds and somehow returned home at the same weight!

Foods such as bread, fruit, vegetables, and cooked meat are available everywhere and usually you can find something not too expensive. If you are a vegetarian that may pose some problems when you are staying with people, especially if there is a language barrier. You might offend some people and their customs if you refuse to eat with them and their food.

It's a good idea to carry some food items with you at all times, such as nuts, fresh bread, bananas, other fruits, and a small canteen of water. European bread is the best in the world. Some days I was to able to survive quite adequately on a loaf of bread which will also help you keep within your "84 Cent" budget. By having food with you at all times, you won't have to go out of your way as often to find some when hunger strikes at unexpected times. Having some food with you will eliminate the need to find a bank to cash a traveler's check to pay for just one meal if your stay in a country is brief.

But if you're following the suggestions in this book for getting rides and accommodation you'll find food to be part of the package. You don't have to steal or beg or forget to pay your restaurant bill either.

Hitch-hiking

The driver who has picked you up will often stop for a meal and if you've made an effort to be an agreeable passenger, he may well offer you one as well. This is a grey area- you can't expect drivers to feed you. Each day you may have four or five drivers stopping at service stations for a meal. If you feel obligated to buy a meal because your driver does, you will be broke before you know it. Many drivers will insist that they treat you to a meal and I found declining politely sometimes actually offended the driver. Sometimes you have to accept. If accepting such generosity from a stranger bothers you, you can only resolve that when you are the driver, you'll do the same thing for the hitch-hikers you pick up.

On no account should you yourself pay the inflated prices charged at highway restaurants. Try to stay within your "84 Cent" budget. If you have some food with you and your driver doesn't offer to stand you to lunch, then there's no problem.

Where to Get Your "84 Cent" Meals

Farmer's Market - food markets are the most interesting places to find reasonably priced food. This is where all the locals shop, the vendors are friendly, and the variety available is amazing.

Universities - many cafeterias have subsidized food prices to help the college student. Even if you are not staying at a university for the night, don't hesitate to cycle or walk to a campus nearby. It is a misconception that all university meals are bad; many of the smaller private schools have excellent meals at reasonable prices.

Hospitals - another place with subsidized food prices. You don't have to be a patient with a white bracelet around your wrist either.

Supermarkets - another very economical place to get food and interesting in themselves in foreign countries.

Government Buildings - many of the larger buildings have their own cafeteria with subsidized food prices.

Cheap Cafes - Ask if you can wash dishes for an hour or two for a hot and hearty meal. See 'Speaking the Language', chapter 18, page 300.

Street Vendors - their only overhead is the sky above them; it's worth trying a Bulgarian hot dog, Russian ice cream, or a falafel in the Middle East.

The most expensive places for food are restaurants in tourist areas, highway restaurants, and four to five star hotels.

Accommodation

Your efforts to find accommodation will often bring you meals too. Your hosts will usually take it for granted that you will eat with them as well. But obviously they have already done enough for you by asking you to stay. If no offer for food is forthcoming, don't ask.

Finding accommodation in private homes will, most of the time, mean that you will also have dinner and breakfast as well, often enough to keep you going for the day. I estimate that meals earned and/or provided to me during my

110-day trip probably saved me about $350 at supermarket prices.

I was in the market square of Turku. Since the Finns don't have too many tourists in the winter, my flag caught their attention. On four occasions in twenty minutes , people working in the market brought me coffee, fruit and conversation. The whole scene was a little bit embarassing. One man even offered me money; needless to say, I refused.

You might be advised that the Middle East is not a good place to hitch-hike or cycle; I found it otherwise. After hitching through Turkey, I found myself near the Syrian border and looking for a ride to Damascus. A Jordanian picked me up. He was a somewhat intimidating looking character, probably six foot four, wearing a three piece suit and driving a Mercedes-Benz. Before he accepted me as a passenger, he put me through a five minute questionnaire on my opinions of the Arab people, the Arab-Israeli conflict, and the world in general. I seemed to pass the test. As we drove
along he asked me how much money I had, reluctantly I said I had only $200 left. He was amazed. He asked how I could possibly travel on such a small amount of money. He then said he was going to charge me $100 for the ride and $100 for a meal at a restaurant when we stopped. After a while he started to sing in Arabic and he was clapping when he wasn't holding onto the steering wheel (luckily the desert road was fairly straight). He requested some songs from me . I did my best and was on what seemed to be the 99th verse of 'Row, Row,Row Your Boat', feeling like a complete idiot, when he pulled into a restaurant. I was his guest for a delicious three-course meal. This was definitely an interesting example of Arabic humor.

I was hitching through the countryside of Sweden when a very nice elderly couple picked me up. After a short ride they dropped me off. Within a matter of minutes, as I stood there waiting for another ride, they returned bringing me a sandwich and chocolate.

7

Saving on Foreign Exchange and Other Matters Monetary

Anyone traveling, whether you're hitch-hiking, cycling, or with a tour group, obviously has to watch the pennies, and if you are entering new countries every few days it is easy to get confused about exchange rates and currencies. Money is business. In Europe all train, bus and airport terminals, and small independent exchange shops in tourist areas and at borders, have the exchange rates posted. The ethical dealers post both the buying and selling rates - this will save you having to shop around for the actual rate. City banks provide the best rates.

Every time you buy or sell currency, the banks or other agencies, private or public, receive a commission and/or a small service fee. If you need only five or ten dollars in the local currency, it's distressing to find yourself paying a hefty service charge. In Israel, for example, to change ten American dollars in a bank, you are charged a one percent commission plus a one-dollar service fee. That's a loss of 11 percent.

The worst places to exchange money are hotel banks or agencies, border banks and airport banks. Before you leave on your trip, go to your own bank and get at least the currencies of the first two countries you are definitely going to visit. Estimate how much money you think you will need for each country, but don't overextend yourself. If you find you will need more money while in the country you are visiting, then simply go to a city bank to exchange more money. But do this as little as possible to avoid bank charges. The idea is to increase your buying power, not reduce it. If you do have money left over, one thing you should not do is exchange your remaining money into dollars, and then change it into another currency. This will cost you twice in commission and/or service charges at the bank. As you travel you will gain experience in dealing with money and estimating how much you will need for each country. Obviously you will need much more money in Switzerland than in Morocco. Sometimes your itinerary may change. You might drop or add a country to your travel plans. Therefore I recommend that you wait to exchange money or cash travelers checks the day before you are to cross into the next country.

Travelers' checks are your best form of money. Cooks, Barclays, Visa, American Express are all very good companies to deal with. American Express has more offices world-wide than the other companies - this is helpful when you are in a small out-of-the-way town with no local currency in hand. But if you are only going to the United Kingdom, then go with Barclay's since they will have more branches at your disposal. Minimize the headache of replacing lost or stolen traveler checks by keeping the serial numbers separate and record the serial numbers of the used checks. This will speed up the process of getting your checks replaced. You should carry 85% of your money in traveler's checks and the rest in cash. For more information on traveler's checks, call one of these major companies in Canada or the U.S.
Thomas Cook MasterCard -1-800-223-7373
Barclays Bank-for Barclays 'VISA traveler's checks call-1-800-847-2245
American Express 1-800-221-7282

Even though using credit cards and bank cards may seem the most convenient way to 'carry' money, there may be less incentive to try creative methods outlined in this book and you ultimately may lose sight of what traveling should be all about. When you are three thousand miles away from home, with not a worry or care in the world, many young travelers will be tempted to over extend themselves. For those who can manage their money responsibly, then by all means, take a credit card or a bank card, but guard it very closely. If your credit card is stolen, report it immediately.

If your bank is a member of the Cirrus network, call 1-800-424-7787 to find out about ATM machine availability in Europe. Also, check with your credit card company to see if you can leave money in their account rather than yours. Credit cards don't advertise this service because they make more money from the interest on your monthly bill. This advance credit will allow you to withdraw money at ATM machines around the world. With all these options available to you , your money matters should be solved. At least carry traveler checks, a small amount of cash and at least investigate the other options mentioned in this chapter.

Sometimes, you might find you aren't able to find a bank when you need one, and you arrive at a border late at night and even the border bank is closed. Now what do you do? Let's say the nearest town across the border is only five miles away, the weather is horrible and the only way to get there is by taxi. Even if you don't have the currency of that country the taxi driver will accept American cash. Be sure to bring at least 50 U.S. one dollar bills. Why? If you give the taxi driver a twenty, both of you may have no idea as to how much you should be getting back in his currency. You may lose money unknowingly. Six, seven or eight one dollar bills will seem like a lot more money to him. You are not being unscrupulous, you just shouldn't rip yourself off if you don't have to. That is why it is helpful to find a local newspaper every two or three weeks and cut out the international exchange rate chart and keep it with you for transactions such as this.

It was late at night in a small German town, traveling without any German currency, when I came upon a small hotel. I had no choice but to try and exchange money with the bartender. Neither of us knew the exchange rates and I found out the next day I lost about 20% or $10 on the exchange. For a person on an "84 Cent" budget, that mistake really hurt!

Ways to Beat the System
Your Driver

Especially in small countries where drivers often cross into neighboring countries on a regular basis for business or pleasure, your driver will often be glad to exchange some of his local currency for the currency you have from a neighboring country. Neither of you will lose on commissions or service charges. Don't expect the driver to exchange large sums of money though, maybe up to $30.

Other Travelers

Spotting other travelers is not hard

to do, some can be spotted a mile away. A traveler in the street will be willing to change a small amount with you, if he or she is bound for a country you have just left or has a surplus of local currency to exchange for dollars or other hard currency.

Black Market

Exchanging money on the black market essentially means buying or selling money in order to make a profit illegally. People make a living at it. Some of them are dishonest, some are not, so watch out. This method works only in countries where the currency's actual value is less than the official value the governments put on it, so be sure you know what the bank rate is and what the going black market rate is. The official rate can be determined by checking newspapers or magazines (Newsweek carries a weekly listing) before you enter the country or at the exchange facilities at the border.

If there's a flourishing black market, you'll be approached in tourist areas when you get off the bus or train - they'll be waiting for you. A sampling of the rates offered to you and the advice of other traveleres will let you know what the going market rates are and whether it's risky or not to exchange. In some countries you can be put in jail for dealing in the black market. In others, authorities turn a blind eye.

Don't exchange money in a

hurry in a crowded spot, where the dealer could suddenly dash away or do a last-minute switch in the roll of bills he gives you. Count the money yourself, even if he has counted it out for you. Overall, I don't think dealing in the black market is worth the risk of being thrown in a roach-infested jail.

Selling Articles

You may find odds and ends in your backpack that you really don't need any longer and which you can sell. You can also take along a few small items from home which can be sold abroad, for example, small calculators, costume jewelry, nail clippers--any small transportable item that does not take up very much room in your backpack. If you are in third world countries you may want to simply give away some of these items to people who have never seen them before. You will realize as you travel just what you have that is surplus, and it's often possible to dispose of used clothing at flea markets and perhaps at the same time find a bargain or two to buy. I took along three tennis racquets to sell for extra money - one to a driver, and two at tennis clubs.

Border Regulations

Money, or the lack of it, can be a problem at borders. Certain countries, particularly some developing and third world countries will insist that you exchange a certain sum of money into their currencies before allowing you in. This can be a lump sum or an amount based pro-rata on the number of days you plan to stay. Getting a visa may be conditional on making this exchange. Fortunately this is not necessary in Western Europe and only one or two Eastern European countries, such as Romania, make this a requirement for entry. Double-check this information at tourist offices or embassies in your country before you go. In some countries you are expected to spend this sum; in others, you will be able to change it back at a bank before you leave. If you are expected to spend it, you can either concentrate your gift or souvenir shopping in that country or use the methods outlined earlier for making unofficial exchanges. Your best bet is to find another tourist who can use some more local currency.

Another border nuisance is the official who demands that you have a certain amount of money to guarantee that you can support yourself while in the country and for onward passage. Never arrive at your first country with four or five hundred dollars and a one way plane ticket. The authorities may be suspicious that you are going to find work illegally, i.e. without a work permit. Being able to tell them where you will be staying - the address of a friend, a relative, a hotel or even a fictitious address may help. Don't worry, though. This usually only happens when you fly to your first destination from North America, And since you will presumably have money for return airfare plus a small emergency fund in the form of travelers' checks it shouldn't be an insurmountable problem.

A letter from your father, if done on an impressive letterhead, promising to be responsible for you, might help. Of course, you may never need to use it or have any intentions of using it, it's just to satisfy the border authorities. It might read something like this:

To Whom It May Concern:

This letter is to advise that my son/ daughter is making a world tour. I will be responsible for any costs which might be incurred in furthering his/ her departure from any country.

Yours truly,
John D. Dad

Another way to enlist parental cooperation without actually costing your parents anything is to have them set up a bank account for you. You can then have the bank arrange drawing rights or a traveler's letter of credit for you in specified foreign countries. (bring a list of the banks' locations for each country). People on lengthy trips often use this method, since their money at home keeps earning interest and they don't need to carry large sums with them in cash or traveler's checks. You will then have a letter from your bank to a specific bank in each country where it's necessary, instructing them to let you withdraw a specific sum of money. It's up to you if you want to use this service, but at the very least you will be able to show the letter at borders where necessary to establish that you have the funds available.

Certain countries will ask you at the border if you are a tourist or transit. If you say tourist, then they will charge you to enter the country. If you say transit, which means you are simply passing through to get to the other country, then they will normally not charge you. Say transit, not tourist, especially if you are only going to stay in the country during the allowed 'transit' period anyway.

Value Added Tax: Refunds

Anytime you buy or rent something be sure to ask for a receipt or depending on the item, ask for the document that declares how much VAT you have paid. Some sales people either forget, don't bother or purposely neglect to advise you on this savings. But the only way you can recoup this tax is by presenting the receipt/papers to border officials when you leave the country. If the amount of VAT is very small, then it is not worth your time to apply for a refund. When you do receive a check from the government it is usually in their currency and by the time you exchange it into dollars you might not be left with very much. Sales taxes range from 6.5%- 25% for car rentals and 15% - 25 % on general purchased items. It would be worthwhile to ask if the refund is going to be in your currency or the foreign currency and if there are any additional charges. Allow at least an extra hour at the airport for processing of VAT refund forms.

VAT Rates

Austria 21 %	Italy 19%
Belgium 25%	Luxemborg 19%
Czech Republic 15%	Netherlands 18%
Denmark 22%	Norway 20%
Finland 19%	Poland none
France 22%	Portugal 17%
Germany 14%	Spain 12%
Greece 16%	Sweden 23%
Hungary 25%	Switzerland 6.5%
Ireland 10%	United Kingdom 15%

Money Crises

If your money is lost or stolen you can have a relative or friend send you money through an American Express MoneyGram. For more information call 1-800-933-3278 in Canada and 1-800-666-3947 in the U.S. The sender pays the service fee.

You can also wire money through the money transfer services operated by Western Union at 1-800-225-5227 or American Express 1-800-543-4080; in Canada 1-800-933-3278

General Advice on Money

• Carry travelers checks in mostly small denominations, 10s & 20s & very few 50s & 100s.
• Carry only a small amount of cash at any time.
• Change all coins for paper currency before you cross a border; banks in other countries won't accept foreign coins.
• Bring 20 to 50 American one-dollar bills for small unofficial foreign exchanges.
• If you don't have the time or opportunity to change your remaining currency before you leave a country, don't feel you have to spend it: you can change it at a bank or with another tourist or with your driver.
• Be careful with black market dealers.
• Keep your list of travelers' check serial numbers separate from your checks.
• The safest way to carry your money, travelers' checks, passport, and other important small paper items, is in a money belt, worn under your clothes. It's a good idea to wrap them in plastic to keep them water-proof.
• If you plan to be in a country for less than a day, bring some food with you - bread and fruit can keep you going all day-so that you won't have to exchange any money at all.
• Sometimes say transit, not tourist, when entering a country.

What the Dollar or Pound is Worth in Foreign Currency

Rates are *only approximate* due to the *constant* changing currency rates. Exchanging money in numerous countries can be confusing and the numbers below are meant to help estimate what something costs in relation to your own currency.

Country	U.S. $	Canadian $	British Pound
Algeria	$1 = 42 dinars $2.40 = 100 dinars	$1 = 30 dinars $3.27 = 100 dinars	1 £ = 133 dinars
Austria	$1 = 9 schillings $11 = 100 schillings	$1 = 7 schillings $15 = 100 schillings	1£ = 15 schillings
Belgium	$1 = 27 francs $3.68 = 100 francs	$1 = 20 francs $4.99 = 100 francs	1£ = 45 francs
Bulgaria	$ = 68 leva $185 = 10,000	$ = 50 leva $251 = 10,000 leva	1£ = 105 leva
Czech Republic	$1 = 22 korun $457 = 10,000 korun	$1 = 16 korun $620 = 10,000 korun	1£ = 37 korun
Denmark	$1 = 5 kroner $19 = 100 kroner	$1 = 4 kroner $26 = 100 kroner	1£ = 8.5 kroner
Egypt	$1 = 3 pounds $38 = 100 pounds	$1 = 2 pounds $51 = 100 pounds	1£ = 5 pounds
England	$1 = 62 pence $1.61 = 1£	$1 = 45 pence $2.17 = 1£	
Finland	$1 = 4 markka $25 = 100 markka	$1 = 3 markka $34 = 100 markka	1£ = 6.5 markka
France	$1 = 4.5 francs $21 = 100 francs	$1 = 3 francs $30 = 100 francs	1£ = 7.5 francs
Germany	$1 = 1.3 marks $74 = 100 marks	$1 = 1 mark $100 = 100 marks	1£ = 2.2 marks
Greece	$1 = 213 drachmas $ 5 = 1,000 drachmas	$1 = 156 drachmas $6 = 1,000 drachmas	1£ = 356 drachmas
Hungary	$1 = 91 forints $ 110 = 10,000 forints	$1 = 67 forints $150 = 10,000 forints	1£ = 173 forints
Ireland	$1 = 60 pence $169 = 100 punts	$1 = 44 pence $230 = 100 punts	1£ = 95 pence

Country	U.S. $	Canadian $	British Pound
Israel	$1 = 2.6 sheqels $38 = 100 sheqels	$1 = 1.9 sheqels $51 = 100 sheqels	1£ 4.3 sheqels
Italy	$1 = 1,473 lire $6.79 = 10,000 lire	$1 = 1,085 lire $9.21 = 10,000 lire	1£ = 2,484 lire
Jordan	$1 = .57 fils $175 = 100 fils	$1 = .42 fils $238 = 100 fils	1£ = 1.02 fils

Luxembourg uses Belgian francs
Liechtenstein uses Swiss francs

Country	U.S. $	Canadian $	British Pound
Morocco	$1 = 7 dirhams $138 = 1,000 dirhams	$1 = 5.3 dirhams $187 = 1,000 dirhams	1£. = 11.6 dirhams
Netherlands	$1 = 1.5 guilders $67 = 100 guilders	$1 = 1.1 guilders $92 = 100 guilders	1£ = 2.4 guilders
Norway	$1 = 6 kroner $17 = 100 kroner	$1 = 4 kroner $23 = 100 kroner	1£ = 9.6 kroner

Monaco uses French francs

Country	U.S. $	Canadian $	British Pound
Poland (new currency)	$1 = 2 zloty $48 = 100 zloty	$1 = 1.5 zloty $65 = 100 zloty	1£ = 4.2 zloty
Portugal	$1 = 136 escudos $7.35 = 100 escudos	$1 = 100 escudos $9.97 = 100 escudos	1£ = 227 escudos
Romania	$1 = 1,529 lei $65 = 100,000 lei	$1 = 1,127 lei $88 = 100,000 lei	1£ = 2,102 lei
Slovak Republic	$1 = 32 koruna $312 = 10,000 koruna	$1 = 21 koruna $431 = 10,000 koruna	1£ = 53 koruna
Spain	$1 = 113 pesetas $9 = 1,000 pesetas	$1 = 84 pesetas $12 = 1,000 pesetas	1£ = 188 pesetas

Scotland uses English pounds

Country	U.S. $	Canadian $	British Pound
Sweden	$1 = 6.5 kroner $15 = 100 kroner	$1 = 5 kroner $20 = 100 kroner	1£ = 10.7 kroner
Switzerland	$1 = 1 franc $94 = 100 francs	$1 = .80 franc $127 = 100 francs	1£ = 1.7 francs
Syria	$1 = 47 pounds $2.50 = 100 pounds	$1 = 41 pounds $2.90 = 100 pounds	1£ = 69 pounds
Tunisia	$1 = .9 dinar $109 = 100 dinars	$1 = .7 dinar $148 = 100 dinars	1£ = 1.7 dinars
Turkey	$1 = 38,762 liras $2.51 = 100,000 liras	$1 = 28,571 liras $3.50 = 100,000 liras	1£ = 73,455 liras

8

Before You Go

Author's Recommendation - Travel Alone

In order to make the ideas in this book really work for you, the author strongly recommends that the male hitch-hiker, at least, travel alone. The cost-saving methods recommended will just not be as successful if you're traveling with someone else. The driver is less likely to invite you to his home; the farmer who finds you on the doorstep is not so apt to give you shelter. Two males traveling together are likely to make a driver suspicious and will get fewer rides than the male-female pair or two women. But the hitch-hiker on his or her own has the best chance of all. Many drivers just do not have room for two people and two backpacks, especially in Europe where most vehicles are small, with little luggage space.

On your own, every moment on your travels is an education in itself. You are forced to cope with the language barriers, being lost or just dealing with the fact that you are in

a whole new world. You learn how to handle the strangers you meet every day, deal with foreign currencies and customs.

But isn't it lonely cycling or hitch-hiking? Aren't you afraid to travel by yourself? Not at all. There is a feeling of you-against-the-elements. It tests your ability to survive on your own. Each day's encounters with people and surroundings present a new challenge. There is complete freedom to go where you please and do what you choose.

You are seldom alone or lonely. You meet more people each day than more conventional tourists do, and certainly more than you do sitting behind an office desk. Most of the experiences will be positive ones, but even the negative ones, especially seen in retrospect, are often learning experiences.

In Turkey, I was picked up by a father and son. I think it was the first time they had ever given a foreigner a ride. The language barrier was almost complete but we exchanged laughs, and also wallets for souvenirs. Then car trouble delayed us for more than three hours. However, the delay proved interesting. We detoured to a shed that turned out to be the local muffler repair shop. I watched as two young boys, neither of whom seemed more than ten years old, used the simplest tools and equipment to repair our muffler. Motorists who venture off the beaten track often report on the skill and ingenuity of the small-town car repair establishment and it was enlightening for me to see this phenomenon for myself.

But isn't travel much pleasanter if you have a friend along to share your experiences? It may be, but you have to balance this against the smaller success you will have, traveling with a companion, in getting rides, food and accommodation. In any case, you will meet many other travelers along the way and when you get home, you'll be able to share stories of your travels with family and friends.

It's a good idea, too, to keep a journal.

Traveling Companions

The decision to travel solo can easily be changed en route. People who start out traveling solo can easily meet other people at youth hostels, on trains and buses, or while cycling. One of the very few people I've ever traveled with was another hitch-hiker who was already a passenger in the car I was getting into. We traveled together for two days, had a great time, then went our separate ways. Essentially, you could have a different traveling companion every week if you wanted to. If you can't find a friend to go with you on your travels, don't let that stop you from going. Sometimes we simply take a friend along for safety. Even though you may be great friends back at school, traveling together seven days a week, 24 hours a day is a different situation altogether. I have heard of many relationships that fell apart because two friends got on each others' nerves or because one person wanted to go to plays, shop, lie in their hotel room while the other one wanted to hike the mountains, cycle, and hitchhike. My best advice is to work out your interests before you leave on your travels to avoid any unnecessary conflict while on the road together. This preparation could save your friendship or marriage and make your travels a fun adventure. If you are committed to going with your school mate or boy friend, I recommend that after traveling together for three weeks, you should travel apart for a few days or a week, then plan to reunite on a certain day and time at a youth hostel or embassy. It's a great way to rejuvenate your relationship. To find out how alike or different you are from your friend, compare the experiences while the two of you were apart.

Women Travelers: Precautions and Concerns

For young women, there's an obvious safety factor in traveling in pairs or in male-female combinations. Male-female combinations will have better luck getting rides than a male by himself. Drivers see couples as very safe passengers.

Women on their own should obviously choose their rides with care. A woman alone should not get in a car with two or more men in it. Just ignore the car or wave it on; waiting for a couple or a family is not a bad idea. So is expertise at self-defence, such as karate. One enterprising woman hitch-hiker suggests that as soon as you get in you take out some fruit and ostentatiously peel it with your hunting knife. You may either have to take a lot of apples or learn to peel very slowly.

For most women, hitch-hiking should not be your main source of transportation, unless your partner is male, or you are athletic and confident about taking care of yourself. You will, however, find hitch-hiking, cycling or simply walking the streets of a foreign city really not that different than walking the streets of an unfamiliar city in your own country. You may get whistled at no matter where you go. Walk with confidence and people will usually leave you alone.

It's impossible to evaluate every country in Europe and Great Britain on relative safety . But a good rule of thumb would be to ask about the crime rate of the country, and the male mentality towards women. To illustrate my point from a male perspective: I was picked up by a 60 year old lady in Sweden and an elderly couple in Norway - those experiences alone suggested to me the Scandinavian people were open and trusting and men were considered generally trustworthy. This is not to say men from other cultures are not trustworthy; they may just have an objectionable way of showing an interest in you. Italian men, I am told, can be forward and aggressive, never intending any harm, but their persistence can be annoying. A firm 'no thank-you' will usually discourage them on the streets. Women should not hitch in Italy. Talk to fellow travelers and ask questions about any concerns you have, and then you can decide which form of transportation you should use. In parts of Asia, the Middle East and Africa, in Moslem areas in particular, it's best to take a train or bus instead, or travel with a male friend. All women should dress conservatively and blondes might want to cover their hair in some countries to draw less attention.

For the reluctant female hitch-hiker, there will be some situations where it will be easier. Let's say you are at a ski resort, the ski hill is just ten miles down the road and you've missed the bus. Rather than wait an hour or two for the next bus, thumb a ride! Most people are driving to the ski resort for the same reason you are. Wait for a car that has skis on the roof. Another way to overcome your concern about hitch-hiking is to take a bus out of a major city to the first small country town. From this point you can hitch-hike from small town to small town using the secondary roads. Small town folk and farmers will be glad to give you a ride.

Cycling on your own should not be of great concern or worry. If you cycle in the Middle East you will draw attention to yourself but not on the same scale as if you were to hitch-hike.

Here's a list of the best hitch-hiking methods for women by themselves or with another female. The following are in no particular order:

- Highway service stations - hop from station to station
- Ride boards at universities
- Yacht-hiking
- Ferry docks - ask drivers for a ride
- Hitching a ride with a bus tour
- Prearranged Rides
- Toll Booths
- Rest areas
- Citizen Band Switch-Over
- Two rides, one driver
- Airplanes at small airports
- Entrance ramps of major highways

What to Take

One of the first considerations when packing your backpack is weight. The second is comfort. No matter what season you travel, temperatures can fluctuate sharply: it can be chilly at high noon in the shadow of the Alps and bitterly cold in the desert at night.

The best solution is to dress in layers, adding or removing as necessary. Even though you may be in Russia in December when it is bitterly cold, unless you plan to spend a few weeks there, I wouldn't take a bulky coat. Once you are in the warmer climates for good, you will find that your coat will take up too much room in your backpack. If you do take one, your best options are to either sell it or trade it at a swap meet or flea market (there are plenty of them throughout Europe) for something useful in your travels. Mailing it home may be too costly, but you could leave it with a friend or relative in the city which will be your point of exit when flying back to your country

In order to facilitate your packing and re-packing every day, you can group similar items together. For example, socks should be put in one clear plastic bag, underwear in another and so on. This will save you time when you want to find just one item in your backpack. Rather than having to take nearly everything out individually, you can remove the bags and get to the bag you need. Also, the bags act as extra protection in case it rains. If you are really organized, then keep a list of what's where in each compartment to save you even more time. Pack as compactly as possible, filling up all spaces, in places such as shoes with miscellaneous items.

Before you finish preparing for your travels, may I suggest that you buy any new clothes and some related items during your travels. You will find buying something in a country to be a lot of fun, and possibly cheaper too! Why not buy sandals in Spain or a Swiss Army knife in Switzerland?

Men and Women

National flags of Canada, United States and/or your state/provincial flag - a minimum 3 feet x 5 feet in size; money belt; passport, money, driver's licence (International one as well), 10 photocopies of passport, 15 passport-size photographs - keep all of this separate from the originals, photocopy of prescription glasses/contact lenses.

- 6 pairs gym socks
- 6 pairs underwear or 2-3 pairs of Tilley's "instant dry" underwear
- 2-6 T-shirts ***
- 1 pair jeans
- 1 cotton turtle neck (winter)
- 1 long-sleeve casual shirt
- 1 jeans jacket
- 1 light sweater
- 1 light down jacket (with hood)
- 2-6 sweatshirts (depends on material thickness) ***
- 1 toque or hat
- 1 scarf (winter)
- 1 poncho or rain cape (can double as groundsheet)
- 1 quick-drying bathing suit
- 1 pair hiking boots-low cut for summer, high cut for snow
- 1 pair running shoes or good walking shoes
- 1 pair sandals

- 1 pair shorts
- 1 towel
- 1 pair of long underwear (very useful in cold climates)
- Clear plastic bags to pack your clothing in groups and for dirty or wet clothing

*** I recommend taking as many T-shirts and sweatshirts as possible to give as gifts and/or trading. Sometimes, I traded for clothing right off the backs of people walking down city streets - it's a fun way to add to your souvenir collection.

Men

- 1 pair dress pants
- 1 dress shirt and tie
- 1 light suit jacket (for dress code occasions or use light sweater, shirt & tie combination)

Women

- 2 bras
- 2 blouses
- 1 skirt (crush-proof, drip dry)

Toilet Kit

Note: carry items in light plastic containers.
For both men and women: toothbrush, toothpaste, soap, shampoo, comb, nail clippers, nail file, nail brush (can also be used for laundry), chapstick, suntan lotion, toilet paper, facecloth, needle and thread, mirror, sunglasses
Men: shaving cream, razor, extra blades.

Women: cosmetics, sanitary aids, hairbrush

Hairdryer: optional and you will need a converter. Sometimes you can style and dry your hair cycling down a mountain road or sticking your head out of a car for a few seconds at 60 m.p.h. It really works!!!

First Aid Kit

Aspirin, band-aids, first-aid ointment, iodine for cuts or scrapes, tensor bandages for sprains, Kaopectate for diarrhea, Halazone tablets to kill bacteria in water, motion-sickness tablets.

Backpack

Choose a bright-colored backpack, preferably orange or yellow, so that you'll be easier to see in the dark and along the highway. Try on the various types available; have the salesperson in the store put weights in them to see how comfortable they are likely to be on the road. Be sure the one you choose rests comfortably on your hips as well as your shoulders. Buy a backpack with an internal frame - an external frame can be uncomfortable against your back, especially if you have a lot of weight in it. Some backpacks are so well-designed that it would take a thief on a crowded bus twenty minutes to figure out how to steal something. Some backpacks convert into what looks like a nice piece of luggage, in case you want to look the part when walking into a five star hotel. You should be willing to spend at least $150 on a good backpack for long journeys and select a "high" pack rather than a "wide" one. It will be easier to load this type into a car and to walk down crowded streets without bumping into people.

I can't say I pride myself in traveling light. I carried approximately 62 pounds which is on the high side. Men should expect to carry at least 50 pounds and women between 40 and 55 pounds. It's not as heavy as you may think, the weight is distributed fairly evenly and a good backpack with thick straps will alleviate any possible strain on your shoulders and back. Carrying a heavy backpack was one of my ways of getting a good workout. No matter how hard we try, especially first-time backpackers, most of us overpack. You will find what is the ideal weight as you travel and you will be able to discard, give away or sell items as you travel to reduce your weight. It's a bit like being on Weight Watchers; your backpack weight will go up and down and hopefully you'll find the weight that suits you.

Tent

If you follow the suggestions in this book you may never have to use a tent. The author carried one for four months and used it only once, on the last day of my travels. It's definitely worthwhile carrying, for the feeling of security it affords. It's reassuring to know you can camp out with a roof over your head if you have to, especially on beaches. One of the best ways to wake up is to see the sunrise over the ocean water. If the beach seems to be somewhat deserted, (non-tourist area) then pitch it. If it's a high traffic area the police and locals may object to your presence; ask before you pitch. A one-or two-person nylon tent of light color, with a screen and zippered closing, can be very light in weight (only 1-2 pounds). If you plan to do a lot of camping, then invest wisely since this may be one of your main abodes on your travels.

Other Equipment

Useful items to have along include a penlight with extra batteries, a spoon and fork, plastic bowl, an all-purpose knife, Michelin maps (more detail than any other maps), writing paper and envelopes, ballpoint pens, magic markers (for making signs) and accompanying cardboard (which you can get at service stations), box of matches, nylon rope, string, water flask. Take at least a 35 millimeter camera with a flash, extra batteries and film, solar-powered calculator, alarm clock, or a wrist watch with a built in alarm-clock; tape-recorder - with a built in transistor radio. It's really interesting to hear our songs in another language, sometimes very poorly translated, listening for instance, to 'Hey Jude' by the Beatles in Hungarian as you walk down a solitary road or through a forest. Earplugs are handy on noisy trains or with snoring room-mates; clothesline to hang clothes in your hotel room or barn.

Make sure you take contraceptives. **Optional items:** portable cooking kit and its accessories ; a small compass; even seriously consider taking a tennis racquet and don't hesitate to visit a sports club. Ask for the pro and he/she might waive any guest or court fees.

Sleeping Bag

The warmest, and most expensive, sleeping bags are filled with down but a small light-weight one is more practical for the traveler. The type that tapers at the feet is ideal if you find it comfortable to sleep in.

Weapons !!??

Sometimes at my lectures Americans ask, should I take a weapon? When you are planning a trip that should be full of fun and adventure, it's rather a sad commentary that you should even consider taking a weapon. As you pack do you say to yourself, 'Hmm, let's see here, I better not forget my toothpaste, my swim suit , my camera, and, oh yes, my gun.' If you are thinking of having to defend yourself every day, then you shouldn't leave home. You cannot carry guns across most borders. An all-purpose knife for eating or whittling a stick could be used to defend yourself, but only in life-threatening situations.Inconspicuous items that could be used to defend yourself are mace (illegal in some countries), and even a tennis or squash racquet, particularly good for defending yourself from wandering dogs.

A Complete Cycling and Camping Equipment List by Jacques Menard

Jacques and his wife Cindy have cycled extensively throughout Europe on five separate occasions. Having experienced the 'ups and downs' on the roads of Europe and with their expertise and thorough knowlege of cycling, I have provided their 'must take' list for the full-time touring cyclist.

Front Bag

Small plastic bag to cover saddle overnight, toilet paper, hat, riding gloves, sunglasses, sunblock, roadlight, camera with 35mm to 80 mm zoom, film, miniature tripod, pen and notepad, pencil with eraser, novel, radio with sw, 1:50,000 route maps, wallet & passport, envelopes for mailing back postcards purchased on route.
Store traveler's check receipts inside end of one handlebar and photocopy of passport in the other.

Camping Equipment (front panniers)

Tent, sleeping bag, self inflating mattress, plastic cover sheet, stuff sack pillow, food cooler (600 square inch) cargo pack for fresh food supplied to be mounted on top of rear pannier rack.

Cooking Kit

Stove, teflon pan, tea pot, lighters, pasta/rice pot, cutlery, plastic spatula, salt tablets, collapsable plastic jug, plastic egg holder, 2 cups, 2 plates, can opener, plastic scouring pad, playing cards, spices, cooking oil, sugar, tea bouillon cubes.

First Aid Kit

Bandages: 10 - 3/8" x 1 1/2", 6 - 3/4" x 3", 1 - 2" x 4", 1 knuckle, 2 fingertip, 2" x 3" bandage, 3.5"bandages, 1" square bandage.
Dressings: 4" x 4" adhesive strips, surgical tape, 2"guaze roll, 1" gauze roll, 1 - 3"x 3" compress, 1 - 2" x 2" compress, 2.5"x 4"compress tweezers, scissors, suture package, finger splints, alcohol swabs, soap, sterile cotton, burn salve, iodine, polysporin, 1 amonia inhalant, ipecac, lypsyl, styptic pencil, nasal spray, headache tablets, anti-acid tablets, alka seltzer, ben gay.

Tools

5" wire cutters, 6" needlenose vicegrips, 6" needlenose pliers, 6"pliers, 6" adjustable crescent wrench, spoke wrench, allen wrenches for all hex sizes on bike, rear gear sprocket remover, air pump, combination screwdriver with tips for all screw heads on bike, duct tape, loctite, grease, tire irons, tire pressure gauge, tire patching kit, oil/chain lubricant, old tooth brush.

Parts

Ball bearings (all sizes on your bike), spare tube, five spokes attached below rear chain stay, leather lace (soak then stretch and bind around broken part and let dry), folding spare tire kept in pannier, spare tube, tent patching kit, brake blocks, spare of longest cable (kept behind frame of rear pannier), spares of the various mounting bolts, nuts, washers, screws you have on your bike, spare light bulbs.

Clothes

Helmet, sun hat, riding shoes, riding gloves, riding shorts, sandals, socks, underwear, t-shirts, riding/rain poncho, handerchiefs, hooded sweatshirt/sweater, wash and wear dress, slacks and shirt, windbreaker, shaving kit, swim suit, towel.

Thanks to Italian red wine, the Leaning Tower of Pisa leans more at night than during the day.

9.

Paperwork

Passports

Before you leave, make sure your passport is valid well beyond your expected date of return, that you have signed it, and that the personal information in it is up to date. If it should expire while you are abroad, it can be replaced at one of the embassies or consulates listed in each country in the chapter, 'Countries in a Capsule'. Replace it as soon as possible. Your passport is the primary identification that allows you into a country.

Passports are often stolen and you should keep yours on your person at all times. Carry it securely in an inside pocket or in your money belt. If you have to give it up at a hotel or hostel desk, or at a foreign embassy where you are applying for a visa, and you do not get it back in reasonable time, get in touch with your nearest embassy or consulate. A hotel or hostel may accept a photocopy of the identification section of your passport instead of the document itself. If you are staying in a hotel with shady characters behind the desk, politely insist that they accept the photocopy since you will need your passport when sightseeing. Take at least 10 photocopies with you.

If you do lose your passport, or it is stolen, report it immediately to your nearest embassy or consulate. Before a replacement can be issued, you will have to provide evidence of your citizenship, photographs, and pay the full fee. You should not carry your passport, other identification, money, travelers' checks, insurance, etc., all in one pocket or container. If you do, you could be left entirely without identification and funds.

How to Get Your Passport
Americans

Americans applying for a passport go to a passport agent at one of the Passport Agencies listed below, or a postal employee designated by the postmaster at selected post offices, a clerk of any State court of record, a clerk of any Federal court, a judge or clerk of selected probate courts, a U.S. embassy in a foreign country.

The applicant must present:
1) Proof of US citizenship in the form of:
a) a certified copy of his/her birth certificate under the seal of the official registrar; or
b) a naturalization certificate; or
c) a consular report of birth or certification of birth; or
d) his/her previous passport.
2) Two recent identical photographs that are good likenesses. Photographs should be clear and show the applicant full-face and with no hat against a plain white or light colored background. Photographs must measure 2in x 2in. Machine photographs are not acceptable.
3) Identification, e.g. a valid driving licence with a signature and containing a photograph or physical description.

The application for a new passport is called Form DSP-11 and is usually processed in ten days or less. Adults cost $65, under 18, $40. The passport is valid for ten years from the date of issue for adults; five years for persons under 18. Passports come in two sizes, the standard 24 page size and the 48 page size. Travelers intending to visit Third World and other countries where visas are required and many entry and exit stamps are entered into passports, should specifically ask for the 48 page passport. An accordion sheet of extra pages can be issued, however, to provide additional space in a valid passport, at any consulate or passport office abroad.

A passport holder can apply for passport renewal in person at any of the places listed above, or in certain circumstances by mail, together with a complete form DSP-82 'Application for Passport by Mail'. This is available from tourist agencies and the places listed above. Provide your previous passport, two new photographs and $55 ($30 for those under 18). Cheques or money orders should be made out to Passport Services, or pay cash in person.

Ask for the booklet "Your Trip Abroad", publication # 044-000-02335-1. This provides general information about passports. It costs $1.25 and you can get it from the U.S. Goverment Printing Office, Superintendent of Documents, P.O.Box 371954, Pittsburgh, PA 15250-7954, tel: (202) 783-3238

US Passport Agencies
Boston - Room E123, John F. Kennedy Building, Government Center, Boston, MA 02203 tel: (617) 223-3831
Chicago - suite 380, Klucynski Federal Building, 230 South Dearborn Street, Chicago, IL 60604 tel: (312) 353-7155
Honolulu - Room C-106, New Federal Building, 300 Ala Maona Blvd., P.O.Box 50185, Honolulu, HI 96850 tel: (808) 546-2130
Houston - One Allan Center, 500 Dallas St., Houston, TX 77002
Los Angeles - Hawthorne Federal Building, Room 2W16, 1500 Aviation Blvd, Lawndale, Los Angeles, CA 90261 tel: (213) 536-6503

Miami - Room 804, Federal Office Building, 51 Southwest First Ave., Miami, FL 33130 tel: (305) 350-4681

New Orleans - Room 400, International Trade Mart, 2 Canal St., New Orleans, LA 70130 tel: (504) 589-6161

New York - Room 270, Rockefeller Center, 630 Fifth Ave., New York, NY 10020 tel: (212) 541-7710

Philadelphia - Room 4426, Federal Building, 600 Arch St., Philadelphia, PA 19106 tel: (215) 597-7480

San Francisco - Room 1405, Federal Building, 450 Golden Gate Ave., San Francisco, CA 94102 tel: (415) 556-2630

Seattle - Room 906, Federal Building, 915 Second Ave., Seattle, WA 98174 tel: (206) 442-7945

Stamford - One Landmark Square, Broad and Atlantic Sts., Stamford, CT 06901

Washington - Passport Office, 1425 K St., NW, Washington, DC, 20524 tel: (202) 783-8170

in the UK

US Embassy, Passport And Citizenship Unit, 24 Grosvenor Square, London W1A 2LQ tel: 01-499-9000 ext 2563/2564 Open: 8:30 a.m.- 4 p.m.

Canadians

Canadians can use one of two methods to obtain a passport. You can get your application from one of the regional offices listed below, and apply personally with proof of Canadian citizenship. Or you can mail your application to The Passport Office, Department of Foreign Affairs and International Trade, Ottawa, Ontario K1A OG3, or call 1-800-567-6868. Do not mail an application to a regional office. If the application is correctly completed and supported by the proper documents, your passport will be mailed back to you in about two weeks.

At time of this publication the fee is $35. You must provide proof of citizenship (original certificates only - no photocopies) in the form of a birth certificate, obtained from Vital Statistics offices in your province of birth, or a Certificate of Citizenship, available from the nearest Federal Citizenship Court.

If you are married, or have been, details of your marriage(s) are required to establish the identity, citizenship, and custody of children.

You must submit two identical unmounted photographs taken from the same negative. Slot-machine photos or those subject to fading or sensitive to heat, or group photographs, are not acceptable. You must sign both photos in the signature slip underneath the picture and your guarantor must sign one photo on the back.

A Canadian passport is valid for five years.

Canadian Passport Agencies
Edmonton - suite 800, 10 Jasper Ave., Edmonton, Alberta T5J

4C3 tel: 1-800 567-6868

Montreal - suite 215, West Tower, Guy Favreau Complex, 200 Dorchester Blvd West, Montreal, Quebec H27 lX4 tel: (514) 283-2152

Quebec City - 10th Floor suite 1000, 2590 Blvd Laurier, Saint-Foy, Quebec GlV 4M6 tel: (418) 648-4990/92

Toronto - 478 University Ave., First Century Tower, Toronto, Ontario, M5G 2L9 tel: (4l6) 973-325l plus four other offices in Greater Toronto: call 973-3251 for other offices in your area.

U.K Citizens

You can pick up your passport applications through the main post office, travel agencies, or from one of the six regional passport offices in Belfast, Glasgow, London, Liverpool, Newport and Peterborough. Be sure to get your application countersigned by your bank manager, a solicitor, barrister, doctor, clergyman, or justice of the peace who knows your personally. Send or drop off the completed form, two recent, identical passport photos and 15 pounds to a regional passport office. Passports are valid for 10 years and for five years for those under 18 and take about three to four weeks to process.

Visas

Canadians, Americans and U.K. citizens do not need visas in Western European countries. U.K. citizens can use either a passport or a Visitor's Passport which is good for Western European travel only to visit a foreign country. The visa requirements change for those wishing to visit some Eastern European Middle Eastern and North African countries. A visa is an official permit to enter a country, granted by the government of that country. Visas are usually stamped in the passport and are valid for a particular purpose and stated time. Visa and tourist card requirements change frequently, depending on the country's political stability at the time and its relationship with your country. Depending on the relationship with a country, a country may not charge one nationality for a visa while it does another. To check the current situation, Americans consult form M-264 Visa Requirements of Foreign Governments, available at any passport agency or get a booklet called "Foreign Entry Requirements". It includes vital information, e.g., the need for an onward or return ticket, proof of sufficient funds, the telephone of the country's embassy in the U.S. You can get this booklet by sending your name, address, and 50 cents - coin or cheque to the Consumer Information Center, Pueblo, CO 8l009. The Bureau of Consular Affairs has a telephone line for current visa information - tel: (202) 663-1225, Mon-Fri. 8:30 a.m.- 4 p.m.

Americans can get the addresses of the nearest consulate or consular agent by consulting the

Congressional Directory, available in most libraries. The U.S. Department of State's **Overseas Citizens Emergency Center** at Room 4811, Washington DC 20520; (enclose a self-addressed stamped envelope) issues Consular Information Sheets, which cover crime, security, political climate, and health risks as well as embassy locations, entry requirements, currency regulations, and other matters. Travel warnings, which counsel travelers to avoid a country entirely, are issued in extreme cases. For the latest information, stop in at any passport office, consulate or embassy or call the interactive hotline - tel: (202) 647-5222.

Canadians can check with Travel Advisory Consular Services at 1-800-267-6788. They can give you general information on visa requirements for many countries (but not all). They can also tell you what the political climate is like in unsettled countries. Canadians can call the Info Center of the Department of Foreign Affairs and International Trade at 1-800-267-8376 to get the booklet 'Bon Voyage...But' or pick it up at a passport office - it gives a list of the Canadian addresses of embassies and consulates around the world and other general information.

United Kingdom citizens contact the 'Travel Advice Unit at 171 27 04 129 for advice on the current situation in foreign countries.

For a quick preview check 'Visa Requirements in a Nutshell' in this chapter for visa requirements and costs, but always double check with travel agents, the country's embassy or the national tourist board to find the most up to date visa situation. For more details refer to each country in the chapter, 'Countries in a Capsule'. If you have a definite itinerary and schedule, you can get any necessary visas from the relevant embassies in your own national capital or nearest consulate office before you leave. If you are going to Western Europe first, then it is often more convenient to get visas for certain Eastern European, Middle Eastern and North African countries in London or in the capital city of the neighboring country. The problem with getting them all in advance, even in London, especially if your itinerary is not definite, is that the visa is only good for a specific period after issue and may expire before you get to use it. You may find you want to visit or work in a country longer than planned. It is a waste of money to have to re-apply for the same visa, stand in line, submit more photographs and endure all the hassles that go along with this process.

Oil rich countries such as Libya, Gabon and Saudi Arabia are not so eager to allow tourists into their country. Since they have a wealth of money, they do not need tourist money or want Western values. With this in mind, it would be wiser to apply for a visa from the embassy in your own country rather than abroad. Embassies in your country may behave more appropriately than at smaller locations in another country where the officials may ignore all the rules set by their goverment and play by their own rules. Sometimes you may find that certain countries will allow you to obtain a visa only in your own country. Algeria, at one point, would not grant visas to cyclists or hitch-hikers. Tourists had to fly into the country, take a boat or have their own car. Despite this warning from the Canadian embassy in Rabat, Morocco, I took a chance since I couldn't afford the airfare or a boat ticket anyway. The embassy was right; I was refused entry. It pays to heed their warnings. In parts of Africa, some visas will be issued only if you fly in and out of the main airport. If you are traveling overland, many countries will not issue a visa unless you already have a visa for the next country en route, so get all your visas in the reverse order in which you will use them. Some visas state the port of entry into the country that you must use and you cannot rely on getting a visa at the border. I was told by an Egyptian ambassador in Jordan that I could do this and I found out this was not the case. I was refused entry.

The escalating costs of visas should be factored into your budget. Most countries will extend a tourist visa two or three times for a fee, but only when the present visa has almost expired and usually only in the capital city. Once it is extended, you will often need an exit visa before you can leave and will also have to provide definite proof of onward travel. If your visa expires, you may be fined or spend some time in jail.

Some countries allow you two or three weeks while in their country before you have to apply for a visa, but be sure to get it before that time period expires or else you will have a lot of explaining to do.

To get a visa you need your passport, passport pictures, and sheets of carbon paper to speed up the business of filling in forms in triplicate. If you plan to visit several countries that require visas, it is wise to have 15-20 passport pictures. You can't always find a photo shop when you need one. Syria, alone, required six photos and three applications for a visa!!! Some Eastern European countries and some other countries around the world require the tourist to purchase daily expenditure coupons or vouchers in the local currency to cover the duration of your trip. The vouchers must be paid for in cash. Countries do this to make sure you don't use your money on the black market instead. This assures the government foreign money is passed through the official banking system. If you are on a tight budget I would recommend skipping these countries for it is sometimes difficult to spend all the vouchers and you cannot cash in any remaining vouchers for hard currency when you want to leave the country.

If you wish to visit Israel and go on to other Arab countries, be sure to ask the Israeli embassy for a visa on a separate piece of paper. If you get the visa stamped in your passport, some Arab countries may refuse you entry into their country.

The Israelis do not volunteer this information and it is up to the discretion of the official whether or not a separate visas will be issued. Be sure to request this before you hand over your passport. The same solution applies for entering Greece with a visa from Cyprus.

If there are strained relations between countries be sure to check at their consulates and your own in a neighboring country to make sure the border is open. You never know when a country may implement martial law. Under those restrictions, border checks are very thorough and time consuming and while in the country you must not arouse the authorities' suspicions. Usually you have to be off the streets by 12 midnight or you might be thrown in jail.

Visa Requirements in a Nutshell
refer to each country in 'Countries in a Capsule' for more information

Country Traveling To:	Canada Cost	U.S. Cost	U.K. Cost
Algeria	$55 Yes	$20 Yes	$60 Yes
Austria	No	No	No
Belgium	No	No	No
Bulgaria	$64 Yes	No-valid for 30 days	$45 Yes
Czech Republic	$50 Yes	No-valid for 90 days	No
Denmark	No	No	No
Egypt	$25 Yes	$25 Yes	$25 Yes
Finland	No	No	No
France	No	No	No
Germany	No	No	No
Greece	No	No	No
Hungary	No-valid for 30 days	No-valid for 30 days	No
Italy	No	No	No
Israel	Free Yes	Free Yes	Free Yes
Jordan	$25 Yes	$65 Yes	$45 Yes
Liechtenstein	No	No	No
Luxembourg	No	No	No
Morocco	No	No	No
Netherlands	No	No	No
Norway	No	No	No
Poland	$55 Yes-valid for 90 days	No-valid for 90 days	No
Portugal	No	No	No
Romania	$34 Yes	No-valid for 30 days	$48 Yes
Slovak Republic	$50 Yes-valid for 90 days	No-valid for 90 days	No
Spain	No	No	No
Sweden	No	No	No

Switzerland	No		No		No
Syria	$45 Yes		$35 Yes		$35 Yes
Tunisia	No		No		No
Turkey	No		$20 Yes-valid for 3 months		$10 Yes
United Kingdom	No		No		N/A

Customs and Duties

Before you leave your own country, register with customs all valuables you are taking that have serial numbers, such as cameras, binoculars, radios, watches, etc. You can do this at your port of exit or at the local customs office. It ensures that you can bring them back into the country without paying duty.

Canadian Customs

Canadians out of the country for more than 24 hours will get a $50 exemption from duties and taxes; of visits out of the country for more than 48 hours it is $200; and over seven days you are allowed to return with $500 worth of goods. These exemptions can be claimed any number of times. Above these limits, you're taxed according to the type of goods you ship home - approximately 30%..(You cannot combine the yearly and 48 hour exemptions, use the $500 exemption only partially, to save the balance for a later trip, or pool exemptions with family members. Duty-free limits are 50 cigars, 200 cigarettes, 2.2 pounds of tobacco, and 40 ounces of liquor which all must be declared in writing upon arrival at customs and must be with you or in your checked luggage. To mail back gifts, label the the package 'Unsolicited Gift-Value under $40. Ask for a copy of the Canadian Customs brochure 'I Declare/Je Declare' from Revenue Canada Customs and Excise Department, Connaught Building, 3rd floor, 555 MacKenzie Ave. Ottawa, Ontario K1A 0L5, tel.(613) 957-0275

U.S. Customs

If you have been out of the country for at leat 48 hours and haven't already used the exemption, or any part of it, in the past 30 days, you may bring home $400 worth of foreign goods duty-free. So can each member of your family, regardless of age; and your exemptions may be pooled, so one of you can bring in more if another brings in less. A flat 10% duty applies to the next $1,000 of goods; above $1,400, the rate varies with the merchandise. You must declare all items bought abroad. You also have to pay tax if you exceed your duty-free allowances: 1 litre of alcohol or wine, 100 non-Cuban cigars or 200 cigarettes, and one bottle of perfume. Gifts valued at less than $50 may be mailed to the U.S. duty-free, with a limit of one package per day per addressee, and do not count as part of your exemption-mark the package 'Unsolicited Gift' and write the nature of the gift and its retail value on the outside. For more information on customs regulations, ask for 'Know Before You Go'. Write to the U.S. Customs Service, Box 7407, Washington, DC 20044, tel. (202) 647-0518 or 927-6724, to register your camera before going overseas call (202) 927-0540

U. K. Customs

Travelers 17 or older who have returned from European Union countries may bring back the following duty-free goods, provided they were not bought in a duty-free shop: 1.5 liters of alcohol over 22% volume or 5 liters of alcohol under 22% volume, 5 liters of still table wine, 300 cigarettes or 150 cigarillos, 75 cigars or 400 grams of tobacco, 75 grams of perfume, and other goods worth up to 250 pounds. Contact the customs office, for more information.

Medical Matters

Before leaving home, talk to your doctor or muncipal or provincial public health offices to find out what immunization you need for the countries you plan to visit. Some travel agents will have this information.

Americans should inquire through the US Public Health Service, National Communicable Disease Center, Atlanta, GA 30333 which deals with health requirements and animal and plant quarantine regulations for the US and other countries and publishes a

small booklet 'Health Information for International Travel, available upon request. The USPHS at 330 Independence Ave., SW, Washington DC 20201, provides information on vaccinations and other immunizations required for visitors to foreign countries and in some cases will also administer the necessary shots.

Canadians can obtain information about vaccinations and other medical information from the following Department of National Health and Welfare Travel Information Offices:

British Columbia HWC, 5th Floor, 2130 Government St., Victoria BC V8W lY3 tel: (604) 566-3387

or HWC, 7th Floor, ll33 Melville St., Vancouver, BC V6E 4E5 tel: (604) 666-6196

Alberta HWC, 40l Toronto Dominion Tower, Edmonton Center, Edmonton, Alberta T5J 2Zl tel: (403) 420-2697

Saskatchewan HWC, l855 Smith St. Regina, Saskatchewan S4P 2N5 tel: (306) 359-5413

Manitoba HWC, Room 500, 303 Main St., Winnipeg, Manitoba R3C OH4 tel: (204) 949-3616

Ontario HWC, 3rd Floor, 55 St.Clair Ave. East, Toronto, Ontario M4T lM2 tel: (416) 966-6245

or 7 Medical Services, HWC, 30l Elgin St., Ottawa, Ontario KlA 0l3 tel: (6l3) 990-3616

or Travel Innoculation Clinic at the Toronto Hospital, 200 Elizabeth St., 1 Eaton North, room 250, M5G 2C4, tel: (416) 340-3670

Quebec Services Medicaux, Sante et

Bien-etre Social Canada, Le Complex Guy-Favreau, 200 Dorchester Blvd., West, Montreal, Quebec H2Z 1X4 tel: (514) 283-4880

New Brunswick HWC, 89 Canterbury St., Room 513, Saint John, NB E2L 2C7 tel: (506) 648-4862

Nova Scotia HWC, 2129 Kempt Rd, Halifax, Nova Scotia B3K 5N6 tel: (902) 426-3998

Newfoundland Health and Welfare Canada (HWC), Room 410, Sir Humphrey Gilbert Building, Duckworth St. PO Box 5759, St. John's, NFLD A1C 5X3 tel: (709) 772-5571

United Kingdom citizens should check with their doctors regarding vaccination requirements for foreign countries or the British Tourist Authority at Victoria Station, Forecourt, 12 Regent St. off Picadilly Circus, tel: 071 730 3488 or the British Travel Centre at 12 Regent St., tel: 071 730 3400.

Because health regulations can change on short notice, depending on local circumstances and the occurrence of epidemics, you should confirm requirements just before you leave and, if you are on a long trip, during your travels. In general, the cost for immunization shots will be higher outside Canada and the United States. You may have difficulty in finding a health plan that covers these shots, and even if you can, it's best to obtain them before you go. It's better to weather any side effects at home rather than while you're on the road.

People who need special medical treatment should carry a doctor's letter, with the brand and generic name of any drug needed. This will help you get medical assistance if your medication is misplaced or your luggage delayed or lost. Allergies should also be documented by your doctor, as should any condition which prevents you from having any required immunization. Take copies of any prescriptions, including those for glasses or contact lenses.

Travel Insurance

If you are paying for health insurance, check to see if it will cover you out of the country. If it doesn't, invest in health travel insurance. And even if it does, the coverage may be so minimal that you will be well advised to buy extra coverage. The cost of medical treatment and hospital care outside North America can vary from prohibitively expensive to free, and while no traveler wants to think of accident or illness marring his trip, it can happen. It would be a major shock to find medical and hospital bills of thousands of dollars, to be paid in cash before you can be released from a foreign institution. It is usually better to deal with a professional insurance broker than with a travel agent whose expertise is booking flights, not advising on insurance.

Make sure your coverage is total rather than giving specified maximum amounts for individual sections such as medical care, hospital beds, ambulances, surgery, etc. Also inquire about personal accident insurance, personal liability, cancellation due to ill health, strike and delay which relates to industrial action, breakdown, or adverse weather conditions which cause a delay on your outward departure. Also ask about travel trade indemnity which covers you in the event an airline goes broke and baggage and personal money loss.

If you buy an International Student Identity Card you are automatically insured for $100 a day for in-hospital expenses, $3000 for accident-related medical expenses and $10,000 for emergency medical evacuation. Make sure you ask for a summary of coverage from CIEE (Insurance Dept, 205 E. 42nd St, New York, NY 10017-5706

In Canada, Liberty Health (formerly Ontario Blue Cross), offers a plan available to people covered by provincial health insurance. For people under 55, traveling for 60 days, the insurance cost would be $193. To obtain all the travel insurance company names and phone numbers call Canadian Life & Health Insurance Association at 1-800-268-8099.

Further information for travelers can be obtained from International Association for Medical Assistance to Travelers, Inc. (IAMAT), 350 Fifth Ave., New York, NY 10001 or 40 Regal Rd., Guelph, Ont. Canada N1K 1B5 tel: (519) 836-0102 and 1287 St.Clair Ave. West, Toronto, M6E 1B8 tel: (416) 652-0137. Here are some U.S. companies that specialize in travel insurance, call them if you feel you are not adequately covered by your own insurance company:

Health Care Abroad 1-800-237-6615 or 1-703-687-3166
Access America 1-800-284-8300
Tele-Trip (Mutual of Omaha) 1-800-228-9792 or 1-402-345-2400
Travel Assistance International 1-800-821-2828 or 1-202-331-1609
Travelers Insurance Company 1-800-243-3174

The best recommendation given by British travel officials is to contact travel insurance agents in the yellow pages.

If possible, claims should be left until you return home. Under no circumstances should you send original documentation by mail overseas, since it can be lost quite easily.

If you find yourself in difficulty because of an accident, illness, or loss of funds, don't hesitate to seek help from your nearest consulate or embassy. Officials there will help you get in touch with a doctor, a hospital, a lawyer, your family, or friends at home, and provide other assistance or advice as needed.

Mail Drops

Your embassy or consulate abroad is usually your best bet for mail delivery. You can leave a list with family and friends, with dates of your expected arrival in each city. The Canadian government pamphlet 'Bon Voyage, But'... lists embassy and consulate addresses, while the American government publishes a pamphlet called "Key Officers of Foreign Service Posts "(contact your local passport agency office). Note that embasssy officials will not forward your mail to another address. After a certain period of time it will be returned to the sender.

In a capital city without Canadian diplomatic representation you can use the British Embassy or American embassies. Similarily, Americans could use the Canadian or British embassies. You can also use General Delivery at any city's main post office. Letters should be addressed with your surname in capital letters and underlined, followed by Poste Restante, City, Country. American Express offices have traditionally been used as mail drop-offs; they prefer that you be a customer. This can be accomplished by using them to book your flight or by carrying their travelers' checks. Their mail facilities in major tourist cities in season often have horrendous lineups.

You can also mail books and tapes to your embassies or post offices so that you will always have something to read or listen to. If you plan to travel through countries with vast climate changes, you could mail some of your winter clothing as well. There is nothing worse then being burdened with too much 'baggage' in your backpack that you can't use for long periods of time.

If you are going to be in a country for any length of time, you should register at your embassy and, particularly if the country is politically unstable, let them know where you are going to be staying. You will find week old newspapers from your country at your embassy in case you want to catch up on your favourite sports team or soap opera.

Drugs & Narcotics
(taken from Bon Voyage But... a Canadian government pamphlet)

"Increasingly severe penalties are being imposed on persons convicted of possessing, smuggling or trafficking in drugs. Heavy fines and/or long prison sentences are becoming more common as part of the major international effort to curtail the use and transportation of drugs: in Singapore, for example, possession of even small amounts carries the death penalty. Tourists should exercise extreme caution about accepting to transport any parcel, however small, across a border, remembering that narcotic drug traffickers will try to use respectable, innocent-looking tourists to carry drugs for them through customs inspection lines. Persons who innocently commit such offences can be held in jail, often in very uncomfortable conditions, for long periods while awaiting trial. Because drug offences are particularly distasteful to some countries, the suspected drug offender, regardless of nationality, may be last to be brought to trial."

10.

Planning Your Route

When to Go

Most people believe the best time to travel in Europe is during the summer months, between May and September. Understandably, college students or families with school children have to wait until school has recessed for the summer. As a result, Europe is inundated with cyclists, hitch-hikers, backpackers and other tourists during those months. You may see so many familiar faces and meet so many compatriots that you'll think you've never left home. I was picked up by a relative of a school friend from Norway while hitching the roads in that country, and also met a person who'd attended one of my lectures and a former church associate. Trains and train stations will be crowded. Cyclists needn't be concerned, but people renting cars can expect delays. You'll have longer delays in getting rides as many other hitch-hikers will be competing for rides at entrance ramps. When you do get a ride, the traffic will be backed up at peak periods in the most popular tourist areas. The situation can be so bad that the BBC customarily broadcasts news of the length of delays to be expected at the most heavily traveled border crossings on summer weekends. Prices for accommodation, transportation, and food are all higher in tourist areas. The cities and many of the places you especially want to see will be too crowded to be enjoyable. And in some countries, particularly in the Mediterranean area, it will be too hot to be comfortable for hitch-hiking.

All this adds up to a very strong argument for traveling off-season if you can, and for students on the semester system this can be ideal. You may think it would be too cold to hitch-hike through Sweden or Finland except in the summer months, but it is perfectly practical, take the train during bad weather conditions.

Where to Go

I suggest, that you plan your routing as much as possible in advance. The worst mistake you could make is to backtrack. If you are returning to your original destination in a particular country, find another route, so that you don't see the same scenery twice, unless it is so spectacular that you want to see it again. There is too much to see in this world and too little time. Avoid having to cross the English Channel and other bodies of water more than once; these costs will really eat into your budget. If you plan your routes intelligently, you should get to the colder climate countries as soon as possible or as late as possible when the cold is not too unbearable. Here are a couple of suggested routes that can be done in a one-semester break from school, or in four months off the job.

September 1 - January 1

Arrive in London and hitch, cycle or take the train through the British Isles for two to four weeks, then travel to Scandinavia by boat from Scotland or England to the Netherlands, Germany, Denmark, Sweden or Norway, taking an optional bus tour from Helsinki to Russia (get your visa in Helsinki and expect to wait at least 5-8 days for it), then work your way through Western and Eastern Europe, to Turkey, Syria, Jordan, into Israel, overland into Egypt, by boat to Greece, by boat to southern Italy (skip former Yugoslavia), along the Mediterranean coast of France to Spain and Portugal. You can include North Africa by crossing from Spain to Morocco or from Sicily to Tunisia. Then back to London and home.

January 1 - May 1
Warning: U.S. & Canadian External Affairs were warning against travel to Algeria for security reasons. Check before you apply for an Algerian visa.

Arrive in London and head through France to Spain and Portugal, cross to North Africa, see Morocco, Algeria, and Tunisia, returning either to Spain or crossing from Tunisia to Sicily, then along the Mediterranean, by boat from Italy to Greece (skipping former Yugoslavia) and by boat from Greece to Egypt (I wouldn't recommend trying to go through Libya-there's too much red tape involved), back through Israel, Jordan, Syria, and Turkey, through Eastern and Western Europe to Scandinavia (arriving approximately mid-March or after) , with the optional Russian bus tour, and back to England for two to four weeks in the British Isles before returning home.

Either of these routes can be adapted for a shorter or longer trip. To help you plan, consult the temperature charts in the appendix.

11.

Airline Matters

The more time you have between the time you decide to travel and the date you leave, the better. Once you understand the different ticketing options available to you, then you can make an intelligent decision. Secondly, do the homework yourself. There are many competent travel agents who will do the research for you to book your ticket, but sometimes the agency may make a better commission on the airline they recommend which may not suit your travel needs. Call every airline using the 1-800 numbers, and compare airfares on four or five possible destinations during the low and high season. Perhaps you can be flexible and leave a week or two earlier than planned and return at the end of your travels during another period that will save you money. Once you have compared all dates and prices with every airline, then, by all means, have the travel agency book the ticket for you. You won't save any money by buying the ticket directly from the airline, so you might as well help the local travel agency stay in business.

Also contact CIEE for student discounts, Travel CUTS in Canada at 187 College St Toronto, Ontario M5T 1P7 tel: (416) 979-2406 and Council Charter tel: (212) 661-0311 or 1-800-800-8222 in the U.S. Student Travel Australia has offices all over the world and offers low-price airfares to cities all over the globe. STA also offers the American Youth Hostels card, the ISIC (International Student Identity Card), the IYC (International Youth Card), free pamphlets on services and rates. In the U.S. contact 5900 Wilshire Blvd., suite 2100, Los Angeles, CA 90036 tel. 213-937-1150

If you do your homework, and are under 26, you should never have to pay full fare for a ticket.

Other options are to check the weekend newspapers for incredibly low airfares and travel agencies on or near college campuses. If the cheapest seats are full, try to get on a waiting list, if you can't then call every day-even two or three times a day to see if there are any cancellations or new cheap seats available. The airline reservationist is usually not allowed to tell you if further cheap seats may become available, so it will pay to keep calling everyday. Off-season tickets will be cheaper and easier to get. Make sure you ask what days are the cheapest to fly.

Airfare Options

Here are options that may suit your needs:

Open Jaw - consider flying into one city and returning from another. The fare is figured simply by taking half of the round trip airfare for each of those destinations.

Standby tickets - are not as popular as in the old days, but you can get a discounted seat at the last moment while waiting at the airport. For students on a low budget, sleeping at the airport overnight might be worth the gamble but could prove to be disastrous especially in the summer when flights are usually full. Try during the off-season. But, hey, you're a student and probably unemployed, so what's the rush? Instead of stand-by, the airline will offer the three-day advance-purchase youth fares for people under 25, you book only within three days of departure. Return flights must also be booked no earlier than three days before departure. This option is better during the off-season as well when the planes aren't as full. You must return within one year of your departure.

Apex (Advance Purchase Excursion) If your timetable is flexible, then buy your ticket in advance, it

will save you a lot of money and promise you a seat. If you are bumped, scream bloody murder, but check in as early as possible to avoid this happening to you. These tickets are bought at least 21 days in advance, **Super-Apex,** when you know your travel plans at least one month in advance; there is a penalty of $50 -$100 if you cancel or change your date of departure.

Consolidators who buy up many tickets at a substantial discount may be the cheapest way to go. These tickets are sold to the travel agent. All restrictions are usually waived, but if the airline can't get you home on schedule, there may be difficulty getting other airlines to accept these tickets. The airlines won't tell you which consolidators they use; you have to phone consolidators or agencies specializing in these tickets, and ask. If the airline you are using, has a sale, - a ticket price lower than the one you have now purchased - you usually can't trade it in. You are usually stuck with that price. Budget airfares usually have non-refundable and non-changeable restrictions. Think about this carefully before you decide on which ticket plan to use.

Another option is Airhitch. This company provides low-price, last-minute seats for flights to Western Europe. One way tickets from the East Coast can cost only $169 U.S. and $269 from the West coast. Contact Airhitch at 2790 Broadway, suite 100, New York NY 10025 tel: (212) 864-2000; 1341 Ocean Ave. suite 62, Santa Monica, CA 90401 tel: (310) 458-1006. Also call Access International 101 W. 31st St. suite 1104, New York, NY 10001 tel: (212) 465-0707 or 1-800-825-3633; UniTravel, 1177 N. Warson Rd. Box 12485, St. Louis, MO 63132, tel: (314) 569-2501 or 1-800-325-2222

Courier flights are possibly worth investigating if you live in the city where the flight is departing, usually New York or San Francisco. Again, you need to be very flexible. You can only save small amounts on airfare if you are willing to deliver a package or letter but you can usually only stay a week or two and you give up your luggage allowance to the freight you are supposed to deliver. Luggage that is small enough for a carry-on is allowed, but if you are only delivering a simple letter, check with the courier company to see if the restriction will apply to your situation. A newspaper called Travel Unlimited will give you the latest in courier and discount airfare. It costs $25 /year-Box 1058, Allston, MA 02134 Also, contact 'Now Voyager' (212) 431-1616 or at 74 Varick St. suite 307, New York, NY 10013. If you are 18 and over, need a cheap airfare, call them especially a couple months in advance. Flights in the summer and during school holidays are in high demand. You can depart form New York, Houston, Newark or Miami. Most flights are only one week long. Round-trip fares start at $99 for emergency situations to $299 from New York to London. **BUT BE AWARE YOU CAN ALSO GET NORMAL AIRFARES FOR ABOUT THE SAME PRICE AND YOU DON'T HAVE TO RETURN IN ONE WEEK. GOING TO EUROPE FOR ONE WEEK IS SENSELESS..** Be prepared to pay for a $50 registration fee. If you want to investigate this courier option call Discount Travel at 1-800-344-9375 for a book called A Simple Guide to Courier Travel;- it costs $17.95 Other courier companies to call are: Discount Travel International in New York at (212) 362-3636 or Halbart Express in NY at (718) 656-8189 and Courier Travel Service, 530 Central Ave. Cedarhurst, NY 11511 tel (516) 374-2299

In Canada the only courier company is FB on Board at 83 Galaxy Blvd, Unit 34, Rexdale, Ontario M9W 5X6, tel: (416) 675-4133. During high season (June-Sept. 15) and December the "administrative" fee is $525, during the low season, Sept. 15-May the fee is $450. The "administrative" fee is really the fee to cover the cost of the flight. But, again you have to go on scheduled flights, into specific cities and return in 8-12 days. Is it worth it?

Charter Flights - Charter companies buy a block of tickets on a regular commercial flight and sells them at a discount or lease the whole plane and offer cheaper seats to the public. Be aware, if the flight does not sell out, then the charter flight may be cancelled or re-scheduled. Ask the charter company about their track record in cancelling flights and their policy on refunds. If a block of tickets is sold on a regular commercially scheduled airline, then the chances of anything happening to you are remote. Check the reputation of the company with the Better Business Bureau.

Round-the-World tickets can be a bargain and can work out to be 50% cheaper, than if you flew to many cities around the world. Scandinavian Airlines allows a minimum of 3 stops and no more than 15, price Cdn. $3,247; British Airways has unlimited stops, but a maximum of 28,500 miles allowed, their cheapest price is Cdn.$3,700. You must book the first sector in advance, you can't backtrack. Tickets are usually valid for 90 days to a year.

For international flights make sure you are at the airport at least two hours before departure, bikes are usually not charged as they can be substituted for a second piece of luggage-make sure you dismantle it and get it packed in a box; make sure all loose straps on your backpack are secure before you give it to the airline as straps can get caught on conveyor belts and destroy your backpack.

Airlines

The following North American airlines serve the major cities in Europe and the United Kingdom: (800 numbers vary from area code to area code)

Air Canada 1-800-268-7277
Canadian Pacific 1-800-363-7530
American Airlines 1-800-433-7300
Continental 1-800-231-0856
Delta 1-800-241-4141
Northwest 1-800-447-4747
United Airlines 1-800-241-6522
Virgin Atlantic Airways Ltd. 1-800-862-8621

European Airlines

Austrian Airlines 1-800-843-0002
Belgium: Sabena Belgian World Airlines 1-800-955-2000
Cyprus: Cyprus Airways (212) 714-2190
The Czech Republic and Slovakia: Czechoslovak Airlines (CSA) (212) 682-5833
Denmark: Scandinavian Airlines (SAS) 1-800-221-2350
Finland: Finnair 1-800-950-5000
France: Air France 1-800-237-2747
Germany: Lufthansa 1-800-645-3880
Great Britain: British Airways 1-800-247-9297; Virgin Atlantic 1-800-862-8621
Greece: Olympic Airways (212) 838-3600 or 1-800-223-1226 outside NY
Holland: KLM Royal Dutch Airlines 1-800-777-5553
Hungary: Malev Hungarian Airlines (212) 757-6446
Iceland: Icelandair 1-800-223-5500 highly recommended one to use
Ireland: Aer Lingus 1-800-223-6537
Italy: Alitalia 1-800-223-5730
Malta: Air Malta (415) 362-2929
Norway: Scandinavian Airlines (SAS) 1-800-221-2350
Poland: LOT Polish Airlines (212) 869-1074
Portugal: TAP Air Portugal 1-800-221-7370
Romania: Tarom Romanian Airlines (212) 687-6013
Spain: Iberia Airlines 1-800-772-4642
Sweden: Scandinavian Airlines 1-800-221-2350
Switzerland: Swissair 1-800-221-4750
Turkey: THY Turkish Airlines (212) 986-5050

12.

Transportation Options and More Vital Information

In the next two chapters, you will find the practical information you need to make your time abrod cost-effective and yet adventurous. The prices given for transportation and accommodation will help you decide whether to hitch, cycle, take the train or bus and if you should stay at a university, hostel, knock on a farmer's door or work in a hotel kitchen for the night. Town locations and telephone numbers for over 3,000 youth hostels are included. Information on 'Must See Tourist Sights', 'Best Scenery', 'Night Life and More', and 'Best Festivals' in each country will help you decide if it's worth it to break your neck to get to a town or city just to see one tourist site. I have chosen many of the best sites and activities based on my own experience and suggestions from the tourist boards for each country. There are many excellent travel books that will give you comprehensive information on museums you should visit, history, plane and train schedules, hotels, restuarants and much more. Some of the best information you get will

be from all the dozens of local people you will meet every day.

Even though you have information about each country, it's often useful to visit a tourist office when you arrive in a town or city. Consult the Tourist Board addresses supplied in the next chapter. Before you leave, brochures from various countries will provide many colored pictures of the ruins, towns, the countryside and festivals to give you a visual idea of what to expect. You can also visit the library and photocopy information needed to plan your travels. This information will help you decide which countries to visit and it will help with your routing. Once you leave the country you can discard the brochures and lighten your load.

While traveling, don't be afraid to change your travel plans at a moment's notice. You may pick up information from your driver or host about something in the area which would be well worth visiting.

Personally, I didn't read up on any countries before I left for my trip. I didn't carry any travel books or brochures with me, I simply followed my instincts, information gathered through school, friends, TV and the local people in every country. But for most first-time travelers who may have to budget their time wisely, you will find the information on each country helpful. I have also included "a little history" of each country and 'peculiar customs and expressions'. This will broaden your knowledge about the people and their past and help initiate some interesting conversations with your hosts or drivers.

You will find Eastern Europe, the Middle East and North Africa, worth every effort to travel there. Languages and customs may seem more foreign to you, the standard of living much lower, sanitary conditions not to your liking, but despite these drawbacks, you will find the contrast with the Western way of life fascinating. You will be able to stretch your dollar much further in these countries. Just be willing to accept the differences you discover and you will probably have a more exciting time than in Western countries more like your own.

For each country, I have provided some selected routes you may want to cycle or hitch-hike on and their distances. When planning your day, it is nice to know the distance between you and your next destination. If you wish to take the train instead, then the distance between each city is not so important, but whether or not you lose out in the adventure getting to your point of interest. Distance will be critical in making your decision for some of you, but don't despair if you don't reach your planned destination. There isn't a youth hostel in every town, but you should still be successful in securing accommodation if you use my methods. If you use most of my hitch-hiking methods you will be able to cover 200- 600 miles in one day, while cycling 250 miles may take 4-8 days depending on the terrain, wind speeds, overall weather and how energetic you feel each day.

Recommended Cycling Routes & Distances

By no means do these routes cover all the scenic beauty of this region of the world.

Oxford, England to Newhaven-253 miles;

York to Edinburgh, Scotland-264 miles;

Brussels to Amsterdam-272 miles;

Brussels to Versailles, France-411 miles;

Versailles to Angers, France-281 miles;

Stockholm to Copenhagen-392 miles;

Copenhagen to Kiel, Germany-165 miles;

Trier to Bingen, Germany-157 miles;

Heidelberg, Germany to Munich-279 miles;

Salzburg, Austria to Vienna-295 miles;

Vienna to Budapest-240 miles;

Prague, Czech Republic to Frankfurt, Germany-367 miles;

Patras, Greece to Athens-559 miles;

Ancona, Italy to Genoa, Italy-414 miles;

Genoa to Carcassonne, France-533 miles;

Seville, Spain to Madrid, via Lisbon-800 miles;
Basel, Switzerland-Strasburg-Mainz-Luxembourg-522 miles;
Salzburg, Austria (Brenner Pass) & Innsbruck to Zurich-407 miles;
Zurich-Vevey-Basel-312 miles;
Verona, Italy, & Venice to Vienna-527 miles;
Vienna to Salzburg-233 miles;
St. Malo, France-Carnac-Les Ponts-Chambord/Bracieux-440 miles;
Chambord, France-Rochechouart-Rocamadour-Carcassonne, France-482 miles;
Carcassonne to Frontignan-Apt-St.Tropez, France-426 miles;
St. Raphael, France to Finale Ligure, Italy-l48 miles ;
Zaragosa, Spain to Lleida/Lerida & Barcelona-217 miles;
The Irish Coast-Tralee-Waterville-Kenmare-Bantry-Cork-242 miles;
Newcastle, England to Malham-Chester-Borth-Bath-721 miles;
Bath, England- Portsmouth-Channel Crossing- St.Malo- Bayeux-250 miles;

Train Passes

Purchase your BritRail or EurailPass before you leave home. You can't buy a BritRail pass in the United Kingdom, or a EurailPass in continental Europe, though you can get it in the U.K.albeit at a slightly higher rate. Contact Council Travel, Travel CUTS or your local travel agent. If you plan to travel for one month just in one country or just for a few days it may be wiser to buy a national train pass in that country. This is a critical decision especilly if you don't want to commit yourself to using the train for a solid two or three months.

BritRail (prices are in Canadian dollars)

BritRail Pass gives you unlimited rail travel in England, Scotland and Wales for periods ranging from 8 days to one month.

	First Class		Standard Class	
	Adult	Senior 60 and over	Adult	Senior 60 and over
8 days	$359	$335	$279	$250
15 days	$580	$539	$420	$370
22 days	$755	$680	$520	$469
1 month	$879	$799	$605	$549

BritRail Youth Pass (ages 16-25, Standard class only)

8 days	$219
15 days	$335
22 days	$415
1 month	$485

BritRail Flexipass -Travel days need not be consecutive.

		Adult	Senior	Youth
4 days/1 month	First Class	$299	$279	-
	Standard	$235	$215	$189
8 days/1 month	First Class	$469	$419	-
	Standard	$339	$305	$269
15 days/1 month	First Class	$699	$629	-
	Standard	$485	$440	-
15 days/ 2 months	Standard	-	-	$390

Children under 5 travel free. Children 5 -15 years pay 1/2 adult fare for Britrail Pass and Flexipass. Youth is 16-25, Senior Citizen is 60 or older. Call 1-800-722-7151 to order your pass.

England /Wales Pass
4 days-first class-$239, Second class-$189; unlimited travel on British Rail services in England(as far north as Berwick and Carlisle) and throughout Wales.

BritIreland Pass-unlimited rail travel in England, Scotland, Wales, Northern Ireland and the Republic of Ireland-includes round-trip Sealink ferry service between Holyhead and Dun Laoghaire, Fishguard and Rosslare or Stranraer and Larne.

	First Class	Second Class
5 days in 15	$519	$395
10 days in 1 month	$759	$559

Children 5-15 pay half fare, under 5 travel free

BritFrance RailPass-unlimited rail travel in Britain and France, plus one round-trip channel crossing by catamaran.

	Adult 1st class	Adult Standard	Youth(12-25)Standard
5 days/15	$425	$320	$220
10 days/1 month	$640	$485	$340

Eurostar Channel Tunnel Tickets
This train service links London to Paris in 3 hours and Brussels to London in 3 hours and 15 minutes.The lowest fare currently available is a 14-day, second class advance purchase at $105, called the "Discovery Special". Tickets are available in Britain, Belgium and France or call 1-800-EUROSTAR or your travel agency.

Please note, if you wish to sleep on trains at night, you can sleep upright for free or expect to pay for sleeping accommodations on the train called berths or couchettes.

Eurail (prices are in U.S. dollars)

Eurailpasses are good for Austria, Belgium, Denmark, Finland, France, Germany, Greece, Hungary, Ireland, Italy, Luxembourg, Netherlands, Norway, Portugal, Spain, Sweden, Switzerland and to Istanbul, Turkey. The pass also gives you access to steamers, ferries and buses either free or at reduced prices. You can get off and on at your convenience.

Eurail Pass is a convenient card for unlimited lst class rail travel throughout 18 countries in Europe. Prices are in U.S. dollars as of Oct.1, 1995

15 days	$498
21 days	$648
1 month	$798
2 months	$1, 098
3 months	$1,398

Eurail Saverpass-for three or more people traveling together. Unlimited lst class rail travel. Same privileges as the regular Eurailpass, but requires that the group always travel together.(Saverpass for two people traveling together is valid between Oct. 1 and March 31 only)

15 day Eurail Saverpass (price per person)	$430
21 day Eurail Saverpass (price per person)	$550
1 month Eurail Saverpass (price per person)	$678

Eurail Flexipass-Unlimited lst class rail, same privileges as the regular Eurailpass

Any 5 days within 2 months	$348
Any 10 days within 2 months	$560
Any 15 days within 2 months	$740

Eurail Youthpass-for under 26 years of age, unlimited 2nd class rail travel through 18 countries in Europe

15 day Youthpass	$398
1 month Youthpass	$578
2 month Youthpass	$768

Eurail Youth Flexipass-under 26, unlimited 2nd class travel

Any 5 days within 2 months	$255
Any 10 days within 2 months	$398
Any 15 days within 2 months	$540

Europass

It is designed for travel in the five most frequently visited countries of Europe.-France, Germany, Italy, Spain, Switzerland. You determine the number of countries visited based on the number of travel days purchased. Optional add-on countries. Austria, Belgium and Luxembourg (considered one country) and Portugal.

	Adult	Youth
3 Countries	1st Class	2nd Class
Any 5 days within 2 months	$280	$198
Any 6 days within 2 months	$318	$226
Any 7 days within 2 months	$356	$254
4 Countries		
Any 8 days within 2 months	$394	$282
Any 9 days within 2 months	$432	$310
Any 10 days within 2 months	$470	$338
5 Countries		
Any 11 days within 2 months	$508	$366
Any 12 days within 2 months	$546	$394
Any 13 days within 2 months	$584	$422
Any 14 days within 2 months	$622	$450
Any 15 days within 2 months	$660	$478
Associate Countries		
Austria	$35	$25
Belgium and Luxembourg	$22	$16
Portugal	$22	$16

Associate countries extend the geographic area of the pass, they do not extend the pass length in days. Youth passes for people under 26 are available. Passes are not refundable in case of loss, theft or once validated. An insurance option is available for $10 per pass, which refunds 100% of the unused portion of the pass in the event of loss or theft. Unused, unvalidated passes must be submitted to the issuing office within one year of issue date. Any refund is subject to a 15% cancellation charge. Please read the "Conditions of Use " on your pass. Prices applicable as of Oct. 1, 1995. Children under 12 pay half price, under 4 travel free.

Here are some sample train fares between cities if you did not want to buy a Eurailpass. Prices, in U.S. dollars.

1st class
Amsterdam-Berlin-$141, Barcelona-Helsinki-$604, Berne-Oslo-$496, Hamburg-Venice-$279, Madrid-Barcelona-$62, Milan-Lisbon-$294, Paris-Budapest-$302, Rome-Athens-$270, Stockhom-Paris-$400, Vienna-Dublin-$510

2nd class
Amsterdam-Paris $67, to London $90, to Rome $232;

London-Edinburgh $91, to Paris $138, to Amsterdam $90;
Munich-Brussels $137, to Innsbruck $101, to Rome $88,
Rome-Florence $24, to Venice $44, to Geneva $99, to Madrid $155
Madrid-Lisbon $40, to Paris $105, to Barcelona $41;
Paris-Amsterdam $67, to Copenhagen $197, to Zurich $75, to Nice $100

Car Rentals

You don't have to rent cars too often to discover how much a car rental will eat into your budget. On our honeymoon a few years ago, we decided to drive through eight countries in 19 days. We had rented a car in England for a day and it was only a last minute decision when we arrived in the port of Calais, to rent again. After comparing prices from all the car rental agencies at the port we decided to use Thrifty, but as I found out when we returned the car at the end of the trip, this was not such a thrifty investment.

The costs for the car rental were:
Car Rental/week-$175 x 3= $525
   unlimited mileage
VAT (value added tax) at 35% of $525=$183.75
Collision Damage Waiver-19 days x $10=$190
Petrol (gas) $20/day x 19= $380
Tolls, Parking = $30
Total = $1,308.75

Our whole vacation cost Cdn.$4,000 including airfare and as you can see, the car rental exhausted a lot of our funds for getting around.

Now for the rest of the story... I found driving through cities such as Rome and Paris to be the most harrowing driving experience I have ever had even though deep down I enjoyed the 'stock car' racing mentality of competing with the drivers and negotiating turns on the narrow streeets of these cities. My wife felt the driving experience was like a bad nightmare. Driving is not for everybody, especially in the major cities. We found that we really didn't need a car in the cities. Besides walking, you will find the local transportation systems the best way to get across town.

One day into the trip we had car trouble in Paris. The radiator had overheated. Not wanting to waste our precious vacation time, I called the number given to us by the rental agency and we were met by their tow truck who took care of the problem fairly quickly. After driving 300 miles I discovered engine problems - there was hardly any oil in the engine! Once in the shop, the mechanics discovered one of the brake lines was going to snap at any time- brakes are obviously important, but even more so through the mountainous regions. Then just outside Venice, on a Sunday morning, we parked our rental car in a deserted parking lot in front of the grocery store, locked our doors, spent less than five minutes in the store and came back to find the door had been professionally pried open. With hardly any damage to the car, our camera and binoculars had been stolen. Depending what country you are in and what licence plates you have, you may be a preferred target for thieves. When I returned the rental car I was confronted by the representative for having the brake lines repaired without notifying them. Also, I wasn't aware the car rental agency should have filled out the forms which declared how much value added tax (VAT) we had paid. Any time you rent or buy something in Europe and the United Kingdom you present the VAT form to the border officials and they mail all or most of the VAT back to your home address. It was great having the car , but we never expected this many problems and hassles in only 19 days.

Since many married or older people travel the more conventional way, here's a comparison of what our honeymoon cost and what travel cost when I was single, footless and fancy free. By myself, I saw 30 countries in four months for just under a $1,000, including return airfare. With my wife, honeymoon or not, this short 19 day trip and eight countries cost over $4,000 for the two of us, including airfare. I didn't expect my wife to travel the way I did as a student. I am still glad we rented a car, but it pays to investigate car rentals before you leave your country. Here are some general tips and helpful telephone numbers...

General Advice and Observations...

- Students should avoid renting cars due to the high cost-you will be hurt by the insurance costs. You will need at least 3-4 people to make it more economical.
- Travelers, especially students, will miss out in meeting the people.
- Rental rates are usually higher for walk-ins. If you are definitely going to rent a car, call all of the numbers below and compare rates.
- The VAT varies considerably from country to country . Countries with a lower VAT may have a higher basic rental rate.
- Make sure you get your International Drivers Licence-check with your American or Canadian Automobile Association.
- Distances are in kilometres in Europe - one kilometre equals 0.62 of a mile.
- Cars solve the problem of carrying your luggage and you can get to some of the most remote parts of a country turning right or left at a moment's notice.
- Get detailed up-to-date city maps and plot your course on the map in advance. If you or your parents are member of CAA or AA ask for travel maps and try to get 'triptyques' from a British association for the continent.
- Stay out of the fast lane-European drivers will appear out of nowhere.
- Take the country roads as much as possible. This is the best way to visit the small towns and see the many castles and other sites not easily accessible from a super highway.
- Keep your gas costs down by renting the smallest of the small cars.
- If you have to leave valuables in the car, make sure you place them in the trunk. At night, take your

valuables to your hotel room.
- Make sure you get unlimited mileage.
- Ask about any restrictions, especially border or ferry crossings, all possible hidden costs, repair facilities, drop-off charges, extra charge for more than one driver.
- Before driving off: check for dents and scrapes, condition and inflation of tires, the location of jack and spare tire, if any spare bulbs and fuses are provided and /or required, warning triangle provided and / or required, sufficient oil and other fluids.
- If you are going for longer than, 21 days, it may be wiser to lease a car.The maintenace service and 24 hour emergency road service is waived once you lease a car. Ask if CAA or AA will cover this for you. There are many variables to consider before leasing, so do your homework. Allow at least two weeks to make these arrangements, signing of contracts etc.
- Petrol prices range from $.90/litre in Poland to $1.50/ litre in Italy and France. When you are only a few kilometres from the next country you are going to visit, it might be wise to find out what the price of petrol is and consider filling up before you cross the border.

Car Rental Companies & 800 #'s

Ansa International 1-800-527-0202
Auto Europe 1-800-223-5555
Avis 1-800-955-1155: (081) 848-8765 in U.K.
Budget 1-800-472-3325; free 0800 181-181 in U.K.

Connex International 1-800-333-3949: (081) 749-9110 in U.K.
DER Tours 1-800-421-4343: (800) 252-0606 in California
Dollar 1-800-421-6878: 1-800- 421-6868 in Alaska and Canada: (071) 935-6796 in U.K.
Europcar 1-800-227-3876: (071) 834-8484 in U.K.
Europe by Car 1-800-223-1516; 1-800-252-9401 in California
Foremost Euro-Car 1-800-423-3111: 1-800-272-3299 in California
Hertz 1-800-654-3001: (081) 679-1799 in U.K.
Kemwel 1-800-678-0678
Kenning 1-800-227-8990: (01246) 208888 in U.K.
Marsans 1-800-223-6114
National 1-800-CARRENT
Thrifty 1-800-367-2277: (081) 203-7666 in U.K.
Woods of Reigate 1-800-526-2915 in U.K.
World Wide Car Hire (0) 273-203366/205025 (24 hours) in U.K.

Besides airfare, your most expensive transportation options are train passes and car rentals. A three week car rental may be comparable to a three week train pass, but 5-10 individual train passes may add up very quickly. Some of the train passes are only economical if you are on the train quite a bit. Don't let Europe become a blur. You should go over your travel plans, study maps and decide what your goals are for that country. To get a complete listing of fares for major routes call 'Rail Europe'at 914-682-2999 or ask your travel agent for a copy of

Eurailtariff manual. If you are under 26 deduct approximately 30% for youth reductions.

Working in Europe

For Canadians and Americans there are two ways to go about working in Western Europe: legal and working 'under the table'. Under the country-by-country listings that follow, you'll find which countries are in need of foreign help and which are not. If you want to use the legal channels expect a certain amount of red tape, possible disappointment and lengthy delays in getting your papers processed. Investigate this possibility as soon as you can. Once in the country, you may find an employer who will hire you and skip the red-tape.

Many of you may want to work sporadically as you travel through many countries without the burden of wasting your holiday time on work permit matters, so if you are willing to do jobs the locals don't enjoy doing you will often be able to work 'under the table'. You might turn up your nose at the same job in your own country, e.g. picking grapes, washing dishes or being a babysitter, but in a different environment and culture the job won't seem that bad. It's only temporary work, it will give you a reason to stay in an area and explore it during your off time and make some money at the same time. Your room and board may also be taken care of. Unless you have an official work permit, never tell the border offi-

cials you are going to work in the country; you will be sent back. Contact the tourist board of the country you are interested in, the addresses in the chapter 'Countries in a Capsule' or check the English newspapers available in the country you are traveling in. Bring any documentation to help prove your qualifications in a particular field and talk to the people running the youth hostels for any help or leads.

If you wish to work in Eastern Europe , North Africa and the Middle East, your best opportunities would be teaching English, (usually only if you're willing to commit to staying for some time), au pair work (babysitting) and working at resorts. Most menial jobs will earn you pocket money, and usually room and board.

Babysitting

I have provided telephone numbers and addresses of babysitting service companies in selected cities. Primarily this service is for travelers who need babysitting services, but it won't hurt for you to call this company to see if YOU can offer your services. It's worth a try to pick up some extra travel money.

Telephone Calls

Calling Home- AT&T, MCI, Sprint and Bell Canada have international services that allow you to call fairly easily and avoids those huge hotel surcharges. Before you leave the U.S. or Canada call one of these companies to find out the procedures to use their service. AT&T USA Direct-1-800-874-4000, MCI World Phone 1-800-444-4444 or Sprint Express 1-800-793-1153. For Canada, call "Canada Direct"at 1-800-561-8868 to get a list of telephone numbers which will allow you to call from any country to Canada using a Canadian operator only. Bell Canada has a different number for each country.

When calling long distance in Europe, area codes start with a zero, are used only when calling within the country. To call outside the country, you may need to drop the '0' or '9' and replace it with the country code. For example, to call someone in Sweden from Finland, dial 990 (international access code for Finland), then 46 (Sweden's country code), then 8 (Stockholm's area code), then the number you are calling. From Canada or the U.S., dial 011-990-46-8-and the number.

To call home from one of the countries the country code for U.S. and Canada is 1. For example, to call New York from anywhere in Spain, dial 07(the international access code) plus 1 (the US country code) plus 212 (area code), plus the local number.

More Than 3,000 Youth Hostels To Choose From

If you want the street addresses, postal codes and any other details for youth hostels in each country, I recommend that you order a copy of the Hostelling International Book - ordering information is available at the end of the last chapter. I have included the name of the **town** only except for some large **cities, the telephone number and reservation number** (if available) for all youth hostels in each country. It will at least be reassuring to know while you're cycling or hitch- hiking that very affordable accommodation is just down the road. To avoid long distance calls, try the first number to make a reservation. I have only added the street address in major cities to help orientate yourself. In any case, small town or big, it wouldn't hurt to call the youth hostel to make sure its' not full and you can ask for the street address and get directions at the same time. A simple phone call will save you time, energy and frustration.

Even though I have provided every single youth hostel location throughout Europe, the Middle East and North Africa, don't feel you have to stay in a youth hostel every night. Remember, you shoud try and stay with the locals as much as possible to learn about the culture.

Please note: If the hostel is listed in bold type, this means the hostel is part of the International Booking Network allowing you to book in advance.

13.

Countries in a Capsule

All prices quoted fluctuate with the exchange rate. If you sense a little propaganda in 'A Little History' please note that much of the information has been provided by national tourist offices of each country.

ALGERIA

A Little History

Algeria was conquered by French forces in the 1830s and annexed by France in 1842. For most of the colonial period, official policy was to colonize with French settlers, and many French citizens became permanent residents. Political and economic power within Algeria was held largely by the white settler minority; the indigenous Muslim majority did not have equal rights. In 1954, the Front de Liberation Nationale (FLN), began a war for national independence, in the course of which about 1 million Muslims were killed or wounded. The French government agreed to independence in 1962.

In 1990, the National People's Assembly adopted a law providing that, after 1997, Arabic would be Algeria's only official language and that the use of French and Berber in schools and in official transactions would be subject to substantial fines. In response, more than 100,000 people demonstrated in Algiers against political and religious intolerance.

Since independence, Algeria has supported a number of liberation movements in Africa and the Middle East in various ways, including the provision of military, financial and diplomatic aid to the Polisario Front in the territory of Western Sahara.

In response to the Iraqi invasion and annexation of Kuwait in 1990, the Algerian government condemned Iraq's action and President Chadli met President Saddam Hussain of Iraq to help mediate in the crisis. In 1992, the establishment of a fundamentalist state was pre-empted by the military's refusal to let the elected government take office. As a result, there has been serious unrest and terrorist incidents and it has not recently been safe for travel.

Contact External Affairs in Canada, the State Department in the U.S. or the Foreign Office of the U.K. to learn about the current situation.

Population - 25,325,000

Capital - Algiers

Government - Single party independent republic

Religion - Moslem

Language - Arabic and French

Money - Dinar (ad) One dinar equals 100 centimes; no restrictions on the amount of money you bring in, you are obliged to buy dinars, keep receipts in case of spot checks when leaving the country.

U.S. $1 = 42 dinars, Cdn $1 = 30 dinars, British £ = 133 dinars

Public Holidays

Please note the weekend in Algeria falls on Thursday and Friday.

Visas

Visas for Americans $20, Canadians $55, U.K. citizens U.S. $60. You need 3 photos and 3 applications. Visas are granted for one month.

Peculiar Customs and Odd Expressions

Handshaking is common when meeting and leaving. Kissing on both cheeks (when greeting one another only) is common among men and women.

Best Festivals

Ouargla-Spring Festival of music and dance at night at ruins of Sedrata

Night Activities & More

Best place for drinking alcohol is in Oran.

Must See Tourist Sites

Algeirs- the casbah - a maze of narrow alleys, Grand Poste building; Place des Martyrs, Mosque of Sidi Abd Er Rhamane, Grand Mosque

Assekrem-near Tamanrasset-ancient villages

Constantine- one of the most Arab beautiful cities in the world, Palace of El Hadju Ahmed, Place de la Breche, Sidi MCid suspension bridge, on the fringe of the Roman ruins of eastern Algeria and the vast Sahara desert.

Ghardaia - l2th century Djemaa Chaaba-underground mosque-prayers held on the roof, large market, ornate cemetery

Oran - great for souvenir shoppers, Place de la Perle-cathedral

Ouargla - Museum of Sahara, ruins of Sedrata

Tamanrasset - in the desert l,000 km south of Ghardaia, for an understanding of life in the Sahara, highest shade temperatures in the world recorded here

Timgad - most complete Roman remains anywhere in the world

Tlemcen - ancient walled city, Sidi Bou Mediene mosque and many others

Places to Avoid

Batna - town is not worth seeing;

Algerian-Moroccan border just north of Mauritania-armed conflict between the Moroccan army and Polisario guerrillas.

Best Scenery

Ouargla - surrounded by half million palm trees;

Rhumel Gorge surrounding Constantine, incredible salt lakes at Les Lacs; journey from Rhoufi to Biskra - 160 km of mountain range, canyons, huge palm trees;

Tassili n'Adjjer mountains - near Libya, world's best open-air museum with tens of thousands of ancient rock paintings going back to 6000 BC, visit only in the cooler months (see climate chart);

Timimoun - built on the Grand Erg Occidental-moonlit views are wonderful.

Transportation

Buses wise choice for long distances in desert area, make sure you take a lot of water to avoid dehydration.

Hitch-Hiking

Good method of travel, if you are going south make sure you secure a long ride, best rides with caravans on trans-Saharan trucks.

Youth Hostels

Federation Algerienne des Auberges de Jeunesse, 213 Rue Hassiba Ben Bouali, B.P. 15, El-Annasser, 16015, Alger, Algeria, tel: (213) (2) 70321/ 674616, fax (213) (2) 674616; many youth hostels and cheap hotels - 40 dinars a night, your stay at a hostel may be limited to three nights.

Youth Hostel Town Locations and Telephone Numbers

A Adrar (7) 258284; Algeirs 213 Rue Hassiba-Ben-Bouali 670032; Annaba (8) 844983; **B** Batna (4) 553807; Bechar (7) 810844; Beni-Abbes no tel. #; Biskra no tel. #; Blida (3) 416601; Bordj-Bou-Arreridj (213) 5699683 ; Bouira (3) 927503; Boussaada (5) 532258; **C** Constantine 695461; **D** Douaouda-Marine no tel. #; **E** El-Kala (8) 650534; El-Kantara (4) 718532; **G** Ghardaia - 2 hostels - 1) MJ Dahane Brahim a Metili Hostel on Wilaya de Ghardaia, tel: (8) 897668; 2) MJ Emir Abdelkader Hostel at Ghardaia Centre, tel: (8) 894403; Guelma (8) 205953; **H** Hammam Bouhadjar (7) 216706; **I** Illizi no tel. #; **J** Jijel - 2 hostels - 1) AJ Jijel Hostel on rue de Freraes Khecha, tel: (5) 460980 ; 2) AJ Taher Hostel on rue du 1 er Novembre, tel: (5) 960427; **L** Laghouat (9) 722303; Lakhdaria 522400; **N** Nakhla no tel. #; **O** Oran - 2 hostels - 1) rue Benadjila Lahouari Hostel on 3 re Benadjila Lahouari, tel: (6) 350245; 2) rue Maoued Ahmed Hostel on 19 rue Maoued Ahmed, tel: (6) 398026; Ouargla - 2 hostels - 1) AJ Mostefa-Ben-Boulaid Hostel in the Quartier Emir-Abdel-Kader, tel: (9) 703003; 2) AJ Rose des Sables Hostel on avenue de la Palestine, tel: (9) 703820; Oum El Bouaghi no tel. #,; **R** Relizane no tel. #; **S** Sidi-Aissa (5) 568530; Skikda 743400; **T** Tala-Guilef 402821; Tamanrasset (9) 734047; Tebessa (8) 975797; Tiaret (7) 288133; Tichy-Bejaia (5) 231460; Tizi-Ouzou (3) 201212; Tlemcen (7) 263226; Touggourt (9) 674709.

Useful Addresses and Tourist Offices
ONAT - tourist office on Rue - Herlisa Boukhelse, Algiers,
Main post office for poste restante at La Grande Poste, 5 blvd. Mohamed
  Khemisti, Algiers
Algerian Embassies (for tourist information, contact the embassies)
in U.S.
2118 Kalorama Rd. N.W. Washington D.C. 20008, tel: (202) 265-2800, fax
  (202) 667-2174
in Canada
435 Daly Ave., Ottawa, Ontario K1N 6H3, tel: (613) 789-8505, fax (613)
  789-1406
in the U.K.
54 Holland Park, London W11 3RS, tel: 44 122 17800
Foreign Posts in Algeria
Algiers
British Embassy, Residence Cassiopee, Batiment B 7 Chemin des Glycines,
  tel: 60 56 01
United States Embassy, BP 549, 4 Chemin Cheikh Bachir El-Ibrahami,
  16000 Alger-Gare, tel: 601 186
Driving Distances (in km)
From Algiers to cities in Algeria:

Adrar 1,543	Guelma 537	Ouargla 800
Batna 435	Jijel 359	Saida 437
Biskra 425	Laghouat 400	Setif 300
Boussada 122	Mascara 361	Tlemcen 540
Constantine 435	Medea 91	Tamanrasset 1,970

Telephone Information: International Code 00, Country Code 213, Main
  City Area Code: Algiers 2; time difference (Eastern Daylight) plus 6 hours.

AUSTRIA

A Little History

For the 640 years the Hapsburg dynasty ruled, much of the history of Europe was made in Austria, an empire on which Charles V was able to boast in the early 1500s with some justification "the sun never set".

In 1955, the day on which Austria's sovereignty was restored, the Austrian Nationalrat enacted the Federal Constitution Law on the permanent neutrality of Austria. In the same year Austria became a member of the United Nations.

Austria has done its part to shape the new Europe: joining the European Union as a full member. The small country stood as a beacon of

116

freedom, democracy and private enterprise and as a bridgehead at the Iron Curtain through more than 40 years. Austria welcomed tens of thousands of people when the Russian tanks rolled into Hungary in 1956, Czechoslavakia in 1968, and Poland in 1980. In low-profile, high-security operations, Austria has been the main conduit in the exodus of Soviet and Iranian Jews. Ever since the civil war in what used to be Yugoslavia began, Austria has been harboring and helping the victims. Austria has done and given much to help bring economic progress, self-determination and free enterprise to neighboring regions which have, as a result, recently emerged as free democratic nations.

Population - 7,620,000
Capital - Vienna
Government - Federal Republic
Religion - Roman Catholic
Language - German, English is widely spoken and understood
Money - Schilling (AS) one Schilling equals 100 Groschen. Coins of 5, 10, 50 Groschen; and of 1, 5, 10, 20 Schillings. Notes of 20, 50, 100, 1,000 and 5,000 Schillings
U.S. $1 = 9 schillings, Cdn. $1 = 7 schillings, British £. = 15 schillings
Public Holidays
January 1 and 6, Easter Monday, Labour Day, Ascension Day, Whit Monday, Corpus Christi, Feast of the Assumption November 1, Feast of the Immaculate Conception December 8, Christmas and Boxing Days. Stores are closed on Saturday afternoons, but in major cities remain open until 5 p.m. on the first Saturday of every month; most stores are open Monday to Friday from 8 or 9 a.m. to 6 p.m. many with a two-hour lunch break.
Visas
Visas are not required for Americans, Canadians or U.K. citizens.
Peculiar Customs and Odd Expressions
The end is good, everything is good- Ende gut, alles gut
The way you shout into the woods is how the echo returns it- Wie man in den Wald hineinschreit, so hallt es zuruck
Love goes through the stomach- Die Liebe geht durch den Magen
All good things are three - Aller guten Dinge sind drei
You are not worth your salt- Du bist Dein Salz nicht wert
Work until you have become somebody- Ehre, leiste, schaffe was, bis Du kannst und hast etwas
Half won is half gone - Halb gewonnen, halb zerronnen
Life is suspended on a silver thread - Dein Leben hängt an einem silbernen Faden
People welcome the spring with masks and ringing of bells at the Carnival and greet people with the salute, 'Grüss Gott'.

In the city a man will often kiss a woman's hand in greeting, the saying is "Küss die Hand,gnadige frau"

Yodeling is the old means of communication and entertainment

Best Festivals

Bregenz Festival - July 20-Aug. 20 a monstrous floating stage on Lake Constance

Graz - Steirischer Herbst Styrian Autumn Festival in October

Innsbruck - Tyrolean Festival of Early Music in Aug.-brass band concerts, folkloric shows, sacred music

Salzburg - most famous music Festival, late July to end of August

Schubert Music Festival mid-June for 2 weeks in Feldkirch, Vorarlberg

Vienna Festival - mid-May to mid-June and Vienna International Music Festival from June to July

Night Activities and More

Skiing - best time, Christmas until the end of April, over 7,000 miles of cross-country trails, most famous area in Kitzbühel, Lech, St.Anton, Innsbruck; other great areas are Montafon, the Otztal, the Zillertal, the Pitztal, the Stubaital, the Gastein Valley & the Dachstein area; a great place for apres-ski is the Gemütlichkeit!

Vienna - visit the cafe culture and relax at a Kaffeehaus for hours over a coffee and an interesting newspaper; capital of music - operas, operettas, waltz concerts etc.; Vienna nightclubs- visit Balls during carnival season and around New Year (you can make reservations or get tickets the same days for some Balls); Seitenstettengasse is a street dubbed the Bermuda Triangle where many bars are located in the area, Rabensteig (street), nearby has many bars; U4 disco is on the U4 subway line.

Must See Tourist Sights

Bregenz - St. Martin's Tower, take aerial tram to top of Pfander for a panoramic view over Lake Constance

Graz - Eggenberg Castle just outside town, the cathedral, mausoleum, take the incline railway from the riverfront up Schlossberg or walk up the steps for a close look at the Clock Tower and panoramic view

Innsbruck - Ambras Castle, Tiroler Landesmuseum, Ferdinandeum Museum, the Old Quarter, the "Golden Roof", Olympic sites

Krems - Dominican and St.Vei churches

Kufstein - 13th century Bruck Castle

Linz - Linz Castle, New Cathedral, medieval main square, Postlingberg monastery of St. Florian

Melk - Benedictine Monastery, Schallaburg Castle

Reutte - Ehrenberg ruins

Salzburg - Mozart Museum, Salzburg Marionette Theater, Salzburg Festspielhaus (opera house), Mönchsberg Mountain, giant ice caves outside of Salzburg, near Werfen (May to Oct.), Hohensalzburg Fortress,

Mirabell Castle, trick fountains at Hellbrunn

Vienna- Albertina Museum (Graphische Sammlung), Schatzkammer-the Imperial Treasury Stephansdom-Gothic church, Uhrenmuseum der Stadt Wien-clock museum, Museum of Fine Arts, Rathaus (city hall)-used for open air concerts, Schonbrunn Palace, State Opera House, Donauturm-viewing tower, Belvedere Palace; ride the giant ferris wheel at the Prater Amusement Park for a panoramic view from more than 200 feet up of the Vienna Woods.

Best Scenery

Salzburg - the Salzkammergut -Sound of Music country

Danube Valley - over 500 castles and fortresses around Vienna, most scenic - between Krems and Melk is the Wachau section of the Danube

Tirol including Innsbruck - some of the best scenery in the Alps.

Bus

More expensive and slower than trains, see the bus station for the Fahrpläne Bundesbus schedule or the tourist office; 1,800 scheduled bus lines.

Cycling

Bicycles can be rented from 170 train stations, rentals-from AS50-AS90 / day, cost to drop off bike at another Austrian train station is an extra AS40.

Hitch-Hiking

To book a ride in advance in Vienna call Mitfahrzentrale Wien at 3 Invalidenstrasse 15 tel: 715 00 66, a ride from Vienna to Salzburg can cost AS230, to Munich AS310.

Train

National rail passes, you can purchase the Austrian Rail Pass for Cdn.$237 1st class, Cdn.$159 2nd class for 4 days of travel in 10 days or a Bundesnetzkarte ticket for one month of travel or the kilometer discount pass. Ask for discount rail ticket if under 26.

Camping

Over 400 campsites, most closed in winter, cost AS30-AS60 per person plus same for tent and a car.

Youth Hostels

They range from AS100 - AS250 including breakfast and linen, no age limits, advance reservations required for groups; for on-the-spot information contact one of the two Associations 1) Osterreichischer Jugendherbergsverband, 1010 Wien, Schottenring 28, Austria tel: (43) (1) 533-5353 or Fax (43) (1) 5350861 or 2) Osterreichisches, Jugendherbergswerk, 1010 Wien, Helferstorferstrasse 4, Austria, tel: (43) (1) 5331833/34 Fax (43) (1) 5331833 ext 81. Many hostels have facilities for skiing.

Youth Hostel Town Locations and Telephone Numbers

A Admont (3613) 2432; Aigen (732)27205507; Ampflwang (732) 772632;

Annaberg (2728) 8496 or (1) 5237167; **B** Bad Aussee (3622) 52238; Badgastein (6434) 2080; Bad Ischl (6132) 26577; Bad Kreuzen (7266) 6636; Bad Leonfelden (7213) 383; Braunau (7722) 4532; Bregenz (5574) 42867; Bruck an der Mur (3862) 56089; **D** Drosendorf (2915) 2257 or (1) 5237158;**E** Ebensee (6133) 6698 or (732) 782720; Engelhartszell (7717) 8115 or (732) 782720; **F** Feldkirch (5522) 7381; Feldkirchen (4277) 2644; Freistadt (7942) 4365;**G** Gosau (6136) 8352 or (732) 7955700; Graz (316) 914876; Grobpertholz (1) 5237158; Grundlsee (3622) 8629; **H** Hallein (6245) 80397; Hallstatt-Lahn (6134) 279; Hard (5574) 70536; Haslach (7289) 71153; Heiligenblut (4824) 2259; Hinterstoder (7564) 5227 or (732) 7817894; Hohentauern (3618) 217; **I** Innsbruck - 5 hostels- 1) Reichenauerstrasse Hostel on Reichenauerstrasse 147, tel: (512) 346179; 2) Studentenheim Hostel on Reichenauerstrass 147, tel: (512) 346179; 3) Rennweg Hostel on Rennweg 17b, Tirol, tel: (5222) 25814; 4) Volkshaus Hostel on Radetzkystr 47, tel: (512) 495882; 5) St. Nikolaus & Glockenhaus Hostel on St. Nikolaus, Innstr 95, tel: (512) 286515; **J** Judenburg (3572) 7355; **K** Kaprun (6547) 8507; Kitzbuhel (5352 3651; Klagenfurt - 2 hostels- 1) Jugendgastehaus Hostel on Universitatsviertel, Neckheimg 6; tel: (463) 230020, 2) Kolping Hostel on Enzenbergstrasse 26, tel: (463) 56965; Klosterneuburg (2243) 83501; Konigswiesen (7955) 344; Krems ((2732) 83452 or (1) 5864145; **L** Lackenhof (7480) 251 or (1) 5237158; Laussa (7255) 7234 or (0732) 467923; Lech (0732) 467923; Lech-Stubenbach (5583) 2419; Linz - 3 hostels- 1) Stanglhofweg Hostel on Oberosterreich (near the stadium) tel: (732) 664434; 2) Blutenstr Hostel on Blutenstr 23, tel: (732) 237078; 3) Kapuzinerstr Hostel on Kapuzinerstr 14, tel: (732) 782720; **M** Maria Lankowitz (3144) 71700; Mariazell (3882) 2669; Maurach am Achensee (5243) 5239; Melk (2752) 2681 or (1) 5237167; Mondsee (6232) 2418; Murau (3532) 2395 or (316) 824481; Mureck (3472) 2164; **N** Neuberg (3857)8495; Neu - Nagelberg (2859) 476 or (1) 5864145; Neusiedl (2167) 2252; Neustift (7284) 8196; **O** Oberndorf (7483) 267; Obertraun (6131) 360 or (732) 782720; **P** Pernitz (2632) 72373; Pfunds (5474) 5244; **R** Rennweg (4734) 364; Reutte (5672) 3039; Reutte - Hofen (5672) 2644; Riegersburg (3153) 217; **S** Salzburg - 6 hostels - 1) **Jugendgastehaus Hostel**, on Josef - Preis Allee 18, tel: (662) 8426700; 2) Aigner Strasse Hostel on Aigner Strasse 34, tel: (662) 623248; 3) **Eduard-Heinrich-Haus Hostel** on Eudard-Heinrich Str 2, tel: (662) 625976; 4) Glockengass Hostel on Glockengasse 8, tel: (662) 876241; 5) Haunspergstrasse Hostel on Haunspergstrasse 27, tel: (662) 875030; 6) Walserfeld Hostel on Schulstrasse 18, tel: (662) 851377; Schladming (3687) 24531; Sillian (4842) 6321; Soboth (3460) 207; Spielfeld (3453) 2344; Spital am Pyhrn (7563) 214; Spittal (4762) 3252; Spittal/Goldeck (4762) 2701; Steinbrunn (2624) 52791; Steyr (7252) 45580; Stummerberg (5283) 29365; St. Gilgen (6227) 365; St.Johann im Pongau (6412) 6222; St. Mar-

tin am Tennengebirge (6463) 7318; St. Michael im Lungau (6477) 630; **T**
Ternitz (2630) 38483; Trofaiach (3847) 2260; **U** Uderns (5288) 2866;
Ulmerfeld-Hausmening (7475) 4080 or (1) 5864145; Ulrichsberg (7288)
6512; **V** Villach (4242) 56368; **W** Weissenbach am Attersee (7663) 220;
Wels (7242) 67284; Weyer (7447) 2844 or (732) 782720; Weyregg (7664)
2780 or (732) 782720; **Vienna (Wien)** - 6 hostels - 1) **Brigittenau Hostel**
on Friedrich Engelsplatz 24, tel: (1) 33282940; 2) Myrthengasse/
Neustiftgasse on Neustiftgasse 85, tel: (1) 52363160; 3) Jugenherberg
Lechnerstrasse Hostel on Lechnerstrasse 12, tel: (1) 7131494; 4) Hostel
Ruthensteiner on Robert Hameringgasse 24, tel: (1) 8934202; 5)
Jugengastehaus der Stadt Hostel on Schlossberggasse 8, tel: (1) 8771501;
6) Schlobherberge am Wilhelminenberg Hostel on Savoyenstrasse 2, tel:
(1) 458503700; Wiener Neustadt (2622) 29695 or (1) 5864145; Zell am
See (6542) 7185.

Work

Need a work permit and residency permit in advance from the Austrian
Consulate, check with tourist offices to arrange a Volunteer Work Permit. Only a prospective employer in Austria can apply for the permit. If
you don't speak German, you will reduce your chances. In Austria, contact ÖKISTA, Türkenstrasse 4, 1090 Wien, Austria.

Babysitting

Innsbruck - call Babysitter Zentrale, tel:294132 on Tues. and Thurs. 9am-
11a.m., Wed and Fri. from 4:30 to 6 p.m.; Vienna-call Babysitting Zentrale
at 95 11 35 Mon.-Fri. from 8a.m.-2 p.m.; Salzburg- call 8044-6001 or
8044-6002, Mon-Thurs. 9am-12 noon & 1:30 to 3:30 pm, Fri. 9 am-12
noon;

Useful Addresses and Tourist Offices
in U.S.

Austrian National Tourist Office P.O.Box 491938, Los Angeles, CA 90045,
tel: (310) 477-3332, fax (310) 477-5141;

Box 1142 Times Square, New York, NY 10108-1142, tel: (212) 944-6880
fax (212)730-4568

in Canada

2 Bloor St. East , suite 3330, Toronto, Ont M4W 1A8 tel: (416) 967-3381,
fax (416) 967-4101

1010 Sherbrooke St. W. suite 1410, Montreal, Quebec H3A 2R7 tel: (514)
849-3709, fax (514) 849-9577

1380-200 Granville St. Vancouver, BC V6C 1S4 tel: (604) 683-5808/9, fax
(604) 662-8528

in the U.K.

30 St. George St., London WIR OAL, tel: 0171/629-0461

in Vienna

Tourist Information Office 1) main office-is at 1 Kärntner Strasse, tel:(1)513

88 92 or Österreich Werbung at Margaretenstrasse l, l040 Vienna, tel: (1) 587-2000 any town/village has a tourist office that will help with accommodation.
Austrian Student Travel Office, at Reichsratstrasse 13 tel: 4087821-accommodation help.
Vienna Tourist Board at Obere Augarten Str. 40, 1020 Vienna, tel: (1) 21114
Student Travel Service at Erlerstrasse l9-25, Innsbruck, tel: 29 997 also at
  Okista, Turkenstrasse 4, A-1090 Wien, tel: 40148/220, fax 401 48 290
Austrian Camping Club (Österreichischer Camping Club)-An der Au, A-3400 Klosterneuburg tel: 02243-85 877

Austrian Embassies
in U.S.
3524 International Court N.W., Washington, D.C. 20008 tel: (202) 895-6700
in Canada
445 Wilbrod St., Ottawa, Ont. KlN 6M7 tel: (6l3) 789-1444
Austrian Consulate - 360 Bay St. suite 1010, Toronto, Ontario M5H 2V6 tel: (416) 863-0649
in the U.K.
18 Belgrave Mews, London, SW1 X8HU, tel: 44 171 23 53 731
Foreign Posts in Austria
Vienna
Canadian Embassy, Dr. Karl-Lueger-Ring 10, A-1010 Vienna, tel: 0222/5333-3691, M-F 8:30-12:30, 1:30-3:30
British Embassy, 1030 Jauresgasse 10, tel: 0222/713-1575, M-F 9:15-12, 2-4
United States Embassy, 1090 Boltzmanngasse 16, A-1090 Vienna, tel: 0222/31339, 3195523, or 3195524 in an emergency, M-F 8:30-5
United States Consulate, Gartenbaupromenade 2, A-1010 Vienna, tel: 0222/31339 M-F 8:30012, 1-3:30 Innsbruck
United Kingdom Consulate, Matthias-Schmid-Str. 12/1, tel: 0512/588320, M-F 9-12

Driving Distances (in km)
From Vienna to cities in Austria:

Bregenz 664	Linz 175
Graz 193	Salzburg 303
Innsbruck 476	St. Pollen 62
Klagenfurt 318	

From Vienna to cities in Europe:

Athens1,870	Budapest 270	Munich 470	Rome 1,230
Belgrade 700	Bucharest 1,330	Madrid 2,78	Stockholm 1,680
Berlin 670	Copenhagen 1,060	Paris 1,370	
Brussels 1,275	Milan 960	Prague 320	

Telephone Information: International Code 00, Country Code 43, Main City Area Codes: Salzburg 662, Vienna 1 or 9; time difference (Eastern Daylight) plus 6 hours. Emergency # 144

A Little History

A war broke out in 1792 between revolutionary France and Austria as French soldiers invaded Belgium. For two years the two factions fought their battle in Belgium which was eventually occupied by France from 1794 to 1814. The foreign regime, distasteful as it was, did transform the country into a modern state. However, the invaders and their ways were not popular and there was a 'Peasants Revolt' in 1798 which was brutally suppressed.

When Napoleon was toppled, following his defeat at Waterloo, the Allies amalgamated Belgium and Holland into the United Kingdom of Netherlands under King William I. Politically, the union worked very poorly, especially since the Dutch King had absolutist and centralizing ideas whereas the Belgians had always stood stiffly for their local liberties under former Hapsburg rulers. The Belgians found it difficult to accept equality of representation in the States General when their population was nearly double that of the northerners and also objected to the insistence on Dutch as the official language. The Revolution started in Brussels in 1830 during a performance of Auber's opera "La Muette de Portici". The audience, on hearing the duet "Amour sacre de la Patrie"(Sacred love of the Fatherland), left the theatre and hoisted the Brabant flag. Similar revolts followed throughout the provinces, but the Belgians were defeated at Hasselt. William's elder son, was sent to negotiate and, after some fighting, withdrew. A provisional government was formed and national independence proclaimed.

The London conference of January 20, 1831, recognized Belgium as an independent and "perpetually neutral state."

After WWII the Benelux Union was formed with the Netherlands and Luxembourg, the formal establishment of Brussels as the "capital" of Europe.

Belgium is a small country and has three regions: Flanders (Flemish), Wallonia (French) and Brussels (Flemish), all have self-government in many spheres. Belgium has retained its old-world charm in the preservation of its ancient buildings and historical traditions.

Population -10,000,000
Capital - Brussels
Government - Constitutional monarchy
Religion - mostly Roman Catholic
Language - French, Dutch (Flemish), German and English is widely spoken
Money - Belgian franc (BF), Coin of 1, 5, 20, and 50 francs. Notes of 100, 500, 1,000, 2,000 and 10,000 francs
    U.S. $1 = 27 francs, Cdn. $1 = 20 francs, British £ = 45 francs

Public Holidays

Public holidays (on which banks and most shops are closed) are: New Year's Day, Easter Monday, Labour Day -May 1, Ascension Day, Whit-Monday, National Festival-July 21, Assumption-August 15, All Saints-Nov. 1, Armistice Day-Nov 11, Christmas Day.

Banks are usually also closed between 12 noon and 2pm on ordinary working days.

Visas

Americans, Canadians, and U.K. citizens do not need visas.

Peculiar Customs and Odd Expressions

Among friends, Belgians touch cheeks and kiss the air three times, alternating cheeks, men do this as well; talking with one's hands in one's pants pockets is rude; it is rude to point with the index finger; snapping the fingers of both hands is a vulgar gesture; in general, avoid gesturing.

C'est une drache nationale - It's a national rain shower (it's raining throughout the country)

Mon petit choux - My little cabbage (my darling)

Best Festivals

Brussels - best is Ommegang - 16th century-style procession in the Grand Place, first Thurs. in July; Flanders Fest.-Aug. & Sept., the Brussels Fest.-June to Sept.-both offer a variety of concerts and recitals

Bruges - Procession of the Holy Blood on Ascension Day

Night Activities and More

Brussels: Brussels Jazz Club; Play-Night-local cabaret; Discos-Griffin's of the Royal Windsor, Mirano, Le Garage; 'Jeux de Nuit'.

Must See Tourist Sites

Alden Biesenin - Limburg near Bilzen-incredible collection of castles

Antwerp - Rubens House, Royal Art Gallery, Mayer van den Bergh Museum-artworks; Steen Castle-contains the National Maritime Museum; Cathedral of Our Lady

Bruges - Belfry Tower, Town Hall, Canals and Lake of Love

Brussels - Grand Place-beautiful square-contains Town Hall, Maison des Brasseurs- brewery; Maison du Roi-city museum; St. Michael's Cathedral

Durbuy - prides itself on being the smallest town in the world-very picturesque

Ghent - Van Eyck's Adoration of the Mystic Lamb at St.Bavo's Cathedral, Gravensteen 12th century castle, St. Michael's Bridge

Liege - the Palace of the Prince-Bishops, St. Lambert & Market Square

Mechelen - St. Rombout's Cathedral, The Town Hall

Namur - 15th century citadel

Ostend - seacoast resorts

Best Scenery

A canal ride from Bruges to Kamme

Ardennes area southwest of Brussels

Dinant - very picturesque town on a river

Bus

Eurail Passes can be used for bus travel between cities, contact DeLIJN bus company in Flanders or TEC in Wallonie.

Cycling

Best in the flat north, can be rented from some train stations for 50BF a day if you have a train ticket, 280BF without a ticket, bikes must be returned to same station.

Hitch-Hiking

Drivers are fast; this method is good in the Ardennes; talk to travel agencies in Brussels about TaxiStop agencies that match you with a driver - very reasonable.

Train

Benelux Tourrail Pass for 3,030BF for under 26, otherwise 4,040BF good for 5 days in a 17 day period in Belgium, Netherlands, Luxembourg; for Belgium only, the Belgium Tourrail Pass for 1,995BF for any age group, or the Half-Fare Card - 570BF for one month, best deal Belgian Go Pass - under 26- ten one-way trips anywhere in the country for 1,290BF.

Camping

Tourist board has list of campsites, average price 50BF per adult and tent, majority of campsites are in the Ardennes and on the Coast.

Youth Hostels

From 300BF-660BF/night includes breakfast. For on-the-spot information contact: l) Vlaamse Jeugdherbergcentrale, Van Stralenstraat 40, B-2060 Antwerpen, Belgium, TX71934 VJHB tel:(32) (3) 2327218 or 2) Les Auberges de Jeunesse, Rue Van Oost 52, B-1030, Bruxelles, Belgium tel: (32) (2) 2153100

Youth Hostel Town Locations and Telephone Numbers

A Antwerpen (3) 2380273 **B** Bokrijk/Genk (89) 356220; Bouillon (61) 468137; **Brugge** (50) 352679; **Brussels** - 3 hostels - 1) **Jean Nihon Hostel** on 4 Rue de l'Elephant, tel: (2) 4103858; 2) Jacques Brel Hostel on Rue de la Sablonniere 30, tel: (2) 2180187; 3) Bruegel Hostel on Heilig Geeststraat 2, tel: (2) 5110436; **C** Champlon (84) 455294; **D** Diest (13) 3113721; Dudzele/Brugge (50) 599321; **G** Ghent (9) 2337050; Geraardsbergen (54) 416189; **H** Herbeumont (61) 411368; Huizingen (2) 3830026; Huy-Tihange (85) 231051; **K** Kortrijk (56) 201442; **L** Liege (2) 2153100; **M** Maldegem (50) 713121; Malmedy (80) 338386; **N** Namur (81) 223688; Nijlen (3) 4110733; **O** Oostduinkerke (58) 512649; Oostende (59)805297; **S** St.-Vith (80) 229331; **T** Tienen (16) 822796; Tilff-Liege (41) 882100;

Tongeren (12) 391370; Tournai (69) 216136; **V** Vleteren (57) 400901; Voeren (41) 811110; **W** Westerlo (14) 547938; **Z** Zoersel (3) 3851642.

Work

For non-EU nationals it is illegal, unless you try to work in hostels, restaurants, resorts etc., you get a permit obtained by the employer before you enter the country, and work is hard to find.

Babysitting

Contact ULB in Brussels at avenue Paul Heger 22, Prefab 4 tel: 650-2171.

Useful Addresses and Tourist Offices

in U.S.

Belgian Tourist Office, 780 Third Avenue, suite 1501, New York, NY l00l7 tel: (212) 758-8130, fax (212) 355-7675

in Canada

Belgian Tourist Office, P.O.Box 760, Succursale N.D.G, Montreal, Quebec tel: (514) 484-3594 H4A 3S2

in the U.K.

Premier House, 2 Gayton Rd., Harrow, Middlesex HA1 2XU, tel: 0181/861-3300

in Brussels

Tourist Information in Brussels is in the Hotel de Ville on the Grand Place near the Town Hall tel:02-513-8940,

Head office - Rue du Marchee aux Herbes-Grasmarkt 63, B-l000 Brussels tel:02/504 03 86 Youth Information Centres - Info-Jeunes rue Marche aux Herbes 27, tel: 02 512 32 74;

SOS Jeunes open all day and night tel: 02 736 36 36.

Belgian Embassies

in U.S.

3330 Garfield St. NW Washington D.C. 20008, tel: (202) 333-6900

in Canada

80 Elgin St. 4th floor, Ottawa, Ontario K1P lB7 tel: (6l3)-236-7267/9

in the U.K.

103 Eaton Square, London, SW1 W9AB, tel: 44 71 235 5422

Foreign Posts in Belgium

Brussels

Canadian Embassy, 2 av. Tervuren, tel: 02/735-80-40, M-F 9-12, 2-4

British Embassy, 85 rue d'Arion, tel: 02/287-62-17, M-f 9:30-12, 2:30-4:30

United States Embassy, 25 blvd. du Regent, tel: 02/513-38-30, M-f 9-12

Driving Distances (in km)

From Brussels to cities in Belgium:

Antwerp 47	Leuven 26
Bruges 96	Liege 98
Eupen 144	Namur 63
Ghent 56	Tournai 83

From Brussels to cities in Europe:

Amsterdam 198	London 325	Paris 292
Cologne 203	Madrid 1,609	Stockholm 1,886
Copenhagen 1,177	Reims 196	Zurich 625
Lille 105	Rome 1,768	

Telephone Information: International Code 00, Country Code 32, Main City Area Codes: Antwerpen 3, Bruges 50, Brussels 2, Gent 9, Liege 41, Namur 81, Tournai 69; time difference (Eastern Daylight) plus 6 hours. Emergency # 900

BULGARIA

A Little History

As many art works and other remains prove, Bulgaria has been inhabited for over 5,000 years, originally by the Thracians. The Greeks established colonies in 600 B.C. and in 336 Philip of Macedonia held sway. The Romans began their invasion at the same time and ruled the country in the 1st Century A.D. Sofia, then called Serdica, was the capital of Roman Thracia. In 400 A.D. the land was taken over by the Slavs who in turn were conquered by the Bulgars whose ancient capital Bulgary still exists on the Volga River. The Bulgars integrated with the Slavs and adopted their culture.

The first Bulgarian kingdom was established by Khan Asparukh in 681. Christianity was introduced in 865. Assaults by the Byzantines started at about that time; they ruled from 1018 to 1185 when a revolt against them established the second Bulgarian kingdom. During that time Bulgaria became one of the most powerful states in Europe with thriving industry and culture. The Ottoman Empire began its aggression in 1393 and after many attacks finally took over the entire country and held it until 1878. Popular uprisings helped by the Imperial Russian army re-established Bulgaria. Before WWII there were a number of governments and territorial wars. In 1944 the People's Republic of Bulgaria was established as a Soviet satellite. With the demise of Soviet power and democratic elections, the present republic was established. Since October 1991 Bulgaria has been ruled by a coalition of democratic parties. The main objectives of government are: transition to market economy, privatization of industry and agriculture, and integration with Western Europe and the U.S.

Population- 9,300,000
Capital-Sofia
Government- parliamentary democracy

Religion - 90% Orthodox Christians, some Roman Catholic and Muslim

Language - Bulgarian, Russian, some German

Money- Leva One leva equals 100 stotinki. Coins of 1, 2, 5, 10, 20, and 50 stotinki, and of 1, 2 and 5 leva. Notes of 1, 2, 5, 10, 20, 50, 100 and 200 leva. Money can only be exchanged at tourist offices, banks, and major hotels in major cities. You should only have to pay for plane tickets and lodging in U.S. currency (U.S. currency is the most preferred), avoid the black market altogether.

U.S. $1 = 68 leva, Cdn. $1 = 50 leva, British pd. = 105 leva

Public Holidays

New Year's Day, January 1st; National Liberation Day, March 3rd; Easter Monday; Labour Day, May 1st; Day of Bulgarian Culture and the Cyrillic Alphabet, May 24th; Christmas, December 25th. Banks open Monday to Friday 8:30 a.m. to 5:30 p.m.

Visas

U.S. citizens do not need a visa for stays under 30 days, over 30 days-the visa costs $34 with a 2 week wait, or $64 to get a visa right away. Visas issued at the airport or at the border $64 in U.S. cash.

Canadians need visas for stays under 30 days - $55 for a 5 day wait, or $100 for a visa the same day, visas at the border or airport cost U.S.$64. A transit visa (staying less than 30 hours) cost $30.

Visas for U.K. citizens cost approximately U.S. $ 45.

Peculiar Customs and Odd Expressions

A nod means 'no'and a shake of the head means 'yes'

Best Festivals

Burgas - Golden Orpheus Festival, international entertainment in June

Koprivstitza Folklore Festival in August

Sosopal (by the Black Sea) - Apolonia Fest. has arts, music and drama, end of Aug.-Sept. 10th

Sofia Musical Weeks in May and June

Valley of the Roses Festival between Sofia and the Black Sea, held on the first Sunday in June - attracts thousands from all over the world for the parade of flowers, folk concerts, entertainment and games.

Night Activities and More

Sofia-dancing-Angel Club, Disco NDK; disco dancing at the National Palace of Culture; Orbylux disco and Sky Club disco

Must See Tourist Sites

Bozhenzi - storybook town with whitewashed houses where many Bulgarian writers and artists find their inspiration

Gabrovo - nearby is Etura - a live museum of Bulgarian Revival

Kiprivshtitsa - romantic town with white stone fences covered with geraniums and ivy

Pliska - near the city of Shumen, imposing fortress and tower

Plovdiv - Forum of Philoppolis, Mosque of Djoumaya Djamiya, Roman amphitheater

Sofia - Bulgarian Jewish Exhibition, Sveti Georgi Rotunda (in Sheraton's courtyard)-4th century church; Natzionalen Archeologicheski (National Museum of Archaeology); Hram-Pametnik Alexandee Nevsky (domed church); Naroden Dvorets Na Kultuata (huge National Palace of Culture)

Sosapol (near Burgas) at the Black Sea - an ancient Bulgarian town with beautiful, typical Bulgarian architecture

Melnik - old Bulgarian town, and a fine winery. near Sofia - famous Rila Monastery - 100 km south of Sofia

Triavna - old town from the Bulgarian Revival, beautiful houses with wood-crafted interiors

Veliko Turnovo - between two steep hills above the Yantara River, a fortress gate provides the only access to the summit, breathtaking views and the Ascension Patriarchal Church

Best Scenery

Nessebur - situated on a small rocky peninsula jutting into the Black Sea, 40 ancient churches and cobblestone streets

Rila Mountains - great scenery and great for walking, mountain huts available

Veliko Turnovo - old home built into the hillside of the limestone cliffs

Valley of Roses between Sofia and the Black Sea - rose oil industry - visit town of Kazanlak

Varna and the Black Sea coast

Transportation

Eurail, InterRail are not valid in Bulgaria; if you are coming from Romania you will still need a $36 transit visa. Buses are better than trains, both stopping in remote towns. Buy train tickets in advance at the Rila Railway Bureau at offices in major Bulgarian cities.

Hitch-Hiking

It is legal, best to get rides on trucks.

Accommodation

Your best bet are university dorms for 150 leva-200 leva/night- contact Orbita tourist office for a list.

Camping

Sites are 100 leva - 260 leva/night.

Youth Hostels

Bulgarian Youth Hostel Federation, Boul Vassil Levski 75, Sofia 1000, Bulgaria, tel: (359) (2) 883821, fax 802414; hostel prices range from 55-140 leva, including sheet rental per night, most serve meals. Orbita arranges stays in private homes. All reservations should be made through 'Pirintourist', 12 Pozitano St, 1000 Sofia fax (359) (2) 650052.

Youth Hostel Town Locations and Telephone Numbers
A Ambaritza (670) 26017; Apriltzi (68) 23683; **B** Bansko (7443) 2271;
Belogradchik (936) 3285; Borovez (721) 2205; Bourgas-Sarafovo (56)
36008; Buntovna 380; Buzludja (431) 22566; **C** Chepelare (3051) 2061;
D Dimitrovgrad (391) 7586; Dryanovo (676) 2332; **H** Harmanli (373)
2432; Hristo Smirnenski (359) 3573; **K** Koprivshtitza (87) 0586;
Kujstendil (78) 22332; **L** Lovech (68) 23683; **M** Madara (5) 7717;
Malyovitza (2) 870687; Martziganitza (331) 22646; Momchil Junak
(301) 21293; **P** Pamporovo (301) 21293; Perushtitza (32) 223958;
Petrohan (9671) 4285; Pleven - 2 hostels - 1) Touristicheski dom
'Pleven'Hostel, no address given, tel: (64) 29013; 2) Hizha 'Pleven'
Hostel at the Middle Stara Planina Mountain (64) 29013; **R** Razlog
(747) 2256; Rila (22) 70; Rilski Ezera (701) 22524; Rousse (82) 28990;
S Sandanski - 2 hostels - 1) Camping Sandanski Hostel in the Sandanski
town, tel: (746) 5167; 2) Yane Sandanski Hostel in the Pirin Mountain,
tel: (746) 5193; Sapareva Banja 214; Skalni Mostove (3051) 3261;
Sliven (44) 22930; Sofia - 5 hostels - 1) "Tourist" Hostel at the Komplex
'Krasma polyana', tel: (2) 881079; 2) Aleko Hostel at the Vitosha Moun-
tain, tel: (2) 881079; 3) Belite Brezi Hostel at the Vitosha Mountain
National Park, tel: (2) 881079; 4) Planinarska Pessen Hostel at the
Vitosha Mountain, tel: (2) 881079; 5) Planinetz Hostel at the Vitosha
Mountain (20km from Sofia) , tel: 573139; Stara Zagora (42) 40076;
Strandja (56) 36008; **T** Tchernatiza (32) 223958; Treshtenik (28) 82;
Troyan (6702) 6017; **V** Varna (52) 222710; Veliko Turnovo - 2 hostels
- 1) Trapezitza Hostel at the Touristicheski dom 'Trapezitza', tel: (62)
20373; 2) Momina Krepost Hostel at the Touristicheski dom 'Momina
Krepost', tel: (62) 20373; Velingrad (359) 3573; Vidin (94) 22351; Vratsa
(92) 22139; Vurbishki Prohod (54) 57717; Vurhovruh (32) 223958; **Y**
Yarorov (474) 5206.
Useful Addresses and Tourist Offices
Bulgaria-Balkan Holiday, 41 E. 42nd St., suite 508 New York, NY 10017,
  tel: (212) 573-5530
in the U.K
18 Princes St., London WIR 7RE, tel: 0171/499-6988
Sofia - Orbita student run tourist office at blvd Stambolijski 45a tel: 801812 ; Pirin
  Travel Agency at blvd Stambolijski 45a tel: 2/88-41-22 info. and hostel
  bookings
Balkantourist and the State Tourist Information Office at Knajaz Dondukov
  37 tel:884430
Plovdiv-Pauldin Tourist office at Bulgaria 34, tel:032/55-38-48 and Orbita
  at Vazrazdane 79, tel: 032/23-23-00
Varna-Balkantourist has 3 offices here, see the one across from the train
  station, tel:052/ 22-56-30

Bulgarian Embassies
in U.S.
1621 22nd St. N.W., Washington D.C. 20008, tel: (202) 483-5885
in Canada
65 Overlea Blvd, suite 406, Toronto, Ontario M4H 1P1 tel: (416) 696-2420, fax:(416) 696-8019
in the U.K.
186 Queen's Gate, London, postal code not available, tel: 584 9400
Foreign Posts in Bulgaria
Sofia
British Embassy: Bulgaria marsal Tolbuhin 65, tel: 87-83-25, M-Th 8:30-5:30, F 8:30-1
United States Embassy, Alexander Stambolijski 1, tel: 02/88-48-01, M-F 9-5
Driving Distances (in km)
From Sofia to cities in Bulgaria:

Blagoevgrad 102	Koulata 188	Smolyan 255
Bourgas 392	Pleven 176	Stara Zagora 234
Dobrich 512	Plovdiv 156	Turgovishte 345
Gabrovo 223	Rousse 324	Varna 470
Kapitan Andreevo 315	Silistra 446	Veliko Turnovo
Yambol 300		

From Sofia to cities in Europe:

Athens 660	London 2,575	Rome 1,585
Belgrade 403	Madrid 3,020	Salonika 303
Berlin 1,580	Milan 1,470	Skopje 208
Brussels 2,124	Munich 1,513	Tirana 505
Budapest 785	Oslo 2,707	Vienna 1,015
Bucharest 395	Paris 2,165	Warsaw 1,504
Copenhagen 1,945	Prague 1,280	

Telephone Information: International Code 00, Country 359, Main City Area Code: Sofia 2, Lovech 68, Plovdiv 32; time difference (Eastern Daylight) plus 7 hours

CYPRUS

Visas
Visas are not needed for Americans and Canadians for up to 3 months.
Youth Hostels
Contact Cyprus Youth Hostel Association, 34 Th Theodotou St., PO Box 1328, Nicosia, Cyprus. tel: (357) (2) 442027; fax (357) (2) 442896., prices range from C£3.00-C£5.00 per night, plus sheet rental if needed at C£1.00.

Youth Hostel Town Locations and Telephone Numbers
A Ayia Napa (3) 723433; **L** Larnaca (4) 621188; **N** Nicosia (2) 444808; **P** Paphos (6) 2325 88; **S** Stavros (6) 722338; **T** Troodos (5) 422400.
Telephone Information: International Code 00, Country Code 357, Main City Area Codes: Nicosia 2, Larnaca 4, Limassol 5, Ayia Napa 3, Paphos 6; Time difference (Eastern Daylight) plus 7 hours.

CZECH REPUBLIC

A Little History

The Czech Republic includes the historical lands of Bohemia, Moravia and Silesia, which have formed the nucleus of the Czech state since the early Middle Ages. The forefathers of its inhabitants settled here during the 5th to 10th centuries A.D. Around the year 868 Prince Borivoj I of the Premyslide family became ruler and his dynasty laid the foundations of the Czech state during the following five centuries. The Luxemburgs ruled from 1310 to 1347, and from the mid-16th century the Hapsburg dynasty. After the disintegration of the Austro-Hungarian empire the independent Czechoslovak Republic was established in 1918. In World War II it was under Nazi occupation, in 1948 came the Communist coup resulting in forty years of isolation. After the November 1989 events, called the "gentle revolution," its democratic traditions were restored and after the peaceful division of the country the Czech Republic came into being on January 1, 1993.

Population - 12,000,000
Capital - Prague
Government - parliamentary democracy
Religion - Roman Catholic and some Protestant
Language - Czech, some Russian and English
Money - Koruny. One koruny equals 100 haleru. Coins of 10, 20, 50 haleru, 1,2, 5, 10, 20 and 50 korun. Notes of 100, 500, 1,000 and 5,000 korun. Change money on weekdays at state bank- 2% commission charge, Chequepoint charges 9%, hotels even more.
U.S. $1 = 22 korun, Cdn. $1 = 16 korun, British £ = 37 korun
Public Holidays
New Year's Day, Jan. 1; Labour Day, May 1; Day of Liberation from Fascism, May 8; Day of Slav Apostels, July 5; Day of Jan Hus death at the stake, July 6; Day of origin of the independent Czechoslovokia, Oct. 28; Christmas Eve, Dec. 24; Christmas, Dec. 25; Easter Monday - 'movable'
Visas
Canadians must apply for a 30 day visa before entering the country, cost is

$50 Cdn., same for a transit visa. Americans and U.K. citizens may enter the Czech Republic for 30 days without a visa.

Peculiar Customs and Odd Expressions

When introduced to a Czech woman or an elderly person, wait to see if he or she extends a hand before offering to shake; never keep your left hand in your pocket while shaking hands with your right; to get someone's attention, raise your hand, palm facing out, with only the index finger extended, avoid waving or beckoning; don't talk to someone with your hands in your pockets or while chewing gum; when invited to dinner at a Czech home, bring a bouquet of unwrapped flowers- the bouquet should have an uneven number of flowers, but not thirteen; red roses are reserved for romantic situations.

During the past century the most wide-spread saying about the Czechs was: "Each Czech is a musician."

On the 5th Sunday before Easter, also called Black or Death Sunday, a straw figure is brought out of the village and is drowned or burnt; on the night before May 1 a witch-burning ceremony takes place followed by singing and music; weddings ususually held after Christmas until Ash Wednesday and then again after the harvest, at times when there was enough food and less work to be done in the fields and around the house.

Best Festivals

Folklore Festivals in Brno - in April; in Pardubice- in June; Sumperk- International folklore festival in August

Night Activities and More

Prague - Club America, Radost, AghaRTA Jazz Centrum, Rock Cafe, Reduta

Beer Fact: the American "Budweiser" has its origins in the town of Ceske Budejovice

(Bohemian Budweis), which has been producing the beer, "Budvar" for 300 years.

Must See Tourist Sites

Brno - Dom na Petrove (Gothic cathedral of St. Peter and Paul) on Petrov Hill; Kapucinske Klaster (monastery)

near Brno - Punkevni caves

Ceske Budejovice - Budvar brewery

Cesky Krumlov - Rozmberk Castle

Karlovy Vary - world-renowned spa

Marianske Lazne - visit Ustredni Lazne mineral baths

Prague - Prague Castle, Castle Gallery, St.Vitus's Cathedral 14th century; Royal Palace and the Garden on the Ramparts; Karluv Most - a bridge with a marketplace; Stare Mesto is the Old Town

Karlstejn Castle - built 1348-1357-most visited castle in the Czech Republic, 20 km. from Prague

Southern Bohemia - Hluboka and Strakonice castles

Near Prague - Krivoklat Hrad-11th century castle; Hradec Kralove-2 1/2 hours train ride from Prague - historic centre of Eastern Bohemia

Pisek - one of the most beautiful towns in Southern Bohemia- 13th century stone bridge

Telc - in South Moravia-outstanding Renaissance and Baroque ancient monuments

Best Scenery

near Brno - Macocha gorge

Cesky Krumlov - beautiful castle, narrow, twisting streets along the winding Vltava River

Karlovy Vary - winding river valley

Marianske Lazne - town set in a forested valley

Southern Bohemia - medieval towns, castles, rolling green hills

Transportation

EurailPasses and InterRail not accepted here. Trains and buses are crowded and slow. Costs are reasonable.

Hitch-Hiking

This is a good way to get around in this country.

Accommodation

Contact Cedok tourist office for private rooms - 220 korun-440 korun.

Youth Hostels

Contact: KMC Club of Young Travellers (Secretariat), Karoliny Svetle 30, 11000 Praha 1, Czech Republic, tel: (42) (2) 24230633, fax (42) (2) 24230633; Hostelling International has 20 hostels-beds cost 90 korun-500 korun a night, including a bed sheet, try university dorms throughout the year-only 50 korun a night.

Youth Hostel Town Locations and Telephone Numbers

B Brno (5) 331111; **C** Ceske Budejovice (38) 38312; Ceska Lipa (425) 52786; Chomutov (396) 5404; **D** Domazlice (189) 2386; **H** Horsovsky Tyn (188) 2319; **J** Jenisov (38) 38312; **K** Karlovy Vary - 2 hostels - 1) Albion Hostel on Zamecky vrch 43/379, tel: (17) 23473; 2) Cajkovsky Hostel on Sadova 32, tel: (17) 28437; Kladno (312) 3252; Kutna Hora (327) 2089; **L** Laznicky (335) 92201; Loucen (68) 38251; **M** Marianske Lazne 2624; **N** Nove Mesto na Morave (616) 916245; **P** Pisek (362) 4983; Plzen (19) 276500; **Praha** - 3 hostels - 1) CKM Juniorhotel on Zitna 12; tel: 292984; 2) **Hotel Beta** on Roskotova 1225/1, tel: (2) 462791; 3) Hotel Standart on Pristavni 2, tel: (2) 876541; **S** Sazava no tel. #; Sobesin tel. # Kacov 94243; **U** Uhersky Brod (633) 3190; Usti n/ L (47) 62215; **V** Vamberk (445) 41259; Velke Pavlovice (626) 922465; **Z** Zivohost tel. # Nahoruby 91181.

Useful Adresses and Tourist Offices

Cedok Tours, 10 E. 40th St. suite 3604, New York, NY 10016 tel: (212) 683-2647 or 1-800-800-8891

in the U.K.
17-18 Old Bond St., London WIX 4RB, tel: 0171/629-6058
Prague-youth travel bureau-Cestovni Kancelar Mladeze (CKM); American Hospitality Center at Na Mustku 7, off Vaclavske nam, tel: 02/262-045 hours - daily 9-9
Prazska Informacni Sluzba (PIS) at Na Prikope 20 - tourist information office tel: 544444
Cedok at Na Prikope 18, Praha tel: 2127111-tourist info. office close to Wenceslas Square
Cedok at Panska 5, Praha tel: 225656/227004 - accommodation service-hotels and private rooms
Czech Embassies
in U.S.
3900 Spring of Freedom, Washington, D.C. 20008, tel: (202) 363-6315/9
in Canada
541 Sussex drive, Ottawa, Ontario K1N 6Z6, tel: (613) 562-3875/7
Consulate General of the Czech Republic, 1305 Pine Ave. West, Montreal, Quebec H3G 1B2, tel: (514) 849-4495, fax: (514) 849-4117
in the U.K.
26 Kensington Palace Gardens, London, W84 QY, tel: 24 31 115
Foreign Posts in the Czech Republic
Prague
Canadian Embassy, Mickiewiczova 6, Hradcany, tel: 42-2-2431-1108/12, M-F 8-12, 2-4
British Embassy, Trziste 15, Mala Strana, tel: 02/533-347, M-F 9-12, 2:45-4
United States Embassy, Trziste 15, Mala Strana, tel: 02/536-641, M-F 8-1, 2-4:30
Driving Distances (in km)
From Prague to cities in Czech Republic:

Brno 198	Liberec 112
Ceska Budejovice 144	Olomouc 255
Hradec Kralove 101	Ostrava 343
Cheb 168	Pardubice 78
Jihiava 118	Plzen 78
Karlovy Vary 122	Sumperk 622

From Prague to cities in Europe:

Amsterdam 1,420	Copenhagen 970	Rome 1,392
Berlin 344	Madrid 2,642	Stockholm 1,679
Brussels 1,202	Munich 360	Vienna 294
Budapest 652	Oslo 1,579	Warsaw 626
Bucharest 1,583	Paris 1,108	

Telephone Information: International Code 00, Country Code 42, Main City Area Code: Prague 2; time difference (Eastern Daylight) plus 6 hours.

A Little History

On June 8 , 793, a convent at Lindisfarne, on the north shore of Scotland, was sacked and the holy inmates were put to the sword or enslaved. Christian Europe woke up with a fierce hangover. Word traveled fast even in those days of rudimentary communications; coastal England and France braced for nasty times. The invaders with peculiar head-gear were called "Vikings" because they gathered at the vik (little fjord) to assemble their ships and sail off for pillage and adventure in foreign lands. Tightly constructed ships and an unchallenged military organization took the Vikings from triumph to triumph over the next three centuries, as kings such as Regnar, Harald Bluetooth and Sweyn Forkbeard made their way through the defenceless coasts to the south. The unfortunate inhabitants paid protection money called Danegeld, but never enough. The English king who played this hapless game - paying enormous sums of silver over and over again to no avail - went down in history as Ethelred the Unready.

The Vikings were not purely sadistic, nor was anarchy their main delight. Population pressures on the Danish mainland drove them to it, and once they got to the places they sacked, they settled and organized as often as they plundered. They gave English the word "law", and created a high degree of social organization. They constructed cities where none had been before. They explored Iceland, Greenland, and North America. They mingled with the existing populations in England and France, acquiring their vernacular and religion, Christianity. By the time the Viking Age ended, Denmark had established itself as a nation, under King Harald Bluetooth.

Denmark is the southern-most and smallest of the Scandinavian countries (excluding Greenland and the Faroe Islands). It has 500 islands, many of them are uninhabited. There are no mountains and no rivers, but the varied landscape includes hills, forests, lakes and small watercourses.

Population - 5, 200,000
Capital - Copenhagen
Government - Constitutional monarchy
Religion - Lutheran
Language - Danish, secondary language are English and German
Money - Krone (kr) One krone equals 100 ore. Coins of 25 and 50 ore, and
   of 1, 5, 10 and 20 kroner. Notes of 20, 50, 100, 500, 1,000 kroner
   U.S. $1 = 5 kroner, Cdn.$1 = 4 kroner, British £ = 8.5 kroner
Public Holidays
January 1, Maundy Thursday, Good Friday, Easter Sunday, Easter Monday,
   Prayer Day-4th Friday after Easter, Ascension Day, Constitution Day,

Whit Sunday, Whit Monday, Dec. 24 from 12 noon, Christmas Day and December 26.

Visas

Americans, Canadians, and U.K. citizens do not need visas.

Peculiar Customs and Odd Expressions

Danes say the traditional greeting 'hiej', which sounds exactly like 'Hi' when both arriving and departing; the gesture North Americans use to indicate that someone is crazy (index finger circling while pointed at one's temple) is used to insult other drivers while on the road; the North American "O.K." gesture (thumb and forefinger forming a circle) can be taken as an insult in Denmark; summon waiters by raising your index finger; at the theater, enter a row with your back to the stage (so that you face people seated in the row). It is considered insulting to squeeze past seated people with your backside facing them; at the beach many women wear topless bathing suits; Skaal-a toasting custom when drinking- you raise your glass, look at the other person in the eye, nod and say "Skaal", finish your whole drink while fixing your eyes upon the person opposite you, after it's finished, raise your glass again, bow slightly and now you can look away.

"man kan ikke vaere venner med alle" - "you can't be friends with everybody"

Best Festivals

Aarhus International Jazz Festival mid-July

Copenhagen Jazz Festival in early July

Frederikssund, Sealand - Viking Festival, approx. June 23- July 9- open-air play performed by 200 bearded Vikings, followed by a Viking banquet in Valhalla.

Odense - Hans Christian Andersen festival at the Funen Village every summer July 19 to August 13

Night Activities and More

Copenhagen - discos - Annabel's, Daddy's - in the Palads Cinema complex; Vin and Olgod-dancing; Jazzhouse Monmartre; On the Rox, U-Matic, Prive, Minefield

Must See Tourist Sights

Aalborg - Viking burial ground

Aarhus - Old Town (Open air Museum), Moesgaard Prehistoric Museum built with original medieval bricks and wood; Fire Protection Museum

Copenhagen - Nationalmuseet (national museum-most museums close on Mondays); visit the Amalienborg Palace, built between 1749 and 1760; Tivoli - amusement park-city center - orchestras play, gardens flourish, great for walking - a must see; climb the City Hall Tower; Kaastellet-The Citadel, at the Langelinie - 300 year old military fortress; Rosenborg Castle

Helsingor near Copenhagen - Kronborg Castle

Esbjerg - Saedden Church-unusual brick structure lit by hundreds of
  lightbulbs
Hillerod - famous for its Frederiksborg Castle
Odense - Hans Christian Andersen museum; St. Canute's Cathedral
Roskilde - Viking Ship Museum

Best Scenery
coming to Elsinore - via the Danish Riviera, a 25 mile stretch.

Bus
Much slower than trains, but much cheaper, train passes are not valid on
  buses, no bicycles allowed, tickets can be bought from the bus driver -
  you should have money or tickets ready upon boarding.

Cycling
You can rent bikes for approximately 50kr a day at train stations - you
  cannot drop off the bike at other train stations in the country or other
  countries; cycling distances are short and the charming countryside is
  dotted with villages and gentle, rolling hills.

Hitch-Hiking
Relatively easy in this country, stay on entrance ramps.

Train
Nordturist Pass valid only in Scandinavia costs 1450 kr youth or 1930kr-
  21 unlimited days of travel; ScanRail (youth 2nd class)-5 days of travel
  within 15 day period for $175 U.S., 10 days within 1 month-$295 U.S., 1
  month consecutive is $425 U.S. Nordturist passes - see the local Danish
  State Railways offices; ScanRail - get your tickets from a travel agency
  in North America.

Camping
Approximately 40kr, over 500 camping sites.

Farm Vacations
There are 370 farms offering accommodation - from a humble stay in a
  modest house to homes with up to 25 beds. Bike trips, bonfires, horse-
  back rides, pottery lessons and smoke-curing fish programs are offered
  at many of them. Costs - for bed & breakfast 155-175kr.

Private Accommodation
Local tourist offices handle rents of rooms situated at a reasonable distance
  from town centres. Tourists can write or call the tourist offices, but may also
  visit them to book overnight accommodation. The tourist offices charge a
  small reservation fee. Average prices for a single room are 120-175kr.

Youth Hostels
There are 130 hostels available, they house 2-6 people per room, students need-
  ing inexpensive shelter should write to Denmarks Vandrehjem which is the
  Youth and Family Hostels Association, at Vesterbrogade 39, DK-1620 Copenhagen V, Denmark, tel: (45) (31) 313612, rates range from 85kr in a
  room with more than 2 people and up to 250 kr/night for a private room.

Youth Hostel Town Locations and Telephone Numbers
A Aabenraa 74622699; Aalborg 98116044; Aeroskobing 62521044; Anneberg 59930062; Arhus 86167298; Arup 64431328; Assens 64711357; **B** Billund 75332777; Blokhus-Hune 98249180; Bork Havn 75280222; Brande 97182197; Bronderslev 98821500; **E** Ebeltroft 86342053; Enderupskov 74821711; Esbjerg 75136833; **F** Faborg 62613508; Fakse 56714181; FAROE ISLANDS - 3 hostels - 1) Klaksvig Hostel on 3870 Klaksvig, tel: 4255403; 2) Oyndarfjordur Hostel on 'Fjallsgardur', tel: 4244522; 3) Gjogv Gjoargardur Hostel on 476 Gjogv, tel: 29823175; Fjerritslev 98211190; Fredensborg 42280315; Fredericia 7592187; Frederikshavn 98421475; Frederiksvaerk 42120766; **G** Givskud 75730500; Gjerrild 86384199; GREENLAND - 2 hostels - 1) Narssarssuaq Hostel on 3923 Narssarssuaq, tel: 92993522; 2) Igaliku Hostel on 150 Narsaq, tel: 29935151; Grena 86326622; Grindsted 75322605; Gudhjem 53985035; **H** Haderslev 74521347; Hadsund 98574345; Hasle 53966434; Helsingor 49211640; Henne St 75255075; Herning 97123 144; Hirtshals 98941248; Hjembaek 53468181; Hjorring 98926700; Hobro 98521847; Holbaek 59442919; Horsens 75616777; Hou 98253212; **J** Jels 74552869; Juelsminde 75693066; **K** Kalundborg 59561366; Katrinedal 75756146; Kerteminde 65323929; Kolding 75509140; Korsor 53571022; Kobenhavn (Copenhagen) - 2 hostels -1) **Amager Hostel** on 2300 Kobenhavn S., tel: 32522908; 2) Bellahoj Hostel on 2700 Bronshoj, tel: 31289715; Koge 53651474; **L** Lyngby 42803074; Laeso 98499195; Logumkloster 74743 618; **M** Maribo 53883314; Marstal 62531064; Mon 55812030; **N** Nakskov 53922434; Naestved 53722091; Nyborg 65312704; Nykobing Falster 54856699; Nykobing Mors 97720617; **O** Odense 66130425; Oksbol 75271877; **R** Randers 86425044; Rebild 98391340 Ribe 75420620; Ringe 62622151; Ringkobing 97322455; Ringsted 53611526; Roskilde 42352184; Roslev 97571385; Rudbol 74738298; Rudkobing 62511830; Ry 86891407; Romo 74755188; Ronde 86371108; Ronne 56951340; **S** Sakskobing 53896045; Samso 86592044; Sandvig 56480362; Sejero 53490290; Silkeborg 86823642; Skagen 98442 200; Skanderborg 86511966; Skaelskor 53594384; Slagelse 53522528; Store Heddinge 53702022; Struer 97855313; Svaneke 56496242; Svendborg 62216699; Saeby 984636 50; Sonderborg 74423112; **T** Thisted 97925042; Tisvildeleje 42309850; Tonder 74723500 **V** Varde 75221091; Vejle 75825188; Viborg 86671781; Vollerup 74423990; Vordingborg53775084; Aeroskobing 62521044
Youth Deal
For a two week period every summer from apporoximately June 24 to July 6 people under 26 can bunk down for free in 50 places around the country. That's right - it won't cost you a cent! All you need is your own sleeping bag and a means of transportation. Pick up a list of participating sleeping quarters from major railway stations and local tourist offices. If the snag in

this deal is transportation, you will be glad to hear that the Danish State Railways in this period has cut its prices on a two-week pass for those under 26.!!!!

Work

Permits are rarely issued to Canadians and Americans. Contact: Danish International Students' Committee, 36 Skindergade, 1159 Copenhagen K, Denmark

Babysitting

Copenhagen contact Minerva at 31-22-96-96, call Mon.-Thurs. 7a.m.-9a.m. and 3 p.m.-6 p.m., Friday from 3 p.m. to 7 p.m., Sat 3 p.m. to 7 p.m.

Useful Addresses and Tourist Offices

in U.S.

Danish Tourist Board, 655 3rd Ave., 18th floor, New York, NY 10017, (212) 949-2322 fax (212) 286-0896;

in Canada

P.O./CP 636, Mississauga, Ontario L5M 2C2, Info Line (905) 820-8984

in the U.K.

Sceptre House, 169-173 Regent St., London WIR 8PY, tel: 0171/734-2637

in Denmark

Danish Tourist Board at Bernstoffsgadel, DK-1577,Copenhagen, tel 33/11-13-25 or Tourist Info. in Copenhagen: Use It at Radhusstraede 13, DK-1204 Copenhagen K, Tel: 33-156518; Inexpensive accommodation for students write to Danmarks Vandrehjem, (Youth and Family Hostels Association), Vesterbrogade 39, DK-1620 Copenhagen V or Danish International Student Committee at Skindergade 28, DK-1159 Copenhagen K tel: 33 11 00 44

Danish Embassies

in U.S.

3200 White Haven St. N.W., Washington D.C. 20008-3683, tel: (202) 234-4300

in Canada

47 Clarence St. # 450, Ottawa, Ontario K1N 9K1, tel: (613) 562-1811

in the U.K.

55 Sloane St., London SW1X 9SR, tel: 171 333 0200 or 235 1255

Foreign Posts in Denmark

Copenhagen

Canadian Embassy, Kristen Bernikowsgade 1, tel: 33-12-22-99, M-F 8:30-4:45

British Embassy, Kastelvej 40, tel: 35-26-46-00, M-F 9-5

United States Embassy, Dag Hammarskjolds Alle 24, tel: 31-42-31-44 M-F 8:30-5

Driving Distances (in km)

From Copenhagen to cities in Denmark:

Aalborg 384	Herning 281	Randers 322
Arhus 286	Hjorring 432	Rodby 163

Ebeltoft 340	Horsens 239	Silkeborg 281
Esbjerg 280	Hundested 67	Skagen 487
Frederkshavn 447	Kalundborg 103	Struer 329
Froslev/Border 293	Kolding 212	Thisted 147
Gedser 152	Middelfart 189	Tonder 297
Halsskov/Korsor 110	Naestved 85	Veljle 215
Helsingor 47	Odense 147	Viborg 305

From Copenhagen to cities in Europe:

Belgrade 1,920	Milan 2,039	Rome 2,136
Berlin 626	Munich 1,259	Stockholm 709
Brussels 927	Oslo 609	Vienna 1,264
Budapest 1,522	Paris 1,267	Warsaw 1,213
Madrid 2,586	Prague 970	

Telephone Information: International Code 00, Country Code 45, Main City Area Code, Copenhagen 31; time difference (Eastern Daylight) plus 6 hours. Emergency # 100

EGYPT

A Little History

The history of Egypt dates back some 5,000 years. The Pharaonic era is divided into three main periods:

The Ancient Kingdom - Its capital was Menf (Memphis), founded by King Mena, the first King of Dynasty I, who united Upper and Lower Egypt. King Zoser built the Saqqara pyramid, the first large-scale stone structure in history. Pharaonic Egypt was at the apex of its civilization when the Pyramids were built.

The Middle Kingdom - Its capital was Thebes. A period characterized by an artistic renaissance, agricultural projects and trade exchange with Bilad al Sham and the Sudan.

The New Kingdom - starts with 18th Dynasty founded by King Ahmos. Its capital was Thebes, except for the short period, when King Akhen-Aton moved his capital to Tel-el-Amarna and lived there with his wife Nefertiti. Among the eminent rulers of the New Kingdom was King Ramses II who left a great architectural patrimony, the most important being the two Temples of Abou-Simbel. After the Pharaonic era came the Persian, the Greek, the Roman and the Byzantine eras.

The Arab Islamic Conquest started in 641 when the Arabs entered Egypt, under the leadership of Amr ibn el Aas, and Egypt became a great islamic bastion.

In 1798, Napoleon Bonaparte, led his expedition to Egypt, which brought Egypt contact with European civilization for the first time. In 1840, Mohamed Aly established his dynasty in Egypt, which it ruled for over 100 years. In 1952, a revolution put an end to monarchy and established a republic.

Population - 60,000,000
Capital -Cairo
Government - Independent state with democratic Presidential system
Religion - Moslem with a Coptic Christian minority
Language - Arabic, English spoken in tourist areas
Money - Egyptian pound (EE) check; one pound equals 100 piastres (pt) ; bank notes:100 pounds,20, 10,5,1; 50 piaster, 25, 10, 5; coins-10P 5P, 1P you must change a certain amount of money for every day you are in the country, not always strictly enforced. When you want to change Egyptian money back to another currency when you leave the country you need to keep 'money exchange receipts' when you want to leave the country. There is a black market where Egyptian currency can purchased at lower than official rates. To get rid of surplus Egyptian currency try the casinos in five star hotels where I changed money with rich Arabs.
U.S.$1 = 3 pounds, Cdn.$1 = 2 pounds, British £ = 5 pounds
Banks close on Fridays and Saturdays, open 8:30 a.m. - 4:30 p.m.and often 6:30 p.m.-8:30 p.m. Banks in major hotels offer 24 hour, 7 day service at the standard rate of exchange.

Public Holidays
Ramadan Bairam Holiday, Feb. 20-23, Sham El Nassem, April 15; Sinai Liberation Day, April 25; Grand Mairam Holidays, April 29-May 3; Labour Day, May 1; Beginning of Kijira calendar, May 20; Evacuation Day, June 18; national Day, July 23; Prophet Muhamed's Birthday, July 29; Armed Forces Day, October 6. Friday is the Muslim holy day, most people do not work on Thursdays either - the workweek runs from Saturday through Wednesday; In addition there are a number of Islamic holidays which are determined by the phases of the moon.

Visas
Visas cost $25 for Americans, Canadians and U.K. citizens. Egyptian authorities are not always consistent in charging the same price for visas - be sure to double check.
Passport authorities are empowered to grant a transit visa or an entry visa on the spot. The foreign tourist has to register within 7 days of his arrival in the country; hotels provide the service automatically. He may renew his residence permit (visa) for 6 months, provided he submits proof that he has transferred the required amount of money, i.e.$180 for each additional month. Visitors arriving through North and South Sinai entry points, should obtain visas in advance- no emergency visas granted- bearing in mind that a transit passenger means that he is transitting through Cairo on an organized trip.

If you are planning to go to Israel and then travel to an Arab country, make sure you ask for a separate visa from the Israelis. Otherwise, an Israeli visa in your regular passport may make it difficult to visit some Arab countries on your travels. To enter Egypt from Israel make sure you check with the Egyptian embassy in Israel that there is no surprise religious holiday and that the border is open. Normally the border is open 24 hours a day seven days a week.

Peculiar Customs and Odd Expressions

Arab men often walk hand-in-hand, although Westernized Egyptians rarely do this - if an Egyptian holds your hand, take it as a sign of friendship; "yes" usually means possibly". Avoid talking about Israel; a traditional Arab male will not necassarily introduce his wife; a traditional Arab greeting between men involves each grasping the other's right hand, placing the left hand on the other's right shoulder, and exchanging kisses on each cheek - kisses are always between members of the same sex - men and women may not kiss in public. The left hand is considered unclean in the Arab world - never eat with the left hand, avoid gesturing with the left hand. Pointing at another person is impolite; as well, traditional Arabs do not cross their legs when sitting - never show the bottom of your feet to an Arab, it is considered offensive. The "thumbs up"gesture is offensive throughout the Arab world. If you are a guest in someone's home, bring a gift of baked goods or chocolates - a great gift is a compass, this allows a devout Muslim always to know where Mecca is. Electronic gadgets make popular gifts - give gifts with the right hand; remember to remove your shoes before entering a mosque.

Best Festivals

Cairo - International Tourist Day, September 27

Cairo - International Arab Travel Market in September

Cairo - King Tut Festival, November 4 and Arab Horse Festival in November

Cairo - an international rowing regatta is held every year in December

Ismailia Folklore Festival, August 24-31

Night Activities and More

Alexandria - night clubs - Crazy Horse and Crevette

Cairo- Sound and Light show of the three pyramids and the Sphinx, beautiful background music, presented after sunset throughout the year, contact: 3852880 or 3857320 in Cairo

South Sinai - many beaches, superb diving, hot sulphuric spring

Karnak - Sound and Light show

Must See Tourist Sites

Alexandria - the catacombs of Kom el Shokafa, the Greco-Roman Museum, Pompey's Pillar, Ras-at-Tin Palace, Montazah Palace, the Roman Theater, great beaches

Aswan - The Aswan Dam-largest modern day structure in Egypt, Tomb of the Agha Khan, Monastery of St. Simon, tombs of the Middle Kingdom, Abu Simbel temple - either take the train to Aswan or the airplane

Cairo - the Sphinx and the Pyramids in Giza; Alabaster Mosque; the City of the Dead in the Citadel area; Egyptian Antiquities Museum includes treasures from the tomb of Tutankhamun; Memphis and the Pyramids of Saqqara; Islamic Museum, camel market every Friday morning; Khan el Khalily bazaar, Abou Serga Church-4th century A.D., the Tree of the Virgin;

Luxor - Valley of the Kings and the Valley of the Queens, the Karnak Temples, the Tombs of the Nobles, the Temple of Luxor, the Karnak Temples

Port Fuad - visit the Yacht Basin/Marina/Club for trying to work on a yacht to another destination

Red Sea coast - visit the ancient desert monasteries of St.Paul and St.Anthony

South Sinai - many great beaches, Sudr fortress

Suez - boats leave here for Jordan every three days, Jordanian visas available on board

Best Scenery

Take a boat trip down the Nile - one of the best trips you'll ever take

If you can climb a pyramid (it's illegal-just throw the security guards a few coins) you'll get the best view of the Cairo area and desert.

Bus

Luxurious buses regularly serve major cities, starting from early a.m. until 8 p.m., Regular public and tourist transport within the cities; donkey rides are a good bet in small towns and tourist resorts.

Hitch-Hiking

Fairly good, but women should dress conservatively, hitch with a male companion or better yet take the trains, which are quite cheap.

Train

Cairo is linked to all Egyptian cities by train, most air conditioned, with sleepers-lst and 2nd class. Students can get a 50% discount. For more information, tel: 753555 or 753147

Accommodation

Hotels - very cheap, ranging from 3 - 20 pounds.

Youth Hostels

Contact: Egyptian Youth Hostels Association, 1 El-Ibrahimy St, Garden City, Cairo, Egypt; tel: (20) (2) 3550329, 3540529, fax (20) (2) 3550329; main centre is at Cr. Abdel Hamid Said St, Marouf, Cairo, tel: 5758099, fax: 5777773 rates are very cheap - 3pounds - 8 pounds per night, includes breakfast.

Youth Hostel Town Locations and Telephone Numbers

A Alexandria 5975459; Assyout 324841; Aswan 322313; **C** Cairo, Hostel at 135 Abdel Aziz Al Saoud St., El Manial, Kobri El Gamaa (University

Bridge), 840729; **D** Damanhour324056; **E** El Fayoum 323682; **H** Hurghada 442432; **I** Ismailia 322850; **L** Luxor 372139; **M** Mersa Matrouh 932331; **P** Port Said 228702; **S** Sharm-El-Sheikh 600317; Sohag 324395; Suez 21945 **T** Tanta 337978.

Places to Avoid & Helpful Hints

Don't pay for rides, prevent any hassles by telling the driver before you get in the car that you have 'no money'. Most people will want to meet you, so unless you really are desperate for a ride save your money for another driver who will not insist that you pay. Visit the Valley of the Kings on a donkey.

Make sure you have enough money to get through no-mans-land from Israel to Egypt-you'll need it to pay for the special bus or if you're running late -for the taxi ride.

Useful Addresses and Tourist Offices
in U.S.

Egyptian Tourist Authority, 630 Fifth Ave., suite 1706, New York, NY 10111, (212) 332-2570

in Canada

Egyptian Tourist Authority, 1253 McGill College Ave. suite 250, Montreal, Quebec H3B 2Y5, tel: (514) 861-4420, fax: (514) 861-8071

in the U.K.

Egyptian Tourist Authority, 168 Picadilly W1, London, tel: 493 5282

in Egypt

Cairo- Tourist Office at 5 Adly St., tel: 3913454, also at the airport, pyramids, train station

Youth Travel Bureau at the Travel Section. 7 Abdel Hamid Saiid St., Maarouf, tel 2-5758099

Luxor - Tourist & State Information office on El Bahr El Nil road - at Tourist Bazaar

Egpytian Embassies
in U.S.

2310 Decatur Place, N.W., Washington D.C. 20008, tel: (202) 232-5400, fax: (202) 332-7894

Consulates are located in New York City, Chicago, Houston, San Francisco

in Canada

454 Laurier Ave. East, Ottawa, Ontario K1N 6R3, tel: (613) 234-4931, fax: (613) 234-9347

Consulate

1 Place Ville Marie, suite 2617, Montreal, Quebec H3B 4S3, tel: (514) 866-8455, fax: (514) 866-0835

in the U.K.

75 South Audley St., London W1, tel: 499 2401

Foreign Posts in Egypt
Cairo
United States Embassy, North Gate 8, Kamal el-Din Salah, tel: 355-7317
British Consulate, Sh. Ahmed Raghab, Garden City, tel: 354-0852
Work
Work permits are required. You can apply during your visit. Teaching English is a possibility. Contact the British Council at l92 Corniche El Nil, Aquza, Cairo tel: 345 3281 and International Language Learning Institute, at 9 Orm;an Villas, Dokki, Cairo, and at Borg el Giza,El Kebly, Giza, Cairo tel: 720431.
Driving Distances (in km)
From Cairo to cities in Egypt

Abu Simbel 1,264	Dahab 610	Newebaa 670
Alamein 304	Fayum 103	Port Said 220
Alexandria 221	Hurghada 504	Qantara Shark 150
Arish 306	Ismailiya 140	Rashid 263
Aswan 982	Luxor 721	Suez 134
Baltim 201	Matruh 490	Tunnel of Ahmed Hamdy 150

Telephone Information: International Code 00, Country Code 20, Main City Area Codes; Alexandria 3, Cairo 2; time difference (Eastern Daylight) plus 7 hours.

FINLAND

A Little History

The forefathers of the present-day Finns arrived in their homeland around the time of the birth of Christ. In the 12th century Sweden annexed Finland and ruled it for about 600 years. Even today, about six percent of the population speaks Swedish as a first language.

In 1809, after the Napoleonic Wars, Finland became a self-governing Grand Duchy of Tsarist Russia. In 1917, at the time of the Russian revolution, Finland declared itself independent and became a parliamentary republic. It is a western democracy with a policy of active neutrality which has made Helsinki a favorite venue for international summit meetings.

Population - 5,000,000
Capital - Helsinki
Government - Independent Republic
Religion - majority Lutheran, Greek Orthodox is a small minority
Language - Finnish and Swedish are the official languages, some English
Money - Markka (mk) One markka equals l00 pennia. Coins of 5, l0, 20,

and 50 pennia and 1 and 5 markka. Notes of 10,50, 100,500 and 1,000 markka
U.S.$1 = 4 markka, Cdn.$1 = 3 markka, British £ = 6.5 markka

Public Holidays

January 1, January 6 (Epiphany), Good Friday, Easter Monday, May 1 (Vappu), Ascension Day, Whit Monday, Midsummer (Juhannus; nearest Saturday to June 24, All Saints' Day, December 6 (Independence), Christmas Day, and Dec. 26.

Visas

Americans, Canadians and U.K. citizens do not need visas.

Peculiar Customs and Odd Expressions

When invited to a Finnish home for dinner, take flowers for the hostess; it is not appropriate to be "fashionably late" to a meal; Scandinavians are known to be heavy drinkers at mealtime; a toast is usually proposed at the beginning of a meal; a firm handshake is the standard greeting for men and women. Even children are encouraged to shake hands; only close friends and family greet with hugs and kisses; it is not polite to talk with one's hands in one's pockets; sitting with the ankle resting on the knee is too casual; Finns are not comfortable with physical contact such as backslapping; a toss of the head is a motion for "come here"; it is not proper to fold one's arms- it signifies arrogance.

For toasting drinks - say 'kippis'

An 'everyman's right' law allows people to temporarily pitch a tent anywhere in the countryside as long as you are not a nuisance - just ask for permission first.

'Tarttis tehdä jotakin... Kyllä se siitä' - Something should be done... Everything will be okay'

'Kylla routa porsaan kotiin ajaa'- 'For certain the frost will drive the pig home'

Oma maa mansikka, muu maa mustikka'- 'One's own country is a strawberry, someone else's is a blueberry'

'Sanasta miestä, sarvesta harkää'l- 'a man's words are to a man, as a bull's horn is to the bull,' which means, a man must mean what he says.

Best Festivals

Helsinki Festival - Aug. 20 - Sept. 3 - biggest in Scandinavia

Lahti - June 7-11 - Midnight Sun Song Festival - popular music concerts

Rock Festivals - summer best time for them, best ones are Provinssirock in Seinajoki - first weekend in June, by the Laituri in Turku-2nd weekend in June and Ruisrock in Turku - late June/early July

Pori - International Pori Jazz Festival - July 16-24-big open-air concerts and jam sessions

Night Activities and More

Saunas - public saunas an experience you should not miss, contact tourist board, cost about 20FIM

Helsinki - drinking and dancing - the Kaivo, Cantina West, Hesperia, Fizz,

Fennia, Page, Cafe Strindberg, Cafe Engel

Kompassi - is a centre for young people in the heart of Helsinki where you can find out what is going on, meet other people of their own age and get help with problems

Turku -Apteekki pub Bors Night club, Casanova, Moritz, discos-Calypso, Submarina, Time Out

Reindeer joring in the winter - only in Lapland-you race in a one-seat chariot pulled by reindeer

Experience the midnight sun in June on the Arctic Circle

Must See Tourists Sights

Helsinki - Kauppatori Market Square, Temppeliaukio-church, Helsinki Cathedral, Uspenski Cathedral, Seurasaari Island - open air museum near Helsinki - boat not necessary, footbridge connects mainland; Suomenlinna - fortress - 15 minute ferry ride from Market Square;

Kristenestad - best preserved wooden town in Finland, dating back to the 17th century.

Tampere - known as the City of Sapphire Lakes with 22 within the city limits

Turku - the Handicraft Museum , Turun Tuomiokirkko Cathedral, Turku Castle

Best Scenery

Most worthwhile scenery surrounds Turku and Helsinki

Rovaniemi - experience the midnight sun starting June 6 just north of this town on the Arctic circle

Kuusamo nature area at its best is the district round Lake Oulujarvi in Northern Finland is very wild and beautiful with vast forests, bogs, deep lakes and rapids

The "Bear Trail" Karhunkierros 75km trekking route starting in the village of Juuma, is 50km north of Kuusamo-the tourist office in Kuusamo-tel: 989/850-2910

Bus

Great for getting to out of the way places-get a Student Coach Discount Card-gets you 30% discount on all fares, tel: 9600-4000. Helsinki Card-buy this at travel agencies or the Helsinki City Tourist Office to get reduced prices or even 'free' prices for saunas, tours, theater, opera, transportation, museums and a sightseeing tour.

Cycling

Great because of flat terrain, rentals 20-50 markka per day, no charge on a train and most buses.

Hitch-Hiking

One of the easiest places to get rides; in the wilderness expect to wait longer.You can find out about rides being offered by phoning Radio City 96.2 MHz tel: 90-694-1566, program called 'Transport for Rovers" every Thursday between 7 p.m. and 8 p.m. You can phone in your message between 11 a.m. and 12 noon at no charge. Helping to pay for gas is welcomed, but not mandatory.

Train

Finnrail pass-unlimited use for 3/days in one month - 505 markka, 5/days/ month-685 markka, 10/days 945 markka, contact the train station-Valtion Rautatiet at Vihonkatu 13, Helsinki tel: 90/7071; Helsinki-St.Petersburg, Russia, 2nd class - 265 markka, Helsiniki-Moscow - 506 markka - for travel to Russia reservations should be sent to Helsinki Ticket Office, address: VR Passenger Traffic Service, Rautatieasema, 00100 Helsinki, tel:358-100 128

Camping

'everyman's right' law - you can temporarily pitch your tent on any property in the countryside; many cheap or free wilderness huts with bunk beds and firewood, over 350 campsites - costs 100 markka for 2 adults,

Youth Hostels

Cheapest in Western Europe. prices range from 45 markka to 150 markka; Finnish Youth Hostel Assoc.- without membership add FIM 15 more, advance bookings through SRM Hostel Booking Center, Yrjonkatu 38 B, 15, 00100 Helsinki, Finland tel: (358) (0) 6940377, fax 9358) (0) 6931349; over 160 hostels, all hostels have family, single or double rooms, some have dormitories for 5-10 people. Many hostels have saunas, bicycles, boats and canoes for the guests.

Youth Hostel Town Locations and Telephone Numbers

A Asnekoski (945) 12711; Ahtari (965) 31467; Akaslompolo (9695) 69234; Akaslompolo (9695) 69234; Alajarvi (966) 74542; Alvettula (917) 45112; Anjalankoski (951) 36560 61; **D** Dragsfjard (925) 424553; **E** Eno (973) 77607; Enonkoski (957) 479 431; Espoo (90) 86701; **H** Hameenkyro (931) 3406191; Hameenlinna (917) 6828560; Hamina (952) 477747; Haukipudas (981) 5401222; Heinavesi (972) 66419; **Helsinki** - 6 hostels - 1) **Eurohostel** on Linnandatu 9, tel: (90) 664452; 2) Stadium Hostel on Pohj Stadiontie 3 B, tel: (90) 496071; 3) Vantaan Hostel on Tikkurilan Urheilupuisto, tel: (90) 8393310; 4) Academica Hostel on Hietaniemenkatu 14, tel: (90) 4020206; 5) Satakuntatalo Hostel on Lapinrinne 1A, tel: (90) 694226; 6) Erotajanpuisto Hostel on Uudenmaankatu 9, tel: (90) 642169; Hetta (9696) 521361; Hoilola (974) 56202; Hyrynsalmi (986) 741711; Hyvinkaa (914) 436747; **I** Iisalmi (977) 23940; Ilmajoki - 2 hostels -1) Viitala Hostel on Ristimaentie 207, tel: (964) 4227657; 2) Palonkortteeri Hostel on Kauppatie 26, tel: (964) 4246473; Ilomantsi (974) 843107; Imatra (954) 4321270; **J** Jamsa (942) 62388; Jarvenpaa (90) 287775; Joensuu - 3 hostels -1) Joensuun Elli Hostelon Laniskatu 18, tel: (973) 225927; 2) Partiotalo Hostel on Vanamokatu 25, tel: 973) 123381; 3) Joensuu Hostel on Ita-Suomen Liikuntaopisto, tel: (973) 1675076; Joutsa (947) 889107; Juva (955) 459622; Jyvaskyla (941) 253355; **K** Kaamanen (9697) 52725; Kaavi (971) 675333;

Kabbole (915) 635643; Kajaani (986) 622254; Kalajoki - 2 hostels - 1) Tapion Tupa Hostel on Hiekkasarkat, tel: (983) 466622; 2) Kaju Hostel on Opintie 1, tel: (983) 462933; Kankaanpaa (930) 22373; Karigasniemi (9697) 61188; Karsamaki (984) 61455; Kaskinen (962) 2227007; Kauhava (964) 43153 50; Kaustinen - 2 hostels - 1)Koskelan Lomatolo Hostel on Kansalantie 123, tel: (968) 8611338; 2) Pauanteen Majatalo Hostel , no address given, tel: (968) 8611881; Kemijarvi- 2 hostels - 1) Matkatupa Hostel on Ulkuniemi PL, tel: 9692) 888517; 2) Kemijarvi Hostel on Lohelankatu 1, tel: (9692) 813253; Keminmaa (9698) 288166; Kerimaki (957) 4827; Kiilopaa (9697) 667101; Kittila - 2 hostels - 1) Kittila Hostel on Valtatie 5, tel: (9694) 642238; 2) Sillankorva Hostel, ask for address in town, tel: (9694) 653428; Kiuruvesi (977) 50222; Kokkola (968) 8314006; Kolari - 2 hostels - 1) Vaattovaaran Hostel , ask for address in town, tel: (9695) 61086; 2) Lappean Loma Hostel, ask for address in town, tel: (9695) 63164; Korpilahti (941) 827437; Kotka (952) 604215; Kouvola (951) 3754771; Kristiinankaupunki (962) 2225611; Kuhmo (986) 6556245; Kuopio - 2 hostels - 1)Tekma Hostel on Taivaanpankont 14B, tel: (971) 2822925; 2) Rauhalahti Hostel on Katiskaniementie 8, tel: (971) 3611700; Kuortane - 2 hostels - 1) Virtaniemen Hostel on Virtala, tel: 965) 5256689; 2) Wilmeikko Hostel on Camping Aholankangas, tel: (965) 5254104; Kuusamo (989) 8522132;Lahti - 2 hostels - 1) Kivik Hostel, ask in town for address, tel: (918) 826324; 2) Mukkula Hostel on Ritaniemenkatu 10, tel: (918) 306554; Lappeenranta - 2 hostels - 1)Lappeenranta Hostel on Kuusimaenkatu 18, tel: (953) 4515555; 2) Karelia Park Hostel on Korpraalinkuja 1, tel: (953) 675211; Leppavirta (972) 42061; Liesksa - 3 hostels - 1) Loma-Kitsi on Kitsintie 86A, tel: (975) 539114; 2) Herranniemi Hostel on 81590 Vuonislahti, tel: (975) 542110; 3) Koli Hostel on Niinilahdentie 47, tel: (973) 673131; **L** Liljendal (915) 616354; **M** Mantta (934) 4888641; Mikkeli (955) 366542; Muonio (9696) 532237; Muurame (941) 3732390; **N** Nerkoo (977) 35281; Nilsia (971) 431803; Nivala (983) 443171; Nurmes - 2 hostels -1) Hyvarila Hostel on Lomatie, tel: (976) 481775; 2) Pompannappi Hostel on Koulukatu 16, tel: (976) 21770; Nurmijarvi (90) 2765879; **O** Oulu - 2 hostels - 1) Otokyla Hostel on Haapanatie 2, tel: (981) 5308413; 2) Valkkyla Hostel on Kajaanintie 36, tel: (981) 3118060; Outokumpu (973) 552309; **P** Parainen (921) 885944; Parikkala (954) 430851; Peera (9696) 532659; Pelkosenniemi (9692) 53402; Pello (9695) 86155; Pietarsaari - 2 hostels - 1)Svanen/ Joutsen Hostel on Nissasorn, tel: (967) 7230660; 2) Bodgardet Hostel on Pitajantie 5, tel: (967) 7246610; Pori (939) 6378125; Porvoo (915) 5230012; Pudasjarvi -2 hostels - 1) Pudas-Maja Hostel on Sahkotie 3, tel: (988) 823220; 2) Kunto-Syote Hostel on PPa 2, tel: (988) 838167; Puumala (954) 81119; **R** Raahe (982) 2238448; Rantasalmi (957) 440124; Rauma - 2 hostels - 1)Poroholma Hostel at the Camping Site, tel: (938) 8224666; 2) Rauma Hostel on

Satamakatu 20, tel: (938) 8240130; Rautalampi (979) 530320; Rautavaara - 2 hostels - 1)Metsakartano Hostel , ask in town for address, tel: (971) 780510; 2) Aiitarinne Hostel on Tulimaentie, tel: (971) 780058 ; Riihimaki - 2 hostels - 1)Riihimaki Hostel on Merkuriuksenkatu 7, tel: (914) 741471; 2) Seurahuone Hostel on Hameenkatu 29, tel: (914) 7721; Ristiina (955) 664101; Rovaniemen Mlk (960) 778086; Rovaniemi (960) 344644; Rymattyla (921) 2521894; Ruotsinpyhtaa (915) 618474; **S** Salo (924) 3084409; Savonlinna - 2 hostels - 1) Malakias Hostel on Pihlajavedenkuja 6, tel: (957) 23283; 2) Vuorilinna Hostel on Kylpylaitoksentie, tel: (957) 5750430; Seinajoki (964) 4144800; Siilinjarvi (971) 423022; Sodankyla - 2 hostels - 1) Lapin Opisto Hostel, ask for address in town, tel: (9693) 211960; 2) Visatupa Hostel on Sodankylantie, tel: (9693) 634133; Sotkamo (986) 6660541; Sulkava (957) 76150; Suomussalmi (986) 723179; Sykarainen (968) 623086; Suvanto (9692) 54112; **T** Taivalkoski ((88) 845762; Tammisaari (911) 2416393; Tampere - 4 hostels - 1) NNKY (the YWCA) on Tuomiokirkonk 12A, tel: (931) 225446; 2) Domus Hostel on Pellervonkatu 9, tel: (931) 2550000; 3) Uimahallin Maja Hostel on Pirkank 10-12, tel: (931) 2229 460; 4) Harmala Hostel on Nuolialantie 50, tel: (931) 2651355; Tenhola (911) 2450633; Tornio (9698) 481682; Turku (921) 2316578; **V** Vaasa (961) 3177850; Valkeakoski (937) 5766405; Vartsila (973) 624176; Veikkola (90) 2773288; Virrat - 2 hostels - 1) Domus Hostel on Sipilantie 3, tel: (934) 54570; 2) Haapamaki Hostel ask in town for address, tel: (934) 58845; **Y** Ylivieska (983) 424583.

Work

You need a permit before entering the country. Best chance are au pair jobs or living with a family, doing odd jobs, teaching English for free board and some money: contact: International Trainee Exchange of the Ministry of Labour, Kalevankatu 16, PL 524, 00101 Helsinki 10, Finland

Useful Addresses

in U.S.

Scandinavian National Office, 655 Third Ave., New York, NY 10017 (212) 949-2333

in Canada

Finnish Tourist Board , P.O.Box 246, Station Q, Toronto, Ontario M4T 2M1 tel: 1-800-346-4636

in the U.K.

66-68 Haymarket, London SW1Y 4RF, tel: 0171/839-4048

in Finland

Finland Tourist Board-Etelaesplanadi 4 , tel 90/4030-1300, across from the City Tourist Office; Helsinki City Tourist Office - at Pohjoisesplanaadi 19, tel 90/169-3757

Finnish Travel Association at Mikonkatu 25, 00100 Helsinki 10 tel: 170 868

Oy Kilroy Travels Finland at Kaivokatu 10 FIN-00100 Helsinki Finland tel:011-358-0-680-7811, Director: Pekka Hagman.

This is the recommended agency for student travel. Finnish Student Travel
   Service (FSTS) at:
Kauppakatu 12, 40100 Jyraskyla 10 tel: 941 17507
Hallituskatu 33, 90100 Oulu 10 tel: 981 222 720
Tuomiokirkonkatu 36, 33100 Tampere 10 tel: 931 309 95
Finland Festivals, Mannerheimintie 40 B 49, PO Box 56, FIN-00101 Helsinki
   tel: 445 686
Finnish Embassies
in U.S.
E 3301 Massachusetts Ave., N.W., Washington D.C. 20008 tel: (202) 298-5800
in Canada
E 55 Metcalfe St., suite 850, Ottawa, Ontario K1P 6L5 tel: (613) 236-2389
Consulate
1200 Bay St. suite 604 Toronto, Ontario M5R 2A5 tel: (416) 964-0066
in the U.K.
38 Chesham Place, London SW1X 8HW, tel: 171 838 6200
Foreign Posts in Finland
Helsinki
Canadian Embassy, Pohjoisesplanadi 25B, tel: 90/171-141, M-Th 8:30-4,
F 8:30-1:30
British Embassy, Itainen Puistotie 17, tel: 90/661-293 M-F 9-12
United States Embasssy, Itainen Puistotie 14B, tel: 90/171-931 M-F 9-12
Driving Distances (in km)
From Helsinki to cities in Finland:

Jyaskyla 272	Rovaniemi 834
Karigasniemi 1,200	Tampere 174
Kilpisjarvi 1,204	Tornio 744
Kuusamo 804	Turku, Abo 166
Nuorgam 1,330	Vaalimaa 188
Oulu 612	Vaasa Vasa 419

Telephone Information: International Code 990, Country Code 358, Main
   City Area Codes: Helsinki 0, Tampere 31, Turku 21; time difference
   (Eastern Daylight) plus 6 hours. Emergency # 002

FRANCE

A Little History

France's earliest recorded histroy dates back to prehistoric times. Wall paintings, the most famous of which decorate the Lascaux caves in southern
France, proving the existence of a fairly advanced civilization 30,000 years
ago. By the first century, various tribes lived in the territory called Gaul

(France) and joined forces to fight the advancing Roman legions. In the centuries that followed, Gaul was invaded by many tribes, including the Franks who settled here. Their influence was so predominant that gradually Gaul became known as France-land of the Franks.

In 1337, the King of England laid claim to the French throne, giving rise to the Hundred Years' War. A young peasant girl, Joan of Arc, was inspired to lead her country against the English. She was eventually captured and burned as a witch. By 1453 the English had been driven out of France.

During the Renaissance period arts flourished, trade developed, French navigators set out to explore the New World. In 1562 the Wars of Religion between Catholics and Protestants started, ending in 1598 when the Protestants were assured civil and religious liberties.

In 1789, during the French Revolution, Parisians stormed the Bastille, an ancient fortress where the kings had imprisoned people without trial. The peasants were given land of their own, the nobles lost their privileges and the king his throne. The First Republic replaced the monarchy, but the new ideas of liberty and equality were deemed dangerous by France's neighbors and war soon broke out. General Napoleon Bonapartes' armies swept across Europe, victorious. He became emperor in 1804, but a new coalition of France's foes was formed and Napoleon was finally defeated at Waterloo (1815).

During WWI, 1,390,000 French people died and half the country was devastated. WWII brought the occupation of half of France by the Nazi armies and the creation of the Free French forces headed by General de Gaulle. France adopted a new constitution in 1946, in 1958, with its Fifth Republic and President, General de Gaulle.

Population - 56,160,00

Capital - Paris

Government - Republic

Religion - majority are Catholic

Language - French

Money - Franc (F) one franc equals 100 centimes. Coins of 5, 10, 20, 50 centimes, and 1, 2, 5, l0 francs. Notes are 20, 50, 100, 500 francs U.S.$1 = 4 francs, Cdn.$1 = 3 francs, British £ = 7.5 francs

Public Holidays

All shops are closed on Sundays, except souvenir shops, bakery-pastry shops, butchers, newspaper-tobacconist shops which are open usually until 1 or 2 p.m. More shops are open in Paris. Everything is open on Saturdays in all cities. Some shops in some areas close on Mondays (either for the morning only or the whole day) while others close on Sundays. Banks are always closed on Sundays and either on Saturdays or on Mondays; on other days they close at 5 p.m. Most shops and banks are closed daily between 12 noon and 2 p.m. but shops remain open until 7 p.m. Museums and art galleries are closed on Tuesdays. Everything closes on: New Year's Day, Easter Monday, Whit Monday, and Christmas day the following public holidays are observed; Labour Day -May 1 & May 8 (end of year), Ascension-variable date in May, Bastille Day-July 14, Assumption-August 15, All Saints' Day-November 1 and Armistice Day-Nov. 11.

Visas
Americans, Canadians and U.K. citizens do not need visas.

Peculiar Customs and Odd Expressions
Zut! or Flute! - Darn it!

C'est genial! C'est super- It's cool or great or awesome

Cul sec! - Bottoms up!

Tomber dans les pommes - means to pass out

Ça craint!, C'est nul! - it sucks! (very popular and used by young people)

L'habit ne fait pas le moine - the garment does not make the monk

Ce n'est pas demain la veille! - it's not for tomorrow! (when something is not likely to happen)

'To live elsewhere, is to live in the relative sense of the world, to live in Paris is to live in the full sense' written by a 14th century schoolboy.

Always greet people by saying, 'Bonjour, Monsieur/Madame/Mademoiselle even in a store.It is usual to shake hands always on greeting and parting from friends and acquaintances and kiss both cheeks of close friends; the "thumbs up"sign means "O.K.", the U.S. "O.K." sign means "zero" in France; slapping the open palm over a closed fist is vulgar. Give a gift to your host , such as wine; when buying fruit, let the shopkeeper pick it out-do not touch the produce; the French consider it an insult to the chef to add salt or other seasoning to your food, even after you have tasted it; bread is supposed to be torn, not cut; summon a waiter by saying 's'il vous plait, not garçon which means boy; to call for the check, make a writing gesture; don't chew gum in public; do not sit on lawns - just admire them.

Best Festivals
Avignon - world-famous Festival d'Avignon - last 3 weeks of July-actor, dancers, musicians - 300 performances a day

Bayonne - first Wed. in August, includes 'running of the cows', not bulls

Bourges - International Music Festival: "Le Printemps de Bourges" - rock, pop, rap, held the last week of April

Cannes - International Film Festival from May 17-28

Menton - The Fête des Citrons (Lemon Festival) is a fun carnival around Feb.16 - March 5

Nice - The Carnival, approx. Feb. 16 to March 5

Quimper - Festival de Cornouaille-music, costumes , held every year between the third and fourth Sundays in July. Bastille Day on July 14 is the country's biggest national celebration.

Night Activities and More

Every city and village has bars, cafés or pubs. Ask any young person on the street where you should go. Most dance clubs in France (Paris excluded) are "free for girls" even on Fridays and Saturdays or "free before midnight"on certain nights

Cannes - the Municipal Casino

Paris - most nightclubs are far too expensive for a student on a budget, ask where you should party for the evening at the youth hostel or wherever you are staying. Try Le Balajo and La Locomotive. Other clubs worth mentioning Club Zed, Balajo, Memphis, Le Sunset, Caveau de la Huchette; Cabarets - if you can afford them - the Crazy Horse, Moulin Rouge, Folies - Bergère

Must See Tourist Sights

Barbizon - great hiking area

Bayeux - serves as the base to visit the D-Day beaches, the Bayeux Tapestry

Bayonne - Cathedrale Sainte Marie, bullfights

Biarritz - some of the best surfing

Carcassonne - beautiful sites-the 11th century St. Nazaire, Comtal Castle,

Courchevel 1850 (1850 meters above sea level) - best skiing in France

Grenoble - great skiing

Les Eyzies de Tayac - some of worlds'oldest artworks in the Musee National de la Pre-histoire, see two caves-Grotte de Font de Gaume & Grotte des Combarelles

Loire Valley - chateaus of Amboise, Chenonceau, Chambord and many others

Lyons - Gallo-Roman Museu, Amphitheatre des Trois where Christians may have been martyred in the 2nd Century

Mulhouse - sports car museum - probably best in world

Paris - get a museum pass for 70 francs for one day, 140 francs-3 consecutive days, 200 francs for 5 days - get it at subway stations, kiosks in Paris, at the museums-it'll save you a lot of money. Louvre Museum, Eiffel Tower, Arc de Triomphe, Montmartre - old Paris - artist square; Pantheon, Notre Dame Cathedral, Picasso Museum, Victor Hugo Museum, Sorbonne University, Catacombs, Marais district (Place des Vosges, the oldest Royal square in Paris), Centre Pompidou and its modern art museum, the Champ Elysées - from the Arc de Triomphe to the Place de la Concorde and the Obelisque; Musée d'Orsay for its impressive collection of Impressionists, The Opera Garnier, La Grande Arche in the new business district of La Defense, you must visit the Montmartre and Latin Quarter districts - old cobblestone streets, friendly atmosphere, street artists

155

Near Paris - Versailles Palace, Chartres Cathedral, Fountainbleau Palace, Monet's Museum and garden in Giverny

French Riviera - Cannes - beaches - best east of St.Tropez, Menton & village of St. Paul de Vence

Nice - the Promenade des Anglais - beautiful waterfront walkway; pebbly beaches

St.Tropez-best beaches, topless sunbathing, some of the most beautiful yachts in the world

Perigueux - close to the prehistoric caves of the Vezere Valley

Rouen - Place du Vieux Marche (accent on last e for Marche) where Joan of Arc was burned at the stake, Notre Dame Cathedral, Palais de Justice

Saint Malo - some of the highest tides in the world - 13 meters above the low-water mark, see the ramparts, Cathedrale Saint Vincent

Strasbourg - 1176 Gothic cathedral, Eglise Saint Thomas

Aside from visiting the above towns and cities, if you have time visit the following areas: in the South West - the old town of Albi, the villages of Cordes, St.Cirq Lapopie, the medieval Sarlat, Collonges la Rouge, Rocamadour, the villages of Espelette, Ainhoa and St. Jean Pied de Port in the Basque country; Toulouse, Banyuls and Collioure close to the Spanish border; the Cirque de Gavarnie in the Pyrenees in the South East - Avignon, Arles, Nimes, Marseilles, Cassis and Les Calanques; Menton

Best Scenery

the quiet region of Auvergne and its ancient volcanoes and cheese-making villages such as St. Nectaire

in the North West: the scenic road along the Cote de Granit to the Pointe du Raz; the beautiful island of Corsica

the Dordogne Valley

Pyrenees Alps, the forests of Barbizon, wine districts of Burgundy, Champagne, Bordeaux, the Rhone Valley; Riviera - the incredibly beautiful scenic road between St.Tropez and Nice (Corniche de l'Esterel); Chamonix-this town is surrounded by the best scenery in the French Alps

Cote d'Emeraude, Cote de Granite Rose and Finistere regions

Airline

One very good deal is the Air Inter (France's domestic airline) Youth & Student Pass: it gives unlimited air travel for any 5 days within one month for Cdn $289 - eligible for people under 25 or students under 27. Try to book at least one week in advance.

Bus

Slightly cheaper, but slower than trains, very few long distance bus services.

Cycling

Most towns have rental bikes by the hour, day and week; most mountain bikes cost 60 - 120 francs a day. They can be rented from major train stations and dropped off at other train stations.

Hitch-Hiking

When using cardboard signs, write s.v.p.(síl vous plait), after the destination; Contact-Allostop-Provoya 84 Passage Brady, near the metro Chateau d'Eau, tel: 1-42-46 00 66. These people will arrange a ride for you, but it can be costly; if you are on a budget - make sure you check all possible charges.

Train

Best deal is the French Flexipass, 4 days - U.S.$125 in a l5 day period, you must buy this pass in your country at a travel agency. There are also several train passes available in North America through the Rail Europe Co.- for example, the France Rail Pass gives unlimited travel for 3 days within one month for U.S. $140, each additional day is $45. The Rail 'n Drive Pass offers 3 days of rail travel and 3 days of car rental within one month for U.S.$139.

Camping

Thousands of seasonal and year-round campgrounds, inquire at a tourist office or get the Guide Officiel Camping/Caravaning or Michelin's Camping/Caravaning France; it is difficult to get a place late in the day in July and especially August. Campsites average U.S.$15.

Youth Hostels

Contact the Federation Unie des Auberges de Jeunesse, 27 ure Pajol, 75018 Paris, France, tel: (33) (1) 44898727, fax (33) (1) 44898710; prices range from 29 francs to 70 francs, breakfast costs l5-17 francs, in Paris - 90-115 francs, includes breakfast.

Youth Hostel Town Locations and Telephone Numbers

A Agen 53661898; **Aix-en-Provence** 42201599; Aix-les-Bains 79883288; Albi 63545365; Alencon-Damigny 33290048; Angouleme 45924580; Annecy 50453319; Anzin 27469063; Arles 90961825; **Arras** 21227002; Arrens 62972464; Aubusson 55661359; Auch 62053480; Avrille-Langeais 47249600; Axat 68205327; **B** Banize 55660793; Beaugency 38446131; Beaulieu-sur-Dordogne 55911382; Belfort 84213916; Belle-Ile en Mer 97318133; Besancon 81884311; Betete 55807891; Biarritz-Anglet 59638649; Blois - 2 hostels - 1) Les Grouets Hostel on 18 rue de l'Hotel Pasquier, tel: 54782721; 2) Monlivault AJ on Cedex 181, tel: 38446131; Bordeaux 56915951; **Boulogne-sur-Mer** 21314822; Bourges 48245809; Brest 98419041; Brive 55243400; Bugarach 68698437; **C** Caen (31521996; Cahors 65539702; Calvi 95651415; Cap Ferret 56606462; Cap Frehel 96414898; **Carcassonne** 68252316; Cassis 42010272; Cepoy 38932545; Cernay 89754 459;

Chalons-sur-Marne 26681356; **Chamonix** 50531452; Chamrousse 76899131; Charleville-Mezieres 24574436; Chaumont 25032277; Chauny 23520996; Cherbourg - new youth hostel in 1996; Chinon 47931048; Cholet - 2 hostels - 1) Les Goelands Hostel on 2 rue Hallouin, tel: 41622357; 2) Les Paquerettes on 5 rue de la Casse, tel: 41713636; Choucan-en-Broceliande 97227675; Clermont-Ferrand 73922639; Colmar 89805739; Concarneau 98970347; Creil 44253766; Crevoux 92431818; **D** Dieppe Offranville 35848573; Dijon 80729520; Dinan 96391083; Dole 84823674; Dunkerque 28633634; **E** Etsaut 59348898; Eu-Le Treport 35860503; Evian 50753587; **F** Fontaine-de-Vaucluse 90203165; Fontenay-le-Comte 51691344; Frejus 94521875; **G** Gannat 70902829; Givet 24420960; Granfontaine 88972076; Granville 33501895; Gray 84648260; **Grenoble-Echirolles** 76093352; Guillestre 92450432; **I** Ile-de-Batz 98617769; Ile-de-Groix 97868138; Imphy 86687200; Inzinzac-Lochrist 97360808; **J** Jausiers 92810649; **L** La Clusaz 50024173; La Foux d'Allos 92838108; La Palud-sur-Verdon 92773872; La Rochelle 46444311; La Toussuire 79567204; Lannion - 2 hostels - 1)Beg Leguer AJ on Route de Goalagorn, tel: 96472486; 2) Les Korrigans on 22300 Lannion, tel: 96379128; Lanslebourg 79059096; Lautenbach 89742681; Lauzun 53941207; Le Bousquet 68205479; Le Mans 43812755; Le Mazet St. Voy 71650035; Le Mont-Dore 73650353; Le Puy en Velay 71055240; Le Trayas 93754023; Les Deux Alpes 76792280; Les Echandes 77357294; Les Gets 50791486; Les Rousses 84600280; Les Sables d'Olonne 51957621; Les Saintes-Maries-de-la-Mer 90975172; Lorient 97371165; Lourdios 59344639; **Lyon-Venissieus** 78763923; **M** Mael-Pestivien 96457528; Manosque 92875744; **Marseille** - 2 hostels - 1) **Bonneveine** on Av J Vidal, tel: 91732181; 2) Chateau de Bois-Luzy on Allee des Primeveres, tel: 91490618; Martinique-Morne Rouge (596) 523023; Menton 93359314; Metz - 2 hostels - 1) on 6 rue Marchant, tel: 87750726; 2) on 1 Allee de Metz Plage, tel: 87304402; Millau 65601595; **Montpellier** 67603222; Montreuil-Sur-Mer 21061083; Morlaix 98881363; Morzine 50791486; Mulhouse 89426328; Munster 89773420; **N** Nantes - 3 hostels - 1) Place de la Manu Hostel on 2 Place de la Manu, tel 40205725; 2) Porte Neuve Hostel on 1 place Ste Elisabeth, tel: 40200080; 3) Port Beaulieu Hostel on 9Bd Vincent Gache, tel: 40122400; Nice - 2 hostels - 1) AJ Nice on route Forestiere du Mont Alban, tel: 93892364; 2) Summer Hostel, ask for address in town, tel: 93892364; Nimes 66232504; Noumea (687) 275879; **O** Oinville 34753391; **P** Paimpol 96208360; **Paris** - 5 hostels - 1) **Le d'Artagnan Hostel** on 80 rue Vitruve, tel: (1)43610875; 2) **Cite des Sciences Hostel** on 1 Rue Jean-Baptiste Clement, tel: (1) 48432411; 3) Jules Ferry Hostel on 8 Boulevard Jules Ferry, tel: (1) 43575560; 4) Arpajon Hostel on 3 rue Marcel Duhamel, tel: (1) 64902885; 5) Relais European Hostel on 52 avenue Rober Schumann, tel: 69848139; Pua-Gelos 59065302; Perigeaux 53535205; Perpignan

68346332; Plouguernevel 96291095; **Poitiers** 49580305; Pontarlier 81390657; Pontivy 97255827; Pontorson 33600018; Puicheric 68437381; **Q** Quiberon 97501554; Quimper 98554167; **R** Redon 99721439; Reims 26405260; **Rennes** 99332233; Roanne 77725211; Rochefort-sur-Mer 46871642; Rodez 65423545; Rodome 68203222; Rouen 35720645; **S** Saintes 46921492; Saint-Barthelemy de Bellegard 53804598; Saint-Brevin 40272527; Saint-Brieux 96787070; Saint-Gaudens 61956537; Saint-Guen 96285434; Saint-Junien 55022279; Saint-Malo 99402980; Saint-Martin des Olmes 73820138; Saint Mihiel 2989 1506; Saint-Pierre de Maille 49489225; Salies-de-Bearn 59382966; Saverne 88911484; Savine 92442016; Seez 79410193; Sequret 90469331; Serre-Chevalier/Le Bez 92247 454; Sete 67534668; Spontour AJ 55275273; **Strasbourg** - 2 hostels - 1) **Parc du Rhin** on rue des Cavaliers, tel: 88601020; 2) **Rene Cassin** on 9 rue de l'Auberge de Jeunesse, tel: 88302646; **T** Tarascon 90910408; Tarbes 62366363; Tignes 79063507; Toulouse 61804993; Tours 47251445; Trebeurden 96235222; Troyes-Rosieres 25820065; **V** Valence 75423200; Ventron AJ 29241956; Vernon 32516648; Verzy 26979010; Vesoul 84764855; Vezelay 86332418; Vienne 74532197; Vierzon 48753062; Villefrance de Rouergue 65450968; **W** Woerth 88540330; **Y** Yvetot 35953701.

Work

Very difficult to get permission, maybe as a grape picker in the autumn as an undocumented helper; babysitting for families as an au pair (mother's helper) very common in France, especially Paris.Usually you have to be studying in the country, otherwise you should have a work permit in advance; contact the French consulate or Paris tourist office.

Babysitting

Nice - call Allo Nursing Service at 93-98-60-98 or the Association Nicoise de Services at 93-85-91-88

Paris - try Allo Maman Poule at 47-48-01-01 or Kid Service at 47-66-00-52

Useful Addresses and Tourist Offices

in U.S.

French Tourist Office

444 Madison Ave, New York, NY 10022 (212) 838-7800

for all of U.S. 1-900-990-0040

645 N. Michigan Ave., Chicago, IL 60611-2836

9454 Wilshire Blvd., Beverly Hills, CA 90212

in Canada

1981 McGill College Ave., suite 490, Montreal H3A 2W9 (514) 288-4264 for Quebec and Eastern provinces

30 St.Patrick St. suite 700, Toronto, Ont. M5T 3A3 tel: (416) 593-4723 for Ontario and Western Provinces

in the U.K.

178 Piccadilly, London W1V OAL, tel: 0171/491-7622
in Paris
French Information Bureau, 127 ave. Champs-Elysees, Paris 75008, tel:
(1)49-52-53-54
Organisation pour le Tourisme Universitaire at av.George Berranos 39, Paris
5e tel: 4723 61 72
French Embassies
in U.S.
4101 Reservoir Rd. NW Washington D.C. 20007-2185 tel: (202) 944-6000
in Canada
42 Sussex Drive, Ottawa, Ont. KlM 2C8 tel: (613) 789-1795; for visa info:
613-789-3486
in the U.K.
58 Knightsbridge, London SW1, tel: 441 71 201 1000
Foreign Posts in France
Paris
Canadian Embassy, 35 av. Montaigne, 8E, tel: 1/44-43-29-00 Metro Subway:
Franklin Roosevelt stop, M-F 8:30-12
British Embassy, 35 rue du Faubourg St. Honore, 8e, tel: 1/42-66-91-42,
Metro Subway stop: Madelaine, M-F 9:30-1, 2:30-6
United States Embassy, 2av. Gabriel, 8e, tel: 1/42-96-12-02, Metro Subway
stop: Con-Corde, M-F 9-6
Driving Distances (in km)
From Paris to cities in France:

Besancon 400	Lyon 471	Rouen 139
Calais 310	Marseille 777	St. Dizier 208
Chalons Sur-Marne 185	Nancy 310	Strasbourg 488
Charleville Mezieres 228	Nice 933	Toulouse 684
Dijon 304	Poitters 335	Troyes 160
Langres 278	Reims 146	Valence 561

From Paris to cities in Europe:

Anvers, Belgium 342	London, 471
Amsterdam 501	Luxembourg 338
Bale, Switzerland 484	Madrid1,317
Barcelona 1,091	Milano 864
Brussels 307	Munich 845
Cologne, Germany 497	Rome 1,428
Copenhagen 1,201	Torino 762
Geneva, Switzerland 546	Vienna 1,316
Hamburg, Germany 278	

Telephone Information: International Code 19, Country Code 33, Main City
Area Codes: Paris 1, other cities- no area codes; time difference (Eastern
Daylight) plus 6 hours. Emergency # 17

A Little History

Everywhere in the Federal Republic of Germnay you will encounter testimonies to a history over two thousand years old. From the very beginning, Germany has been a federal country; it never really became a centralized state. The separate Germanic tribes, Saxons, Franks, Swabians and Bavarians to this day, give the German regions their distinctive identities. The Romans incorporated the western and souther regions into their empire. After the decline of the Roman Empire, and following the interim period of the Carolingian Empire, the "Holy Roman Empire of German Nations" came into existence some 1,000 years ago. It was a loose federation of German princely states in an elective monarchy with an Emperor at its head.

This empire came to an end in 1806 as a result of the French Revolution and the Napoleonic Wars. In the 19th century, the new political order led to a late national unification: In 1871 the remaining 25 German states were united under Prussian leadership to form the German Empire. The end of WW I in 1918 sealed the fate of the monarchy; the German Empire became a republic.

The end of WW II led to the division of the country into West and East. The Federal Republic of Germany was established out of 11 federal states. In the East the German Democratic Republic was formed. In 1990 both German states were united. The five states of the German Democratic Republic joined the Federal Republic of Germany, which now comprises 16 federal states.

Population - 80,000,000
Capital - Berlin
Government - Parliamentarian, democratic, with 16 states
Religion - all denominations, predominantly Roman Catholics and Lutherans
Language - German (also Danish and Sorbic)
Money - Deutschmark (DM) One Mark equals 100 Pfennig. Coins of 1, 2, 5, 10, 50 Pfennige and of 1, 2, 5, Mark. Notes of 5, 10, 20, 50, 100, 500, 1,000 Mark.
U.S.$1 = 1.3 marks, Cdn.$1 = 1 mark, British £ = 2.2 marks
Public Holidays
Whit Monday, October 3rd, National Day; Christmas Day, December 26; January 1; Good Friday, Easter Monday, May 1, Ascension Day May 25

Visas

Americans, Canadians and U.K. citizens do not need visas.

Peculiar Customs and Odd Expressions

Shake hands both upon meeting and upon departing; never keep your left hand in your pocket while shaking hands with your right - Germans shake hands frequently, with strangers and friends, but it is declining in importance among young people; men stand when women enter a room; when entering or leaving a store, it is considered polite to say "hello"and "good-bye"to the sales clerk; Germans are open and generous with close friends, but they are more formal and reserved in public - you do not see many smiles or displays of affection on German streets; to get someone's attention, raise your hand, palm facing out, with only the index finger extended - don't wave or beckon; don't talk to someone with your hands in your pockets or while chewing gum; expect to be hushed if you so much as cough while attending an opera, play, or concert. German audiences remain extraordinarily silent, rarely even shifting in their seats; in restaurants summon the waiter or waitress by raising a hand- address a waiter as "Herr Ober," a waitress as "Fraulein".

Sauer macht lustig - Sour makes you happy (i.e. when biting in a sour apple or pickle, it makes you smile.)

Das ist zum Mause melken - This makes one milk nice (i.e. This drives one nuts.)

Reden ist Silber, Schweigen ist Gold - Talking is silver, silence is gold

Das Auge ibt mit - The eye eats as well (i.e. It is important to garnish the dinner plate nicely.)

Man soll den Tag nicht vor dem Abend loben - One shouldn't praise the day before evening (or better before the end of the day)

Bowling teams go to a town called Assmannshausen, swap partners, kiss and fondle each other before going for their next bowl-these are married people swapping mates!!

Cheek kissing is common among males and females who know one another.

Re: "Hello" in Germany - "Guten Tag" is common throughout Germany. But, in northern Germany they say "Moin, Moin"- it sounds like "morning, morning" and it is used all day long, "goodbye" is "Tschub". "Servus" is used among southern Germans for welcoming and saying goodbye. Bavarians greet each other with "Brub Gott", and the Swiss-Germans say "Gruetzi mitenand". Don't be surprised to hear young people say, "Hi, hallo"and "Bye, bye".

Best Festivals

Bad Segeberg - Karl-May-Festspiele in July and August

Bayreuth - Richard Wagner Festival in July and August

Carnivals in Cologne, Mainz and Munich - dates vary, beginning of spring- Feb.- March.

Dresden - International Dixieland Festival every year in the first half of May

Hanover - Maschsee-Lake-Festival early August

Kiel - the Kieler Woche - yachting regatta - last week of June

Munich Opera Festival in July and August, and infamous Oktoberfest Festival - starts 16 days before the first Sunday in October

Schleswig - Holstein Music Festival, end of June until mid August

Starkbierzeit - Strong Beer Festival during Lent

Night Activities and More

Berlin - over 450 clubs and taverns, disco-Annabel's, Beehive, Milch Bar, Orpheus, Metro-pol, Chez Nous

Dusseldorf - you'll find a bar or pub in every building in the old town

Hamburg - Reeperbahn (Red Light)

Munich - infamous Hofbrauhau - great for beer drinking, Nachtcafe, Babalu, Unterfahrt, Jenny's Place in the Blue Note

Must See Tourist Sights

Aachen - The Cathedral, Puppet Fountain in the market, Post Wagen tavern - possibly oldest in Europe

Berlin - remains of the Berlin Wall, Brandenburg Gate, Funkturm-Berlin Radio Tower, Zoo Aquarium-best collection in the world, Kaiser Wilhem Memorial Church, Charlottenburg Castle, Hitler's Bunker

Bonn - most of the foreign embassies located here

Bremen - Market Place surrounded by eight century old buildings, St. Petri-Dom cathedral

Cochem and Koblenz - between these two cities is Germany's best medieval castle- the Eltz Castle

Cologne - the Dom-largest Gothic Cathedral in the world - a must see, has the largest working bell in the world - 24-tons..

Dusseldorf - in the old town you'll find a bar or pub in every building

Ettal - Linderhof Castle (Bavarian Alps)

Freiburg - magnificent "Munster" Gothic cathedral - a masterpiece

Frankfurt - Dom-a 13th century church, apple wine taverns, Stadel art gallery

Fussen - Neuschwanstein Castle, outstanding, two hours outside of Munich by car

Eisenach - pretty town on the edge of the Thuringian Forest, Wartburg castle nearby

Garmisch - Partenkirchen-Alpine resort - great view of German and Austrian Alps, many winter sports

Hamburg - great art galleries-Kunsthaus, Kunstverein, Deichtorhallen, Kunsthalle; one of the more notorious red-light districts

Heidelberg - world's largest wine barrel - 58,000 gallons, one of best Gothic castles

Lake Chiemsee - on the lake is Herrenchiemsee Castle (Bavarian Alps) 1 hour south of Munich

Leipzig - best site is the Volkerschlachtdenkmat-Battle of Nations Monument, the Renaissance Town Hall

Lubeck - medieval town, the Holstentor - fortified gate with huge twin towers

Magdeburg - Cathedral

Munich - Marienplatz-medieval square, Peterskirche-beautiful church, Residenz (Royal Palace), Neues Rathaus-New Town Hall-contains world-famous Glockenspiel, many museums such as Deutsches Museum; Frauenkirche - Cathedral of Our Lady 1488.

Naumburg - beautiful little medieval town

Nurnberg-Kaiserburg - the Imperial Palace, churches-St.Lorenz and St. Sebaldus, many ancient sites

Passau - tunnels and archways in the old town, the Dom St. Stephan has largest church organ in the world

Regensburg - Cathedral, medieval Old Town, 12th century bridge-one of oldest in Europe

St. Goar - incredible Rhine castle called Rheinfels overlooking this town

Trier -Germany's oldest town, most Roman ruins north of the Alps

Wurzburg - Prince-Bishops' Palace, Marienberg Fortress

Warnemunde - eastern Germany's most popular beach resort

Best Scenery

The Romantic Road runs north-south through western Bavaria, from Wurzburg to Fussen near the Austrian border, passing through Rothenburg ob der Tauber, Dinkelsbuhl and Augsburg

The Bavarian Forest near the Czech border is great for hiking

Black Forest near Baden-Baden, Karlsruhe and Basel; the Mosel Valley; Harz Mountains; Rhine River Valley

Bus

A little cheaper than trains but not as punctual.

Cycling

Many bikes can be rented from train stations, prices range from 10-15DM a day, you can go from hostel to hostel, trains charge aprroximately 5-8DM for carrying a bike, the only rail pass that allows free transport of bikes is the Tramper Ticket.

Hitch-Hiking

Check with Mitfahrzentrale agencies in most German cities-check with the local tourist agencies to locate them or look the title under the yellow pages. You will have to help pay for the petrol, costs to the driver, and a reservation fee to the agency.

Train

Individual train passes are expensive, unless you have a Eurail, InterRail or Junior Flexipass (Deutsche Bundeshahn -DB) for travelers under 26-

good on most Europabus and DB buses-5/day within 30 day period-$138, l0/day-$188, l5/day-$238-to get DB rail passes before leaving your country call DER Tours 1-800-782-2424. Prices are in U.S.$

Camping

Over 2,000 campsites, many open year round; Deutscher Camping Club, Mandlstrasse 28, 80802 Munich, local tourist boards can help as well. Campsites average 25DM per person.

Youth Hostels

Over 620 (more than any other country), contact Deutsches Jegendherbergswerk, Hauptverband, Postfach 1455, 32704 Detmold, Germany, tel:(49) (5231) 74010, fax (49) (5231) 740149; costs range from 14-25DM, breakfast is usually included; lunch, dinner costs from 4-9DM.

Youth Hostel Town Locations and Telephone Numbers

A Aachen (241) 71101; Aalen (7361) 49203; Affalter (37754) 6208; Albersdorf (4835) 642 Alpirsbach (7444) 2477; Altena (2352) 23522; Altenahr (2643) 1880; Altenau (5328) 361; Altenberg (35056) 2318; Alglashutten (7655) 206; Altleinin"ge"n (6356) 1580; Amberg (9621) 10369; Amorbach (9373) 1366; Annweiler (6346) 8438; Arneburg (3932 1) 2386; Arnsberg (2931) 10627; Aschaffenburg (6021) 930763; Ascheffel-Aschberg (4353) 307; Augsburg (821) 33909; Augustusburg (37291) 20256; Aurich (4941) 2827; **B** Bacharach (6743) 1266; Bad Bentheim (5922) 2480; Bad Bergzabern (6343) 8383; Bad Berleburg (2331) 35070; Bad Blankenburg (36741) 2528; Bad Brambach (37438) 541; Bad Doberan (38203) 2439; Bad Driburg (5253) 2570; Bad Durkheim (6322) 63151; Bad Ems (2603) 50384; Bad Endorf-Hemhof (8053) 509; Bad Essen (5472) 2123; Bad Gandersheim (5382) 2967; Bad Herrenalb (7083) 2430; Bad Hersfeld (6621) 2403; Bad Homburg (6172) 23950; Bad Honnef (2224) 71300; Bad Iburg (5403) 2422; Bad Karlshafen (5672) 338; Bad Kosen (34463) 597; Bad Kreuznach (671) 75351; Bad Lauterberg (5524) 3738; Bad Marienberg (2661) 5008; Bad Munstereifel-Rodert (2253) 7438; Bad Neuenahr-Ahrweiler (2641) 34924; Bad Oldesloe (4531) 504294; Bad Saarow-Pieskow (33631) 2664; Bad Sachsa (5523) 8800; Bad Salzungen (3695) 2208; Bad Schandau-Ostrau (35022) 2408; Bad Segeberg (4551) 2531; Bad Sulza (36461) 567; Bad Urach (7125) 8025; Bad Wimpfen (7063) 7069; Bad Zwischenahn (4403) 2393 Baden-Baden (7221) 52223; Balingen (7433) 5911; Bamberg (951) 56002; Barth (38231) 2843; Bautzen (3591) 44045; Bayerisch-Eisenstein (9925) 337; Bayreuth (921) 25262; Bayrischzell (8023) 675; Beckerwitz (38428) 362; Bederkesa (4745) 406; Benediktbeuern - 2 hostels - 1) "JH Don-Bosco Hostel on Don-Bosco-Str 3, tel: (8857) 88350; 2) "JH fur Madchen on Bahnhostr 58, tel: (8857) 9050; Bergen (8662) 8246; Bergneustadt (2261) 41203; Berlin - 3 hostels - 1) Ernst Reuter Hostel on Hermsdorfer Damm 48-50, tel: (30) 4041610; 2) Kluckstr Hostel on Kluckstr 3, tel: (30) 2611097; 3) YGH am Wannsee

Hostel on Badeweg 1, tel: (30) 8032034; Bernburg (3471) 25167; Bernkastel- Kues (6531) 2395; Bersenbruck (5439) 704; Biberach (7351) 21885; Biedenkopf (6461) 5100; Bielefeld (521) 22227; Biggesee (2761) 6775; Bilstein (2721) 81217; Bingen-Bingerbruck (6721) 32163; Binz (38393) 32597; Bischofsheim (9772) 371; Bischhofsmais- Oberbreitenau (9920) 265; Bispingen (5194) 2375; Blaubeuren (7344) 6444; Blockhaus (2265) 8628; Blomberg (5235) 7255; Bockswiese (5325) 2256; Bodenmais Am Kleinen Arber (9924) 281; Bodenwerder (5533) 2685; Bollendorf (6526) 200; Bonn - 2 hostels - 1) Bad Godesberg Hostel on Horionstr 60, tel: (228) 3175; 2) Venusberg Hostel on Haager Weg 42, tel: (228) 289970; Bonndorf/Schw (7703) 359; Borger (5953) 228; Borgwedel (4354) 219; Bork (33976) 437; Borkum (4922) 579; Born-Ibenhorst (38234) 229; Brandenburg (3381) 5211040; Braunlage (5520) 2238; Braunsdorf (33633) 635; Breisach (7667) 7665; Bremen (421) 171369; Bremen-Blumenthal (421) 601005; Bremerhaven (471) 5902533; Bremervorde (4761) 1275; Bremsdorfer Muhle (33654) 272; Brieselang (33232) 39408; Brilon (2961) 2281; Brodenbach (2605) 3389; Brotterode (36840) 32125; Bruggen (2163) 5161; Buchheim (34345) 2657; Buckow (33433) 286; Budingen (6042) 3697; Burg auf Fehmarn (4371) 2150; Burg an der Wupper (212) 41025; Burg Breuberg (6165) 3403; Burg Hessenstein (6455) 300; Burg/Spreewald (35603) 225; Burg Stargard (39603) 20207; Burg Wildenstein (7466) 411; Burghausen (4834) 2436; **C** Calw (7051) 12614; Cappenberger (2306) 53546; Carolinensiel (4464) 252; Celle (5141) 53208; Chemnitz (371) 71331; Chossewitz (33673) 5757; Clausthal-Zellerfeld (5323) 84293; Coburg (9561) 15330; Cochem (2671) 8633; Colditz (34381) 3335; Cottbus (355) 22558; Creglingen (7933) 336; Cuxhaven-Duhnen (4721) 48552; **D** Dahlen (34361) 51355; Dahmen (39933) 552; Dahn (6391) 1769; Darmstadt (6151) 45293; Dassow-Holm (38826) 614; Daun (6592) 2884; Demmin (3998) 223388; Dessau (340) 619452; Detmold (5231) 24739; Diez (6432) 2481; Dinelsbuhl (9851) 9509; Donauworth (906) 5158; Dornstetten (7443) 6469; Dorsten (2369) 8722; Dreisbach (6868) 270; Dresen - 3 hostels - 1) Hubnerstr Hostel on Hubnerstr 11, tel: (351) 4710667 2) Oberloschwitz Hostel Sierksstr 33, tel: (351) 36672; 3) Radebeul Hostel on Weintraubenstr 12, tel: (351) 74786; Duderstadt (5527) 73001; Duisburg (203) 724164; **Dusseldorf** (203) 724164; **E** Eberbach (6271) 2593; Ebersberg (8092) 22523; Ebrach (9553) 271; Eckernforde (4351) 2154; Ehrenfriedersdork (37346) 253; Eichstatt (8421) 4427; Eisenach - 2 hostels 1) Mariental Hostel on Mariental 24, tel: (3691) 203613; 2) Bornstrabe Hostel on Bornstrabe 7, tel: (3691) 732012; Eisenberg (36691) 3462; Ellwangen (7961) 53880; Emden (4921) 23797; Erbach (6062) 3515; Erfurt (361) 5626705; Erlangen (9131) 862555; Erpfingen (7128) 1652; Esborn (2335) 7718; Eschwege (5651) 60099; Esens-Benserseil (4971) 3717; Essen-Werden (201) 491163; Esslingen (711) 381848; Eutin (4521) 2109; **F** Falkenhain (3727) 2952;

Fallinbostel (5162) 2274; Feldberg (39831) 20520; Feldberg/ Schw (7676) 221; Feuchtwangen (9852) 842; Finnentrop (2721) 7293; Finnentrop-Heggen (2721) 50345; Flensburg (461) 37742; Flessenow (3866) 435; Forbach - 2 hostels - 1) "Heinrich-Kastner-Jugendherberge"on Birket 1, tel: (7228) 2427; 2) Herrenweis Hostel on Haus Nr 33, tel: (7226) 1318; Frankfurt (69) 619058; Frauenau (9926) 543; Frauenstein (37326) 307; Freiburg (761) 67656; Freudenstadt (7441) 7720; Freusburg (2741) 61094; Friedrichroda - 2 hostels - 1) Friedrichroda Hostel on Waldstr 25, tel: (3623) 4410; 2) Wanderhuten Heuberg Hostel on Waldstr 25, tel: (3623) 4410; Friedrichshafen (7541) 72404; Friedrichstadt (4881) 7984; Frobersgrun (37431) 3256; Fulda (661) 73389; Furth im Wald (9973) 9254; Fussen (8362) 7754; **G** Garmisch-Partenkirchen (8821) 2980; Geesthacht (4152) 2356; Geising (35056) 5465; Gelnhausen (6051) 4424; Gemund (2444) 2241; Georgsmarienhutte (5401) 2568; Gerolstein (6591) 4745; Gersfeld (6654) 340; Geyer (37346) 1364; Giessen (641) 65879; Glorsee (2338) 434; Glorsee (2338) 434; Gluckstadt (4124) 2259; Gommern (39200) 50031; Gorenzen (34782) 384; Gorlitz (3581) 406510; Goslar (5321) 22240; Gossweinstein (9242) 259; Gottingen (551) 57622; Graal-Muritz (38206) 520; Grabow (38756) 7954; Grafenroda (36205) 290; Gravenwiesbach (6086) 520; Greetsiel (4926) 550; Greiz (3661) 2176; Grethen (3437) 3449; Grobenhof (3881) 4411; Grob Reken (2864) 1023; Grober Inselsberg (36259) 2329; Grumbach (37343) 2288; Gunzburg (8221) 34487; Gutersloh (5241) 822181; **H** Hagen (2331) 50254; Haidmuhle-Frauenberg (8556) 467; Haldensleben (3904) 40386; Halle (345) 24716; Haltern (2364) 2258; Hamburg - 2 hostels - 1) Auf dem Stintfang Hostel on Alfred-Wegener-Weg 5, tel: (40) 313488; 2) Horner Rennbahn Hostel on Rennbahnstr 100, tel: (40) 6511671; Hameln (5151) 3425; Hamm (2381) 83837; Hankensbuttel (5832) 2500; Hannover - 2 hostels - 1) Hannover Hostel on Ferdinand-Wilhem-Fricke-Weg 1, tel: (511) 1317674; 2) Hannover Hostel on Hermann-Bahlsen-Allee 8, tel: (511) 691493; Hann.Munden (5541) 8853; Haren (5932) 2726; Hartenstein (9152) 1296; Hattingen (2324) 60453; Heide (481) 71575; Heidelberg (6221) 412066; Heidenheim (7321) 949045; Heilbronn (7131) 172961; Helgoland (4725) 341; Hellenthal (2482) 2238; Helmarshausen (5672) 1027; Heppenheim (6252) 77323; Heringsdorf (38378) 22325; Hermeskeil (6503) 3097); Hertlingshausen (6356) 281; Hilders (6681) 365; Hildesheim (5121) 42717; Hinsbeck (2153) 6492; Hitzacker (5862) 244; Hochspeyer (6305) 336; Hof (9281) 93277; Hohe Fahrt (5635) 8142; Hohenberg (9233) 1587; Hohenstaufen (7165) 438; Hoherodskopf (6044) 2760; Hohnstein (35975) 202; Holzhau (37327) 322; Holzminden (5531) 4411; Homburg (6841) 3679 Hormersdorf (37346) 396; Horn-Bad Meinberg (5234) 2534; Hornum (4653) 294; Hoxter (5271) 2233; Hude 94408) 414; Hurth (2233) 42463; Husum (4841) 2714; **I** Idar-Oberstein (6781) 24366; Igersheim (7931) 6373; Ihrlerstein-Kelheim (9441)

3309; Ilmenau (3677) 24131; Ingolstadt (841) 34177; Insmuhlen (4188) 342; Isny (7562) 2550; Itzehoe (4821) 62270; **J** Jever (4461) 3590; Johanngeorgenstadt (3773) 2194; Jonsdorf (35844) 220; Juist (4935) 1094; **K** Kandern (7626) 484; Kappeln (4642) 8550; Karlsruhe (721) 28248; Kassel (561) 776 455; Katzhutte (36781) 37785; Kehl (7851) 2330; Kempten (831) 73663; Kevelaer (2832) 8267; Kiel (431) 731488; Kirchberg (7954) 230; Kitzingen (9321) 4251; Klausdorf (33703) 634; Klein Koris (33766) 730; Kleve (2821) 23671; Klingenthal (37467) 22094; Koblenz (261) 73737; Kochel (8851) 5296; **Koln** - 2 hostels - 1) **Deutz Hostel** on Siegesstr 5a, tel: (221) 814711; 2) Riehl Hostel on An der Schanz 14, tel: (221) 767081; Konigsberg (9525) 237; Konigsbronn (7328) 6600; Konstanz (7531) 32260; Korbach (5631) 8360; Kothener (33765) 555; Kretzschau (3441) 212678; Kreuth-Scharling (8029) 552; Kronach (9261) 94412; Kronenburg-Baasem (6557) 339; Kulmbach (9221) 7243; **L** Lam (9943) 2936; Lanshut (871) 23449; Langeleben (5353) 8582; Langenwetzendorf (36625) 305; Langeoog (4972) 276; Laubach (4153) 2598; Lauenburg (4153) 2598; Lauterbach (6641) 2181; Leer (491) 2126; Leichlingen (2175) 2917; Leinburg-Weissenbrunn (9187) 1529; Leipzig - 2 hostels - 1) Centrum Hostel on Kathe-Kollwitz-Str 64-66, tel: (341) 470530; 2) Auensee Hostel on Gustav-Esche-Str 4, tel: (341) 57189; Lenggries (8042) 2424; Lensahn (4363) 2241; Leuchtenburg (36424) 23216; Lichtenfels (9571) 71039; Lichtenstein (37204) 2718; Leipnitzsee (33397) 21659; Limburg (6431) 41493; Lindau (8382) 5813; Lindlar (2266) 5264; Lingen (591) 97306-0; Linsengericht (6051) 72029; List (4652) 397; Lochen (7433) 37383; Lohne-Gohfeld (5731) 81012; Lohr (9352) 2444; Lorrach (7621) 47040; Lubben (3546) 3046; Lubeck - 2 hostels - 1) Gertrudenkirchhof Hostel on Am Gertrudenkirchhof 4, tel: (451) 33433; 2) JGH Hostel on Mengstr 33; tel: (451)7020399; Ludwigsburg (7141) 51564; Ludwigstein (5542) 1812; Luneburg (4131) 41864; **M** Mainz (6131) 85332; Malente (4523) 1723; Manderscheid (621) 822718; Mannheim (621) 822718; Marburg (6421) 23461; Mardorf (5036) 457; Marktredwitz (9231) 81082 Martinfeld (36082) 9339; Mauth (2651) 2355; Mayen (2651) 2355; Meinerzhagen (2354) 14341; Meisdorf (34743) 8257; Meissen (3521) 453065; Melle (5422) 2434; Melsungen (5661) 2650; Memmingen (8331) 494087; Mendig (2652) 4777; Menzenschwand (7675) 326; Meppen (5931) 2771; Merzalben (6395) 6271; Meschede (291) 6666; Milow (3386) 280361; Mirow (39833) 20726; Mittenwald (8823) 1701; Mohnesee (2924) 305; Molln (4542) 2601; Monchengladbach (2161) 559512; Monschau - 2 hostels - 1) Burg Hostel on Auf dem Schloss 4, tel: (2472) 2314; 2) Hargard Hostel on Hargardsgasse 5, tel: (2472) 2180; Montabaur (2602) 5121; Morbach (6533) 3389; Morsbach (2294) 8662; Mosbach (6261) 7191) Mosenberg (5681) 2691; Much-Berghausen (2245) 3828; Muden (5053) 225; Muhldorf (8631) 7370; Muhlhausen - 2 hostels - 1) "Am Schwanenteich"on Popperoder Gasse, tel: (3061) 71137; 2) Tonberg Hostel on Auf dem Tonberg 1, tel: (3601) 3318; Mulheim (208) 382191;Munchehofe (33432) 8734;**Munchen (Munich)** 2 hostels - 1) **Neuhausen JH** on wendl-Dietrich Str 20, tel: (89) 131156; 2) Thalkirchen Hostel on Miesingstr 4, tel: (89) 7236550; Munster (251) 532470; Murchin (3971) 2732; Murrhardt (7192) 7501; Mutzschen (34385) 51241; Mylau (3765) 34584; **N** Naumburg (3445) 703422; Neckargemund-Dilsberg (6223) 2133; Neidenberga (36737) 262; Neschwitz (35933) 5370; Neubrandenburg (395) 4225801; Neudorf (37342) 8282; Neugersdorf (3586) 702729; Neuhaus (3679) 2862; Neumunster (4321) 403416; Neureichenau-Rosenbergergut (8583) 1239; Neuschonau-Waldhauser (8553) 6000; Neuss-Uedesheim (2131) 39273; Neustadt (6321) 2289; Nideggen (2427) 226; Niebull (4661) 8762; Norddeich (4931) 8064; Nordenham (4731) 88262; Norderney - 2 hostels-1) Sudstr Hostel on Sudstr 1, tel: (4932) 2451; 2) Dunensender Hostel on Am Dunensender 3, tel: (4932) 2574; Nordlingen (9081) 84109; Northeim (5551) 8672; Nottuln (2502) 7878; Nurnberg (911) 221024; **O** Oberammergau (8822) 4114; Oberbernhards (6657) 240; Oberhundem (2723) 72640; Oberoderwitz (35842) 26544; Oberreifenberg (6082) 2440; Oberstdorf-Kornau (8322) 2225; Oberwesel (6744) 7046; Ochsenfurt (9331) 4949; Oerlinghausen (5202) 2053; Ohorn (35955) 2762; Oldenburg/Holstein (4361)7670; Oldenburg (441) 87135; Ortenberg (781) 31749; Osnabruck (541) 54284; Ossa (34346) 60587; Osterode (5522) 5595; Ottenhofen (7842) 2629; Otterndorf (4751) 3165; Ottobeuren (8332) 368; **P** Paderborn (5251) 22055; Panschwitz-Kuckau (35796) 357; Papenburg (4961) 2793; Passau (851) 41351; Pforzheim (721) 962100; Pirna-Copitz (3501) 527316; Plau am See (38735) 345; Plauen (3741) 522125; Plon (4522) 2576) Plothen (36648) 22329; Pockau (37367) 9589; Porta Westfalica (571) 70250; Pottenstein (9243) 1224; Prebelow (33921) 222; Prien (8051) 2972; Prora (38393) 32844; Prum (6551) 2500; Pullach (89) 7930643; **R** Raben (33848) 221; Radevormwald (2195) 1063; Radis (34953) 39288; Rathen (35024) 425; Ratingen (2102) 22997; Ratzeburg (4541) 3707; Ravensburg (751) 25363; Rechenberg (7967) 372; Regensburg (941) 57402; Rendsburg (4331) 71205; Retzstadt (9364) 1367; Rheine (5971) 2407; Rinteln (57551) 2405; Rittersgrun (37757) 260; Rochlitz (3737) 2131; Rochsburg (37383) 6503; Rodinghausen (5746) 8173; Rosbach (2292) 5042; Rostock (381) 716224; Rostock-Warnemunde (381) 52303; Rotenburg/Wumme (4261) 83041; Rotenburg/Fulda (6623) 2792; Rothenburg/Tauber (9861) 4510; Rothenfels (9393) 1015; Rottweil (741) 7664; Rudesheim (6722) 2711; Rurberg (2473) 2200; Ruthen (2952) 483; Ruttelerfeld (4452) 416; **S** Saarbrucken (681) 33040; Saarburg (6581) 2555; Sachsen-Anhalt (3907) 712629; Saldenburg (8504) 1655; Sandhatten (4482) 330; Sargenroth (6761) 2500; Sayda (37365) 277; Scharbeutz-Klingberg (4524) 428; Schellerhau (35052) 4227; Schillighorn (4426) 371; Schleswig (4621) 371; Schliersee-Josefsthal

(8026) 71068; Schluchsee - 2 hostels - 1) Im Wolfsgrund Hostel on Im Wolfsgrund 28, tel: (7656) 329; 2) Seebrugg Hostel on Haus 9, tel: (7656) 494; Schmallenberg (2972) 6098; Schonberg (4344) 2974; Schonbrunn (36651) 87064; Schoneck (37464) 87064; Schoningen am Elm (5352) 3898; Schonwalde (4528) 206; Schwabisch Gmund (7171) 2260; Schwabisch Hall (791) 41050; Schwarzburg (36730) 22223; Schweinfurt (9721) 21404; Schwerin (385) 213005; Sigmaringen (7571) 13277; Silberborn (5536) 568; Singen (7731) 42590; Soest (2921) 16283; Solingen-Grafrath (212) 591198; Sorpesee (2935) 1776; Sosa (37752) 8268; Spalt-Wernfels (9873) 515; Speyer (6232) 75380; Spiekeroog (4976) 329; Springe (5041) 1455; St. Englmar-Maibrunn (9965) 271; St. Goar (6741) 388; St.Goarshausen (6771) 2619; St. Ingbert (6894) 6102; St. Michaelisdonn (4853) 923; Stade (4141) 46368; Steinbach/Donnersberg (6357) 360; Stralsund (3831) 292160; Straslund-Devin (3831) 270358; Straubing (9421) 80436; Strehla (35264) 733; Strub-Berchtesgaden (8652) 2190; Stuttgart (711) 241583; Syke (4242) 50314; **T** Taltitz (37421) 23019; Tambach-Dietharz (36252) 6149; Tauberbischofsheim (9341) 3152; Tecklenburg (5482) 360; Teterow (3996) 172668; Thale (3947) 2881; Thaallichtenberg (6381) 2632; Thaarandt (35203) 37272; Tholey (6853) 2271; Thulsfelder Talsperre (4495) 475; Titisee - 2 hostels - 1)"JH Rudenberg" Hostel on Haus Nr 6, tel: (7651) 7360; 2) "JH Veltishof" Hostel on Bruderhalde 27, tel: (7652) 238; Todtnauberg (7671) 275; Tonning (4861) 1280; Torfhaus (5320) 242; Tossens (4736) 716; Traben-Trarbach (6541) 9278; Traunstein (861) 4742; Travemunde (4502) 2576; Triberg/Schw (7722) 4110; Trier (651) 29292; Tubingen (7071) 23002; **U** Uberlingen (7551) 4204; Ueckermunde-Bellin (39771) 22411; Uelsen (5942) 718; Uelzen (581) 5312; Ulm (731) 384455; Urfeld (5571) 2298; V Velbert (2051) 84317; Verden (7721) 54149; Vlotho (5733) 4063; **W** Walchensee-Urfeld 98851) 230; Waldeck (5623) 5313; Walmunchen (9972) 244; Walldurn (6282) 283; Waltersdorf (35841) 2650; Wandlitz (33397) 22109; Wangerooge (4469) 439; Waren (3991) 2261; Warmbad (37369) 437; Warmensteinach-Oberwarmen-Steinach (9277) 249; Weener (4951) 555; Weikersheim (7934) 7025; Weilburg (6471) 7116; Weimar - 3 hostels - 1) Weimar "Germania" Hostel on Carl-August Allee 13, tel: (3643) 202076; 2) "Am Poseckschen Garten" Hostel on Humboldstr 17, tel: (3643) 64021; 3) Maxim Gorki Hostel on Zum Wilden Graben 12, tel: (3643) 3471; Weinheim/Bgstr (6201) 68484; Weiskirchen (6876) 231; Werdau (3761) 3514; Wertheim (9342) 6451; Westensee (4305) 542; Westerstede (4488) 3006; Wetzlar (6441) 71068; Wewelsburg (2955) 6155; Wieden (7673) 538; Wiehl (2262) 93410; Wiesbaden (611) 48657; Wiesenttal-Streitberg (9196) 288; Wildeshausen (4431) 2223; Wilhelmshaven (4421) 60048; Willingen (5632) 6347; Windischeschenbach-Tannenlohe (9637) 267; Winischleuba (3447) 314159; Wingst (4778) 262; Winterberg (2981) 2289; Wipperfurth (2267) 1228;

Wirsberg (9227) 6432; Wittdun (4682) 2010; Wittenberg (3491) 3255; Wolfsburg (5361) 13337; Wolfstein (6304) 1408; Worms (6241) 25780; Worpswede (4792) 1360; Worthsee-Steinebach (8153) 7206; Wunsiedel (9232) 1851; Wuppertal-Barmen (202) 552372; Wurzburg (931) 42590; Wustewohlde (4708) 234; Wyk auf Fohr (4681) 2355; **Z** Zeven-Bademuhlen (4281) 2550; Zielow (39923) 2547; Zingst (38232) 465; Zinnwald - 2 hostels - 1) Jagerhutte Hostel on Bergmannsweg 8, tel: (35056) 5825; 2) Georgenfeld Hostel on Hochmoorweg 12, tel: (35056) 5882; Zoblitz (37363) 920; Zuflucht (7804) 611; Zwiesel (9922) 1061; Zwingenberg (6251) 75938.

Work

Legally impossible, but check German newspapers under the heading Biete-employers looking for unskilled help. To investigate an opportunity to work contact: Zentralstelle fur Arbeitsvermittlung, Feuerbachstrasse 42, D-6000 Frankfurt am Main, Germany.

For visa inquiries check with the German Embassy.

Babysitting

Munich-contact 22-92-91 for possible work.

Useful Addresses and Tourist Offices

in U.S.

German National Tourist Office

52nd floor 122 East 42nd St., New York, NY 10168 (212) 661-7200 fax 212-661-7174

11766 Wilshire Blvd., suite 750, Los Angeles, CA 90025 (310) 575-9799 fax 310-575-1565

in Canada

175 Bloor St. E. suite 604 , Toronto, Ontario M4W 3R8 (416) 968-1570 fax (416) 968-1986

in the U.K.

Nightingale House, 65 Curzon St., London W1Y 7PE, tel: 0171/495-3990

in Germany

headquarters is at Beethovenstrasse 69, 60325 Frankfurt/Main tel: 069-7 57 20

Berlin - Tourist Information Office at Berlin, Europa Center, Budapesterstrasse tel: 030 262 60 31

Munich- Munich Student Travel Service at Munich 2, Luisenstrasse 43 tel: 523000 also, Tourist Information Office at Munich, Rindermarkt 5 tel: 23911

German Embassies

in U.S.

4645 Reservoir Rd. Washington D.C. 20007-1998, tel: (202) 298-8140

in Canada

275 Slater St. 14th Floor, Ottawa, Ontario K1P 5H9 tel: (613) 232-1101

Consulate General of the Federal Republic of Germany

77 Admiral Rd. Toronto, Ont. M5R 2L4 tel: (416) 925-2813

in the U.K.
23 Belgrave Square, London SW1X 8PZ, tel: 4471 235 5033
Foreign Posts in Germany
Frankfurt
British Embassy, Bockenheimer Landstr. 42, tel: 069/170-0020
United States Embassy, Siesmayerstr. 21, tel: 069/75360 Munich
Canadian Embassy, Tal 29, tel: 089/290650, M-Th 9-12, 2-5, F 9-1:30
British Embassy, Burkleinstr. 10, tel: 089/211090
United States Embassy, Koniginstr. 5, tel: 089/28880, M-F 8a.m.-11:30 p.m.
Berlin
Canadian Consulate, Friedrichstr., 95, tel: 030/261-1161
British Consulate, Unter den Linden 32-34, tel: 030/220-2431 Hamburg
British Consulate, Harvestehuder Weg 8A, tel: 040/446071, M-F 9-12, 2-4
United States Consulate, Alsterufer 27-28, tel: 040/411710, M-F 9-12
Driving Distances (in km)
From Berlin to cities in Germany:

Dresden 205	Frankfurt 555
Hamburg 284	Munich 584
Heidelberg 619	

From Berlin to cities in Europe:

Amsterdam 633	Copenhagen 461	Rome 1,529
Athens 2,556	London 1,302	Sofia 1,699
Barcelona 1,829	Madrid 2,561	Stockholm 1,070
Belgrade 1,317	Milan 1,106	Warsaw 590
Brussels 963	Oslo 1,040	Vienna 657
Bucharest 1,514	Paris 1,100	Zurich 845
Budapest 1,196	Prague 349	

Telephone Information: International Code 00, Country Code 49, Main City Area Codes, Berlin 30; time difference (Eastern Daylight) plus 6 hours. Emergency # 110

GIBRALTAR (THE ROCK)

contact Gibraltar Information Bureua, 710, The Madison Offices, 1155 Fifteenth St. N.W., Washington D.C. 20005 (202) 542-1108

GREECE

A Little History

In order to study "Greek" history, it is necessary to go back as far as 6,000 years. A sketch of Greek history cannot be undertaken in the same way as a history of Canada or England because Greek history is not the story of a single state. It could almost be called the story of civilization. Greece gave the world the incredible sophistication and beauty of the Minoan civilization on the island of Crete. Greece gave birth to democracy thousands of years ago; introduced literature to the world with Homer's immortal stories of Ulysses and Helen of Troy, that gave us the fundamentals of philosophy, medicine and mathematics in the genius of Plato, Aristotle, Socrates, Pythagoras and Hippocrates. Greece gave us art that is as exquisite, if not as complete, as it was when it was first chiselled from marble thousands of years ago. Greece gave us the first great statesmen, such as Pericles, and the first great adventurers, such as Alexander the Great, who journeyed as far as India.

Like virtually every part of Europe, Greece came under Roman rule. There followed the "Byzantine" Period, from the mid 7th century A.D. to about the 10th century. From the mid 15th century to the early 19th century, Greece was under Turkish rule. This led to a series of struggles which culminated in independence in 1821.

Between the early 1800s and 1924, Greece was a monarchy. A republic was declared in 1924 and lasted until 1935 at which time the monarchy was restored.

Greece was occupied by the Germans during WWII and suffered terribly at their hands. The years following the war saw a great deal of political upheaval and confusion. Finally, a constitution was ratified in 1952. Modern Greece is a democracy with a constitution and parliamentary system. The seat of Federal government is in Athens. Greece is a member of the European Union.

Geographically speaking...

The Greek peninsula, covers an area of 131,944 square kilometers and consists of mainland Greece (Attica, Peloponnese, Central Greece, Thessaly, Epirus, Macedonia, Thrace) and the islands. The Ionian Islands (Zante, Ithaca, Corfu, Cephallonia, Kithira, Lefkas and Paxi) form a chain off Greece's western shores in the Ionian Sea. The Cyclades consist of 39 islands of which 24 are inhabited, the Sporades have four islands, the Dodecanese consist of twelve islands and the Saronic Gulf has five islands including Mt. Olympus.

Population - 10, 264, 000
Capital - Athens
Government - Republic
Religion - Greek Orthodox
Language - Greek and some English
Money - Drachma (DR) Coins of 5, 10, 20, 50, and 100 drachmas. Notes of 100, 500, 1,000, 5,000 and 10,000 drachmas

U.S.$1 = 212 drachmas, Cdn. $1 = 156 drachmas, British £ = 356 drachmas

Public Holidays

National holidays on January 1, January 6, March 25, Ash Wednesday, Good
 Friday, Easter Monday, Whit Monday (note that Greek Easter is fixed in
 accord with Julian calendar which may be later than in the West), May 1,
 August 15, October 28, December 25, 26

Visas

Americans, Canadians and U.K. citizens do not need visas.

Peculiar Customs and Odd Expressions

Greetings can take many forms in Greece- a handshake, an embrace, or
 a kiss can all be encountered at first meetings or among friends and
 acquaintances; to indicate "no", use an upward nod of the head, to
 indicate "yes", use a downward nod of the head; anger is sometimes
 shown by a smile; after giving or receiving a compliment, Greeks
 sometimes make a puff of breath through the lips to ward off the "evil
 eye". If you are invited to a home, compliment the children of the
 household and give them a small gift; flowers or a cake is also appropriate for the hostess. Patrons at restaurants, after a few drinks, liven
 up the place by breaking saucers; Greeks of the Greek Orthodox
 Church wear a special little blue stone to ward off evil spirits for
 extra assurance a special prayer is recited.

Best Festivals

Athens Festival - mid-June to end of Sept.- with plays, concerts, ballet in
 the Herodes Atticus Theatre

Dafni - Wine Festival - Aug. to mid-Sept.

Epidaurus - Drama Festival - July-Sept.

Patras - Carnival in Jan. and Feb. and Patras Festival - in July and Aug.-
 music, dance theatre events

Night Activities and More

Athens - Disco's Take Five, Studio 54, Ergostasio, Nine Plus Nine and
 many more

Must See Tourist Sights

Athens - Parthenon and other ruins on the Acropolis, Erechtheion Temple,
 Theatre of Dionysus, Theatre of Herodes Atticus, many museums, The
 Proplaea, Monastiraki flea market, Hadrian's Library, Temple of Zeus,
 Aghios Nikodimos-oldest and largest Byzantine church in Athens,
 Kaissariani Monastery - 5 km outside Athens

Atticus - along the Apollo Coast - Temple of Poseidon at Sorenion - beautiful
 view

Corinth - ruins of ancient city, Temple of Apollo, Acrocorinth ruins of an
 ancient citadel

Delphi - the Oracle, Theatre and Museum, Monastery of St.Luke nearby

Monemvassia - Byzantine town, great fortress

Mycenae - Tombs of the Kings, and Lion Gate

Mystra - fantastic palaces, monasteries and the Church of Perivleptos

Nafplion - Palamida Fortress - 1,000 steps, great view

Olympia - the Stadium, the Museum, Temple of Zeus

Sparta - temples of Athena and Artemis,

Thessaloniki - walking along the waterfront worth the visit and the White Tower

The Islands - Aegina - Temple of Aphaia; Delos - entire island is one large archaeological site; Corfu, Crete-visit Knossos & Phaestos- many Minoan ruins, Kos, Patmos, Rhodes - City Walls; Saronic Islands - Spetses is the most beautiful island of this group; Mykonos-one of the most visited islands, great beaches, even nude ones at Paradise, Super Paradise and Hell; there are hundreds of islands-check with the Greek tourist office to get their recommendations

Best Scenery

Over 7,000 caves, abysses, 3,400 are located on the island of Crete and 420 are in Attica.

Akti Apollon - beautiful coastline

Diakofto to Kalavryta - take a train - one of the best railway journey's in the world

Nauplia - beautiful coastal highway

Crete - beaches, plains, rolling foothills, rugged mountains

Meteora -huge smooth rocks, cliff-top monasteries

Mt. Olympus - many good walking trails

Mykonos - beautiful white island

Zagoria region - visit the Vikos Gorge - nearly 48 villages in this area

Islands with fewer tourists - Kassos, Shinoussa, Iraklia, Kastellorizo, Anafi, Koufonisi,

Crete - the Samaria Gorge;

Santorini - incredible island

Cycling

Mountainous terrain makes it challenging, not a lot rental stores, rentals - 1,000 -3,000dr a day.

Bus

More reliable than trains, in summer buy tickets a couple hours in advance, if you don't find the bus stop, then flag a bus to stop for you.

Hitch-Hiking

Fairly good, take lots of water in the summer to avoid dehydration.

Train

Slow service but cheaper than buses; make reservations to avoid long line-ups.

Camping

Over 300 campsites, costs - 900dr/person, 600dr/tent, some open all year, ask the tourist board for Camping in Greece brochure.

Youth Hostels

About 30 in Greece, 7 on Crete, 1 on Corfu; costs 700-1500dr, for more information and to obtain an International Guest Card, visit the Greek Association of Youth Hostels in Athens, at 4 Dragatsanious St. tel: 323-4107. If there is no written response contact IYHF Secretariat, 9 Guessens Rd., Welwyn Garden City, Hertfordshire, AL8 6QW, England, tel: (44) (1707) 324170, fax (44) (1707) 323980.

Youth Hostel Town Locations and Telephone Numbers

Due to the large number of islands and the hostels locations, double-check with the Greek Tourist Board before you leave your country or when you arrive in Athens, if necessary.

Athens - 5 hostels - 1) **IYHF Athens International Youth Hostel** on 16 Victor Hugo St. tel: (1) 5234170; 2) Athens Youth Hostel on 1 Agiou Meletiou, tel: 8225860; 3) Athens Youth Hostel on 57 Kypselis St., tel: 8225860; 4) Y.M.C.A. on 28 Omirou St., tel: 362 6970; 5) Y.W.C.A. on 11 Amerikis St., tel: 3624294;

In Thessaloniki (Salonika): Y.M.C.A., Hanth Square, (031) 274000; Y.W.C.A. , 11 Aghias Sophias St., (031) 276144; Mainland of Greece: Delphi (0265) 82286; Litochoron (0352) 21311; Thessaloniki (031) 225946; Peloponnese (connected to the mainland by a bridge): Mycenae (0751) 66224; Nafplion (0752) 27754; Olympia (0624) 22580; Patra (061) 427278; Corfu: Kontokali Youth Hostel on Kontokali Beach in Kerkyra (0661) 91102; Santorini: Thira Youth Hostel, Kontokori, Aghios Elefterios, Santorini (0286) 22722;

Crete: Aghios Nikolaos YH on 3 Stratigou Koraka, Aghios Nikolaos (0841) 22823; Hania YH on 33 Drakonianou St., Hania (0821) 53564; Heraklion YH on 24 Handakos St., Heraklion (081) 222947; Mythios YH on St. Basil, Rethymnon Province (0832) 31202; Mallai YH on Mallia Beach (0897) 31338/285075; Rethymnon YH on Pavlou Vlastou St., Rethymnon (0831) 22848; Sitia YH on 4 Therissou St., Sitia, (0843) 22693.

Work

Unemployment is high, best to find work under the table, i.e. fruit picking, nanny, hotel work. Work permits are required from prospective employers before coming to the country. Contact the Greek National Tourist Office or in Greece, Ministry of Labor, 45 Piraeus St. Athens.

Useful Addresses and Tourist Offices

in U.S.

Greek National Tourist Organization 645 Fifth Ave., New York, NY 10022 (212) 421 5777 fax (212) 826-6940

611 West Sixth St., suite 2198, Los Angeles, California 90017 tel: (213) 626-6696 fax 213-489-9744

168 N. Michigan Ave. Chicago, IL 60601 tel: (312) 782-1084 fax (312)782-1091

in Canada

1233 Rue de la Montagne, suite 101, Montreal, Quebec H3G lZ2 tel: (514) 871-1535

Upper Level, 1300 Bay St. Toronto, Ont. M5R 3K8 tel: (416) 968-2220, fax: (416) 968-6533

in the U.K.

4 Conduit St. London W1R ODJ, tel: 0171/734-5997

in Greece

Greek National Tourist Organization, 2 Amerikis St. P.O.Box 1017 Athens tel:01-3223-111/9

National Tourist Information Office at 2 Karageorgi St., Athens and at Syntagma Square tel: 322 25 45

ISYTS (for students) at 11 Mikis St. Athens l0557, tel: 322 12 67

Greek Embassies

in U.S.

2221 Massachusetts Ave.N.W., Washington, D.C. 20008 tel: (202) 332-2727, fax (202) 265-4931

in Canada

80 Maclaren St. Ottawa, Ont. K2P 0K6 tel: (6l3) 238-6271, fax (613) 238-5676

in the U.K.

1A Holland Park, London, W11 3TP, tel: 727 8040

Foreign Posts in Greece

Athens

Canadian Embassy, 4 Genadiou, tel: 01/72-54-011, M-F 8:30-3

British Embassy, 1 Ploutarchou, tel: 01/72-36-211, M-F 9-3

United States Embassy, 91 Vasilissis Sofias, tel: 01/72-12-951, M-F 9-3

Driving Distances (in km)

From Athens to cities in Greece:

Patrai 192

Thessaloniki 513

Telephone Information: International Code 00, Country Code 30, Main City Area Code: Athens 1; time difference (Eastern Daylight) plus 7 hours.

HUNGARY

A Little History

One of the oldest remains of prehistoric man in Europe was found in Hungary and there are many traces of the people who lived here in very early times, especially the Avars. There are remains of the Roman Empire which extended up to the line now running through the centre of the country, the

Danube. All the major architectural styles, Romanesque, Gothic, Renaissance, Baroque, Neo-classical and Art Nouveau have left behind distinctive momentos of interest. The 1100 year old chequered history of the country, once the independent kingdom of Hungary, later dominated by the Turkish sultans and then progressing from Austrian rule to the dualist monarchy.

During recent history, Hungary allied itself with Nazi Germany before WWII and obtained additional territory when Czechoslovakia was partitioned in 1938. Having sought to break the alliance in 1944, Hungary was occupied by German forces. In 1945, Hungary was liberated by Soviet troops and signed an armistice, restoring the pre-1938 frontiers. It became a republic in 1946. In 1947, the Communists became the largest single party.

Discontent against Communist domination provoked demonstrations in 1956. Fighting broke out and Soviet troops suppressed the uprising.It is estimated 200,000 people fled during this period. In 1990 it was reported 2,500 Hungarian citizens had been killed in another uprising. In 1988, on the 140th anniversary of the 1848 Hungarian uprising against Austrian rule, some 10,000 people marched in Budapest and demanded freedom of the press, freedom of association and the introduction of genuine reforms. The protest was not halted by the police. In 1989 a multi-party system was agreed to and also the Constitution guaranteeing the party's leading role in society was abandoned.

Hungary's relations with Western nations improved steadily in the late 1980's. Hungary became a member of the Council of Europe in 1990. In 1991, Hungary signed treaties of co-operation with Russia and Ukraine, and in 1992 the Russian President, Boris Yeltsin, made an official visit to Hungary, during which time several outstanding compensation claims between the two countries were settled.

Population - 10,300,000
Capital - Budapest
Government - Parliamentary democracy
Religion - mostly Roman Catholic and Protestant
Language - Hungarian, some German and English
Money - Forint, One forint equals 100 fillers. Coins of 50 fillers, and of 1, 2, 5, 10 and 20 forints. Notes of, 50, 100, 500, 1,000 and 5,000 forints. - traveler's checks are accepted in major cities, make small transactions at a time as it is difficult to change forints back into hard currency; show your ISIC card as much as possible to get 50% off bus and train rides.
U.S.$1 = 91 forints, Cdn.$1 = 67 forints, British £ = 173 forints
Public Holidays
New Year, 1 January; 15 March; Easter Monday, 17 April; 1 May; Whitsun Monday, 5 June; 20 August; 23 October; Christmas, 24-26 December.

Visas

Americans, Canadians and U.K. citizens do not need visas for stays less than 90 days.

Peculiar Customs and Odd Expressions

A handshake is customary not only when being introduced, but also when departing; old fashioned Hungarian men will sometimes bow to a woman while shaking her hand; only close friends will greet each other with an embrace - for men, they shake hands, embrace, make cheek-to-cheek contact on the left cheek, then on the right cheek; close female friends do the same but do not shake hand; if you are staying in someone's home, avoid giving wine as a gift as Hungarians are proud of their wine; sounding of car horns is strictly prohibited; shorts are uncommon in the city.

Best Festivals

Budapest - March - Spring Festival, August - Formula One Auto Race at Hungaroring, Sept.- Dreher Beer Festival and Wine Festival

Gyula - Castle Theatre in June, historic dramas, jazz concerts

Szeged-Open-Air Theatre Festival July 20 - August 20 - plays, ballets

Visegrad Festival - 2nd Sunday in July- horse tournament-duellists from Hungary and abroad, dressed in medieval costumes, fight with sword, battle-axe and mace, on horse-back or on foot, also the 'Toldi' competition-winner in this mill - stone throwing and bar holding contest is judged to be the strongest man in Hungary, later concerts with medieval music

Night Activities and More.

Budapest - 123 natural hot springs-best at Gellert Hotel or the Szechenyi Baths; Clubs - Black and White Jazz Pizzeria, Fortuna, Picasso Point, Sancho American-Mexican Pub, Tilos Aza, Nightspots with dancing- Citadella, Pipacs, Nirvana, Olympia, Regina

Best Scenery

Szentendre - town-near Budapest - village of cobblestone roads, trees, art galleries

Transdanubia - region of mountains, hills, Danube river, sunflower fields

Must See Tourist Sites

Budapest - Orszaghaz-huge neo-Gothic parliament building, Nagy Zsinagoga-synagogue, St.Stephen's Basilica, Matyas Templom-13th century Matthias Church on Varhegy; Hungarian National Museum, Budapest Opera House

Eger - outdoor cafes , student town, caves

Esztergom - beautiful Cathedral

Holloko - 13th century castle - great for picnics

Koszeg - fortress town, St. James Church

Pecs - many interesting buildings

Szeged - one of Hungary's best squares

Szekesfehervar - Garden of Ruins, may be Hungary's oldest settlement; cathedral

Visegrad - lies on the best part of Danube Bend river; Nagy Villam Hill Lookout Tower - great views; Royal Palace

Bus

In Budapest, buses go from Erzsebetter Station. Prices are very reasonable.

Hitch-Hiking

Hitch-hiking is pretty good; the people will be curious to meet you.

Train

EurailPasses, InterRail, and European East passes are valid in Hungary. People under 26 can get a discount train pass for 7-10 days of unlimited travel - buy it only if you are going to spend a lot of time on it.

Camping

There are 1, 2 and 3 star campsites and on-site bungalows to rent as well, contact the tourist offices or Magyar Camping es Caravanning Club, Kalvin ter 9, tel: 11 85259.

Private Rooms

Get private rooms through tourist offices-over 20,000 available-reservations can be made at IBUSZ Fizetovendegszolgalat, 1054 Budapest Bajcsy-Zs. u. 58, or Cooptuourist, 1055 Budapest, Kossuth L. ter 13-15; average cost 950 forints a night.

Youth Hostels

270-1,800 forints/night, includes sheets. All hostels serve meals or use restaurants near by. Youth hostel assoc.: Magyarorszagi Ifjusagi Szallasok Szovetsege, H-1065 Budapest, Bajcsy-Zsilinszky ut 31. II/3. Postal Address: H-1396 Budapest PF 483, tel: (36) (1) 1319705, fax (36) (1) 1319705. Two hostels open all year - Budapest Citadella, Gellerthegy and Budapest Csucshegy, Menedekhaz utca 122.

Youth Hostel Town Locations and Telephone Numbers

Baja (79) 324022; Balaton - 6 hostels - 1) Alsoors Hostel refer to "Dunaferr Gyermekudulo", tel: (86) 347138; 2) Balatonfenyves Hostel refer to Youth Camp, Bacs-Kiskun megyei Gyermek es Ifjusagi Alapitvany Tabora, Kolcsey u 45, tel: (85) 361686; 3) Balaton-foldvar Hostel refer to Express Intnational Youth Centre, Hotel Juventus, Jozsef Attila u 9, tel: (84) 340313; 4) Csopak Hostel refer to sort u 9, tel: (86) 346505; 5) Zanka Hostel refer to Gyermekudulo Centrum, 8250 Zanka/Balaton Nord, tel: (87) 348440; 6) Siofok Hostel refer to Hotel Ezustpart, Liszt F setany 3, tel: (84) 350622; Balinka (22) 411519;

Budapest has 33 hostels, just mention the name(s) of the hostel to someone on the street and you should be directed to the nearest one. Hostels and hotels are both very inexpensive - 270-1,800 forints/ night, most are 450-900 forints/night.

Budapest: 1 (area code) followed by the telephone number

1) Csilleberci Gyermek 1- 1565772; 2) Hotel Express 1- 1753082; 3) Hotel Lido 1-2504576; 4) Hostel Zuglo 1- 2512455; 5) Hostel Vasarhelyi

1-1852216; **6)** Hostel Rozsa 1-1666677; **7)** Hostel Landler 1-1667305; **8)** Hostel Kek 1-1852369; **9)** Hostel Selye Janos 1-2100326; **10)** Hostel Bakfark no tel: #; **11)** Hostel Donati no tel. #; **12)** Hostel Felvinci no tel. #; **13)** Hostel Universitas 1-1868110; **14)** Raday 1-2184766; **15)** Kinizsi 1-2173033; **16)** Hostel Diaksportszallo 1-1298644; **17)** Otto es Viktor 1-2670311; **18)** Hostel River Club 1-2214167; **19)** Hotel Nova 1-2775374 **20)** Hotel Campona 1-2273690; **21)** Hotel Goliat 1-2701456; **22)** Hotel Flandria 1-2703181; **23)** "Limes" 1-1575399; **24)** Hotel Eben 1-2523333; **25)** Hotel Touring 1-2503184; **26)** Hotel Griff 1-1667276; **27)** Hotel Platanus 1-1135014; **28)** Hotel Ventura 1-1820306; **29)** Hotel ELM Street no tel. #; **30)** Siraly 1-1530501; **31)** Ananda 1-2202413; **32)** Schonherz 1-1665460; **33)** Barczy 1-1213526; **D** Danfok (663) 341830; Debrecen (52) 349117; Doboz (66) 362348; Domsod (24) 385605; Dunaujvaros (25) 310434; **K** Kecskemet (76) 321916; **N** Nyiregyhaza (42) 402011; **P** Pecs (720) 315829; **S** Szolnok-Tiszaliget (560 424705; Szentendre (26) 312511; **T** Torokbalint (600 348620; **V** Veroce-Danube Bend (27) 350166.

Useful Addresses and Tourist Offices
in U.S.
Hungarian Tourist Board, l50 East 58th St. 33rd floor, New York, NY l0l55, tel: (212) 355-0240

in the U.K.
Danube Travel Ltd., 6 Conduit St., London W1R 9TG, tel: 0171/493-0263
Budapest - IBUSZ - cover all concerns, plus maps and brochures, at Tanacs korut 3c tel: 1186866, at Felszabadulas ter 5 tel: 1-186866, at Petoofi ter 3 tel:1-185707 also in the three main train stations
Tourinform at Sutoo u. 2 tel: 1179800 Tourist info service, and advice on accommodation possibilities - they don't do the booking
Express Youth and Student Travel Bureau at Szabadsag ter l6 tel: 131-7777, Semmelweis utca 4, tel: ll7860; and in Keleti train station
Coopturist at Bajcsy Zsilinszky ut l7 tel: l310992
Budapest Tourist at Roosevelt ter 5-6 tel: ll86000

Hungarian Embassies
in U.S.
3910 Shoemaker St. N.W., Washington, D.C. 20008, tel: (202) 362-6730
Consulate: 223 E 52nd St., New York, NY 10022, tel: (212) 752-0661

in Canada
299 Waverley St ,Ottawa, Ontario K2P OV9, tel (613) 230-96l4
Consulates
l200 McGill College Ave., Montreal, Quebec H3B 4G7 tel: (514) 393-3510
l02 Bloor St. West, suite l005, Toronto, Ontario M5S lM8 tel: (416) 923-8981

in the U.K.
35 Eaton Place, London, SW1X 8BY tel: 4471 235 7191

Foreign Posts in Hungary
Budapest
Canadian Embassy, 11 Budakeszi ut 32, tel: 1/176-7688, M-Th 9-11
British Embassy, V. Harmincad u.6, tel: 1/118-2888, M-F 8:30-11:30, 12-2
United States Embassy, V. Szabadsag ter 12, tel:1/112-6450 or 1/132-8933,M-F 8:30-1, 2-4

Driving Distances (in km)
From Budapest to cities in Hungary:

Debrecen 299	Pecs 198
Eger 128	Sopron 210
Gyor 123	Szeged 171
Kecskemet 85	Zalaegerszeg 224
Miskolc 179	

From Budapest to cities in Europe:

Athens 1,570	Milan 1,10
Barcelona 2,020	Oslo 1,900
Belgrade 400	Paris 1,460
Berlin 910	Prague 570
Brussels 1,370	Rome 1,250
Bucharest 830	Stockholm 1,920
Copenhagen 1,290	Warsaw 680
London 1,760	Vienna 250
Madrid 2,620	

Telephone Information: International Code 00, Country Code 36, Main City Area Code: Budapest 1; time difference (Eastern Daylight) plus 6 hours.

ICELAND

Youth Hostels: contact Bandalag Islenskra Farfugla, Sundlaugavegur 34, P.O. Box 1045, 121 Reykjavik, Iceland, tel: (354) (1) 38110, fax (354) (1) 889201; prices range from Kr 1,000-1,250 plus linen if needed.

Youth Hostel Town Locations and Telephone Numbers
A Akureyri-Storholt - 2 hostels - 1) Storholt Hostel on Storholt 1, tel: (96) 23657; 2) Lonsa Hostel refer to Lonsa, Glaesibaejarhr, tel: (96) 25037; **B** Bakkafjorour (97) 31621; Berunes (97) 88988; **F** Fljotsdalur (98) 78498; Fossholl (96) 431108;.**H** Hafnarfjorour - 2 hostels - 1) Arahus Hostel on Strandgata 21, tel: (91) 655267; 2) Hraunbyrgi Hostel on Hraunbrun 57, tel: (91) 650900; Hamar (93) 71663; Hofn (97) 81736; Husey (97) 13010; Hverageroi (98) 34198; **L** Leirubakki (98) 76591; Lonkot (95) 37432; **N** Njarovik (92) 15662; Njarovik-Strond (92) 16211; **O** Osar (95) 12678; **P** Patreksfjorour (94) 1280; Pingvellir (98) 12915; **R** Reydarfjordur (97)

41447; Reykholt (98) 68831; Reykjavik (91) 38110; Reynisbrekka (98) 71106; Runnar (93) 51262 **S** Seyoisfjorour (97) 21410; Saeberg (95) 10015; Stafafell (97) 81717; Stykkisholmur (93)81095; **V** Vestmannaeyjar (98) 12915.
Telephone Information: International Code 90, Country Code 354, Main City Area Code: Reykjavik 1; time difference (Eastern Daylight) plus 4 hours

REPUBLIC of IRELAND

A Little History

In 1541, Henry V111 of England, in an attempt to gain control of Ireland, forced the Irish Parliament to declare him King of Ireland and tried to force Protestantism on the Irish. His daughter, Mary 1, gave counties in Ireland to English settlers, and Elizabeth 1 outlawed Catholic religious services. This religious persecution continued through the 1600s. In 1801, the Act of Union made Ireland part of the United Kingdom of Great Britain and Ireland. The Irish Parliament was dissolved, but the Irish eventually won the right to send representatives to the British Parliament.

Additional misfortunes afflicted the Irish people because of their overreliance upon the potato as a staple of diet. In 1845, a plant disease wiped out the potato crop. From 1845 to 1847, about 750,000 people died of starvation or disease, and hundreds of thousands of others left the country.

The whole of Ireland was formerly part of the United Kingdom. In 1920 the island was partitioned, the six north-eastern counties remaining part of the United Kingdom, with their own government. In 1922, the 26 southern counties achieved dominion status, under the British Crown, as the Irish Free State. The dissolution of all remaining links with Great Britain culminated in the adoption, by plebiscite, of a new constitution, which gave the Irish Free State full sovereignty within the Commonwealth from 1937. Formal ties with the Commonwealth were ended in 1949, when the 26 southern counties became a republic. The partition of Ireland remained a contentious issue, and from 1969 a breakaway group from a volunteer force, the Irish Republican Army (IRA), calling itself the Provisional IRA, conducted a violent campaign to achieve reunification. The Irish government was opposed to any British military withdrawal from Northern Ireland. In 1985, Britain gave Ireland an advisory role in Norther Ireland's government, but terrorist acts have continued into the 1990s.

Population - 3, 550,000
Capital - Dublin

Government - Parliamentary democracy

Religion - Roman Catholic

Language - English

Money- Irish Punt or Pound(IR) Notes of 1, 5, 10, 20, 50, 100 U.S.$1 = 60 pence, Cdn. $1 = 44 pence, British £ = 95 pence

Public Holidays

St. Patrick's Day (March 17), Good Friday, Easter Monday, Whit Monday, First Monday in June, First Monday in August, Last Monday in October, Christmas Day, Boxing Day and New Year's Day.

Visas

Americans and Canadians do not need visas.

Peculiar Customs and Odd Expressions

'Blarney'- it is the name of a village, a castle, a woodland grove, a special stone and a style of speech; the Leprechaun-legend has it they are no more than 24 inches tall, dressed in bright colors, skilled as shoe makers, and, if caught by surprise, can lead you to a pot of gold. 'slainte'- most familiar toast; the glass for a toast is always raised with the right hand; the glass is held straight out from the shoulder. The reason: when toasting began, it was not unusual to find a sword, dagger or other weapon in the right hand, or concealed nearby. The traditional toasting position proved that you had come in friendship. It is traditional to clink glasses after the toast has been proposed but before it is drunk. This tradition is rooted in the earliest human history: people have always made a noise to frighten away the evil spirit. Some toasts:

Birthday - May you die in bed at 95 years, shot by a jealous husband (or wife).

Wedding - May you have many children and may they grow as mature in taste and healthy in color and as sought after as the contents of this glass.

Anniversary - I have known many, liked not a few, loved only one, I drink to you.

General - May we be alive at the same time next year; Here's a health to your enemies' enemies!; Here's to you, as good as you are. Here's to me, as bad as I am. As good as you are and as bad as I am, I'm as good as you are, as bad as I am.

Best Festivals

Cork - one of the largest jazz festivals in Europe, last weekend of October

Dublin - Bloomsday on June 16 - various events to celebrate Leopold Bloom's Joycean journey around the town; Theatre Festival-late Sept. early Oct.; the All Ireland Hurling (1st weekend of Sept.) and Football finals take place two weeks later.

Galway - Arts Festival late July

Night Activities and More

Dublin - many old pubs - Brazen Head, O'Donoghue's-music pub, Baggot Inn; Leeson St. for the discos

Must See Tourist Sights

Alwee Caves in the region of Burren in County Clare

Athlone - Athlone Castle-open to public in summer

Bantry - between mountains and the waters of Bantry bay, visit the Bantry House

Cork - Blarney Castle nearby

Dublin - St.Patrick's Cathedral, Dublin Castle, Merrion Square, National Museum, Guinness Brewery, James Joyce Museum, Kilmainham Jail, Malahide Castle nearby

Enniskillen - the popular Marble Arch Caves nearby

Killarney - St.Mary's Cathedral

Kilkenny - Kilkenny Castle

Kinvarra - just north is the Dunguaire Castle

Limerick - the 1210 King John's Castle, and the 1172 St.Mary's Cathedral

Newgrange - one of the best Celtic passage tombs in Ireland

St. Patrick's Rock (a wonderful medieval site) in northern Ireland

Tipperary- Rock of Cashel-spectacular group of medieval buildings, Holycross Abbey

Best Scenery

The southwest countrside through Bantry, Ballylickey, Kenmare to Killarney and Dingle Bay, the L54 coastal to Ballyvaughan is also spectacular

Cliffs of Moher

Donegal and Connemara coasts

Dunmore Cave - Ballyfoyle, Co. Kilkenny

Wicklow Way - from County Dublin to County Carlow - one of the best walks - 132 km

Bus

Rides are free with Eurail or InterRail Passes. Without one of these passes, if you are under 26 with an ISIC, purchase the Travelsave Stamp for approx. U.S.$13. This stamp will reduce train prices by 50%, bus prices by 30% and ferries by 25-30%. Available at USIT-student travel service-in Dublin, Galway and Cork. Consider the bus and rail Emerald Card (Ireland & Norther Ireland)-£105 for 8 days in a 15 day period, £180 for 15 days in a 30 day period; Irish Explorer Rail/Bus - Republic of Ireland only- 8 days in a15 day period £90 ; Irish Rambler Bus only -Republic of Ireland only - 3 days in a 8 day period - £28 , 8 days in a 15 day period - £68, 15 days in a 30 day period - £98 .

Cycling

Rental companies: The Bike Store Ltd., they have 8 offices in the country, head office - 58 Lower Gardiner St., Dublin l tel: 01-872-5931, costs - £6 to £l0 a day, or £30 to £35 /week one way rentals an extra £5; Irish Cycle Hire has many depots located at train stations, pick-up and drop-off available from all depots, location-Mayoralty St. Drogheda, Co. Louth tel: (041) 41067, 42338, 35369; Raleigh Rent-a Bike have over 60 dealers throughout the country - for information and reservations call/write c/o C.Harding for Bicycles, 30 Bachelors Walk, Dublin 1, tel: (353) 1-873-3622, fax: (353) 1 - 873-3622

Hitch-Hiking

One of the best ways to see the island, Irish are very friendly.

Train

Irish Rover RailPass good for all trains in the Republic and Northern Island-prices-5 days in a 15 day period- £75; Irish Explorer Rail (Republic of Ireland) - 5 days in a 15 day period - £60; train rides free with Eurail or InterRail Pass.

Camping

Cost £4 to £6, some hostels have campsites.

Youth Hostels

Prices range from £3 to £7, check with Irish Youth Hostel Association 61 Mountjoy St. Dublin 7, Republic of Ireland, tel: (353) (1) 8304555, fax (353) (1) 830 5808 or Independent Holiday Hostels- ask tourist board for information on Independent Hostel Owners in Dublin, tel: (073)-301 30

Youth Hostel Town Locations and Telephone Numbers

A Aghavannagh (402) 36102; Allihies (27) 73014; Aranmore Island no tel. #; Arthurstown (51) 89411; **B** Ball Hill (73) 21174; Ballinclea (45) 54657; Ballinskelligs (66) 79229; Ballydavid Wood House (62) 54148; Baltyboys (45) 67266; Ben Lettery (95) 34636; Black Valley (64) 34712; **C** Cape Clear Island (28) 39144; Cong (92) 46089; Cork (21) 543289; Crohy Head (75) 21950; **D** Doorus House (91) 37512; **Dublin** - 2 hostels - 1) **Dublin International YH** on 61 Mountjoy St., tel: (1) 8301766; 2) Harcourt St. Hostel on 69/70 Harcourt St., tel: (1) 750430; Dun Chaoin (66) 56121; **E** Errigal (75) 31180; **F** Foulksrath Castle (56) 67674; **G** Galway (91) 27411; Glanmore Lake (64) 83181; Glencree (1) 2864037; Glendaloch (call an Ogie office); Glenmalure (call an Ogie office) **I** Indreabhan (91) 93154; **K** Killala House Youth Hostel (96) 32172; Killarney (64) 31240; Killary Harbour (95) 43417; Knockree (1) 2864036; **L** Limerick (61) 314672; Loo Bridge (64) 53002; **M** Mountain Lodge (52) 67277; **O** Omeath (42) 75142; **P** Pollatomish (97) 84511; **R** Rosslare Harbour (53) 33399; **T** Tiglin (404) 40259; Tra na Rosann (74) 55374; Traenlaur Lodge (98) 41358; **V** Valentai Island (66) 76141; **W** Westport (98) 26644

Work

Unemployment around 20%, work under the table in pubs, restaurants.

Useful Addresses and Tourist Offices

in U.S.

Irish Tourist Board - 345 Park Ave. 17th floor New York, NY 10154 (212) 481-0800 or 1-800-223-6470, fax: (212) 371-9052

in Canada

160 Bloor St. East, suite 1150, Toronto, Ont. M4W 1B9 tel: (416) 929-2777

in the U.K.

Ireland House, 150 New Bond St., London W1Y 0AQ, tel: 0171/493-3201

in Ireland

Tourist Info: in Dublin, at the airport and 14 Upper O'Connell St.tel: 74 77 33
   best source is called Bord Failte Eireann at Baggot St. Bridge in Dublin

Independent Holiday Hostels, UCD Village, Bellfield, Dublin 4 tel: 01-
   260-1634

Union of Students in Ireland Travel, l9 Ashton Quay, Dublin 2 tel: 01-679-8833

Irish Embassies

in U.S.

2234 Massachusetts Ave. NW, Washington, DC 2008 tel: (202) 462-3939

in Canada

130 Albert St., Ottawa, Ont. K1P 5G4 tel: (6l3) 745-8624

in the U.K.

17 Grosvenor Place, London SWIX 7HR, tel: 171 235 2171

Driving Distances (in miles)

From Dublin to cities in Ireland and Northern Ireland

Belfast 104	Galway 136	Londonderry 176
Cork 178	Killarney 233	

Telephone Information: International Code 00, Country Code 353, Main
   City Area Codes: Dublin 1, Cork 21, Limerick 61, Galway 91; time difference (Eastern Daylight) plus 5 hours. Emergency # 999

ISRAEL

A Little History

Israel, the Promised Land of the Bible, is today a thriving, modern country. But the echoes of its ancient past still reverberate at the sites of many of the most stirring events in mankind's history. Jerusalem, a Holy City for Christians, Jews and Moslems, retains its aura of sanctity and welcomes a constant stream of pilgrims of all faiths. The contemporary city of Be'er Sheva (Beersheeba) stands at the threshold of the Negev Desert, as it did in the days of the Patriach Abraham. Eilat, Israel's busy port on the Read Sea, was a seaport in the days of King Solomon.

As Palestine, largely inhabited by Arabs, the country was part of Turkey's Ottoman Empire from the 16th century until World War I, when it was occupied by the British. The Zionist movement in Europe led to the Balfour declaration by Britain in 1917 favouring establishment of a Jewish homeland in Palestine. The struggle between Jewish settlers and Palestinian Arabs and neighbouring Arab states has continued from the 20s to the present. There have been three wars...in 1947, 1967, and 1973. The State of Israel was proclaimed in 1948 at the end of the British mandate. An exodus of Arab refugees, an influx of Jews from all over the world, and widespread Jewish settlement in former Palestinian Arab areas has resulted in a population 82% of whom profess Judaism, and 14% Islam.

Capital - Jerusalem, diplomatic capital is Tel Aviv
Population - 4,800,000
Government - Democratic
Religion - Jewish, Moslem and Christian minorities
Language - Hebrew, English and Arabic
Money - Sheqel, One sheqel equals 100 agorots, Coins of 5 and 10 shekalim, 1 sheqel and 10 & 50 agorots, Notes of 10, 20, 50, 100, 200 sheqels.; due to high inflation exchange money as few times as possible and use travelers cheques of higher denominations - the charge per cheque is approx. $4-$6; you can reduce these charges greatly by using your ATM card; keep all exchange receipts to change your sheqels back to hard currency.
U.S.$1 = 2.6 sheqels, Cdn.$1 = 1.9 sheqels, British £ = 4.3 sheqels
Major Jewish Holidays
1st Day of Pessah, 15 April; 7th Day of Pessah, 21 April; Pentecost, 4 June; Rosh Hashana, 25/26 September; Yom Kippur, 4 October; 1st Day of Sukkot, 9 October; Simhat Torah, 16 October.
Visas
Canadians, Americans and U.K. citizens can obtain their visa at port of entry in Israel at no charge. Make sure you ask for your visa stamp to be put on a separate piece of paper (it should be pointed the separate piece of paper is not always granted) - most Arab countries will not allow you in if they see this stamp in your passport. Don't get your visa for Egypt in Israel as it will state it was issued in Tel Aviv (this advice is only given if you plan to visit other Arab countries). Visas may be extended (for a nominal fee) at offices of the Ministry of the Interior in the following locations: Afula, Akko (Acre), Ashqelon, Be 'er Sheva, Eilat, Hadera, Haifa, Herzelia, Holon, Jerusalem, Nazareth, Netanya, Petah Tiqva, Ramat Gan, Ramla, Rehovot, Safed, Tel Aviv and Tiberias.
The Allenby Bridge, near Jericho, about 40 km (25miles) from Jerusalem, is one of the border checkpoints for tourists between Israel and Jordan. Bus and taxi service is available to the bridge, but no private vehicles are permitted to cross. Canadians and Americans can get the Israeli visa at the bridge.
For Egypt - there are three crossing points: Rafiah, Taba and Nitzana. Four bus companies maintain routes between Cairo and Tel Aviv and Jerusalem via Rafiah. Egged Bus No. 362 leaves Tel Aviv for the Rafiah Terminal daily at 8:50 a.m. and Rafiah for Tel Aviv at 3:00 p.m. Egged Bus No.

l00 leaves Tel Aviv for Cairo and Cairo for Tel Aviv daily at 8:00 a.m. (further information is available at travel agencies in Egypt or Israel).

Taba, just south of Eilat, is open 24 hours a day. Visitors may enter Israel on foot, by private car or in organized tour buses. Regular bus service is available between Taba, Santa Katerina in Sinai and Cairo.

Peculiar Customs and Odd Expressions

Most Israelis speak at a much closer distance than North Americans are used to. Do not back up or shy away. There is also more physical contact, and conversations often involve touching; when an Israeli Arab says "yes", it usually means "possibly"; Israelis love to argue and are rarely at a loss for an opinion; when Israelis constantly gesture with their hands when speaking, they avoid pointing at another person; if you are staying in an Israeli home give candy or flowers as a gift, give or receive your gifts with the right hand; despite Israel's heat, conservative tradition dictates that most of the body remain covered; for hitch-hiking do not use your thumb, point at the ground with your fingers. It is odd to see a Hassid in Jeruselum wearing a fur hat in middle of summer.

Best Festivals

Eilat - an annual festival, highlighted by water sports and moonlight pageants and a summer Jazz festival - contact tourist board for dates in Israel

En Gev Music Festival - held during the Intermediate Days of Passover at Kibbutz En Gev on the Sea of Galilee, it varies each year and changes according to the Jewish calendar

Jerusalem - The Israel Festival approximately May 20 - June 10 - country's leading musical and dramatic talent and world-famous visiting companies and artists. In 1996, a $17 million, 3000th birthday party with festivities and several special performances each month. Tickets for all Jerusalem 3000 events from Bimot, 8 Shammai St. Jerusalem 94631, tel: 011-972-2-250-905 or 240-896. Fax 011-972-2-244-535

Night Activities and More

Jerusalem - visit Yemin Moshe - a restored neighborhood and artists colony with its windmill landmark

Tel Aviv - Israel's round-the-clock city, the country's main nightlife centre

Rent scuba equipment in Eilat and see the coral reefs

Must See Tourists Sites

Acre - north of Haifa - the city walls, El-Jazza Mosque and many other mosques, Crusader's Subterranean City, Turkish Citadel

Beersheba - main city of the Negev desert, interesting place to see the Bedouins chit-chat in the middle of nowhere, Museum of the Negev

Bethlehem - visit the Church of Nativity where Christ was said to have been born; Herodian-fortified mountain palace near Bethlehem; Solomons's Pools

Haifa - Elijah's Cave, Carmelite Monastery, the Bahai Temple and Gardens

Jerusalem - the holiest of cities shared by Jews, Moslems, and Christians; The Citadel, Tower of David, Jaffa Gate, Damascus Gate, Lions' Gate, Church of the Holy Sepulchre, Church of the Ascension, Great Synagogue, the Western Wall, Via Dolorosa where Jésus walked bearing the cross, Dome of the Rock, Mahaneh Yehuda Market- best place for fruits and vegetables

Tel Aviv - Jaffa - visit the bazaars in the old city

Tiberias - Hammt Gader-2,000 year old Roman bath houses

Best Scenery

Caesarea National Park - see the Roman aquaduct, the Roman Theater, Crusader Moat, Crusade gate house

Dead Sea - an incredible tranquil setting, lowest point on earth - 1,312 feet below sea level, your eardrums may hurt from the descent; you can float on the water and read a newspaper without getting it wet; the salt content is ten times that of regular sea water, absolutley nothing lives in the Dead Sea

Eilat - some of the best coral reefs in the world in this resort town south on the Red Sea

Haifa - beautiful beaches

Masada - get to it from Beersheba; great rock overlooking the western shores of the Dead Sea - site of Herod's Palace

Tiberias - resort town of great beaches on the western side of the Sea of Galilee

Places to Avoid

Since absolutely everything closes on the Jewish Sabbath-Friday sunset to Saturday sunset, do not bother trying to get to the borders; avoid staying in the Arab hostels - security is not good or very clean. Don't sleep outside in Jeruselum.

Bus

Somewhat expensive. The Egged Bus Cooperative operates nearly all inter-city bus lines and urban service in most cities and towns as well.

Hitch-Hiking

The best country in the world for hitch-hiking, even the soldiers do it regularly.

Train

There is train service to a few towns from Tel Aviv. There is no railway service on Sabbaths and major religious holidays.

Camping

The campsites are outstanding, offering full sanitary facilities, electric current, restaurants and /or food shops, telephones, postal services, first aid, campfire areas and more; prices are affordable. For site locations, bookings, and other details, contact the Israel Camping Organisation, 22100 Nahariyya. tel: (04) 925392.

Rooms for Rent

An increasing number of Israel's rural settlements (kibbutzim and moshavim) are supplementing their incomes by offering rooms for rent at reasonable prices. Contact your nearest Israel Governmentt Tourist Office. In Jerusalem, contact the government agency called "Good Morning Jerusalem" to book private rooms (Bed & Breakfast) with Jerusalem families range from U.S.$30 to $60, Reservation Center at the main entrance of Binyaney Haóoma opposite the Egged Bus Terminal, tel: 02-511270.

Youth Hostels

More than 30 hostels for all ages. All offer dormitory accommodations and most also provide meals and self-service kitchen facilities. The Israeli Youth Hostel Assoc. arranges individual package tours, called 'Israel on the Youth Hostel Trail' for 14, 21, or 28 days. These include nights in any of 25 hostels, with breakfast and dinner, unlimited bus travel, a half-day guided tour, free admission to National Parks, a map and other informative material. For further information, contact the IYHA. Hostels average U.S. $14 a night including breakfast and sheets. Pay foreign currency to avoid paying the 17% Value Added Tax .

Israel Youth Hostels Association (IYHA), PO Box 1075, 3 Dorot Rishonim St, Jerusalem 91009, Israel, tel: (972) (2) 252706, fax (972) (2) 250676.

Youth Hostel Town Locations and Telephone Numbers

A Akko(Acre) (4) 911982; Arad (7) 957150; **B** Beersheba / Beer Sheva (7) 277444; Bet Meir (2) 342691; **D** Dead Sea, Beit Sara Hostel (57) 84165; Taylor Hostel at Massada along the Dead SeaShore, (57) 84349; **E** Elat (59) 72358; Eilat (7) 370088; Ein Gedi (7) 584165;**G** Golan Heights, Hispin Hostel, (6) 763305; **H** Haifa (4) 531944; Hevel Katif (7) 847596; **J** Jeruselem - 7 hostels - 1) Louise Waterman Wise Hostel on 8 Hapisga St., tel: (2) 420990 2) Ein Karem Hostel ask for street address, tel: (2) 416282; 3) Bet Bernstein Hostel at Town Centre, 1 Keren Hayesod St., tel: (2) 228286; 4) Forest Hostel ask for street address, tel: (2) 416060; 5) Old City Hostel on 2 Rehov Ararat, Jewish Quarter, tel: (2)288611; 6) Beit Shmuel Hostel on 13 King David St., tel: (2) 234748; 7) "Hadavidka" Hostel on 67 Ha nevi'im St., tel: (2) 384555; Judean Hills, Bar Giora Hostel, (2) 911073 **K** Karei Deshe (6) 720601; Kfar Etzion (2) 935133; Kfar Vitkin (9) 666032; Kiryat Anavim (2) 342770; **M** Maayan Harod (6) 531660; Metzada (Massada) (7) 584650; Mitzpe Ramon (7) 588074; **N** Negev Great Crater, Mitzpeh Ramon Hostel (57) 88258; **P** Petah Tiqva (30 9226666; Poriah (6) 750050; **R** Ramat Yohanan (4) 442976; Rosh Haniqra (4) 821330; Rosh Pina (6) 937086; **S** Shlomi (4) 808975; **T** Tel Aviv (3) 5441748; Tiberias (6) 721775; **U** Upper Galilee, Tel Hai Hostel (6) 940043; Upper Galilee, Nature Friends Hostel, (6) 937086; **W** Western Galilee at Nahariyya, Kalman Hostel, (4) 920355; Western Galilee, Sulam Zor Hostel, (4) 823345; Western Galilee, Kiryat Tivon Hostel (4)931482 Central

Galilee, at Safed, Beit Benyamin Hostel, (6) 931086; Cental Galilee, Hankin Hostel, (6) 531660; **Z** Zfat (6) 921086.

Useful Addresses and Tourist Offices
in U.S.
Israel Ministry of Tourism Office, 800 Second Ave. 16th floor, New York, NY 10017, tel: (212) 499-5650, fax (212) 499-5645, other offices in Chicago, Los Angeles, Dallas, Miami
in Canada
Israel Government Tourist Office, 180 Bloor St. West, suite 700, Toronto, Ontario M5S-2V6, tel: (416) 964-3784, fax: (416) 964-2420 or 1-800-669-2369
in the U.K.
Israel Government Tourist Office, 18 Great Marlborough St., London W1V 1AF, tel: 71 434 3651
in Israel
Jerusalem - Government Tourist Information Office, 24 King George St.,tel: 02 241281
Tourism Police, at Kisleh, Old City, tel: 273222; Israel Students Tourist Association, 5 Eliasmar St. tel: 02 225258
Tel Aviv - Government Tourist Inforamtion Office, 5 Shalam Aleichem St. tel:660259/60
Israel Students' Tourist Association at 109 Ben Yehuda St. POB 4451, tel: 247 164
Israeli Embassies
in U.S.
3514 International Drive, Washington, D.C. 20008, tel: (202) 364-5500, fax: (202) 363-4156
in Canada
50 O,Connor St, #1005, Ottawa, Ontario K1P 6L2, tel: (613) 567-6450
in the U.K.
2 Palace Green, London W8 4QB, tel: 957 9500
Foreign Posts in Israel
Tel Aviv
United States Embassay, 61 Hayarkon St., tel: 654338
British Embassy, 1 Ben Yehada St. tel: 5100166
Work
Working on a kibbutz can be a good experience; just make sure you get what is due to you. An alternative is working for a farmer on a moshav (similar to a kibbutz), but the hours can be very long. Think about working at resorts. For kibbutz work contact: your Israeli tourist office before you leave your country or in Israel: contact 1) Ichud Hakevutzot Vehakibbutzim, Hayarkon St. 53 A, Tel Aviv or 2) Hakibbutz hameuchad, Soutin St. 27, Tel Aviv 3) Hakibbutz Haártzi, Leonardo da Vinci St. 13,

Tel Aviv 4) Hakibbutz Hadati, Dubnov St. 7, Tel Aviv. For work on a moshav contact: Workers Moshavim Movement, Leonardo da Vinci St. l9, Tel Aviv. You won't get rich working on a kibbutz or a moshav but you will make some great international friends.

Driving Distances (in km)

From Tel Aviv to cities in Israel:

Akko 117	Haifa 99	Mezada (Masada) 169	Tiberias 132
Ashqelon 63	Hebron 97	Nazareth 102	Zefat (Safed) 168
Be'er Sheva 113	Jericho 101	Netanya 29	
Bet She'an 117	Jerusalem 62	Rehovot 24	
Elat 354	Metulla 196	Rosh Haniqra 137	

Telephone Information: International Code 00, Country Code 972, Main City Area Codes: Jerusalem 2, Tel Aviv 3; time difference (Eastern Daylight) plus 7 hours.

ITALY

A Little History

Italy is one of the oldest countries on the planet. Three thousand years ago the history of Italy was already in full swing. It is also one of the newest, for it united under one government only a hundred years ago. It is generally considered the country of art. But as you delve into its history , you will find that it is also the country of law-makers, builders, and thinkers. Many of the great ideas that guide the world today were born there. In 1753 B.C., Rome was founded by Romulus who, with his twin brother Remus - so runs the tale - had been abondoned as a child on the banks of the river Tiber, and suckled by a she-wolf. Even before this, the future Romans, descendants, they claimed, of Aeneas of Troy, had founded other towns on the Alban Hills.

Romulus was the first of the seven kings of Rome. A republic followed. It lasted for 500 years, the first enduring democratic system of government in the world. Two elected consuls ruled Rome, and a senate made its laws. The Roman legions proved invincible in their many wars and the republic grew and grew so that, by the time Christ was born, it ruled the entire known world. But by this time, emperors (Julius Caesar was the first) had taken the place of the Consuls. As a universal empire, Rome continued for another 400 years establishing everywhere the principles of law by which we still live.

The break-up of the Roman Empire did not mean the end of Italy. Christianity had made its world centre in Rome, and Rome converted and absorbed, through the work of the popes of the Middle Ages, the waves of northern barbarians who poured down into Italy. One thousand years after Rome fell, Latin was still the common language of educated people in the West.

As far back as the dawn of this millennium, the Italian city-states -- Milan, Venice, Florence, Pisa and a hundred others-- emerged from the night of the Middle Ages, and elbowing their way between empire and church, asserted their independence.They governed themselves as republics, with officers elected by the medieval guilds. Many became highly prosperous, and developed the first banking systems known in the West. But while the great nations of Europe were forming, Italy was split up in a dozen separate states, and did not achieve political unity until the 19th century.

In the first World War, Italy fought against the Austrian Empire and, by defeating its armies on the Plave river in 1918, brought about its dissolution. After WW I , in a struggle between the Communists and the Fascists, the dictator, Benito Mussolini, came to power. He ruled for little over 20 years and made the fatal decision, in 1940, to join Hitler's war, but when, in 1943, he was finally ousted by the King, the Italians rose against the Fascists and the Germans and fought on the side of the Allies for the last 18 months of the war.

Population - 57,576, 000
Capital - Rome
Government - Republic
Religion - Roman Catholic
Language - Italian
Money - Lira (L) Coins of 50, 100,200, 500, lire. Notes of 1,000, 2,000, 5,000, 10,000 50,000, and 100,000 lire
U.S.$1 = 1,473 lire, Cdn.$1 = 1,085 lire, British £ = 2,484 lire
Public Holidays
January 1 and 6, Easter Sunday, Easter Monday, April 25, May 1, Ascension Day, June 2, Whit Sunday, Corpus Christi, August 15 (Assumption), November 1, December 8, Christmas Day, December 26
Visas
Americans, Canadians and U.K. citizens do not need visas.
Registration by Tourists
The formality of registering with the police within three days of arrival in Italy is attended to by hotel management. If staying with friends or in a private home, the visitor has to register in person at the nearest police station. In Rome there is a special police information office to assist tourists. Interpreters are available, tel: 461-950 or 486-609
Peculiar Customs and Odd Expressions
Dolce far niente - It's sweet to do nothing (Italians have a relaxed approach to time)

Handshakes may include grasping the arm with the other hand; women may "kiss" good friends on either cheek; close friends and male relatives often embrace and slap each other on the back; Italians "talk with their hands"; a disgruntled man quickly strokes his finger tips under his chin and thrusts them forward- this is a sign of defiance. Suggested gifts to give if you are in someone's home are chocolates, pastries, but never an even number of flowers. If you give wine, be certain it is of excellent vintage. Anyone with bare legs or a sleeveless top will have difficulty getting into any Italian church and especially the Vatican. Rome - you can guarantee your return to Rome if you throw coins into the Trevi fountain while looking the other way!

Best Festivals

Cagliari - May 1-4 - one of the largest and most colorful processions in the world. Several thousand pilgrims wearing costumes dating back to 1657, accompany the statue of a saint on foot, in cars and on horses

Florence - Scoppio del Carro means Explosion of the Cart using fireworks on Easter Sunday

Gubbio - May 15 - one of strangest events - men race carrying huge wooden constructions called ceri

Holy Week Festival (the week before Easter) - best in Sicily and Assisi.

Perugia - Umbria Jazz event in July

Rome - Festa di San Giovanni on June 23 and 24-dancing and eating in the streets

Siena - Il Palio Fest on July 2 and Aug.16-extraordinary horse race in the town's main piazza

Spoleto - Festival of Two Worlds -music, theatre and ballet, late June to late July

Venice - Gondola races on the first Sunday in Sept.; carnival 10 days before Ash Wednesday

Night Activities and More

Florence - best nightclub is Jackie-O; Space Electronic, The Red Garter

Rome - spend the evening sitting outdoors in the piazza San Marco; night-clubs - Radio Londra, Carusso Caffe, Metropolis and many more - visit the tourist board

Must See Tourist Sights

Assisi - Basilica of St. Francis, Roman Forum, Basilica of Santa Chiara; beautiful scenery.

Bologna - oldest university in the world, museums and palaces

Florence - Baptistry of St.John the Baptist, dome of Santa Maria del Fiore (Duomo), Piazzale Michelangelo, Galleria dell Áccademia -see Michelangelo's *David;* 2 major art galleries: Uffizi, Pitti Palace; Straw Market, Centrale market Islands - visit Capri where the Roman emperors vacationed, oldest vacation resort in Italy, and the island of Ischia, bigger with fewer people

Mt. Etna - one of the world's most active volcanoes and largest live one in Europe

Naples - Vesuvius, Castel Nuovo; one of the most beautiful bays in the world

Orvieto - one the most beautiful cathedrals in this town - region of Umbria

Padua - the Wooden Horse (replica) from the Trojan War, Church of Sta. Sofia, Scrovegni Chapel

Palermo - many art treasures and historic buildings

Perugia - hill top town, Gothic Cathedral, Etruscan-Roman Museum, Church of St. Domenico, Paolina Fortress

Pisa - Leaning Tower, Duomo, Gothic church

Pompeii - excavation sites, Roman amphitheatre

Portofino - beautiful but crowded with tourists

Positano - beautiful village built into the mountainside above the sea

Rome - watch out for pick-pockets, Colosseum, Janiculum Promenade, Arch of Constantine, Roman Forum, Baths of Caracalla, Trevi Fountain, National Roman Museum, Piazza Navona - many cafes, artists and tourists; the Spanish Steps; outside Rome - the incredible Catacombs of San Callisto-underground burial place of early Christians

Salerno - one of most scenic regions of Italy

San Gimignano - near Florence, 14 incredible medieval towers

Sardinia - Porto Cervo yacht basin, beautiful beaches

Siena - Town Hall, Music Academy, Duomo, Pinacoteca

Sorrento - beautiful beaches, mountains, fishing village and resort

Vatican City - Basilica of St.Peter, largest in the world, entry will be denied if you wear shorts; Vatican Museum

Venice - Basilica di San Marco, Palazzo Ducale; visit the prisons reached by Bridge of Sighs, San Stefano-Gothic Church, Rialto district, try a gondola, Museo Correr

Best Scenery

Amalfi Drive just south of Sorrento is beautiful

Cortina D'Ampezzo - beautiful mountains

Italian Lakes

Perugia - dramatic view from the hilltop town

Positano - houses climb the mountainside

Rapallo - another mountainside village

Santa Margherita - enchanting resort and an intriguing fish market

Sardinia - powder white beaches, 30 miles of coves, cork trees, mountains

Sicily in the spring

Taormina - 1000 feet above the Straits of Messina, beautiful views

Bus

Basically used where trains can't go - in the mountainous areas; buy tickets on the bus, tobacco shops, at bars by bus stops and of course at the bus station.

Cycling

Best is in Sardinia and along its coast between Alghero and Bosa, in the southern section of this region cycle along the coast of Apulia; and from Florence or Siena to San Gimignano and Volterra. Rentals cost from L8,000-L15,000 a day, rentals available in most towns in Rome- rental locations-Via di Porta Castello 43, near St.Peter's and at Piazza Navona 69, next to Bar Navona. Ask tourist board for all addresses while in Rome.

Hitch-Hiking

Women should avoid Sicily and Sardinia and for the rest of Italy, do it with a male friend. Otherwise, one of the most scenic countries for getting rides in all of Europe.

Train (prices in $U.S.)

Since train passes are affordable, consider the Italy Flexi Railcard- 4 days of travel in 9 days-$116; 8 days in 21 - $164, 12 days in 30 - $210 or the Italian Rail Pass-unlimited travel for 8 days-$152, 15 days-$190, 21 days-$220, 30 days-$264.

Camping

Over 1,700 campsites- prices range from L6,000- L15,000 per person, check with tourist offices.

Accommodation in Private Homes

Available in most cities and towns. Contact the official tourist office of the city or town that interests you and request "un elenco di affittacamere" (list of persons renting rooms). Private homes are not rated by the tourist office.

Meet the Italians

Italy does not have an established 'Meet the Italians' program. However, each city and most towns in Italy have an official tourist office (called either Azienda di Promozione Turistica, or Ente Provinciale per il Turismo, Azienda Autonoma di Soggiorno e Turismo) which could possibly handle arrangements to stay with or meet with an Italian family. Arrangements of this type are usually for tourists staying a considerable length of time (several weeks or more) in an Italian city and not for those staying for brief visits. Requests for these arrangements should be sent several months prior to departure in order to give the tourist offices the time needed to complete final preparations. Since there are over 100 local tourist boards (too many to list), simply contact the Italian Tourist Board to get the list.

Youth Hostels

Nightly charges range from L15,000-L20,000 which include sheets and breakfast in most hostels. More than 50 hostels - youth hostels are called 'ostelli per la gioventu', check with Associazione Italiana Alberghi per la Gioventu, Via Cavour 44, 00184 Roma, Italy, tel: (39) (6) 4871152, fax (39) (6) 4880492.

Youth Hostel Town Locations and Telephone Numbers

A Abetone (573) 60117; Agerola-San Lazzaro (81) 8025048; Agropoli-Paestum (974) 838003; Alghero-Fertilia (79) 930353; Arbus (70) 977155; Ascoli Piceno (736) 259007; Asiago (424) 455138; Assisi (75) 816767; **B** Bari-Palese (80) 5300282; Bergamo (39) 3521126; Bologna - 2 hostels - 1) San Sisto 1 Hostel on Via Viadagola 14, tel: (51) 519202; 2) San Sisto 2 Hostel on Via Viadagola 5, tel: (51) 501810; Bomba Lake (872) 860475; **C** Castroreale (90) 9746398; Como (31) 573800; Cortona (575) 601392; **D** Domaso (344) 96094; **E** Erice (923) 552964; **F** Finale-Marina (19) 690515; **Florence** (55) 601451; **G** **Genoa** (10) 2422457; Guastalla (522) 824915; **L** Lipari (90) 9811540; Lucca (583) 341811; **M** Mantova (376) 372465; Marina di Massa e Carrara (585) 780034; Menaggio (344) 323 56; Milano (2) 39267095; Montagnana (429) 81076; **N Naples** (81) 7612346; **P** Parma (521) 581546; Pesaro (721) 55798; Pescocostanzo (864) 641247; **R** Ravenna (544) 420405; Reggio Emilia (522) 454795; Rieti-Terminillo (746) 261169; Rimini-Miramare (541) 373216; Riva del Garda (464) 554911; **Rome** (6) 3236267; Rovereto 464) 433707; **S Salerno** (89) 790251; San Lazzaro di Savena (51) 6258352; Savona - 2 hostels - 1) Franceschini Hostel on Via alla Stra 29, tel: (19) 263222; 2) Priamar Hostel on Fortezza Priamar, tel: (19) 812653; **Sorrento** (81) 8781783; Soveria Mannelli (968) 6660 79; **T** Tavarnelle Val di Pesa (55) 8077009; **Turin** (11) 6602939; Trieste-Grignano (40) 224102; **V Venice** (41) 5238211; Verona (45) 590360.

Work

If you do find a job the employer will have to get a permit before you start working; getting a permit is very difficult, main legal employment is teaching English, try to work in bars, restaurants, fields.

Babysitting

For au pair work contact: Au Pairs-Italy, 46 The Rise, Sevenoaks, Kent TN13 lRJ, England or L'Aguilone, Mrs. Barbara Merra, via G. Pascoli, 15, 20129 Milano, Italy tel: 02/29529639, fax: 02/657 1563

Useful Addresses and Tourist Offices

in U.S.

Italian Government Tourist Office

630 Fifth Ave., suite 1565, New York, NY 10111 tel: (212) 245-4822 fax: (212) 586-9249

12400 Wilshire Blvd, suite 550, Los Angeles CA 90025 tel: (310) 820-0098, (310) 820-6357

in Canada

1 Place Ville Marie, suite 1914, Montreal, Quebec, H3B 2C3 tel: (514) 866-7667, fax: (514) 392-1429

in the U.K.

1 Princes St., London W1R 8AY, tel: 0171/408-1254

in Rome

Compagnia Italiana Turismo at piazza della Repubblica, contact Dr. Cesare Della Pietra, General Manager

Rome - State Tourist Office in Termini train station, and at via Parigi 5, tel: 06/48899253; Centro Turistico Studentesco at Via Genova 16 tel 46791

Italian Embassies
in U.S.

Embassy - 1601 Fuller St. N.W. 20009 tel: (202) 328-5500

Consulates - 690 Park Ave. New York tel: (212) 737-9100

2590 Webster St. San Francisco tel: (415) 931-4925

There are other consulates in Los Angeles (3), Miami, Orlando, Atlanta, Chicago, New Orleans, Boston, Detroit, Philadelphia, Houston

in Canada

Embassy - 275 Slater St. 21st Floor, Ottawa, Ontario K1P 5H9 tel: (613) 232-2401

Consulates - 136 Beverley St., Toronto, tel: (416) 977-1566

1200 Burrard St. suite 705, Vancouver, B.C. V6Z 2C7 tel: (604) 684-7288

3489 Drummond St., Montreal, Quebec H3G 1X6 tel:(514) 849-8351

in the U.K.

14 Three Kings Yard, London, W1, tel: 3122 200

Foreign Posts in Italy

Venice

British Embassy, Dorsoduro 1051, near the Academia, tel: 041/522-7207

Rome

Canadian Embassy, Via G.B. de Rossi 27.00161, tel: 06/44598750 M-F 8:30-3

British Embassy Via XX Settembre 80A, tel: 06/482-5441 M-F 9:30-12:30, 2-4

United States Embassy, Via Vittorio Veneto 119A, tel: 06/46741 M-F 8:30-12, 2-4

Milan

Canadian Consulate via Vittor Pisani 19, tel: 02/669-7451, M-F 9-12:30, 1:30-5:15

British Consulate, Via San Paolo 7, tel: 02/869-3442, M-F 9:15-12:15, 2:30-4:30

United States Consulate, Via P. Amedeo 2/10, tel: 02/290-045-59 M-F 9-1

Driving Distances (in km)
From Rome to cities in Italy:

Agrigento 1,073	Genova 526	Padova 530	Sestriere 778
Ancona 294	Lucca 335	Palermo 1,043	Torino 702
Assisi 175	Matera 523	Perugia 176	Trieste 715
Bologna 408	Messina 785	Pisa 334	Udine 684
Catania 881	Milano 681	Ravenna 375	Venezia 684
Cortina 716	Napoli 232	Reggio Calabria 799	Verona 549

From Rome to cities in Europe:

Berlin 1,573   Munich 969
Brussels 1,615   Paris 1,532
Copenhagen 2,352   Vienna 1,168
Madrid 2,099

Telephone Information: International Code 00, Country Code 39, Main City Area Codes: Florence 55, Milan 2, Naples 81, Rome 6, Venice 41; time difference (Eastern Daylight) plus 6 hours. Emergency # 113

JORDAN

A Little History

Jordan is a land of history, and new details of its ancient civilizations are coming to light every year, as archaeological teams probe into the Jordanian earth in search of the past. The most recent archaeological work indicates that nomadic Stone Age inhabitants lived along ancient river beds and former lakes as far back as half a million years ago, and by 8,000 B.C., permanent villages of stone and mudbrick houses started to appear on the scene. In the Early Bronze Age, about 3,200 B.C., the start of the true urban life is recorded in a series of small, walled "cities" that appear throughout Jordan.

Situated as it was between the great civilizations of Egypt to the west and Mesopotamia to the east, Jordan was destined to be a busy crossroads. In the Iron Age, during the first millennium B.C., several small kingdoms prevailed. The Arab Nabataeans established their kingdom in southern Jordan at the end of the 1st millenium B.C., with its secure capital at Petra, but finally succumbed to Roman control in the early 2nd Century A.D. The Romans ruled Jordan for several centuries, until the Byzantine empire, with its capital at Constantinople, brought Christianity to the area for some 400 years. In the 7th Century A.D. the armies of Islam came out of Arabia and established the Umayyad Caliphate at Damascus, and Jordan has been Islamic ever since.

In 1916, the Sherif Hussein of the Hijaz launched the Great Arab Revolt against the Ottomans, and by the early 1920s the Emirate of Transjordan was established under the rule of the Emir Abdallah, grandfather of King Hussein. In 1952 eldest son to King Talal, Prince Hussein succeded to the throne at the age of 16. Jordan became fully independent from Great Britain in 1946.

Following the 1948 Arab-Israeli war, the east and the west banks of the Jordan river were united in order to save the parts of Palestine which remained under Arab control at the end of the war from further Israeli occupation. The second mahor Arab-Israeli war (June 1967) resulted in the occupation of the West Bank by Israeli forces.

Capital - Amman
Population - 4, 0l0,000
Government - Monarchy
Religion - Moslem
Language - Arabic, and English
Money - Dinar (JD) one dinar equals 1,000 fils. Coins are 5, 10,50, 100, 250 fils. Notes of 500 fils and 1, 5, 10, 20 dinars
U.S.$1 = .57 fils, Cdn.$1 = .42 fils, British £ = 1.02 fils

Public Holidays

Jordan celebrates the Muslim New Year, the Feast of Ramadan, the Prophet's Birthday, his Nocturnal Journey, and the Feast of Sacrifice. National holidays include Labor Day, May 1, Independence Day, May 25, Arab Renaissance, June 10, King Hussein's accession to the throne on August 11 and King Hussein's Birthday on November 14. Friday is the official weekly day of rest, though many Christian shopkeepers close on Sunday instead.

Visas

You should obtain a tourist visa from any Jordanian embassy or consulate before reaching the country; travelers arriving in Jordan without a visa can obtain one at the airport or border post, usually valid for a months visit and renewable in Amman for two more months. Visas for Americans cost $25, Canadians $65, U.K. citizens $45. You can get a visa in person at the embassy or at the Jordanian border or airport.

Travelers can obtain a permit from the Interior Ministry of Amman allowing them to cross the bridges to occupied West Bank and its Holy Land sites in the Jerusalem-Bethlehem region. Visitors coming into Jordan from the occupied West Bank can return to the West Bank across the Jordan River bridges. Travelers with Israeli stamps or visas in their' passports are now allowed to enter Jordan.

Peculiar Customs and Odd Expressions

If you are asked to have dinner in a Jordanian home by the host, it is customary to refuse twice before accepting. You should refuse seconds of any dish offered unless the host insists a couple of times.

Best Festivals

Aqaba water sports festival - every year in mid-November, includes international class competition in water skiing and other aquatic sports.

Jerash Festival for Culture and Arts - two weeks in August, includes daily performances by Jordanian, Arab and international folklore troupes and performing artists.

Night Activities and More

Most bars and discos are in the hotels.

Must See Tourist Sights
Amman - Roman Theatre, the Temple of Hercules at the Citadel
Aqaba - resort on Red Sea (next to Eilat, Israel) - coral reefs
Jerash - perhaps the best preserved and most complete provincial Roman city in the world
Kerak - capital city of the ancient kingdom of Moab, 12th century castle occupies one third of the city, built in the 12th century
Pella - many outstanding remains in the northern Jordan Valley
Petra - one of the most amazing sights in the world, homes carved out of the rock by the Nabataean Arabs. Nearby, there is an old style tourist village called Teba.
Wadi Rum (near Aqaba) -black, wind-sculptured hills, described as 'valley of the moon'
There are hundreds of Roman, Greek and Islamic sites all over the country.
Best Scenery
Dead Sea - see Israel for facts; the King's highway south of Madaba is beautiful
Mt. Nebo - where Moses first saw the promised land, spectacular view across the Jordan valley and the Dead Sea
Rabad Castle on the way to Jerash
Moujeb Valley, a great canyon on the way to Kerak
Places to Avoid
Be careful with the water, get malaria tablets before you enter the country.
Transportation
Buses are fairly good, tourist buses going into Petra won't stop for you, locals may ask for a little money for a ride. (One man had a shot gun next to him so I ended up throwing him a few coins when he demanded money.) There are two buses to Petra a day in case you can't get a ride.
Hitch-Hiking
Generally good; females, as in other Arab countries should hitch only with a male companion.
Accommodation
Hotels for students cost around U.S.15-$30 for a single, no youth hostels. Try to sleep in the caves in Petra with the Bedouin; women should not sleep outside.
Useful Addresses & Tourist Offices
Jordan Information Bureau, 2319 Wyoming Ave. Washington D.C. 20008, tel: (202) 265-1606, fax: (202) 667-0777
in the U.K.
no tourist office location
Amman- Student Office at IAESTE Office, Faculty of Engineering, University of Jordan, tel: 843 555 ext 1789
Ministry of Tourism in Amman call 42 3 11 for information

Jordanian Embassies
in U.S.
3504 International Drive N.W. 20008, tel: (202) 966-2664 for visas ext 104
in Canada
100 Bronson Ave. suite 701, Ottawa, Ontario K1R 6G8, tel: (613) 238-
8090, fax: (613) 232-3341
in the U.K.
no embassy representation
Foreign Posts in Jordan
Amman
Canadian High Commission, Shmessani Bldg. P.O.Box 815403, tel: 666124
United States Embassy, P.O.Box 354, Jabal, tel: 644 371
British Embassy, P.O.Box 87, Abdain, tel: 832 100
Driving Distances (in km)
From Amman to cities in Jordan and Jeruselem:

Aqaba 337	Madaba 32
Jerash 48	Petra 265
Jeruselem 108	Salt 29
Kerak 132	

Telephone Information: International Code 011, Country Code 962, Main
City Area Code: Amman 6; time difference (East. Daylight) plus seven hours.

IRAN- A DANGEROUS COUNTRY-AVOID IT
IRAQ- A DANGEROUS COUNTRY -AVOID IT
LEBANON- A DANGEROUS COUNTRY-AVOID IT
LIBYA - A DANGEROUS COUNTRY - AVOID IT
FORMER YUGOSLAVIA BEST TO AVOID AT THIS TIME

I don't recommend visiting these countries, but in case you wish to be
adventurous contact their embassies regarding visas.

LIECHTENSTEIN

Population - 25,200
Capital - Vaduz
There is not a lot to say about this country, the capital, Vaduz, has only
5,000 people. The tourist office is at Stadtle 37, tel: 075-232 14 43, they
have a free room-finding service and information on the whole country.
Bikes can be rented from Melliger Ag Kirchstrasse 10, for Sfr20 day, tel:
232 16 06. Climb to the castle (not open to public) for a great view of Vaduz
and the mountains. Malbun is the country's ski resort.

Visas

Americans and Canadians do not need visas.

Telephone Information: International Code 011, Country Code 41, Main City Area Code: Vaduz 75; time difference (Eastern Daylight) plus 6 hours.

LUXEMBOURG

A Little History

The Grand Duchy of Luxembourg is a small state, yet it is older than a thousand years. The passing of the Celts and the presence of the Romans have left significant traces. The Grand Duchy dates back to 963 when Siegfried, count of the Ardennes and founder of the Luxembourg dynasty, had a castle built in a coveted strategic position. This fortress, known as the Gibraltar of the North was beseiged and devastated more than twenty times in four centuries. Burgundians, Spaniards, French, Austrians and Prussians battled to conquer it.

In 1815 the Congress of Vienna settled the destiny of the country by raising the former Duchy of Luxembourg to the rank of a Grand Duchy and by giving it as a personal property to the Dutch King. The personal union between Luxembourg and the Netherlands lasted until 1890. In the same year, after the death of William III, King of Netherlands and Grand Duke of Luxembourg, who left no male descendant, the crown of the Grand Duch passed to the elder branch of the House of Nassau. Since that date Luxembourg has had its own dynasty. In 1964 the present Grand Duke Jean succeeded his mother, Grand Duchess Charlotte who, after having reigned for 45 years, abdicated in favour of her son.

Luxembourg lived long years of oppression and suffering during both World Wars despite its neutrality. A strong resistance was organized in 1944 and many Luxembourgers joined the fighting Allied Forces. In 1948 Luxembourg gave up its neutrality and is now a member of the EC and NATO.

Population - 400,000

Capital - Luxembourg

Government - Constitutional Monarchy

Religion- Roman Catholic, Jewish minority

Language - French (official), Luxembourgeois (National), English widely spoken

Money - francs - same value as Belgian money, but can't be used in Belgium U.S.$1 = 27 francs, Cdn.$1 = 20 francs, British £ = 44 francs

Public Holidays
New Year's Day, Easter Monday, May 1, Ascension Day, Whit Monday, National Day on June 23. Assumption Day-August 15, All Saints Day on Nov. 1, Christmas Day and Boxing Day.

Visas
Americans, Canadians and U.K. citizens do not need visas.

Peculiar Customs and Odd Expressions
Remich- March 1 Ash Wednesday - young people carry a great straw doll round the streets. On the Moselle bridge they set fire to it and throw it into the river to herald the end of a joyful carnival.

Grand Duchy-May 1- Spring Fete, members of local societies go into woods to cut off the first green branches, which they fashion into crowns (symbol of the reawakening of nature), which is carried in processions, led by bands in villages.

Dé neishct wot, Dé neischt wennt; Dé neischt sicht, Dé neischt fennt - The one who doesn't risk anything, doesn't win anything; the one who doesn't seek, doesn't find anything

Bleif jidderén bei sengem Handwierk, da faelllt ké Schneider a ké Scho'ster vum Dâg - If everybody sticks to his business, neither taylor nor shoemaker will fall off the roof

D'Honn dé vill billen, beisse net - Dogs which bark a lot do not bite.

Wien zwe'n Huesen zugleich nolaeft, kritt kén - The one who chases two hares at the same time, will catch neither

Besser eng Kûscht and der Taesch, ewe' eng Fieder um Hut - Better to have bread in your pocket, than a feather on your hat

Vunn âner Leits Lieder, ass gutt Rimme schneiden - It is easy to cut belts from other people's leather

Best Festivals
Echternach - June 6, Whitsun Tuesday - dancing procession -unique medieval religious tradition. The dancers, joined by a line of white handkerchiefs, leap together in a rythmic step - accompanied by musicians who play a haunting polka.

Luxembourg City - Schueberfouer - 14 day fun fair, Aug. 19 to Sept. 11 - includes decorated sheep led by shepherds dressed in folk costume on Sunday, Sept. 3.; also, the Octave - an annual pilgrimage from May 7 to May 21, on May 21 the Luxembourg royal family and foreign Chatholic dignitaries take part in the procession.

Moselle Valley - many wine festivals from August to November.

Night Activities and More
Luxembourg City - in the old center-bars/cafes- Interview, Um Piquet; in the Grund area - the Cafe des Artistes, Scott's Pub

Must See Tourist Sites
Beaufort - castle, wooded hills, gorges

Bourglinster - Baroque parish church, tombs of the knights of Linster

Clervaux - see the Benedictine Abbey of St.Maurice and St. Maur

Luxembourg City - the 'Promenade de la Corniche'; a walking city with many great views, 1000 year-old Three Turrets, museums, the remains of the Luxembourg castle on the Bock rocks; the Grand Ducal Palace; town hall (1830-1838), Cathedral of Notre Dame, Grand Duke Adolphe Bridge

Moselle Valley - visit wine cellars (caves) such as Caves Cooperative, Caves Bernard-Massard

Vianden - 9th century castle, picturesque location on riverbanks of the Our

Best Scenery

Clervaux - feudal castle, Benedictine abbey

Esch-sur-Sure - tiny village on a rocky peninsula, steep cliffs, ruined castle, many tourists

Echternach in region of Little Switzerland - great for hiking, cycling

Luxembourg City - the night-time view of the illuminated Petrusse Valley

Moellerdall and the Ardenne with its feudal castles

Vianden - chair-lift up the mountain for a spectacular view

Bus and Train

Eurail Passes and Benelux Tourrail Pass accepted on the trains; every locality has bus connections: tickets available 1) Network ticket costing 140F, valid for one day from punching until 8 a.m the next day. A book of 5 tickets costs 540F. 2) For small trips, you can buy "short distance" tickets at 35F each, valid for one hour, and for a distance of plus or minus 10 km. A 10 journey ticket costs 270F.

Cycling

Popular activity, bikes can be rented for 400F per day, local tourist offices have cycling maps and rental details, you can take the bike on the train for 35F.

Hitch-Hiking

Stay on the entrance ramps on major highways, except for secondary roads or where there is little traffic, then stay well over on the shoulder to get rides.

Camping

Ask tourist board about campsites, price range from 45-100F, plus the tent.

Youth Hostels

Prices range from 320-620F for one night and breakfast, hostels are located in scenic areas between 16 and 32km apart joined by footpaths. Contact the Centrale des Auberges de Jeunesse Luxembourgeoises, 18 Place d'Armes, BP 374, L-2013 Luxembourg, tel:(352) 225588, enclose an international reply coupon.

Youth Hostel Town Locations and Telephone Numbers

B Beaufort 86075; Bourglinster 78146; **E** Echternach 72158; Eisenborn 78355; Ettelbruck 82269; **G** Grevenmacher 75222; **H** Hollenfels 307037; **L** Larochette 87081; Lultzhausen 89424; **Luxembourg City-Mansfield** 226889; **T** Troisvierges 98018; **V** Vianden 84177; W Wiltz 958039.

Work

No permit needed for seasonal grape picking in the Moselle Valley from mid-Sept. for 6 weeks, wages approximately 1,000F a day plus accommodation and meals. For other work your employer will have to get the permit from the Administration de l'Emploi before you enter the country.

Useful Addresses & Tourist Offices

in U.S.

Luxembourg National Tourist Office-17 Beekman Place, New York, NY 10022 tel: (212) 935-8888 fax (212) 935-5896

in the U.K.

122-124 Regent St., London W1R 5FE, tel: 0171/434-2800

in Luxembourg

The Office National Du Tourisme in Luxembourg has offices at the Luxembourg Air Terminal (just by the main railway station) tel. 481199 or the main office at 77 Rue d'Anvers, PO Box 1001, Luxembourg City tel: 400808; Luxembourg City Tourist office is at place d'Armes tel: 222809

Luxembourg Embassies

in U.S.

2200 Massachusetts Ave.NW Washington DC 20008 tel: (202) 265 4171

in Canada

3877 Ave. Draper, Montreal, Quebec H4A 2N9 tel: (514) 489-6052

in the U.K.

27 Wilton Crescent, London, SW1X 8SD, tel: 235 69 61

Foreign Posts in Luxembourg

Consulate of Canada c/o Price Waterhouse & Co., 24-26 Ave. de-la-Liberte, L-1930, Luxembourg, tel: 352-4024-201

British Embassy, 14 Blvd Roosevelt, L-2450, Luxembourg, tel: 352 22 98 64

United States Embassy, 22 Blvd. Emmanuel-Servais, 2535 Luxembourg, tel: 352 460 123

Driving Distances (in km)

From Luxembourg to cities in Luxembourg:

Beaufort 42	Remich 22
Bourglinster 15	Vianden 46
Clervaux 64	

From Luxembourg to cities in Europe:

Belgrade 1,870	Madrid 1,695	Prague 1,029
Berlin 790	Milan 1,200	Rome 1,701
Brussels 213	Munich 659	Vienna 1,104
Budapest 1,351	Oslo 1,694	Warsaw 1,377
Copenhagen 1,085	Paris 376	

Telephone Information: International Code 00, Country Code 352, Main City Area Code: Luxembourg no area code; time difference (Eastern Daylight) plus 6 hours.

A Little History

Monaco, because of its natural, scenic beauty, strategic position on the Mediterranean and excellent port, has always been prized territory. During the Roman era it was part of the Alps-Maritimes Province, and Julius Ceasar launched his Greek campaign from its port. In 1997, the Grimaldi family will celebrate its 700th anniversary ruling Monaco. In the 13th century, much control of Monaco was a point of contention between two rival Italian factions, the Guelphs and the Ghibellines. The Guelphs, from whom the Grimaldis descended, held Monaco for a short time in the 13th century under the leadership of Rainier I. They were overthrown in 1295 by the Ghibellines, who claimed the fortress of Monaco for the Republic of Genoa. In retaliation, Francois Grimaldi disguised himself as a monk and successfully led a small army against the fortress in 1297. Today the legacy of his daring victory is recorded on the coat of arms of Monaco, which bears two monks brandishing swords.

The French Revolution took a toll on European royalty and the Grimaldis were not exempt. During the rule of Prince Honore III, Monaco was annexed by France, members of the Monegasque royal family were imprisoned and Monaco was renamed Port Hercules. The annexation was cut short with the abdication of Napoleon in 1814, when all rights of the Grimaldis were restored. But with Napoleon's downfall, Moncaco was placed under the protection of the King of Sardinia as specified by the Treaty of Paris in 1815. In 1861, Monaco agreed to relinquish half its territory to France in exchange for cash and its recognition as an independent state. On the throne arrived Prince Charles III who realized that most of Monaco's lands and natural resources had been lost. To re-establish an economic base in the Principality he decided that the answers to his nation's predicament were tourism and gambling. Prince Charles III established the Societe des Bains de Mer which consisted of a handful of hotels, a theater and a casino. Three years later, Prince Charles III created the opulent district of Monte-Carlo.

Population 30,000
Language - French, English and the old language called Monegasque
Money - see France
Peculiar Customs and Odd Expressions
Cun de pan e de vin se po envita u vizin - With bread and wine invite your
neighbor
L'Agliufa drisa u bataglio - Garlic makes the ... raise
Ku manessa lechessa - Who cooks, licks

Metew ou luvasu fo save da u metelu per ave u luvasu- You must give up
the small fish to have the bigger one
Dopu ave ben mangiau e ben bevu una pipa va un scu - After drinking and
eating, nothing is better than a pipe
E megliu u vin caudu che l'aiga fresca ku manessa lechessa - Mulled wine
is better than cool water

Best Festivals
Monte Carlo International Tennis Championships in April; Monte Carlo Grand
Prix: May; Fireworks Festivals: July 18th, organized by Italy, August 15th,
organized by Sweden, Aug. 19th, organized by the Canary Islands.

Night Activities & More
Monte Carlo Casino - Le Cabaret
Disco's - Tiffany's, L'X Club, Boccaccio, Jimmy's
Monte Carlo Tennis Open - in May
Monte Carlo - Grand Prix de Monaco - held in May

Must See Tourist Sites
Old Monaco - tiny antiquated village that sits on the rock, Yacht Harbour,
National Museum, Oceanographic Museum, Wax Museum, the gardens
of the Principality, Princess Grace Rose Garden, colorful changing of
the guard at 11:55 a.m. daily at the palace

Best Scenery
Take the winding roads up the mountain hills and see the princely yachts
with the beautiful ocean and coastline below.

Useful Addresses & Tourist Offices
in U.S.
Monaco Tourist Office, 845 3rd Ave., New York, NY 10022 (212) 759-
5227 or 1-800-753-9696, fax (212) 754-9320
42 S. Dearborn St. suite 550, Chicago, IL 60605 tel: (312) 939-7863
in the U.K.
Monaco Government Tourist and Convention Office, 3-18 Chelsea Garden
Market, Chelsea Harbour, London, SW10 OXE, tel: 171 352 9962
in Monaco
National Tourist Office, 2a Boulevard des Moulins, Monte Carlo tel: 92 16 61 16
Telephone Information: International Code 19, Country Code 33, Main
City Area Code: Monte Carlo 93, time difference (Eastern Daylight) plus 6 hours.

MOROCCO

A Little History

Morocco has been inhabited since man appeared on Earth by a people of
shepherds living in tents. Some led a semi-nomadic life farming and set-

tling in villages. The origin of the fair-skinned Berber people remains a mystery.

In ancient days Phoenicians and Carthaginians established trading posts along the Moroccan coast. Succeeding the Phoenicians, the Romans made northern Morocco an imperial province and named it Mauritania Tingitania. The Roman hold waned and once again the Berbers became masters of their country.

Although the first Moslem expedition, viewed by the natives as an invasion, was repelled, the second, led in 708 by Moussa Ibn Noussair, was welcomed as the tribes felt the need for organized religious docrine. Thus, the arrival of Islam.

From 1757 onwards Moroccan trade was open to free competition among European nations. However, drought and famine led the sultans to return to a more isolationist policy.

Some Western countries engaged in complex intrigues in the hope of claiming Morocco as their own. Under the French Protectorate, established through the treaty of 1912, Morocco was occupied for 44 years, but the resistance of King Mohmmed V and the people brought the Protectorate to an end in 1956.

Population - 25,208,000
Capital - Rabat
Government - Constitutional monarchy
Religion - Islam, with freedom of religion for Jewish and Christians minorities
Language - Arabic, French and Spanish widely spoken, Berber in certain regions, English in cities and tourist resorts
Money - Dirham (dh) One dirham equals l00 francs. Coins of 5, l0, 20, 50 francs, and of l, 5 dirhams. Notes of 5, l0, 50, 100 dirhams. Travelers'cheques are accepted at nice hotels restaurants and many shops-some charge 5-6% transaction fee-barter for a lower rate. Best place to exchange money at banks - spend all your dirhams before you go.
U.S.$1 = 7 dirhams, Cdn.$1 = 5 dirhams, British £ = 12 dirhams
Public Holidays
New Year's Day, Jan. 1st; Independence Manifest, Jan. 11th; Throne Day, March 3rd; Labour Day, May; National Holiday, May 23rd; Youth Day, July 9th; Reunification Day, Aug. 14th; Revolution of the King and the people, Aug. 20th; Green March Anniversary Nov. 6th; Independence, Nov. 18th; These religious holidays dates vary according to the muslim calendar: Idul Fitr, Idul Adha, Moharrem 1st, Idul Mawlid Ennabaoui.
Visas
Canadians, Americans and U.K. citizens don't need them for stays up to 90 days.

Peculiar Customs and Odd Expressions

Many hustlers who want to sell you something, befriend you , invite you into their home and won't take 'no 'for an answer. You are not in danger, but you may find their behaviour annoying. Try to shop with a local so you don't get ripped off-prices quoted are always exaggerated; be sure to remove your shoes when entering a Moroccan home or a mosque.

Shaking hands is common, and friends will usually greet each other by kissing.

Best Festivals

1996, January 21 starts the Ramadan month long fast-no eating,drinking, smoking during the daylight hours, at sunset things get a little wild

Marrakesh - National Folklore Festival in early June

Night Activities and More

Night-clubs, discos, oriental cabarets in major cities. There is a rich and varied folklore, with traditional dances and songs.

Must See Tourist Sites

Casablanca - visit the old medina area

Fez - Talaa Kebira - streets of merchants, donkeys; Bou Inania Medersa-beautiful 14th century school; Kairaouine Mosque; Attarine Medersa-large bronze door

Dar el-Makhzen - the royal palace with the golden doors

Marrakesh - Place Djemaa El Fna-fun-filled plaza with snake charmers, trained monkeys, salesman on microphones, interesting foods, 200 foot-tall Koutoubia Minaret; Souks-interesting collection of markets; Ben Youssef Medersa - school; Majorelle Gardens

Rabat - Kasbah des Oudaias - fortified camp-10th century; Hassan Mosque; Mohammed V Mausoleum; Chellah Necropolis - fortified walls; Musee Archeologique - museum

Taza - nearby are the Friouato caverns that reach a depth of 180 metres - a staircase leads down into a veritable underground palace

Places to Avoid

Algerian - Moroccan border just north of Mauritania-armed conflict between the Moroccan army and Polisario guerrillas.

Tangier - many hustlers present, little to see or do

Best Scenery

Mediterranean coast

Valleys and Gorges of the Dades and Ziz

Valley of the Draa and Todra Gorge

Massive sand dunes of Merzouga, the Souss, the Sahara

Tetuan - beautiful view of the coast and Rif mountains

High Atlas Mountains - views of desert-beautiful, near Marrakesh by bus.

Transportation
ONCF - national rail co., only InterRail accepted here; CTM - buses are cheap and fairly comfortable, splurge and go lst class.
Hitch-Hiking
Fairly good, as is the case in all Arab countries, women should hitch with a man.
Camping
There are more than 85 campsites situated near beaches and in wooded areas, pay 10 dirhams/person, 10 dirhams/tent.
Youth Hostels
Contact Federation Royale Marocaine des Auberges de Jeunes, Parc de la Ligue Arabe, BP No. 15998, Casa-Principale, Casablanca 21000, Morocco, tel: (212) (2) 470952, fax (212) (2) 472024; HI-affiliated hostels in l6 cities - very cheap -10-40 dirhams per night.
Youth Hostel Town Locations and Telephone Numbers
A Asni (44) 7713; Azrou (56) 3733; **C** Casablanca (22) 0551; Chefchaouen (98) 6031; **F** Fes (62) 4085; **L** Laayoune (10) 3402; **M** Marrakech (44) 7713; Meknes (52) 4698; **O** Oujda (68) 0788; **R** Rabat (72) 5769; **T** Tanger (94) 6127.
Useful Addresses & Tourist Offices
in U.S.
Moroccan National Tourist Office, 20 East 46th St. suite 120l, New York, NY l00l7 (212) 557-2520, fax (212) 949-8148
in Canada
2001 Rue Universite, suite l460, Montreal, Quebec H3A 2A6 tel: (514) 842-8111
in the U.K.
205 Regent St., London W1R 7DE, tel: 0171/437-0073
in Morocco
contact either Syndicat d' Initiative or ONMT -abrochures and maps, advice, hotel information in most towns and cities.
Morocco Tourist Agency at rue el Jazair 22, Rabat tel: 662 65
Student Union of Morocco at rue Zayanes 55, Agdal, Rabat
Main post office (for poste restante) at Poste Principale, Rabat
Moroccan Embassies
in U.S.
1601 21st St. N.W. Washington, D.C. 20009, tel: (202) 462-7979, fax: (202) 265-0161
in Canada
38 Range Rd., Ottawa, Ontario K1N 8J4, tel: (613) 236-7391, fax: (613) 236-6164
in the U.K.
49 Queen's Gate Gardens, London, SW 75NE, tel: 071 581 5001

Foreign Posts in Morocco
Rabat
Canadian Embassy, 13 Rue Jaafar Assadik, tel: 07/77-13-75
British Embassy, 17 Blvd. Tour Hassan, tel: 07/72-09-05/6, M-F 8-11:30, and 2-5 for British Citizens
United States Embassy, 2 Av. de Marrakesh, tel: 07/76-22-65 M-F 8:30-12:30, 2:30-5:30
Tangier
British Consulate, 9 Rue Amerique de Sud, tel: 09/03-58-07, Open summer, M-Th 9-12, 2-5, F 9-12, fall-spring M-Th 9-12:30, 2:30-5:30, F 9-12
Driving Distances (in km)
From Rabat to cities in Morocco:

Agadir 602	Fes 198	Meknes 138	Tanger 278
Alhoceima 445	Kelaa 316	Nador 537	Tarfaya 1,146
Beni-Mellal 260	Kenitra 40	Ouarzazate 528	Tetouan 294
Casablanca 91	Khemisset 81	Oujda 541	Tiznit 699
Chaouen 239	Khouribga 205	Safi 347	
Errachidia 482	Laayoun 1,251	Settat 157	
Essaouira 442	Marrakech 321	Smara 153	

Telephone Information:
International Code 00, Country Code 212, Main City Area Codes: Meknes 5, Tangier 9, Casablanca 2, Rabat 7; time difference (Eastern Daylight) plus 5 hours.

NETHERLANDS

A Little History

During the Middle Ages, the area now known as the Netherlands comprised a group of autonomous duchies (Gelre and Brabant) and counties (Holland and Zeeland) together with the bishopric of Utrecht. Under Charles V (1500-1558) these territories, together with present-day Belgium and Luxembourg, formed the Low Countries which were part of the Burgundian-Hapsburg Empire. In 1568 a number of the provinces rebelled against Philip II of Spain, sovereign ruler of the Burgundian-Hapsburg domains. The revolt, led by Prince William of Orange, who has gone down in Dutch history as 'the father of the Netherlands', marked the beginning of the 80 Years War of Independence. The Peace of Westphalia (1648) recognized the Republic of the Seven United Provinces as an independent state.

In the 17th century, Dutch merchants formed the Dutch East India Company and established trading posts all over the world. The need to protect trading interests led to several wars, notably against England. The prosperity brought a great flourishing of culture, notably painting, 17th century Dutch artists such as Rembrandt, Vermer and Frans Hals are famous all over the world.

The Netherlands remained independent until the French Revolution. In 1795 it became a vassal state of the French Empire and in 1810 was annexed to France by Napoleon.When the French occupation ended in 1814, the Kingdom of the Netherlands came into existence, comprising the Netherlands and present-day Belgium and Luxembourg. Belgium became independent in 1839. The country was a major colonial power until WWII, but after 1945, Indonesia became independent, as did Surinam in 1975.

Population- 15,500,00
Capital - Amsterdam (government seat is in The Hague)
Government - Constitutional monarchy
Religion - Protestant and Roman Catholic
Language - Dutch and English
Money- Guilder (florin) (f) One guilder equals 100 cents. Coins of 5, 10, 25 cents, and of 1, 2 1/2 and 5 guilders. Notes of 5, 10, 25, 50, 100, 250, 1,000 guilders
U.S.$1 =1.50 guilders   Cdn.$1 = 1.10 guilders   British pd = 2.4 guilders
Public Holidays
New Year's Day, Good Friday, Easter Monday, Queen's Birthday April 30,
   Ascension Day, Whit Monday, Christmas and Boxing Day.
Visas
Americans, Canadians and U.K. citizens do not need visas.
Peculiar Customs and Odd Expressions
Personal compliments should only be given when people know each other
   well; when using the telephone, one should say "Good morning, this is
   Mr. White speaking," instead of just "Hello"; do not shake hands with
   your left hand in your pocket; aside from handshakes, there is very little
   public contact in this country, close friends or relatives may hug briefly.
   If you see someone in the distance that you know, it is considered rude to
   shout at the person to get their attention; Sucking one's thumb is a way
   of saying "I don't believe you"; to indicate that someone is miserly or
   cheap, glide the forefinger down the bridge of your nose a few times. To
   indicate someone is a little deranged the Dutch will brush away imagi-
   nary insects flying in front of one's face. Offering a tiny applause by
   tapping the thumbnails together is a snide gesture which means "We are
   not amused". Don't talk to someone while chewing gum. Gifts to give
   your host are chocolate or candy, avoid giving wine.
Best Festivals
Amsterdam - Holland Festival, every June-music, dramas, concerts, opera, ballet

The Hague - mid- June for 10 days the Pasar Malam Besar Fesival - largest Eurasian Festival in the world runs for 11 days and nights

Den Haag - Parkpop- Europe's biggest free pop festival June 25

Lisse (1 hr. from Amsterdam by car) - tulip festival, starts late April, early May

Maastricht - Netherlands largest carnival fest. before Lent

Ootmarsum - ritual of vloggelen at Easter-bonfires, hymn-singing and a lot of hand-holding as the daily processions wind through the old streets

Night Activities and More

Amsterdam - Holland Casino and the Lido; Disco's -PH 31, Escape, Mazzo, Bamboo Bar, Cafe Alto, Juliana's, Paradiso and Milky Way offer an eclectic variety of small, up and coming bands

Must See Tourist Sights

Aalsmeer - permanent flower wholesale market open Mon-Fri. 7:30 a.m.- 11:00 a.m.

Amsterdam - Royal Palace, Oude Kerk -14th century church, viewing tower open June-Sept., Nieuwe Kerk-New Church next to Royal Palace, Anne Frank House, Westerkerk -Western Church, Rijksmuseum Museum, Art Gallery, De Waag, Munt-Mint Tower 1490, Heineken Brewery, walk through the Red Light District with a friend

Den Bosch - St.Jans Cathedral

Groningen - low-tide walks in mud that can come up to your thighs-can be risky-tours in summer only

Haarlem - Frans Hals Museum

Maastricht - Fine Art Fair in March, Basilica of Our Lady, Basilica of St.Servis, south of the city are limestone caves of mount St. Pietersburg with more than 198 miles of tunnels

Rotterdam - busiest port in the world, Ethnology Museum, spectacular view from the Euromast of the Rhine-Mass delta

The Hague - Houses of Parliament, Royal Palace, Peace Palace, Madurodam- miniature city

Utrecht - Domkerk/Domtoren - Holland's oldest Gothic chruch and high- est tower - supervised climb to the top

Places to Avoid

avoid the drug-infested Oude Zijds Achterburgwal

Best Scenery

Keukenhof garden - spring tulips

Hoge Veluwe - country's largest national park, one hour east of Amster- dam by car

Bus

There is a nationalized bus system-very cheap and reliable-good for get- ting to out of the way places. Information for buses and trains call toll- free, the national transportation line at 06-9292.

Cycling

There are 10,000 km of bike lanes - bikes can be rented at 100 railway stations, rentals cost 9-15 guilders one way/day, 9 guilders for taking it on a train, you must return the bike to the same train station where you rent the bikes from. Cycle the Gelderse Vallei route from Leusden on the easter edge of Utrecht province, through Gelderland and Overijssel, all the way to Drenthe.

Hitch-Hiking

Very good. Stay off the highways, stay at the entrance ramps, try the International Lift Centre (Nieuwezijds Voorburgwal 256, tel. 020/622-4342). You pay a 10 guilder fee plus 10-20 guilders for processing it-they will find you drivers to go anywhere in Europe-you pay the driver 6 cents per km.

Train

Very reliable, frequent and inexpensive, you can get to most cities by train. Day Pass - 58 guilders 2nd class; Link ticket to bus/tram network - 6.50 guilders; Summer Tour -3 days unlimited travel by train within a 10 day period in June, July, and August - one person 79 guilders 2nd class, two persons 134 guilders 2nd class; Tour Time - allows unlimited train travel on any 4 days within a specified 10 day period in Holland and Belgium - 65 guilders (including public transport link rover in Holland 80 guilders extra). These tickets are available in June, July, and August to passengers under 19 years of age from any of the main Dutch railway stations. None of these passes are available in North America.

Camping

Prices average 5 guilders adult, tent 2 guilders, over 1,000 sites, contact NBT for list of sites.

Youth Hostels

Prices range from 21-24 guilders, 5 guilders more if you are a non-member, prices include breakfast, over 38 hostels in the country; hostels are open to anyone regardless of age who has an international youth hostel card. Stichting Nederlandse Jeugdherberg Centrale NJHC, Prof Tulpstraat 2, 1018 HA Amsterdam, Netherlands, tel: (31) (20) 5513155; fax (31) (20) 6234 986.

Youth Hostel Town Locations and Telephone Numbers

A Ameland (5191) 54133; **Amsterdam** - 2 hostels - 1) **Vondelpark Hostel** on Zandpad 5, tel:(20) 6831744; 2) **Stadsdoelen Hostel** on Kloveniersburgwal 97, tel: (20) 6246832;Apeldoorn (55) 553118;Arnhem (85) 420114; **B** Bakkum (2518) 52226; Bergen op Zoom 1640) 33261; Bruinisse (1113) 1480; Bunnik (3405) 61277; **C** Chaam (1619) 1323; **D** Domburg (1188) 1254; Doorwerth (85) 334300; Dordrecht (78) 212167; **E** Egmond (2206) 2269; Elst (8384) 1219; **G** Gorssel (5733) 1615; Grou (5662) 1528; **H** Den Haag (The Hague) (70) 3970011; Haarlem (23) 373793; Heeg (5154) 42258;Heemskerk (2510)

32288; Hoorn (2290) 14256; **M** Maastricht (43) 434404; Meppel (5220) 51706; **N** Nijverdal (5486) 12252; Noordwijk (2523) 72920; **O** Den Oever (2271) 1272; Oldebroek (5255) 1335; **R** Roderesch (5908) 19114; **Rotterdam** (10) 4365763; **S** Scheemda (5979) 1255; Schiermonnikoog (5195) 31257; Sneek (5150) 12132; Soest (2155) 12296; **T** Terschelling (5620) 2338; Texel - 2 hostels - 1) Panorama Hostel on Schansweg 7, tel: (2220) 15441; 2) De Eyercoogh on Schansweg 7, call the Panorama Hostel for res. **V** Valkenswaard (4902) 15334.

Work

Only European nationals can legally work, try under the table work in the bulb fields from June to Oct. To work legally, you must have a permit before entering the country. Contact: Studenten Werkbureau Amsterdam, Koniginneweg 184a Amsterdam.

Babysitting

Amsterdam - students contact Kriterion, 24 Tweede Rozendwaarstraat, tel: 624-58-48 office hours: 5:30 p.m. - 7 p.m.

Useful Addresses & Tourist Offices

in U.S.

Netherlands National Tourist Office

355 Lexington Ave. 21st Floor, New York, NY 10017 tel: (212) 370-7360

225 N. Michigan Ave.,suite 326, Chicago IL 60601 tel: (312) 819-0300 fax::(312) 819-1740

9841 Airport Blvd. Los Angeles, CA 90045 tel: (310) 348-9015, fax (310)-348-9344

in Canada

25 Adelaide St. East, suite 710, Toronto, Ontario M5C 1Y2 (416) 363-1577, fax: (416) 363-1470

in the U.K.

25-28 Buckingham Gate, London SW1E 6LD, tel: 0171/630-0451

Amsterdam - tourist office location is opposite the Central Station and at Leidsestraat 106, tel: 626 64 44; in Rotterdam-at Coolsingel 67 and the Central Station; in The Hague-in Scheveningen at Gevers Deynootweg 126 and the Central Station

Dutch Embassies

in U.S.

4200 Linnean Ave, N.W. Washington DC 20008 tel: (202) 244-5300, fax: (202) 362-3430. Consulates in over 35 cities.

in Canada

350 Albert St. ste. 2020, Ottawa, Ont. K1R 1A4 tel:(613) 237-5030 fax: (613) 237-6471

Consulates in all major cities

in the U.K.

38 Hyde Park Gate, London, SW7 5DP, tel: 71 584 5040

Foreign Posts In Netherlands
Amsterdam
British Embassy, General Koningsln, tel: 020/676-4343, visa information,
   tel: 020/675-8121, open weekdays 9-12, 2-3:30
United States Embassy, Museumpl. 19, tel: 020/664-5661, M-F 1:30-5:15
The Hague
Canadian Embassy, Sophialn 7, tel: 070/361-4111 M-F 9-1, 2:15-3:30
Driving Distances (in km)
From Amsterdam to cities in the Netherlands:

Assen 102	Haarlem 12
Broda 65	Maastricht 133
Eindhoven 75	Rotterdam 45
The Haag 35	Utrecht 24
Groningen 125	

From Amsterdam to cities in Europe:

Belgrade 2,272	Madrid 1,877	Rome 1,986
Berlin 685	Milan 1,382	Stockholm 1,418
Brussels 218	Munich 1,100	Vienna 1,495
Budapest 1,753	Oslo 1,318	Warsaw 1,242
Copenhagen 709	Paris 558	

Telephone Information: International Code 00, Country Code 31, Main
   City Area Codes: Amsterdam 20, The Hague 70, Rotterdam 10; when
   dialling within the Netherlands all area codes should be prefixed with a
   '0'; time difference (Eastern Daylight) plus 6 hours. Emergency # 222222

NORWAY

A Little History

A number of small communities in what is now Norway gradually or-
ganized into larger regions in the 9th century, at the end of which King
Harald Fairhair unified the realm and became its first ruler. In the Mid-
dle Ages, Vikings from Norway settled communities in England, France,
Ireland and Iceland. Viking seafarers found their way to the shores of
North America 500 years before Columbus. Norway and Denmark
formed a kingdom from 1380 to 1814, when Norway adopted its own
Constitution and entered a union with Sweden after the Napoleonic Wars.
In 1905, Sweden and Norway went separate ways and Norway was again
an independent state.

The country is long, narrow and mountainous, with more than 30
per cent of land covered by forests, rivers and lakes. Of the over 4 million
population, 30,000 Norwegians are Samis, otherwise known as Lapps,

an ethnic minority with a language and a culture all their own. Most live north of the Arctic Circle.

Oil and gas fields in the North Sea have for the past two decades been a cornerstone of the economy. More than 80 per cent of all Norwegian exports go to other Nordic countries and the European Union.

Population - 4,249,800
Capital - Oslo
Government - Constitutional monarch
Religion - Lutheran
Language - Norwegian, English widely spoken
Money - Krone One krone equals 100 ore. Coins of 50 ore, and 1, 5, 10 & 20 kroner. Notes of 50, 100, 500, 1,000 kroner
U.S.$1 = 6 kroner, Cdn.$1 = 4 kroner, British £ = 9.6 kroner
Public Holidays
New Year's Day; Labour Day, May 1; Constitution Day, May 17; Easter, Ascension, Whitsun and Christmas.
Visas
Americans, Canadians and U.K. citizens do not need visas.
Peculiar Customs and Odd Expressions
Nar varen kommer, er vinteren glemt- When spring arrives, winter is forgotten
Den som lever lenge, far mang lide- One who lives long, will suffer much
Det hev alle sett vogga, men ingen si grav - Everybody has seen their cradle, but nobody's seen their grave
En mork morgen kan bli en lys dag - A dark morning can turn into a bright day
Om hundre ar er allting glemt - In a hundred years everything will be forgotten
The handshake is standard greeting for men and women; people greet each other by saying "Morn" (which means "morning") at any time of day. Avoid speaking loudly as Norwegians are fairly quiet people. A toss of the head means "come here"; talking with one's hands in one's pockets is considered too casual. Examples of gifts to give to your host in their home are flowers, wine, and chocolates. Wearing shorts is not common in urban areas. On the great national holiday, May 17, people celebrate Midsummer with bonfires and dancing. Private parties, family gatherings and especially weddings are always an excuse for great celebrations. A real country wedding lasts three days.
Best Festivals
Bergen International Music Festival - for 12 days, late May early June when the sun is up the most
Forde International Folk Music Festival - Norway's largest folk music fest. with 200 musicians and dancers from around the world, July 4-7
Holmenkollen Ski Festival - outside of Oslo - Feb. 18-March 17

Molde International Jazz Festival - over 400 jazz musicians, late July

Oslo - Opera Festival in June, Jazz Festival in August

Tromso - Northern Lights Festival - classical & contemporary music performances-celebrates the return of daylight, Feb. 3-12, also in Tromso-Midnight Sun Festival - international choir festival

Night Activities and More

Oslo - Concert Hall performances, as well as the Norwegian Folk Museum and Munch Museum; discos-Barock, Night Cap, Watefront, Smuget, Rockefeller

Must See Tourist Sights

Aalesund - the breathtaking view from the Aksla Mountain summit

Lillehammer - home of the 1994 Winter Olympics

Oslo - Akershus Festning og Slott-Akerhus Castle and Fortress, Norwegian Folkemuseum, Norsk Sjofartsmuseum-Maritime Museum, Vikingskiphuset-Viking Ship House Domkirken-Old Cathedral, Gamle Aker Kirke - church built in 1100

Trondheim - best cathedral in Scandinavia

Best Scenery

between Eidfjord and Fossli - Voringsfoss waterfall and waterway

Bergen - gateway to the fjords, take the funicular to Mt. Floien - spectacular view of the city and fjords

Jotunheimen National Park - beautiful mountains

Midnight Sun viewing - in Alta May 21-July 23; Bodo June 4-July 8, Nordkapp May 14-July 30, Stamsund May 28-July 17, Tromso May 21-July23

Molde - offers a spectacular view of 87 mountain peaks

Sognefjord - from the glaciers to the ocean, one of Norway's best fjords-62 miles long

Oslo - lakes, hiking trails and forests on the outskirts of the city

Peer Gynt mountain country - near Rondane, Jotunheimen, and Lillehammer

Bus

Best for going through the fjords and to go north of Bodo; students using Nordturist, Scanrail, InterRail can get discounts from companies; great for getting off the beaten path, get a pay-as-you-go open-ended bus ticket.

Cycling

Bikes can be rented at train stations and must be dropped off at the same train station. Rental prices are very reasonable.

Hitch-Hiking

A great way to see Norway, people of all ages will give you a ride.

Train (Cdn. prices)

Norway Rail Pass - 2nd class May-Sept.- 7 days $189, 14 days $243, 3 days/1 month-$129; Scanrail pass bought outside of Scandinavia - prices for 2nd class -5 days in a 15 day period $159, youth- $140, any 10 days in

1 month -1st class $275, 2nd class $239; one month unlimited 1st class $399, 2nd class $339. Eurail and InterRail also good for free travel in Norway.

Camping
There are approximately 520 campgrounds, sites cost 40-150 kroner, 10-15 kroner extra per person; camping in the woods is allowed, at no cost.

Farm Stays
Enjoy hiking, fishing, horseback riding, while working on a farm - two night minimum, prices start at U.S.$75/night based on double occupancy, to book-Borton Overseas 1-800-843-0602 or 1-612-824-4415; or Scan World Tours 1-800-323-8308 or 1-312- 792-2053

Meet the Norwegians
Meet the locals on a personal basis. The organization 'Friends Overseas' has been helping tourists since 1972 to get in touch with Norwegians. Send a self-addressed, stamped envelope to Friends Overseas, 68-04 Dartmouth St. Forest Hills N.Y. 11375, with your name, age, address, telephone number, occupation or occupational goal, whether you are traveling alone or with a friend, spouse or family, and approximate date of trip. Inquiries from outside the U.S. should include an International Postal Coupon.

Youth Hostels
Contact Norske Vanrerhjem, Dronningensgate 26, N-0154 Oslo, Norway tel: (47) 22421410, fax (47) 22424476; 100 youth and family hostels for people of all ages- 40-165 kroner includes breakfast - all you can eat.

Youth Hostel Town Locations and Telephone Numbers
A A (yes that is the name of the town!) 76091121; Andalsnes 71221382; Alta 78434409; Alvdal 62487074; Andenes 76141222; **B** Balestrand 57691303; Bardufoss 77836336; Bergen 55292900; Bo i Telemark 35950800 Bodo 75525666; Borlaug 57668750; Bomlo 53425300; Boverdalen 61212064; Byrkjelo 57867321; **D** Dombas 61241045; **E** Evje 37930422; **F** Fauske 75646706; Flam 57632121; Folldal 62493108; Forde 57826500; **G** Geilo 32090300; Gjovik 61171011; Graddis 75694341; Grungebru 35072765; **H** Halden 69180077; Hamar 62526060; Harstad 770641154; Hellesylt 70265128; Helligskogen 77715460; Hemsedal 32060315; Hitra 72445979; Honefoss 32122903; Honningsvag 78473377; Horten 33073026; Hovden 37939522; **J** Jorpeland 51748382; **K** Kabelvag 76078103; Kalvatn 70050130; Karasjok 78466135; Karmoy 52820040;Kongsberg 32732024; Kongsvinger 62817222; Kragero 35983333; Kristiansand 38028310; Kristiansund 71671104; Kviteseid 35053261; **L** Lakselv 78461476; Leira 61362025; Levanger 74081638; Lillehammer 61262566; Lillesand no tel. #; **M** Mandal 38261276; Melbu 76157106; Meraker 74810234; Mjolfjell 56518111; Mo i Rana 75150963; Moss 69255334; **N** Narvik 76942598; Nesbyen 32071397; Nordreisa 77764960; Notodden 35010460; **O** Odda 53641411; Oppdal 72421330; Orje 69811750;

Osen 62444934; Oslo - 2 hostels - 1) Haraldsheim Hostel on Haraldsheimvn 4, tel: 22222965; 2) Holtekilen Hostel on Michelets vei 55, tel: 67533853; **R** Rjukan 35090527; Roros 72411089; Rost 76096109; Rovaer 52718011; **S** Sand 52799901; Sarpsborg 69145001; Sjoa 61236200; Sjusjoen 62363409; Skien 35599551; Skjolden 57686615; Skjak 61214026; Snasa 74151057; Sogndal 57672033; Stamsund 76089334; Stavanger 51532971; Stryn 57871106; Sunndalsora 71691301; Svalbard 79022450; **T** Tonsberg 33312848; Tromso 77685319; Trondheim - 2 hostels - 1) Rosenborg Hostel on Weidemannsvei 41, tel: 73530490; 2) Jarlen Hostel on Kongensgt 40, tel: 73513218; Tvedestrand 37164109; **U** Ulefoss 35945770; Uvdal 32743020; **V** Vaeroy 76095375; Val 74394190; Valdresflya 94107021; Valldal 70257511; Voss 56512017.

Work

You need a work permit before entering the country-if you are successful in finding a job, then apply to your nearest Norwegian embassy- it can take 3 months to process. Best chances for work are at hotels, and fish-processing plants. If you want to work on a farm for bed and board and pocket money contact: Norwegian Committee for International Information and Youth Work, Akersgate 57, Oslo l, Norway.

Babysitting

Oslo- contact 22-60-73-70

Useful Addresses & Tourist Offices
in U.S.

Norwegian Tourist Board
655 Third Ave. New York, NY l00l7 tel: (212) 949-2333
in the U.K.

Charles House, 5-11 Lower Regent St., London W1N 7DE, tel: 0171/839-6255

Oslo Tourist Information Office- located at City Hall (Radhuset) and Central Station tel: 22830050;

Norwegian Embassies
in U.S.

Royal Norwegian Embassy, 2720 34th St.N.W., Washington, D.C. 20008-2714, tel: (202) 333-6000
in Canada

Royal Norwegian Embassy, Royal Bank Centre, 90 Sparks St. ste. 532, Ottawa, Ontario KlP 5B4, tel: (613) 238-6570
in the U.K.

Royal Norwegian Embassy, 25 Belgrave Square, London, SW1X 8QD, tel: 44 171 2357 151, fax 245 6993

Foreign Posts In Norway

Oslo
Canadian Embassy, Oscargate 20, N-0352, tel: 22/46-69-55, M-F 8-3:30

British Embassy, Thomas Hefyes Gate 8, tel: 22/55-24-00, M-F 9-12:30
United States Embassy, Drammensveien 18, N-0255 Oslo, Te. 22/44-85-
   50, M-F 9-12
Driving Distances (in km)
From Oslo to cities in Norway:

Beitostolen 225	Lillehammer 170	Tyinkrysset 262
Dombas 328	Lom 345	
Fagernes 187	Otta 281	
Gjovik 127	Ringebu 230	

From Oslo to cities in Europe:

Amsterdam 1,311	Bucharest 3,163	Prague 1,572
Belgrade 2,530	Copenhagen 609	Rome 2,614
Berlin 1,228	Madrid 3,195	Stockholm 530
Brussels 1,536	Munich 1,861	Vienna 1,873
Budapest 2,132	Paris 1,876	Warsaw 1,822

Telephone Information: International Code 095, Country Code 47, Main
   City Area Codes - no area codes; time difference (Eastern Daylight) plus
   6 hours. Emergency # 000

POLAND

A Little History

The Polish state is over a thousand years old. Poland had gaps in its historical biography: 123 years of partitions and captivity (1795 - 1918) and the
Nazi occupation during World War II. But even before these two episodes,
there had been periods when the Polish state had been half awake - during
the regional partitions, which meant dispersion of the center of authority in
the 12th and 13th centuries, the Swedish deluge in the 17th century and the
many years of Polish soil being ruled by various powers.

   In 1980 a mass labour movement and strikes spread throughout the
country over the introduction of higher prices for meat. In addition, pro-
testers began to advance political demands, such as forming free trade
unions. Lech Walesa was the leader of Solidarity which was involved in
the Gdansk strike. In 1981, martial law was imposed throughout the country, resulting in violent clashes and thousands of arrests, including Walesa.
In 1982 Walesa was released, martial law suspended and by 1984 35,000
detainees had been released.

   In 1990 internal divisions within Solidarity, reflected disagreements
regarding the pace of reform between Walesa and Mazowiecki who favored
a more cautious approach. He and Walesa formed their own alliance,and
President Jaruzelsi agreed to resign to permit direct presidential elections.

Walesa won overwhelmingly and became President in 1990.

Poland became a member of the European Community in 1991. Following the disintegration of the communist bloc, Poland became a member of NATO in 1994.

Population - 38,000,000
Capital - Warsaw
Government - Parliamentary democracy
Religion - Roman Catholic
Language - Polish, some German and English
Money - Old Zloty Notes of 100, 200, 500, 1,000, 2,000, 5,000, 10,000, 20,000, 50,000, 100,000, 500,000 1,000,000 and 2,000,000. New zloty notes of 10, 20 and 50. Coins 1, 5, 10, 20, and 50 zloty; best exchange rates at private exchange office (Kantory Wymiany Walut), also go to banks, some hotels, and Orbis offices - higher commission charged there. U.S.$1 = 2 zloty, Cdn.$1 = 1.5 zloty, British £ = 4.2 zloty(New currency.)
Visas
Americans and U.K. citizens do not need a visa for up to 90 days. Canadians-need a visa-1) you can get a transist visa-valid for 2 days 2) single-entry visa-valid up to 90 days 3) double-entry visa-allows 2 entries within 90 days. Apply for visas outside the country and allow one week for processing. Visas for Canadians cost $55, $85 if you want it the same day.
Peculiar Customs and Odd Expressions
Poles love to stay up late, talking and drinking - leaving early may insult them, so be prepared for a long night; vodka is the main drink - don't get trapped in a vodka-drinking contest, you'll lose, your glass will be refilled every time until the vodka runs out; shake hands when you meet a Pole and when you leave. Close Polish friends or relatives may greet each other effusively, with much hugging and kissing of cheeks; when a Pole flicks his finger against his neck, he is inviting you to join him for a drink. Don't chew gum while speaking to someone; Poles are shocked at the sight of anyone throwing trash anywhere but in a trash receptacle; avoid loud behaviour in public; Poles tend to be quiet. When asking directions from strangers, a woman should approach either a policeman or another woman - approaching a man will probably be interpreted as flirting. Give a gift to your host that is in short supply in Poland such as coffee, perfume, or American cigarettes.

Gosc w dom, Bog w dom - A guest in your house is God in your house
Czym chata bogata tym rada - Whatever riches are in our house, are yours
Best Festivals
Warsaw - Jazz Jamboree in September
Zakopane - International Festival of Highland Folklore, Aug. 19-27-folk art fairs, song performances, shows of folk costume and concerts

Night Activities and More
Krakow - student clubs- Pod Jaszczurai, Rotunda
Warsaw - Guinness Bar, Heineken Bar, Riviera Remont, Akwarium Jazz
Club; discos - Stodola, Hybrydy
Must See Tourist Sites
Gdansk - home of Solidarity, marketplace, waterfront walkway, in the Old
Town - St.Catherine's Church
Lublin - beautiful 13 century castle, with its Chapel of the Holy Trinity and
cellars
Oswiecim is Auschwitz - German concentration camp
Krakow-Kazimierz - Jewish ghetto on south side, Stara Synagoga -old syna-
gogue; Jagiellonian University built 1364; Pauline Church and Monas-
tery on the Cliff; Rynek Glowny - Europe's largest medieval market-
place; Wawel Cathedral - built 1364, Wawel Castle
Malbork - started in 1230 - huge Castle of the Teutonic Knights
Poznan -Town Hall, nearby Kornik and Rogalin estates
Torun - Rynek Staromiejski -Old Town Square; 14th century Ratusz - town hall
Tyniec - The 15th century Benedictine Abbey - beautiful, along a river
Warsaw - Plac Zamkowy-the Stare Miasto plaza-see King Zygmunt 111
statue; 14th century Zamek Krolewski (Royal Castle); Rynek Starego
Miasta(Old Town Square); Jewish Ghetto; Lazienki Park and Palace;
Mausoleum of Struggle and Martyrdom; near Warsaw - town of Wilanow
- beautiful baroque palace
Best Scenery
near Krakow -Wieliczka Salt Mines and the Ojcow National Park - gorges,
caves, Prudnik River
Carpathians and Sudetes mountains along the southern border
Ojcow National Park in the Pradnik river valley, many Stone Age caves
Tatra Mountains (highest ones in the Carpathian chain)-below is the town
of Zakopane
Transportation
EurailPasses and InterRail passes not accepted. Look into the Polrail
Pass - U.S.$35-8 days, U.S.$50-1 month; buses are modern and com-
fortable.
Cycling
There are only a few rental offices. Obtain addresses at tourist office.
Hitch-Hiking
Actually encouraged - one of the best places in the world. You don't need
to use your thumb, just stand there or wave to the car to get a ride. The
government used to reward drivers with a gift for the number of hitch-
hikers they picked up!!!!!!
Accommodation
Inexpensive hotels charge U.S.$10-$30/night.

Camping

Over 200 campsites, pitch a tent in rare primeval forest areas and in the centres of major cities, contact, Polish Federation of Camping and Caravaning, ul. Grochowska 331, Warsaw, tel (22) 106-050.

Youth Hostels

More than 170 hostels, most in countryside, contact Polish Association of Youth Hostels for more information: Polskie Towarzystwo Schronisk Mlodziezowych, 00-791 Warszawa, ul. Chocimska 28, Poland, tel: (48) (22) 498354, 498128, fax (48) (22) 498354, 498128. Expect to pay about 60,000 -120,000 zl (U.S.$3-$6 per night), plus linen if needed. Here's a good sample of hostels covering the whole country.

Youth Hostel Town Locations and Telephone Numbers

B Bialogard 2257; Bialowieza 12560; Bialystock 524250; Bieca 14; Bielsko-Biala 27466; Bobrka k/Krosna (Chorkowka 13097); Bobrka k/Soliny (Solina 61); Brzeg 3620; Bydgoszcz 227570; **C** Chelm 640022; Chmielno no tel. #; Ciechanow 2404; Cieszanow 14; Czarnkow 2744; Czestochowa 243121; **D** Dabrowka (Kazimierz Dolny 10202); Deblin 354; Dzialdowo 2753; **E** Elblag 326125; Elk (87) 2514; **F** Folusz no tel. #; Frombork 7453; **G** Gdansk -3 hostels - 1) Walowa Hostel on ul Walowa 21, tel: (58) 312313; 2) Grunwaldzka Hostel on Grunwaldzka 244, tel: (58) 411660; 3) Kartuska Hostel on ul Kartuska, tel: (58) 326044; Gdynia no tel. #; Gliwice 313799; Glogowek 780; Glucholazy 340; Gniezno (66) 264609; Gora Sw Anny 7976; Gorzow Wielkopolski 27470; Grudziadz 20821; **H** Hawa no tel. # **I** Inowlodz 101122; Istebna Zaolzie 49; **J** Jablonki 26; Jaslo 3464; Jelenia Gora 25746; **K** Kalisz 72636; Kamien (Mirsk 336); Kamien Pomorski 20784; Karpacz - 2 hostels -1) Pegaz Hostel on ul. Karkonoska 17, tel: (75) 19264; 2) Liczyrzepa Hostel on ul Gimnazjalna 9, tel: 19290; Katowice 1555968; Kazimierz Dolny 10327; Kedzierzyn-Kozle 23182; Kielce 23735; Klebowo 1360; Kletno 358; Klodzko 2524; Kobylnica 150103; Konin-Goslawice 427235; Koronowo 822229; Koszalin 426068; Krakow - 3 hostels -1) Oleandry Hostel on ul Oleandry 4, tel: (12) 338822; 2) Kosciuszki Hostel on ul Kosciuszki 88, tel: (12) 221951; 3) Szablowskiego Hostel on ul Szablowskiego 1C, tel: (12) 372441; Kudowa Zdroj (Kudowa 661); Kuraszkow 102571; **L** Ladek 645; Lanckorona 7589; Lebork 6211905; Legnica 25412; Lesko 6269; Lidzbark Warminski 3147; Lidzbark Welski 178; Lubiel Nowy (Wyszkow 1019); Lublin 30628; Lubsko 720398; Ludwikow 336178; Laka Prudnicka 72952; Lacznik 76378; Lagow kKielc 104; Lagow k Zgorzelec 6608; Lazy no tel. #; Leba 661435; Lodn - 2 hostels -1) Zamenhofa Hostel on ul Zamenhofa 13, tel: 42) 366599; 2) Obroncow Stalingradu Hostel on ul Obroncow, tel: (42) 330365; Lubowo (66) 7618; **M** Machocice 112165; Malbork 2511; Miedzyzdroje (91) 80344; Mikolajki no tel. #; Mosina 132734; Myczkow (Polanczyk 5); Mysliborz no tel. #; **N** Narty (Jedwabno 77); Nowa Kaletka (89) 130883; Nowa Slupia 16; Nowy Jaromierz no tel: #; Nowy Sacz

23241; Nysa 3731; **O** Olawa (71) 33156; Olsztny - 2 hostels - 1) Kopernika Hostel on ul Kopernika 45, tel: 276650; 2) Zolnierska Hostel on ul Zolnierska 13 A, tel: (89) 277534; Opole 33352; Osieczna 350134; Ostroleka 2135; **P** Paczkow 6441; Paslek 2431; Pawelki no tel. #; Pila (67) 32583; Pilsudskiego (89) 2745 10; Pisz no tel. #; Pobierowo 62107; Polanica Zdroj (Polanica 212); Polom 75469; Poznan - 3 hostels - 1) Berwinskiego Hostel on Berwinskiego 2/3, tel: 663680; 2) Biskup- inska Hostel on ul Biskupinska 27, tel: 221063; 3) Gluszyna on ul Gluszyna 127, tel: 788461; Przechlewo 25; Przemkow 465; Przemysl (10) 6145; Pulawy (831) 3367; **R** Radom 40560; Radomsko 4495; Rawicz 452014; Rozdziele (Zegocina 87); Rybnica Lesna no tel. #; Rzeszow 34430; **S** Sandomierz 22652; Sanok 30925; Sepolno Krajenskie (88) 2686; Sieradz 5652; Slawkow Niwa 193 1100; Slupca 752018; Slupsk 24631; Smigiel 30; Smoldzinski Las 116348; Stalowa Wola 20429; Strzelno 89567; Stuposiany no tel. #; Szamotuly (668) 21165; Szczecin - 2 hostels - 1) Monte Cassino Hostel on ul Monte Cassino 19a, tel: 224761; 2) Grodzka Hostel on ul Grodzka 22, tel: 332924; Szczyrk 78933; Szczytno 3992; Szklarska Poreba 172141; Szydlowiec 171374; Swieta Katarzyna 112206; **T** Tarnobrzeg 222212; Tarnow 216916; Torun - 2 hostels - 1) Rudacka Hostel on ul Rudacka 15, tel: 27242; 2) Zolkiewskiego Hostel on ul Zolkiewskiego 49, no tel. #; Trzemeszno 80031; **U** Ustron 3501; **W** Walbrzych 77942; Walcz 2749; Warsaw - 6 hostels - 1) Karolkowa Hostel on ul Karolkowa 53a, tel: 328829; 2) Smolna Hostel on ul Smolna 30, tel: 278952; 3) Reytana Hostel on ul Reytana 6, tel: (22) 499164; 4) Lokalna Hostel on ul Lokalna 51, tel: 129521 5) Klopotowskiego Hostel on ul Klopotowskiego 36, tel: 185317; 6) Solidarnosci Hostel on Al Solidarnosci 61, tel: 184989; Wloclawek 362410; Wolin 61637; Wroclaw - 2 hostels - 1) Kielczowska Hostel on ul Kielczowska 43, tel: (71) 253076; 2) Kollataja Hostel refer to Killataja 20, tel: (71) 38856; **Z** Zagorz 22022; Zakopane 66203; Zamosc 6011; Zaniemysl 57289; Zawoja (Zawoja 106); Zieleniec no tel. #; Zielona Gora 79840; Zlotoryja 783674; Zerkow 15; Zywiec 2639.

Useful Addresses & Tourist Offices
in U.S.
Polish Tourist Office, 275 Madison Ave. suite 1711, New York, NY 10016
   tel: (212) 338-9412 fax (212) 338-9283
Chicago - 333 N. Michigan Ave. IL 60601, tel: (312) 236-9013
in the U.K.
82 Mortimer St., London W1N 7DE, tel: 0171/580-8028
in Poland
Warsaw-Almatur-student-travel organization-info on university dorms-at
   UI. Kopernika 23 tel: 022/26-35-12 PTTK has general info and runs
   youth hotels-Swietokrzyska 32, tel: 022/24-14-18; Orbis -government
   tourist agency-not too helpful , at ulica Bracka 16 tel.022/26-02-71;
Center for Tourist Information at plac Zamkowy 1 tel. 02/635-1881
Polish Association of Youth Hostels at Chocimska 28

Polish Embassies
in U.S.
2640 16th St. N.W., Washington, D.C. 20009, tel: (202) 234-3800.
Consulates in Chicago tel: (312) 337-8l66, New York City tel: (212) 370-
  5300, Los Angeles tel: (310) 442-8500
in Canada
443 Daly St. Ottawa, Ontario KlN 6H3 tel: (6l3) 789-0468, fax: (613)
  789-1218
Consulates in Toronto tel: (416) 252-5471, Vancouver tel: (604) 688-3530,
in the U.K.
47 Portland Place, London, W1N 3AG, tel: 580 4324
Foreign Posts in Poland
Warsaw
Canadian Embassy, UI, Matejki 1-5, tel: 022/29-80-51, M-F 8:30-1, 2-5
British Embassy, Al. Roz, tel: 022/28-10-01
United States Embassy, AI. Ujazdowskie 29-31, tel: 2/628-3040, M-F 8:30-5
Krakow
United States Consulate, ul Stolarska 9, tel: 012/22-77-93, M-F 9-3
Poznan
United States Consulate, ul. Chopina 4, 61-708 Poznan, tel: 61/52-95-86
Driving Distances (in km)
From Warsaw to cities in Poland:

Gdansk 343	Poznan 303
Katowice 285	Wroclaw 348
Krakow 294	Zakopane 398

From Warsaw to cities in Europe:

Berlin 586	Madrid 2,423	Rome 1,790
Belgrade 1,810	Milan 1,386	Stockholm 1,025
Brussels 1,906	Munich 1,095	Vienna 690
Budapest 1,786	Oslo 1,490	
London 1,570	Paris 1,481	

Telephone Information:
International Code 00, Country Code 48, Main City Area Codes: Warsaw
  2 or 22, Krakow 12, Poznan 61; time difference (Eastern Daylight) plus
  6 hours.

PORTUGAL

A Little History

Portugal was founded as a independent kingdom more than eight centuries
ago, having established its frontiers, virtually as they are today, by the mid-

dle of the 13th century. Dom Dinis (1279-1325) built 50 fortresses along the border with Castile and signed a pact of friendship with England (1308). Relations with England, Portugal's oldest ally, have always been favourable since this early pact, later cemented by the Treaty of Windsor (1386) and the marriage of England's Philippa of Lancaster to Dom Joao I. Their third son, Prince henry the Navigator, spent the early 15th century developing the national nautical skills. Vasco da Gama found the sea route to India and Bartolomeu Dias rounded the Cape of Good Hope at the southernmost tip of Africa. From Madeira and the Azores, India, Africa and Japan, and to Brazil to the west, the extraordinary voyages initiated by the Portuguese during the 15th century led to discoveries of new peoples and cultures.

Portugal in the 16th century became the hub of a world-wide maritime empire that brought riches beyond belief to the tiny country. When Dom Sebastiao launched a doomed crusade aginst the Moors, he and most Portugal's nobility were killed, leaving Portugal without a ruler and allowing his uncle Philip II of Spain to force his family claim to the vacant throne by invading the country in 1580. Thus Portugal endured sixty years of Spanish domination, becoming unwillingly involved in Spanish wars against England, Holland and France. After a coup in 1640, Dom Joao IV succeeded in regaining Portugal's independence. A devastating earthquake in 1755 severely damaged much of the Algarve and razed Lisbon, killing up to 60,000 people. After becoming a republic in 1910 and living through the 40 year Salazar regime, democracy was established in 1974.

Portugal has been a member of the European Community since 1986. At present it enjoys a climate of political stability, with a high rate of industrial and economic growth. Some 800 km long from north to south it is about 250 km wide.

Population - 10,421,000
Capital - Lisbon
Government - Republic
Religion - Roman Catholic
Language - Portuguese
Money- Escudo ($) One escudo equals 100 centavos. Coins of 50 centavos, and 1, 2 1/2, 5, 10, 20, 50, 100, 200 escudos. Notes of 500, 1,000, 2,000, 5,000 and 10,000 escudos
U.S.$1 = 136 escudos, Cdn.$1 = 100 escudos, British £ = 227 escudos
Public Holidays
January 1, Shrove Tuesday, Good Friday, April 25, May 1, June 10, Corpus Christi, Aug. 15, Oct. 5, Nov. 1, Dec. 1, Dec. 8 and Christmas Day. In addition each town celebrates the feast of its own patron saint (St. Anthony in Lisbon, June 13).

Visas
Americans, Canadians and U.K. citizens do not need visas.

Peculiar Customs and Odd Expressions
It is impolite to eat while walking down the street. A warm, firm hand-shake is the standard greeting. For social occasions, men greet each other with an embrace; women kiss on both cheeks. "Come here" is indicated with the hand down and waving fingers or hand. It is impolite to point. To call a waiter to your table in a restaurant, simply raise your hand. Chocolates or other candy is a preferred gift to give to your host.

Best Festivals
Check with Portuguese National Tourist offices for exact dates:

Braga - Holy Week - hundreds of barefoot penitents carrying torches

Lisbon - Feast Day of St. Anthony-June-singers, musicians, dances, bon-fires etc.

Santarem - National Agricultural Fair-bullfights, dancing, folk singing

Oporto - St. John's Festival from June l6-24, on the 23rd at night the locals amicably hit each over the head with plastic hammers and leeks

Ovar - Carnival Festival weekend before Lent, a very lively occasion with masked processions, carnival floats and battles of flowers

Tomar Festival - June/July-every two years the harvest is celebrated by young couples dressed in traditional costumes with towering displays of flowers on their heads

Viseu- in the mountains - Calvacade of Vila de Moinhos in June, cavalcade of horsemen, folk song and dance groups

Night Activities and More
Lisbon-must see fado tavern, the Machado; discos- Banana Power, Mundial, Beat Club, Crazy Nights, Fragil, Plateau, Alcantara Mar

Must See Tourist Sights
Abrantes - great castle

Alcobaça - Real Abbey of Santa Maria-monastery 1178, a small stream runs through the kitchen to catch the fish; Tombs of Dom Pedro, Inês de Castro

Batalha - Santa Maria da Vitória monastery

Çoimbra - the Old Cathedral, Santa Cruz church, Machado de Castro Museum

Evora - walled city, hilltop cathedral, superb Roman temple of Diana (2nd Century A.D.)

Fátima - the Shrine of Our Lady - pilgrims come from all over the world, more notably May 13 and Oct. 13, see night procession with candles

Faro - Bones Chapel - l250 human skulls

Guimaraes - beautiful medieval town, visit the Peneda Geres National Park, mountainous countryside

Lagos -1000 year old Moorish castle, St.Anthony's Church

Lisbon - Coach Museum-unique vehicle collection, Old Moorish Castle, Tower of Belem, Jerónimos Monastery, Naval Museum, the Old Cathedral, Ancient Art museum-best museum in Portugal, 12th century St.George's Castle, Praca do Comercio-magnificent 'Black Horse' Square and its Arch, charming ancient moorish quarter with narrow winding steets and picturesque white-washed houses

Madeira Islands - if you can afford to fly there, check with tourist office, Zarco Bay is breathtaking

Monsaraz - walled town, beautiful views, medieval atmosphere

Nazaré - enchanting fishing village

Óbidos - medieval walled town with a castle

Oporto - Vila Nova de Gaia wine lodges, Ferreira caves

Porto - hilltop cathedral, the Torre dos Clerigos - a baroque church

Sagres - great fishing, fortress and lighthouse - spectacular

Sesimbra - bustling fishing village with good beaches, brightly painted boats and old Moorish castle

Sintra - a definite 'must see' 800 year old Moorish ruins, fairytale palaces-Pena Palace

Tomar - one of the oldest and most charming towns in Portugal, magnificent Chapter House Manueline window, 15th century Gothic Church of St.John the Baptist

Best Scenery

Albufeira - the 'St.Tropez of Portugal'

Algarve Province - along the southern coast, unusual rock formations

Azores Islands - nine islands a haven of tranquility and great natural beauty where pollution is unknown

Madeira Island - walk along the footpaths which follow the unique and complex Madeiran irrigation system of 'levadas' (the intricate channels which carry water from high up in the mountains down through the terraced farms, and to villages

Porto - picturesque riverside area, impressive bridges

Serra da Estrela - highest mountain range in the country - lies between Guarda & Castelo Branco

Sintra - beautiful mountain road through a national forest preserve, gardens, Royal Palace

Tomar - Castle of the Templars - medieval military structure

Bus

The best bus company is Rede Expressos, giving good service, and fair prices.

Cycling

Not common, rentals in tourist areas for 1500$ a day, charges range from 250$ to 1000$ for taking a bike on a train, register early so it can be registered as baggage.

Hitch-Hiking
A wonderful way to see this country.

Train
Portugal's trains are either slow or too expensive.some sample one way fares, 2nd class from Lisbon: to Oporto 1760$, to Coimbra 1760$, to Faro 1600$, along the Lisbon coast one class only from Lisbon to Estoril 170$, to Sintra 170$; or try the Tourist Pass: for 7 days 17,000$, 4 days 27,000$, 21 days 38,000$.

Country Houses and Manor Accommodation
You can stay at manor or residential houses, rustic houses in the countryside and farm-houses. It is advisable to book in advance, either directly with the owners of the houses, your travel agent or one of the associations. A deposit may be required; full payment is required before arrival. Prices include board and breakfast; other meals can sometimes be arranged by prior request, contact:

ACT - Associacao das Casasem Turismo Alto da Pampilheira, Torre D-2, 3. A-2750 Cascais, tel: (01) 284 29 01/ 284 44 64 or Privetur - Associacao Portuguese de Turismo de Habitacao, Rua Castilho, 209-1. Ft. -1000 Lisboa, tel: (01) 65 49 53/ 286 82 32, Reservations: Pan Europa, tel: (01) 56 34 01

or

Turihab - Associacao de Turismo de Habitacao, Praca da Republica, 4990 Ponte de Lima; tel: (058) 94 27 29

Camping
Very cheap, prices average at 350$ plus 380$ for a tent the best sites are in remote areas. It is advisable to have a camping carnet.

Youth Hostels
Contact: Associacao de Utentes das Pousadas de Juventude, Av Duque de Avila 137, 1000 Lisboa, Portugal, tel: (351) (1) 3559081; fax (351) (1) 3528621; or Movijovem at Avenida Duque d' Avila 137, l000 Lisbon tel:01 355 9081; hostels are called pousadas de juventude, prices range from 1,100-2,000$ per night which includes bedlinen and breakfast, reserve ahead if possible, fewer than 25 hostels in the country.

Youth Hostel Town Locations and Telephone Numbers
A Alcoutim (81) 46004; Areia Branca (61) 422127; **B** Braga (53) 616163; **C** Coimbra (39) 22955;Foz do Cavado (53) 981793; **L** Lagos (82) 761970; Leiria (44) 31868; **Lisbon**- on rua Andrade Corvo 46, tel: (1) 3532696; Lisboa - Catalazete YH - outside of Lisbon- on 2780 Oeiras, tel: (1) 4430638; **M** Mira - 2 hostels - 1) PJ de Mira Hostel on 3070 Praia de Mira, tel: (31) 471275; 2) Mira Youth Camping Park in the Parque de Campismo de Jovens, tel: 31) 47275; **O** Ovar - opening Jan., 1995; **P** Penhas da Saude (75) 25375 ; Portimao(82) 85704; Porto (2) 6065535; **S** Sao Martinho (62) 999506; Sintra (1) 9241210; **V** Vila

Nova de Cerveira (51) 796113; Vila Real de Santo Antonio (81) 44565; Vilarinho das Furnas (53) 351339.

Work

Best chance is teaching English, contact - Intercultura, Avenida Almirante Reis 219, R/C Esq, Apartado 1395, Lisbon 1011 tel: 01 849 3505. For jobs lasting longer than 30 days contact the Ministry of Labour to get a work permit; for jobs under 30 days all you need is written permission from the Ministry of Labor.

Useful Addresses & Tourist Offices
in U.S.

Portuguese National Tourist Office
590 Fifth Ave., New York, NY 10036-4704 tel: (212) 354-4403, fax: (212) 354-4403

in Canada

Portuguese Trade & Tourism Office, 60 Bloor St. West, suite 1005, Toronto, Ontario M4W 3B8, tel: (416) 921-7376, fax: (416) 921-1353

in the U.K.

22-25A Sackville St. London, WIX 1DE
Lisbon - Tourist Office at Palácio Foz, Praça dos Restauradores, tel: 34 636 43/58

Portuguese Embassies
in U.S.

2125 Kalorama Rd., N.W. Washington D.C. 20008 tel: (202) 328-8610

in Canada

645 Island Park Dr. Ottawa, Ontario K1Y 0B8 tel: (613) 729-0883

in the U.K.

11 Belgrave Square, London, SWI X8PP, tel: 4471 2355 331

Foreign Posts in Portugal

Lisbon

Canadian Embassy, Av. da Liberdade 144-156, 4th floor, tel: 01/347-4892, M-Th 8:30-5, F 8:30-12:30

British Embassy, Rua S. Domingos a Lapa 37, tel: 01/396-1191/47, M-F 9-12: 45, 2:30-5

United States Embassy, Av. das Forcas Armada 16, tel: 01/726-6600, M-F 8:30-12:30

Driving Distances (in km)
From Lisbon to cities in Portugal:

Aveiro 252	Evora 150	Santarem 78
Beja 186	Faro 297	Setubal 48
Braga 366	Guarda 359	Viana do Castelo 383
Braganca 503	Leiria 133	Vila Real 404
Catelo Branco 262	Oporto 312	Vila Real de Santo Antonio 350
Coimbra 201	Portalegre 228	Viseu 292

From Lisbon to cities in Europe:

Amsterdam 2,485	Copenhagen 3,229	Oslo 3,783
Athens 4,465	Frankfurt 2,474	Paris 1,815
Berlin 2,287	Helsinki 4,927	Rome 2,709
Brussels 2,114	London 2,227	Vienna 3,200
Budapest 3,475	Madrid 636	

Telephone Information: International Code 00, Country Code 351, Main City Area Codes: Faro 89, Lisbon 1, Porto 2; time difference (Eastern Daylight) plus 5 hours

ROMANIA

A Little History

Romania has been inhabited since the Palaeolithic period. The Dacians, fierce warriors were subdued by the Romans under Trajan in two extremely difficult campaigns at the beginning of the 2nd century AD. The relatively brief Roman occupation, 165 years, nevertheless left as a lasting legacy the Latin language which survived the many subsequent invasions of migratory peoples. Over the years a Romanian identity progressively developed. The feudal states of Wallachia and Moldavia developed in the 13th and 14th centuries. Centuries of struggles against the Turks ensued in these states. Meanwhile Transylvania was successively occupied by the Ottoman and Austro-Hungarian Empires. Finally Moldavia and Wallachia were united in 1859, independence was achieved in 1877, and union with Transylvania in1918. Communist rule, established after the 2nd world war, lasted 45 years and was ended by the December revolution of 1989.

Population - 23,190,000
Capital - Bucharest
Government - Parliamentary democracy
Religion - mostly Orthodox Christians
Language - Romanian; English and French taught in schools
Money - Lei One lei equals l00 bani. Coins of 1 leu, l0, 20, 50 and l00 lei. Notes of l00, 200, 500, 1,000, 5,000 and 10,000 lei. Money will go a long way in this country.
U.S.$1 = 1,529 lei, Cdn.$1 = 1,127 lei, British £ = 2,102 lei
Visas
Americans do not need visas for visits less than 30 days. U.K. citizens require visas - cost is approx. £24, Canadians require visas, cost is Cdn.$34, $48 for business people, and U.S.$15 at any Romanian border point; transist visa (allowing three days for transit) is U.S.$22. If you are

part of an organized tour the visa is free. Make sure you ask for a tourist visa at embassies or consulates or you will be charged for a business visa.

Peculiar Customs and Expressions
Romanians shake hands constantly: when they are introduced, when they leave someone, and every time they meet. No matter how many times they run into each other during the day, they will shake hands each time. Some older Romanians will kiss a woman's hand. Good friends greet each other expansively; men may kiss each other on both cheeks or the mouth. Romanian farmers wear Tyrolean hats similar to the type worn by Chico Marx - do not insult them by laughing at their head gear. The "fig" gesture - the thumb between the index and middle fingers of a clenched fist - is an insult. If you are a guest in someones home bring an item that is in short supply such as perfume or coffee. Offer to help with a household chore, although your offer will probably be refused.

Best Festivals
Brasov - the International Jazz Festival May 5-7
Mamaia - National Festival of Light Music of Mamaia-July-August
Sfantu Gheorghe - International Festival of Amateur Theatricals "Concordia Days", January 10-20; also the secular Winter Customs Festival in February

Night Activities and More
Bucharest - Efes Pub, Karioka-jazz, Vox Maris Disco, Lido, Ambassador, Club A Blue Moon night club and Sexy Club

Must See Tourist Sites
Brasov - interesting medieval fortresses; near Brasov- Castelul Bran (Bran Castle 1377)
Bucharest - Casa Republica - 2nd largest government building in the world; Muzeul de Istorie Nationala (museum of national history); Muzeul Satului-open air Village Museum; Palatul Voievodul - stone remains of the 13th century Princely Court; Stavropoleus Church
Deva -13th century citadel built on top of a volcano, nearby the incredible castle at Hunedoara
Sinaia - "Pearl of the Carpathians", home of the Royal Castel in the Prahova Valley
Suceava - monastery; nearby - many other worthwhile monasteries-such as, Moldovita, Putna, Voronet, Humor, Sucevita
Timisoara - in 1989 this city became a watchword for freedom during the revolution, protests against Ceausescu began here and within one week he was overthrown

Best Scenery
Bukovina - north east Romania - most isolated part of country - many monasteries

Sibiu - one of the most beautiful towns in Romania

Transylvania - many quaint well-preserved towns - central part of country surrounded by the Carpathian mountains

Sighisoara - medieval village - cobblestone streets, mountains, forests, and a river

Transportation

Romania does not accept EurailPasses or InterRail, buy the Romanian Pass - it costs $99 1st class for any 5 days in 15 days, trains are often over-booked, make reservations; buses and trains across the country only cost $l0-$15.

Hitch-Hiking

Well accepted, drivers may want some money, use your own judgement as to how much you offer.

Accommodation

Private rooms-U.S.$5-$15/night, hotels and state-run hotels are usually U.S.$25 a day per person.

Camping

U.S.$2-$5 a day, for locations, ask for the 'Romanian Tourist and Road Map'.

Useful Addresses & Tourist Offices

Romanian National Tourist Office, 342 Madison Ave. suite 210, New York, NY 10173 tel: (212) 697-6971

Look for the Tourist sign in the Gara de Nord-helpful-maps, brochures tel:0l/6l7-2160

ONT Carpati S.A., changes money at the official rate, at B-dul, Magheru 7 tel:6 l45l60

in the U.K.

17 Nottingham Pl., London W1M 3RD, tel: 0171/224-3692

Romanian Embassies

in U.S.

Embassy

1607 - 23rd St. N.W., Washington D.C. 20008, tel: (202) 332-4829

Consulates: 200 E. 38th St. New York, NY 10016, tel: (212) 682-9120 11766 Wilshire Blvd., suite 1230, Los Angeles, CA 90025, tel: (310) 444-0043

in Canada

Embassy

655 Rideau St., Ottawa, Ontario, K1N 6A3, tel: (613) 789-5345, fax: (613) 241-7069

Consulates: 1111 Rue St. Urbain, suite M.01, Montreal, Quebec H2Z 1Y6, tel: (514) 876-1792

111 Peter St., suite 530, Toronto, Ontario M5V 2H1, tel: (416) 585-5802

in the U.K.

4 Palace Green, Kensington, London, W84 QD, tel: 071 937 9666

Foreign Posts in Romania
Bucharest
Canadian Embassy, Calea Nicolae Iorga 36, tel: 01/312-0365, M-F 9-5
British Embassy, Str. Jules Michelet 24, tel: 01/312-0303, M-F 9-1, 2-5,
United States Consulate, Str. Snagov 26, tel: 01/312-4042, in emergencies,
    01/312-6386, M-F 8-12, 1-3
Driving Distances (in km)
From Bucharest to cities in Romania:

Arad 526	Suceava 438
Brasov 171	Timisoaria 567
Focsani 181	Tulcea 263
Sibiu 273	

From Bucharest to cities in Europe

Amsterdam 2,241	Helsinki 2,225	Rome 2,040
Athens 1,200	Lisbon 4,206	Sofia 336
Belgrade 632	London 2,645	Stockholm 2,710
Bratislava 194	Luxembourg 2,110	Tallin 2,266
Brussels 2,280	Madrid 3,506	Warsaw 1,235
Budapest 890	Oslo 2,765	Vienna 1,146
Copenhagen 2,140	Paris 2,460	Zagreb 1,020
Dublin 2,913	Prague 1,450	

Telephone Information: International Code 011, Country Code 40, Main City
    Area Code: Bucharest 1; time difference (Eastern Daylight) plus 7 hours.

SLOVAK REPUBLIC

A Little History

In the 5th century, Slavic tribes from which the Slovaks derive their ethnic
origin, began settling the area of modern Slovakia. The political and constitutional programme of the Slovaks emerged in 1848. The Slovak
National Council struggled for an autonomous Slovakia within the frame-
work of the Kingdom of Hungary. The Czecho-Slovak Republic was created
in 1918 after the disintegration of the Austria-Hungarian Monarchy. Then
in 1939, after the declaration of the independent Slovak Republic it became a puppet state of Nazi Germany. The Czecho-Slovak Republic in
1945 was re-established, but a communist coup in 1948 installed a dictato-
rial totalitarian regime totally dependent on the USSR. In 1968, the Prague
spring invasion of the Warsaw Pact troops into Czecho-Slovakia occurred.
From 1970-1980, the Catholic Church and the intelligentsia-circles of ecolo-
gists, artists and scientists were the primary forces which led to the demise
of the totalitarian regime and the renovation of the democracy in Czecho-

Slovakia in 1989. Finally, on January 1, 1993 there was the declaration of an independent and sovereign Slovak Republic, which emerged after the division of the Czecho-Slovakia. In the same year, Slovakia became a member of the United Nations and the Council of Europe.

Population - 5, 269,000
Capital - Bratislava
Government - Parliamentary democracy
Religion - Roman Catholic 60%, Slovak Evangelical 6%, some Greek Catholic
Language - Slovak, some Russian, and more English
Money - Slovenska Koruna (Sk) = 100 halierov (h), Slovak crown = 100 hellers; in denominations: 10h, 20h,50h, 1Sk, 5Sk, 10Sk (coins), and 20Sk, 50Sk, 100Sk, 500Sk, 1,000Sk, 5,000Sk (bank notes).
U.S.$1 = 30 koruna, Cdn.$1 = 21 koruna, British £. = 53 koruna

Public Holidays

Establishment of the Slovak Republic, Jan. 1; Epiphany (the Three Kings and Christmas holiday in Orthodox Christians); Good Friday, Easter Monday; Labour Day, May 1; Liberation of the Republic, May 8; Holiday of St.Cyril and St. Methodius, July 5; The Slovak National Uprising, August 29; Constitution Day of the Slovak Republic, Sept. 1; Our Lady of Sorrows, Sept. 15; All Saints' Day; Christmas Eve, Dec. 24, 1st Christmas Day, Dec. 25, 2nd Christmas Day, Dec. 26

Visas

Americans and U.K. citizens can enter Slovakia for 90 days without a visa; Canadians need a visa before entering the country - apply at a Slovakian embassy/consulate - the visa is good for 90 days and costs Cdn $50, supply 2 photos. The visa is good for four entries. To extend your visa, you have to apply at least three days before it expires. Visa holders must register with the Foreign Police Office within 3 week days after entry. You need not register with the police if you are staying at a hotel.

Peculiar Customs and Odd Expressions

Slovaks are very friendly with foreigners who are often invited to Slovak homes and offered national food and drinks (Borovicka or Slivovica)
Vsade dobre, doma najlepsie - East, West, home is best
Nenos drevo do leba - Don't carry coals to Newcastle
Visc hlav vi ac vie - More heads, more brains
byt' chudobny ako kostolna mye - to be as poor as a church mouse
nebyt' hodný šestáka - not to be worth the candle

Best Festivals

Bratislava - International Rock Pop Bratislava, June 20-25, Music Festival, Oct. 1-14
Bratislava Jazz Days, Oct. 20-22

Senica - Festival of the Theatre of Youth, July 7-17
Stara Tura - Country Rodeo Sept. 22-24
Vychodna Folklore Festival in July

Night Activities and More

Bratislava - bars and discos - Bratislava Club in Hotel Bratislava, Hotel
Forum, Luna Bar at Hotel Kyjev, Bajkal, Qeen's Pub, Discobarin Hotel
Danube, V-Klub, Junior Club, Jalta, Devin at Hotel Devin

There are over 23 natural curative spas with various kinds of mineral waters - the best is Piestany, other good ones are Trencianske Teplice,
Bardejovske Kupele, Bojnice -contact the tourist office for the locations

Must See Tourist Sites

Banska Stiavnica - medieival town with two castles in the heart of the
mountains, many gothic and renaissance houses. Open air gold mining
museum; swim in the 10 lakes in the area

Bardejov - medieval town- access through four gates in the town walls,
14th century townhall

Bratislava - Bratislava Castle; Stara radnica (Old Town Hall), Dessewffy
Palace, Gothic St. Martin's Cathedral, Devin Castle, Roland's Fountain,
cloisters and churches - Francisca Ursuline of Clare nuns

Kosice - St. Elisabeth's Minster with cathedral and gothic chapel of St. Michael

Spis - region of the greatest number of best preserved historical medieval
towns, best is Levoca dating back to1271

Trencin - in the valley of river Vah, surrounded by Strazovske hills;
Laugaricio Castle

Trnava - archaeological evidence includes finds from the Neolithic Age, it
became a town in 1230, population only 71,000

Best Scenery

The Low Tatra mountains - Magura and the Greater Tatra

The National Park of Pieniny

The oldest glacial cave in Europe at Dobsina

Banská Bystrica - town encircled by hills and mountains in the Hron valley

Vysoké Tatry - beautiful High Tatra mountain scenery and Stary Smokovec resort

Transportation

Very similar to Czech Republic; hitching is a little easier.

Accommodation

Intertravel tourist office arranges bookings at hostels and private rooms

address - Rauchova 14, Bratislava, tel: 7/ 259-711, prices for private rooms
are approx. 450 koruna.

Youth Hostels

Contact: Ubytovne Mladych Na Slovensju (UMS), Prazska 11, 81336
Bratislava, Slovak Republic; tel: (42) (7) 417271, 498672, fax (42) (7)
494715; hostels charge appoximately 10 koruna a day. All bookings
should be made through the national office.

Youth Hostel Town Locations and Telephone Numbers
B Blahova (709) 968196; Bratislava - 2 hostels - 1) Juniorhotel on Drienova 14, tel: (7) 238000; 2) Iuventa Hostel on Karloveska 64, tel: (7) 722686; **D** Domasa-Valkov (938) 91333; **J** Jahodnik (805) 92234; Jasna (849) 915713; **K** Kovacov (810) 8301; Kremna (963) 95114; **P** Piatrova (842) 84389; **T** Tatranska Strba (969) 96291; **U** Upohlav (822) 83148.

Useful Addresses & Tourist Offices
Slovak Travel Bureau, 10 East 40th St, suite 3604, New York, NY 10016
   tel: (212) 689-9720 or 1-800-800-8891
in the U.K.
17-18 Old Bond St., London W1X 4RB, tel: 0171/629-6058
Slovak Association of Travel Agencies, Kocelova 9, 824 79 Bratislava,
   tel: 42 7/ 202 82 67
Bratislava Tourist Information (BIS) at Panska 18 tel. 07/33715 or 07/334370
   is in the Old Town; Accommodation call 07/ 33 43 25
Slovak Travel Agency Slovakia at Mileticova 1, 842 72 Bratislava, tel: 7/632
   01 or Satur Travel Agency at Jesenskeho 5 tel 07/52002 helps with accommodation and provide information on Bratislava and surrounding areas
BIPS (Bratislava Information & Publicity Service) at Rybarska brana, tel:
   333715/334325
Slovak Embassies
in U.S.
Embassy of the Slovak Republic, 2201 Wisconsin Ave. N.W., Washington
   D.C. 20007 tel: (202)965-5161, fax (202) 965-5166
in Canada
Embassy of the Slovak Republic, 50 Rideau Terrace, Ottawa, Ontario K1M
   2A1 tel: (613) 749-4442, fax: (613) 749-4989
in the U.K.
Embassy of the Slovak Republic, 25 Kengsington Place Garden, London,
   W84 QY, tel: 243 0803, fax 727 5824
Foreign Posts in Slovakia
Bratislava
United States Embassy, Hviedzdoslavovo nam. 4, 811 02, tel: 07/33 08 61
Canadian Consulate, Kolarska 4, 81106 Bratislava 1, tel: 42-7-361-220/
   277
British Embassy, Grosslingova 35, 81109, Bratislava, tel: 42-7-364420
Slovakian Misson for Canada in the Czech Republic, Mickiewiczova 6,
   125 33 Praha 1, tel: 2/312 02 51, fax 2/311 27 91
Driving Distances (in km)
From Bratislava to cities in Slovakia:

Bardejov 480	Spis 365
Banska Stiavrnica 240	Trnava 55
Kosice 409	Trencin 124

From Bratislava to cities in Europe

Amsterdam 1,273	Lisbon 3,039	Rome 1,314
Athens 1,886	London 1,602	Sofia 1,029
Belgrade 65	Luxembourg 1,060	Stockholm 1,735
Bern 873	Madrid 2,507	St. Petersburg 2,829
Bonn 991	Moscow 2,104	Warsaw 616
Bucharest 1,138	Oslo 1,705	Vienna 65
Helsinki 1,724	Paris 1,359	
Kiev 1,288	Prague 321	

Telephone Information: International Code 011, Country Code 42, Main City Area Code: Bratislava 7; time difference (Eastern Daylight) plus 6 hours.

SPAIN

A Little History

The Spaniards were especially well prepared by history to conquer, occupy, populate and exploit new lands and assimilate new people. After Christopher Columbus discovered America in 1492, Spaniards settled in Mexico on the Atlantic and Peru on the Pacific in the 16th century.In 1936, after a military coup General Franco became head of the government and commander of the armed forces. The new regime was first characterized by: fierce political repression and economic hardship. Even though Spain declared itself neutral during World War II it remained isolated from Europe and the UN. From the 1970s onwards, opposition to Franco's regime increased. In 1975 when Franco died, Juan Carlos I became King of Spain and a chapter of Spanish history was closed; the doors of freedom and hope were opened for the Spanish people".

Population - 39, 887,140

Capital - Madrid

Government - Constitutional monarachy

Religion - Roman Catholic

Language - Spanish

Money - Peseta (pta) Coins of 1,5, 10, 25, 50, 100, 200, and 500 pesetas. Notes of 1,000, 2,000, 5,000, 10,000 pesetas

U.S.$1 = 113 pesetas, Cdn.$1 = 84 pesetas, British £. = 188 pesetas

Public Holidays

January 1 and 6, March 19, Good Friday and Easter Monday, May 1, Corpus Christi (second Thursday after Whitsun), June 24, 18 and July 25, August 15, Oct. 12, Nov. 1, Dec. 8 and Christmas Day. In addition to these national fiestas each town celebrates the feast day of its patron saint.

Visas

Americans, Canadians and U.K. citizens do not need visas.

Peculiar Customs and Odd Expressions

De noche, todos los gatos son pardos - All cats are alike in the dark

Poderoso caballero es Don Dinero - Money makes the mare go

Lo que algo vale, algo cuesta - You can't make an omelette without breaking eggs

Aunque la mona se vista de seda, mona se queda - You can't make a silk purse out of a sow's ear

When eating, push food onto the fork with knife, when you are finished, place knife and fork side by side on the plate - if they are crossed or on opposite side of the plate, you will be offered more food. Hands should be kept above the table. Pay compliments to your host and the waiters in a restaurant. A handshake is a normal greeting; among close friends, Spanish men will add a pat on the back or a hug; women lightly embrace and touch cheeks while kissing the air. To beckon another person, turn the palm down and wave the fingers or whole hand; snapping the hand downward is used to emphasize a point. The A.- O.K. gesture (making a circle of the first finger and thumb) is rude. If you are staying a Spanish home give chocolates, pastries or flowers. Shorts are not acceptable in public. Don't be put off by the sight of paper and peanut shells on the floors of bars; the more there is the more popular the place

Best Festivals

Granada - International Festival of Music and Dance in June and July

Madrid - San Isidro Labrador Festival May 15 takes place over several days

Pamplona - Running of the Bulls - Fiesta of San Fermin - July 6-14

Seville - the spectacular Easter Feria, held for six days

Valencia - Las Fallas de San Jose - unique - March 12-19 - fireworks, bonfires, music, all - night parties

Night Activities and More

Barcelona - bars/discos - Otto Zutz Club, Ciro', Sno, Le Clochard, Nich Havanna

Madrid - Teatro Real (Royal Theater) authentic flamenco dancing - Zambra, Casa Patas, Torres Bermejas; discos - El Callejon, Abre Vilma; jazz - Whisky Jazz Club, Cafe Berlin, Clamores; Bullfights - best month is in May

Must See Tourist Sights

Algeciras - gateway to Gibraltar, Roman aquaduct, Chapel of our Lady of Europe

Alicante - museums of Archaeology and 20th Century Art, La Asegurada, Santa Barbara Castle, San Nicolas de Bari Cathedral, Santa Cruz district, Santa Maria Church

Avila - one of the world's best preserved, and most impressive walled cities

Barcelona - many museums, Picasso Gallery, Templo Expiatorio de la Sagrada Familia - huge cathedral,

Burgos - great white limestone Cathedral-13th century

Cordoba - the 1000 year old, giant Mezquita (Mosque), visit the Old Town 3-4 four miles away- the incredible ruins of Medina Azahara - the palace is a mile long by and one/half mile wide

Costa del Sol - sunny coastline of southern Spain includes some worthy stops in the towns of Fuengirola, Malaga, Marbella, Torremolinos

Granada - visit Alhambra, Generalife, Alcazaba, the Cathedral, Carlos V's palace, the Albaicin

Madrid - San Nicolas de los Servitas Plaza, museo del Prado, church-San Pedro El Viejo, San Sebastian, Plaza Mayor Fortress, San Isidro Cathedral, church-San Antonio de los Alemanes, Apollo Fountain, Sabatini Gardens, Palacio Real-Royal Palace, Thyssen-Bornemisza Museum-a must see, also see the Cathedral near Madrid - Valle de los Caidos - impressive memorial chapel built inside a mountain

Mallorca Island - students check with tourist board - cost of flying there may be prohibiive, check boat service as well

Ronda - one of Spains' prettiest and most historic towns

Salamanca - Plaza Mayor and the bells rung at midnight

Santillana del Mar - famous Altamira Caves

Segovia - incredible Roman aqueduct, nearby Granja de San Ildefonso - 18th century palace

Seville - Alcazar of King Don Pedro, 12th century Giralda, the cathedral

Toledo - one hour south of Madrid - "the most perfect and brilliant record of genuine Spanish civilization", incredible Gothic cathedral

Valencia - fascinating Palacio de Marques de dos Aguas

Zaragoza - towering Basilica del Pilar

Best Scenery

Barcelona - 30 miles away is the famous Monastery of Montserrat - unusual vista and mountain formation

Ciudad Encantada (Enchanted City) near Cuenca - unusual shaped rocks

Cuenca - the old town which hangs from sides of cliffs- 2 hour car ride from Madrid, Cánadas del Teide National Park in the Canary Islands

Ercina Lake in the Covadonga National Park in Northern Spain

Nerja - beautiful views, interesting caves

Cycling

Not easy to find rentals, bring your own bike, ask at tourist offices, some of the best is in southern Spain.

Bus

Cheapest and best way to go versus the train, bus costs approximately 4,500 pesetas Barcelona to Madrid.

Hitch-Hiking
You'll have better luck on the secondary roads.
Train
RENFE, the national rail company, has expresos or rapidos trains, 20% discount for students under 26, best to travel on non-peak days, Barcelona to Madrid costs 4,500 pesetas.
Warning
Do not sleep on beaches due to thieves, it is forbidden by law.
Camping
Over 800 campsites, prices average 450 pesetas/person and 450 pesetas/tent, if you wish to camp on private land, it is necessary to obtain the owner's permission.
Youth Hostels
Approximately 160 'albergues juveniles', prices range from 650 pesetas - 1,700 pesetas breakfast is usually included, most open only from mid-July to mid-September. Instituto de la Juventud/Red Espanola de Albergues Juveniles, c/ Jose Ortega y Gasset 71, Madrid 28006, Spain, tel: (34) (1) 3477700, fax (34) (1) 4018160.
Youth Hostel Town Locations and Telephone Numbers
A Aguadulce (950) 340346; Aguilas-Calarreona (968) 413029; Albarracin - 2 hostels -1) Rosa Brios Hostel on Santa Maria 1, tel: (974) 710005; 2) Aben-Racin Hostel on Cta Teruel-Albarrracin, tel: (974) 60189; La Alberca (968) 164429; Alborache (96) 2508123; Alburquerque (924) 400041; Alcudia (971) 545395; Algerciras (956) 679060; Alhama de Murcia (968) 630023; Alicante (96) 5113044; Almeria (950) 263342; Almoguera (908) 803763; Almorox (91) 8623265; Alsasua (948) 562304; Altafulla (977) 650779; Arbejal (988) 870174; Arrondas (98) 5840334; Aunon (911) 350120; Avila (920) 221716; **B** Barbastro (974) 311834; **Barcelona** - 4 hostels - 1) **Mare de Deu de Montserrat** on Passeig Mare de Deu del Coll41-51, tel: (93) 2105151; 2) Hostal de Joves on Passeig Pujades 29, tel: (93) 3003104; 3) Pere Tarres on Numancia 1490-151, tel: (93) 4102309; 4) Studio Hostel on Duquesa d'Orleans 58, tel: (93) 2050961; Los Batanes (91) 8691511; Bejar (923) 400702; Benicarlo (964) 470836; Benicasim (964) 300949; Biar (96) 58108 75; Biel (976) 669001; Bimenes (976) 867844; Branavieja - no tel. #; Burgo (947) 220362; **C** Cabrera del Mar (93) 7594448; Canfranc (974) 293025; Castellon - 2 hostels - 1) El Maestrat Hostel on Av Hnos Bou 26, tel: (964) 220457; 2) Mare de deu del Lledo Hostel on Orfebres Santalinea 2, tel: (964) 202290; Cazorla (953) 720329; Cercedilla - 2 hostels-1) Villa Castora Hostel on Cta de las Dehesas, tel: (91) 8520334; 2) Las Dehesas Hostel on Cta de las Dehesas, tel: (91) 8520135; Constantina (95) 5881589; Cordoba (957) 290166; Cortes de Pallas (96) 2517134; La Coruna - 2 hostels - 1) Bergondo Hostel on Gandario Sada, tel: (981) 791005; 2)

Marina Espanola Hostel on Gorbeiroa-Bergondo, tel: (981) 620118; **D** Daroca (976) 800312; Deltebre (977) 480136; Donostia-San Sebastian- 2 hostels -1) La Sirena Hostel on Igeldo Pasealekua 25, tel: (943) 310268; 2) Ulia-Mendi Hostel in the Parque de Ulia, tel: (943) 310268; Dosrius (93) 7955014; L'Escala (972) 771200; El Bosque (Cadiz) (956) 716212; El Escorial - 2 hostels - 1) 'Santa Maria del Buen Aire' Hostel , ask re: address, tel: (91) 8903640; 2) Reidencia Hostel on Residencia 14, tel: (91) 8905924; L'Espluga de Francoli (977) 870356; **E** Espinosa (947) 120449; Ezcaray (941) 354197; **F** Felechosa (98) 5487345; Figueres (972) 501213; **G** Girona (972) 218121; Granada (958) 284306; Guia (928) 882728; **H** Hondarribia (943) 641550; Huelva (959) 253793; **J** Jaca (976) 360536; Jerez de la Frontera (956) 342890; **L** Lago de Sanabria (980) 622083; Layos (925) 376585; Leon - 2 hostels - 1) Europa Hostel on Paseo del Parque 2, tel: (987)200206; 2) Infanta Dona Sancha Hostel on Corredera 2, tel: (987) 203414; La Seu d'Urgell (973) 353897; Les (973) 648048; Llanes (98) 5232 054; Lleida (973) 266099; Logrono (941) 291145; Luarca (98) 5640676; Lugo - 3 hostels- 1) Eijo Garay Hostel on Pintor Corredoira 4, tel: (982) 220450; 2) Area Hostel in Playa de Area-Viveiro, tel: (982) 560851; 3) Hermanos Pedrosa Hostel on Pintor Corredoira 2, tel: (982) 221090; **M** Madrid - 2 hostels - 1) Marcenado Hostel on Calle Sta Cruz de Marcenado No. 28, tel: (91) 5474532; 2) Richard Schirrmann Hostel on Casa de Campo, tel: (91) 4635699; Las Majadas (969) 283050; Malaga (95) 2308500; Mallorca (971) 260892; Manresa (93) 8750396; Marbella (95) 2771491; El Masnou (93) 5555600; Mazagon (959) 536262; Miranda de Ebro (947) 320932; La Molina (972) 892012; Mora de Rubielos (974) 8000 00; Moraira (96) 6492030; Munilla (941) 394213; **N** Navamorcuende (925) 811186; Navarredonda de Gredos (920) 348005; Nuria (972) 732043; **O** Ocana (925) 130055; Olot (972) 264200; Onis (98) 523112; Orea (91) 7176697; Orense (988) 252412; Oveido (98) 5232054; **P** Palencia - 2 hostels - 1) Escuela Castilla Hostel on Avda de Burgos, tel: (979) 721475; 2) Vitorio Macho Hostel on Avda Cardenal Cisneros 12, tel: (979) 720462; Penaranda de Bracamonte (923) 540988; Piles (96) 2893425; Planoles (972) 736177; Poble Nou Del Delta (977) 742203; Pontevedra (986) 554081; Portomarin (982) 545022; Puerto de Navacerrada (contact YH Assoc. in Madrid 5804216); Punta Umbria (959) 311650; **R** Ribadeo (982) 123300; Ribadesella (98) 5861380; Roncesvalles (948) 760015; Rucandio no tel. #; Ruidera (926) 528053; Ruiloba (720172; **S** Sada (981) 620118; Salardu (973) 645271; San Juan del Plan (974) 506049; San Pablo de les Montes - 2 hostels - 1) Banos del Robledillo Hostel on del Robledillo, tel: (925) 415300; 2) Banos del Sagrario Hostel, ask for street address, tel: (925) 415411; San Rafael (921) 171457; Santander (942) 227031; Segovia (921) 420027; Sesena (91) 8936152; Sevilla (95) 4613150; Sierra Nevada (958) 480305; Siguenza (91) 5523490; Solorzano (942) 676342; Soncillo (947)

120449; Soria - 2 hostels - 1) Juan A Gaya Nuno Hostel on Paseo de San Francisco 1, tel: (975) 221789); 2) Antonio Machado Hostel on Plaza Jose Antonio 1, tel: (975) 221789; Soto de Cameros (941) 291100; **T** Tarragona (977) 240195; Tarrega (973) 313053; Teruel (976) 601712; Toledo (925) 224554; Toribon de Llanos (98) 5341968; Tragacete (969) 222654; **U** Uncastillo (974) 679400; **V** Valdeavellano de Tera (975) 271211; Valencia (96) 3617459; Valencia de Alcantara (927) 580041; Valladolid (983) 251550; el Vendrell (977) 680008; Vic (889) 4938; Vigo (986) 290808; Villamanin (987) 598243; Villanua (974) 378616; Viver (96) 3869899; Viznar (958) 543307; **Z** Zaragoza (976) 551387; Zarautz (943) 132910.

Work

Visas must be applied from your country, may be able to teach English, work in bars etc. Unemployment is approximately 20%. Information on vacation work: Spanish Union of Students, Bolsa Universitaria de Trabajo, Glorieta de Quevedo 8, Madrid 8.

Babysitting

Madrid- check with "Servicio Domestico"in the telephone directory for agencies.

Useful Addresses & Tourist Offices
in U.S.

Spanish National Tourist Office

665 Fifth Ave., New York, NY 10022 tel: (212) 759-8822 fax: (212) 980-1053

845 North Michigan Ave. Chicago, IL 60611 tel: (312) 642-1992 fax: (312) 642-9817

8383 Wilshire Blvd., suite 960, Beverly Hills, CA 90211, (213) 658-7188 fax (213) 658-1061

1221 Brickwell Ave., Miami, FL 33131 tel: (305) 358-1992 fax: (305 358-8223

in Canada

102 Bloor St. West, 14th Floor, Toronto, Ontario M5S 1M8 tel: (416) 961-3131 fax (416) 961-1992

in the U.K.

57-58 St. James St. London, SW1A 1LB, tel: 499 1169

in Spain

Barcelona - Barcelona Information - 24 hour service, call: 010; office at Gran Via de las Cortes Catalanas, 658, tel:(93) 301 74 43, 317 58 29

Madrid - Tourist Information Office at Plaza Mayor 3, Madrid tel: 266 48 74

main Madrid tourist office is on the ground floor of the Torre de Madrid in Plaza de Espana tel 91/541-2325; also Madrid Provincial Tourist Office at Duque de Medinacelli 2 tel: 91/4294951

Spanish Embassies
in U.S.
2375 Pennsylvania Ave., N.W. Washington D.C. 20037 tel: (202) 581-5921
Consulates in New York, L.A. San Francisco, Chicago, Miami
in Canada
350 Sparks St., suite 802, Ottawa, Ontario KlR 7S8 tel: (6l3) 237-2193
in the U.K.
39 Chesham Place, London, SW1X 8SB, tel: 235 5555
Foreign Posts in Spain
Madrid
Canada Embassy, C. Nunez de Balboa 35, tel: 91/431-43-00, M-F 9-12:30
British Embassy, C. Fernando el Santo 16, tel: 91/308-52-08, M-F 8-2:30
United States Embassy, C. Serrano 75, tel: 91/577-40-00, M-F 9-12:30, 3-5
Sevilla
Canadian Consulate, Av. de la Constitucion 30, 2nd floor, tel: 95/422-94-13, M-F 10-2
British Consulate, Pl. Nueva 8B, tel: 95/422-88-75, M-F 9-2
United States Consulate, Paseo de las Delicias 7, tel: 95/423-18-83/85, M-F 10-1
Barcelona
Canadian Consulate, Via Augusta 125, tel: 93/209-06-34, M-F 9-1
British Consulate, Av. Diagonal 477, tel: 93/419-90-44, M-F 9:30-1:30, 4-5
United States Consulate, Passeig Reina Elisenda 32, tel: 93/280-22-27, M-F 9-12:30,3-5
Driving Distances (in km)
From Madrid to cities in Spain:

Algerciras 686	La Coruna 637	Sevilla 538
Barcelona 627	Malaga 544	Valencia 350
Badajoz 401	Murcia 378	Vitoria 351
Cadiz 651	Pamplona 407	Zamora 248
Granada 434	Santander 394	Zaragoza 324

From Madrid to cities in Europe:

Amsterdam 1,730	London 1,725	Salzburg 2,136
Berlin 2,485	Munich 1,991	Stockholm 3,295
Brussels 1,556	Oslo 3,133	Venice 2,004
Budapest 2,709	Paris 1,317	Vienna 2,717
Copenhagen 2,539	Prague 2,284	Warsaw 3,268
Lisbon 629	Rome 2,086	Zurich 1,696

Telephone Information: International Code 07, Country Code 34, Main City Area Codes: Barcelona 3, Bilbao 4, Granada 58, Madrid 1, Sevilla 5, Valencia 6; time difference (Eastern Daylight) plus 6 hours. Emergency # 091

A Little History

Scandinavia was home to the Vikings. In 793, they invaded the monastery at Lindisfarne, Scotland, sending shock waves throughout Europe. Later, Vikings conquered England and were given Normandy (Norsemen's Land) by the French King. Four generations later the Normans, led by William the Conqueror, successfully invaded Britain.

As incredible as it may seem, Vikings from Sweden founded the first Russian state, which they ruled for hundreds of years. The czars that descended from these Vikings ruled Russia as late as the 16th century. The Vikings even visited Istanbul, where they were given a royal welcome. Around the year 1000, Leif Eriksson sailed from Iceland and discovered North America. His father, Erik the Red, discovered Greenland. They were that kind of family.

Swedes have been emigrating to and trading with the U.S. for more than 350 years. In 1638, a small fleet of Swedish settlers reached Delaware. They founded a colony at the mouth of the Delaware River called "Nya Sverige"or New Sweden. The colony celebrated its 350th anniversary in 1988, and reminders of the early settlement still exist today. In fact, Swedes introduced the log cabin to America.

Great tides of immigration began in the 19th century. Many Swedes settled in the upper Midwest, where the geography and climate are somewhat similar to that of their home. That's probably why we have the Minnesota Vikings, and not the Miami Vikings.

Population - 8,590,000
Capital - Stockholm
Government - Constitutional monarchy
Religion - Lutheran
Language - Swedish, English widely spoken
Money - Krona (Skr) One kroner equals 100 ore. Coins of 50 ore, and 1,5 kroner. Notes of 10, 20, 50, 100, 500, 1,000, 10,000 kroner
U.S.$1 = 6.5 kroner, Cdn.$1 = 5 kroner, British £. = 10.7 kroner
Public Holidays
January 1 and 6 , Good Friday, Easter Monday, May 1, Ascension Day, Whit Monday, Midsummer Day (nearest Saturday to June 24), All Saints' Day, Christmas Day and Dec. 26
Visas
Americans, Canadians and U.K. citizens do not need visas.
Peculiar Customs and Odd Expressions
'Skoal' is the Swedish 'cheers', wait until your host has said skoal before

touching your drink for the first toast at dinner. The handshake is the standard greeting; good friends (especially among the young) who see each other often do not bother to shake hands. If a woman asks you to dance three times she will invite you back to her place; but do not mistake a Swedish woman's forwardness for a sexual invitation. Swedish women often speak to strangers, especially foreigners when they want to practice the foreigner's language. Suggested gifts for your host are flowers, liquor, wine, cake or chocolates or candy for the children. Swedes do not use many gestures - avoid talking with your hands. A toss of the head means "come here"; look people directly in the eye when you speak to them; Swedes do not like physical contact with anyone except close friends, except for the handshake; do not touch, backslap, embrace, or put an arm around a Swede. Students greet Spring with bonfires and singing; nation-wide custom is the holding of crayfish suppers by lantern light, often outdoors towards the end of summer and midsummer celebrations.

Det ar gott att finna en van pa vagen - Nice to find a friend along the road

Best Festivals

Kalott Jazz and Blues Festival in Haparanda, Sweden and in Tornea, Finland - within walking distance of each other. Dancing: 'Halsingehambon' July 8, hundreds of people dancing the Hambo. Starting on Harga field, dancing continues in Bollnas and Arbra. Finals in Jarvso, where hundreds of couples will be dancing.

Stangaspelen - 'Viking Olympics' July 7-9, 1,700 competitors

Stockholm - best festival is Midsummer's Eve-celebrated on the weekend around the summer solstice (approx.June 23-25). Stockholm Jazz & Blues Festival international stars, beginning of July. Stockholm Water Festival - August 11-20.-concerts, races, a lot of drinking

Night Activities and More

Stockholm - discos- Daily News, Galaxy, Downtown; dancing - Cafe Opera, Berns, King's Cross for cheap beer, Glenn Miller Cafe, Borsen - biggest nightclub, Cabaret Club

The Midnight Sun - when the sun never sets in the summertime: Abisko - June 12 - July 4, Bjorkliden - May 26-July l9, Gallivare - June 4- July 6, Jokkmokk - June 8-July 2, Kiruna - May 28-July 14

Must See Tourist Sights

Gotland - the medieval island - Eketorp - ancient fortress on Oland; the Lummelunda Caves

Gothenborg - historic canals, Elfsborg Fortress, Tjoloholm Castle

Kalmar Castle - by the Baltic Sea, Sweden's best preserved renaissance castle

Lund - many historical buildings

Malmo - one of Sweden's oldest cities, City Square dates back to 1530, Svaneholm Castle-Malmohus Castle, Backaskog Castle

Norrkoping - interesting rock carvings

Sandhamn - tall sailing ships, Royal Swedish Yacht Club

Stockholm - Stadshuset (City Hall), Kungliga Slottest - Royal Palace, Kaknastornet-TV tower - best view of city, Riddarhomskyrkan - church, Vasa museum - world's oldest restored warship, many museums

Best Scenery

Tallberg region by far the most colorful

Central and Northern Sweden, vast mountain ranges, villages of Dalarna and Sami in the Lapland area

Land of the Midnight Sun above the Arctic Circle

Bus

Lower fares available from Sept. to May. Compared to trains, prices are a little bit better, use Swebus or Svenska Buss for travel in the south and Linjebuss in the north; tickets can usually be bought on the bus. Students get a 50% discount Mon.-Wed. and Saturdays.

Cycling

Sweden has many signposted cycle trails throughout the country from north to south. Tourist offices in Sweden can give you information on bike rentals. For more information contact the Swedish Cycling Association: Svenska Cykelsallskapet, Box 6006, S-164 06 Kista, tel: 46-8-751 62 04, fax 46-8-751 19 35

Hitch-Hiking

Fairly easy from the entrance ramps, illegal on the shoulders of the highways.

Train

Within Scandinavia only - use the Nordturist card - 1,480kr for 21 consecutive days of travel, or purchase the Scanrail pass outside of Scandinavia - for 2nd class-5 days of travel within 15 days only U.S.$159, 10 days within 1 month - U.S.$239, one month unlimited travel - U.S.$399. A Reslust Card for 150kr will give you a 50% discount on all prices in Sweden for a year.

Camping

65kr for tents, or you can pitch your tent anywhere in the open - it's a Swedish law called 'every man's right '-you must be 100 meters from any dwelling - for one night only.

Meet the Swedes

Contact Friends Overseas at 68-04 Dartmouth St. Forest Hills, NY 11375- they will set up meetings for you with individuals, families or couples in Sweden. Write a letter with a stamped self-addressed envelope.

Farm House Holidays

Working farms with livestock or produce. Most farms offer accommodations by the week. Bed and Breakfast accommodations are also available and can be booked for one or a few nights. Rates from U.S.$35 include bed linen, towels and a big farm breakfast. Contact: Borton Overseas 1-800-843-0602.

Youth Hostels

Contact: Svenska Turistforeningen (STF), Drottninggatan 31-33, PO Box 25, 101 20 Stockholm, Sweden, tel: (46) (8) 7903100, fax (46) (8) 201332; 290 youth and family hostels ranging from mansion houses, farms and former prisons, to modern buildings and renovated sailing ships; most have two-and four-bed rooms; members 65-95kr a night, non-members 125kr/night - they have laundry facilities, luggage storage, kitchens, best to make reservations, hostels are run by Svenska Turisforeningen, part of Hostelling International, after 6 nights (six welcome stamps) non-members pay member rates.

Youth Hostel Town Locations and Telephone Numbers

A Abisko (980) 40200; Adelso (8) 56051450; Ahus (44) 248535; Algaras (506) 40450; Alingsas (322) 36987; Almhult (476) 71600; Alvdalen 9251) 10482; Alvkarleby (26) 82122; Alvsbyn (929) 11630; Amal (532) 10205; Amotfors (571) 22008; Aneby (380) 40295; Angelholm (431) 52364; Ann (647) 71070; Aradalen (687) 14054; Aras (515) 91051; Are (647) 30138; Asa (340) 655010; Asa-Lammhult (472) 63110; Asarna (687) 30230; Askersund (583) 81087; Avesta (226) 80623; **B** Backakra (411) 26080; Baskemolla (414) 26173; Bassholmen (522) 651308; Bastad (431) 75911; Bengtsfors (531) 10148; Bjorkvattnet (672) 23024; Bjornlunda (158) 20014 Boda (485) 220038; Boda (another town) (481) 24230; Bollnas (278) 23092; Boras (33) 121434; Borghamn (143) 20220; Borgholm (485) 10756; Borgsjo (690) 20075; Borlange (243) 227615; Boson (8) 6056600; Brunskog (570) 52141; Bruzaholm (381) 20200; Burtrask (914) 11013; **D** Docksta (613) 13064; **E** Ed (534) 10191; Edsbyn (271) 34462; Eksharad (563) 40590; Eksjo (381) 36180; Enkoping (171) 80066; Eskilstuna (16) 113080; **F** Falkenberg (346) 17111; Falkoping (515) 85020; Falun (23) 10560; Fargelanda (528) 20350; Faro (498) 223639; Finnerodja (584) 440074; Finnhamn (8) 54246212; Finnskoga-Holjes (564) 20100; Fjallbacka Valo (525) 31234; Fjardlang (8) 50156092; Frillesas (340) 650028; Fryksta-Kil (554) 40850; **G** Gallivare (970) 14380; Gammel-Granome (174) 13108; Garda (498) 491391; Gardserum (120) 20134; Gardstanga (46) 52087; Gavle - 2 hostels - 1) Sodra Radmansgatan Hostel on Sodra Radmansgatan 1, tel: (26) 621745; 2) Engeltofta Bonavagen Hostel on Bonavagen 118, tel: (26) 96160; Gnosjo (370) 31115; **Goteborg** - 3 hostels - 1) **Molndal Hostel** at the Torrekulla turistation, tel: (31) 7951495; 2) Ostkupan Hostel on Mejerigatan 2, tel: (31) 401050; 3) Karralund Hostel on Olbersgatan, tel: (31) 252761; Grangesberg (240) 21830; Granna (390) 10275; Gronklitt (551) 20786; Gullspang (551) 20786; **H** Hagelby (8) 53062020; Hagfors (563) 18800; Hallekis (510) 40085; Hammar (583)

7705 56; Hammaro 954) 510440; Hano (456) 53000; Harnosand (611) 10446; Haparanda (922) 11171; Hassela (652) 40444; Hassleholm (451) 68234; Hastveda (451) 30273; Havang (414) 74071; Haverud (530) 30275; Hedemora (225) 11350; Hedenaset (927) 30350; Hedvigsfors (653) 24049; Helsingborg - 2 hostels - 1) Villa Thalassa Hostel on Dag Hammarskjolds vag, tel: (42) 210384; 2) KFUM Hostel on KFUM Nyckelbo Scoutstigen (420 92005; Hemavan (954) 30002; Hjo (503) 10085; Hogbonden (613) 23005; Hogsby (491) 21600; Hokarangen (8) 941765; Hokensas (502) 50024; Horby (415) 14830; Horndal 9226) 40815; Hoor (413) 25510; Hornefors (930) 20480; Hovenaset (523)37463; Hovra (651) 26055; Huddinge (8) 7469480; Hudiksvall (650) 13260; Hunneberg (521) 220340; Hunnebostrand (523) 58730; I Idre (253) 20228; Immeln (44) 96090; J Jadraas (297) 45140; Jarbo (290) 70151; Jarvso (651) 49511; Jokkmokk (971) 55977; Junsele (621) 32010; K Kalix (923) 10733; Kall (647) 41012; Kalmar (480) 12928; Kalv (325) 51000; Kapellskar (176) 44169; Karlsborg (505) 11600; Karlshamn-Asarum (454) 29985; Karlskoga (586) 56780; Karlstad (54) 566840; Katrineholm (150) 10225; Kinna (320) 12235; Kiruna (980) 17195; Klavrestrom 9474) 40944; Klintehamn (498) 241558; Koping (221) 24495; Kopmanholmen (660) 33496; Korro (470) 34249; Kristianopel (455) 66130; Kristinehamn (550) 14771; Kungalv (303)18900; Kungsbacka (300) 19485; Kyrktasjo (671) 20004; L Laholm (430) 13318; Lanskrona (418) 12063; Langasjo (477) 50310; Larbro (498) 225 786; Leksand (247) 10186; Liden (692) 10567; Lidkoping (510) 66430; Lindesberg (581) 81175; Linkoping (13) 149090; Ljuder (478) 20400; Ljugarn (498) 493184; Ljungdalen (687) 20285; Loftahammar (493) 61110; Loka Brunn (5910 13570; Lommeland (526) 42027; Lonneberga (495) 40036; Lonsboda (479) 20705; Lovanger (913) 10395; Lulea (9200 52325; Lund (46) 142820; Lycksele (950) 14670; M Malexander (142) 30037; Malmo (40) 82220; Malung (280) 14040; Margretetorp (431) 54650; Mariestad (501) 10448; Medevi (141) 91100; Mjolby (142) 10016; Moheda (472) 40052; Motala (141) 57436; N Nas (498) 489116; Nora (587) 14676; Norrahammar (36) 61075; Norrkoping - 2 hostels 1) Turistgarden Hostel on Ingelstadsgatan 31, tel: (11) 101160; 2) Abborreberg Hostel on Abborreberg, tel: (11) 119344; Norrtalje (176) 71569; Norsjo (918) 10181; Nybro (481) 10932; Nykoping (155) 211810; Nynashamn (8) 52020834; Nysater (533) 30030; O Ockelbo (297) 40201; Odeshog (144) 10700; Ohns Gard (500) 441317; Olands Skogsby (485) 38395; Omberg (144) 33045; Orebro (19) 240921; Oreryd Hestra (370) 3370 35; Orkelljunga (435) 53588; Ornskoldsvik (660) 70244; Orrefors (481) 30020; Orsa (250) 42170; Orust (304) 50380; Osby (479) 11830; Oskarshamn (491) 88198; Osterbybruk (295) 21570; Osterbymo (381) 60103; Ostersund (63) 139100; Ottenby (485) 62062; Overum (493) 30302; P Persasen (643) 40180; Pitea (911) 96385; Prassebo (520) 67024; R

Ramsele (623) 10510; Ramsjo (651) 50373; Rantajarvi (927) 23000; Ransater (5520 300 50; Rattvik (248) 10566; Regna (151) 70127; Romelestugan (46) 55073; Ronneby (457) 26300; Rorback (522) 650190; **S** Saffle (533) 10620; Sala (224) 13659; Sandslan (612) 50541; Sandviken (26) 245200; Sanga Saby (80 56042160; Sankt Anna (121) 51312; Sarna - 2 hostels - 1) Bjorkhagen Hostel, ask for address, tel: (253) 10308; 2) Turistgarden Hostel on Sjukstugev 4, tel: (253) 10437; Sater-Havero (690) 30137; Savsjo (382) 12280; Saxnas (940) 70044; Sigtuna (8) 59258200; Skane Tranas (417) 20330; Skara (511) 12165; Skaralid-Klippan (435) 42025; Skelleftea (910) 37283; Skepparholmen (8) 7478800; Skovde (500) 4716 33; Skurup (411) 42251; Smadalaro (8) 50153073; Smedjebacken (240) 76645; Smygehuk (410) 24583; Snoa Bruk (281) 24018; Soderhamn (270) 45233; Soderkoping (121) 10213; Sodertalje (8) 55098025; Sodra Ljunga (372) 16011; Solleftea (620) 158 17; Solvesborg (456) 19811; Sorsele (952) 10048; Sproge (303) 82120; Stenungsund (303) 82120; **Stockholm - 5 hostels - 1)** "af Chapman Skeppsholmen" Hostel on Skeppsholmen, tel: (8) 6795015; 2) Skeppsholmen Vastra Brobanken Hostel on Skep. V. Bro., tel: (8) 6117155; 3) Backpackers Inn on Banergatan 56, tel: (8) 6607515; 4) Zinken Hostel on Zinkensvag 20, tel: (8) 6168100; 5) Langholmen Hostel on Kronohaktet, tel: (8) 6680510; Stora Karlso (498) 240500; Stora Segerstad (371) 21160; Storuman (951) 11730; Storvallen-Storlien (647) 70050; Strangnas (152) 16861; Stromsholm (220) 43774; Stromsnasbruk (433) 20050; Stromstad (526) 10193; Stromsund (670) 10805; Sundsvall (60) 612119; Sunne 9565) 10788; Surahammar (220) 33008; Sveg (680) 10338; **T** Tanndalen (684) 22111; Tjaro (454) 60063; Tjorn Ronnang (304) 677198; Tollarp (44) 310023; Tranas (140) 15166; Tranemo (3250 76710; Trollhattan (520) 12960; Trosa (156) 53228; Trysunda (660) 43038; Tyreso (8) 7700304; **U** Uddevalla (522) 15200; Ulricehamn (321) 13184; Ulvon (660) 34068; Umea (90) 111650 Upplands-Bro (8) 324220; Uppsala (180 324220; Uto (8) 50157660; **V** Vaddo (176) 50078; Vadstena (143) 10302; Valadalen (647) 35110; Vannas (935) 144 93; Vara (512) 10838; Varberg 9340) 41173; Varmskog (570) 61134; Varnamo (370) 19898; Vasteras 921) 185230; Vaxjo (470) 63070; Vilhelmina (940) 14165; Vimmerby (492) 10225; Vindelgransele (950) 82085; Visby (498) 269842; **Y** Ystad (411) 66566.

Hostels in the Archipelago:
F Finnhamn (8) 54246212; **G** Gallno (8) 57166117; **S** Skeppsmyra (176) 94027; St. Kalholmen (8) 54246023.

Work

You will need a work permit before entering the country. Contact: International Association for the Exchange of Students for Technical Experience, Imperial College, London SW7, UK or Arbetsmarknadsstyrelsen, Fack, S-17199 Solna, Sweden

Useful Addresses & Tourist Offices
in U.S.
Swedish Tourist Board
655 Third Ave., New York, NY 10017 tel: (212) 949-2333
in the U.K.
29-31 Oxford St., 5th Floor, London W1R 1RE, tel: 0171/437-5816
in Sweden
Stockhom Information Service-go to the Sweden House tel.08/789-2495
and City Hall (summer only)
Sveriges Forenade Studentkarer (Student Travel Department) at Kungsgatan
4, Stockholm tel: 34 01 80
Stockhom - Central Railway Station - Hotelcentrallen - hostel beds for
12kr, hotels - 25kr
1501 M Street, N.W., Washington, D.C. 20005, tel: (202) 467-2600, fax
(202) 467-2699
Swedish Embassies
in U.S.
Consulate-One Dag Hammarskjold Plaza, 45th Fl., 885 Second Ave. New
York, NY 10017, tel: (212) 751-5900, fax: (212) 755-2732
in Canada
377 Dalhousie St. Ottawa, Ontario, K1N 9N8, tel: (613) 241-8553
in the U.K.
11 Montagu Place, London, W1H 2AL, tel; 71 917 6400
Foreign Posts in Sweden
Stockholm
Canadian Embassy, Tegelbacken 4, S-161 29 Stockholm, tel: 011-46-8-
613-9900, M-F 9-5
British Embassy, 6 Skarpgatan, tel: 08/667-0140, M-F 9-5
United States Embassy, Strandvagen 101, S-115 89 Stockholm, tel: 011-
46-8-783-5300, M-F 9-6
Driving Distances (in km)
From Stockholm to cities in Sweden:

Haparanda 1064	Malmo576
Gothenburg 489	Ostersund 596
Kalmar 411	Umea 688

From Stockholm to European cities:

Belgrade 2,089	Madrid 3,295	Rome 3,000
Berlin 1,335	Munich 1,968	Vienna 1,973
Brussels 1,636	Oslo 530	Warsaw 1,922
Budapest 2,231	Paris 1,976	

Telephone Information: International Code 009, Country Code 46, Main
City Area Codes: Helsingborg 42, Malmo 40, Stockholm 8, Goteborg
31; time difference (Eastern Daylight) plus 6 hours. Emergency # 90000

A Little History

Switzerland was not originally a nation but a league of communities, a Confederation that wanted self-rule. Federal elements still characterize its political organization. The Federal State of 1848 with its 22 cantons (23 currently) was the expression of the common will. The partners were republics, communities with their own history, of differing ethnic origin, with different languages and outlooks. This explains why three languages exist: German, French and Italian. German has its centres in Zurich, Basel and Bern; French in Lausanne and Geneva and Italian in Lugano.

At the Congress of Vienna in 1815 the European powers promised Switzerland "recognition and sanction of everlasting neutrality". The country interferes in no foreign conflicts and enters into no pacts. In the eyes of many people, this makes Switzerland a mere spectator on the scene of world events but offers the Swiss full freedom of movement and action in the field of international business. It assumes the role of host, especially in Geneva, for many international organizations. By a popular referendum, Switzerland decided against joining the United Nations, but it cooperates in most international organizations, particularly in the area of development. It makes a corps of volunteers available to assist in case of natural catastrophes.

Population - 6,870,000
Capital - Berne
Government - Swiss Confederation
Religion - Roman Catholic and Protestant
Language - German 65%, French 18%, Italian 10%, Romansh 1%, English - is the 'fifth language'
Money - Swiss franc (SFr) One franc equals 100 centimes (French), centesimi (Italian) or Rappen (German), coins of 5, 10, 20 and 50 centimes and 1,2, 5 francs. Notes of 10, 20, 50, 100, 500, 1,000
U.S.$1 = 1 francs, Cdn.$1 = .7 francs, British £. = 1.7 francs
Public Holidays
Federal holidays when banks, stores and offices are closed are Jan. 1, Good Friday, Ascension Day, Dec. 25 and 26, Easter Monday, Whit Monday, August 1. The first four have Sunday transport services.
Visas
Americans, Canadians and U.K. citizens do not need visas.
Peculiar Customs and Odd Expressions
In all parts of Switzerland, the word used for thanking someone is always the French "merci". The Swiss use it often and are impressed when visitors do the same. The Swiss consider it impolite to keep your hands in

your pockets during conversation; the standard greeting is the handshake. Even children are encouraged to shake hands; in the German areas of Switzerland, women sometimes embrace, but men do not; in the French and Italian areas, both men and women may embrace. The French also kiss each other three times on the cheek. Gum chewing in public is inappropriate; backslapping is not appreciated. Flowers or chocolates are good gifts to give to your host.

Mid-April, in Zurich, a procession takes place wherein an effigy of winter is burned to the accompaniment of the church bells.

Best Festivals

Geneva Festival - second weekend of Aug. the 10-13, fireworks and parades

Lucerne - International Music Festival - mid August to mid September

Montreux - famous international Festival of Jazz on second Friday of July

Neuchatel - August14-19, International street musician festival (buskers festival)

Neuchatel - Wine Festival with parade Sept. 22-24

Salzburg - Salzburg Fest. in August - if you like opera - one of the world's best

Valais - cow fights in villages, they take place on many Sundays after April, the grand final is on Ascension Day in Aproz

National Day, August l, is celebrated in the country districts with processions in local costume, dancing, fireworks and bonfires lit to the surrounding heights

Night Activities and More

Bern - night club-Hollywood East

Davos - great for skiing

Geneva - dancing-New Mylord

Lenzerheide - Valbella - great for skiing

Lugano - Titanic discoteca

Zermatt - some of the best skiing in the country

Zurich - discos - Mascotte, Le Petit Prince; jazz-Casa Bar, Moods

Must See Tourist Sites

Bellinzona - a city of castles

Berne - Zeitglockenturm - clock tower, Cathedral - Old City, many fountains and museums

Fribourg - most of the medieval buildings of Switzerland

Geneva - Cathedrale St.Pierre-north tower gives best view, United Nations headquarters - Palais des Nations, Jet d'Eau 425 foot-high fountain

Grindelwald - Europe's longest gondola lift

Lucerne - Glacier Gardens, the covered bridge, Lion Monument, Transport Museum

Montreux - 13th century Chateau Chillon

Zurich - Rietberg Museum, Kunsthaus-paintings, Fraumunster Church, Grossmunster Cathedral built around 1100.

Best Scenery

Arosa - beautiful scenery from a hot air balloon

Ascona - great view of Lato Maggiore (lake)

Burgenstock - view overlooking Lake Lucerne

Crans-Montana - beautiful hills

Geneva and its lake and mountains

Grindelwald - gondola lift allows great views

Interlaken - mountain railway to the top of the Jungfrau

Lake Constance - incredible beauty

Lausanne - nestled on the north shore of Lake Geneva

Locarno - great view from Monte Bre mountain, half-way up is the Madonna del Sasso church

Mont-Pelerin - high above Lake Geneva - great view

Valais - impressive Alpine scenery

St.Moritz - best resort in case you are looking for a job

St. Moritz - three beautiful lakes nearby

Ticeno region - near Lugano, known for its' "Mediterranean Mood" (quite warm in winter - Switzerland's Florida)

Zermatt - the Matterhorn - most famous peak in the Alps

The valley between Lauterbrunnen and Grindelwald

Cycling

Rent from train stations for 19fr per day and returned to any station with a rental office, bikes can be transported on trains, but not city trains; 250 train stations available.

Bus

Eurail passes not valid, but Swiss passes are great for getting to out of the way villages.

Hitch-Hiking

Stay on the entrance ramps; much easier on secondary roads.

Train (prices in $U.S.)

Swiss Pass-8 day pass - 1st class - $280, 15 day pass - $328, 1 month - $452; 2nd class-8 day pass - $196, 15 day - $226, 1 month - $312 good for travel on trains, buses and ferries; Swiss Flexi Pass - 3 days of travel in a 15 day period - 1st class - $234, 2nd class - $156; The Half-Fare Travel Card - 1st class - $126 or 2nd class - $104 obtained at Swiss train stations, gives you 50% discounts on trains, buses, steamers and a free round-trip to the airport.

Camping

There are approximately 360 campsites, prices from 7-15 fr/person, plus 3-5 fr/tent, list available from Switzerland Tourism.

Farm Stays

To live on a farm with a Swiss family contact Schweizerischer Bauernverband CH-5200 Brugg tel. 056/42-32-77- they have a list of families - one week stay is required.

Youth Hostels

Contact: Schwizer Jugenherbergen, Schaffhauserstr 14, Postfach 161, 8042 Zurich, Switzerland, tel: (41) (1) 3601414, fax (41) (1) 3601460; 80 hostels - costs 17-30fr a night, nearly all include breakfast, non-members an extra 7fr, sheets 2fr, book in advance between June and September, no age limit, except people under 25 have priority.

Youth Hostel Town Locations and Telephone Numbers

A Arosa (81) 311397; Avenches (37) 752666; Avers (81) 631134; **B** Baden (56) 216796; **Basle** (61) 2720572; Beinwil am See (64) 711883; Le Bemont (39) 511707; Bern (31) 3116316; Biel (32) 412965; **Bonigen-Interlaken** (36) 224353; Braunwald (58) 841356; Brienz (36) 511152; Brugg (56) 411020; Bruson (26) 362356; **C** Champex (26) 831423; Chateau d'Oex (29) 46404; La Chaux-de-Fonds (39) 284315; **D** Davos-Wolfgang (81) 461484; Delemont (66) 222054; **E** Engelberg (41) 941292; **F** Fallanden (10 8253144; Faulensee (33) 541988; Figino (91) 601151; Filzbach (58) 321342; Flumserberg (81) 7331047; Frauenfeld (54) 213680; Fribourg (37) 231916; **G** Geneve (22) 7326260; Gersau-Rotschuo (41) 841277; Goschenen (44) 65169; **Grindelwald** (36) 531009; **H** Herzogenbuchsee (63) 611018; Hoch-Ybrig (55) 561766; Hospental (44) 67889; **J** Jona-Rapperswil (55) 279927; **K** Klosters (81) 691316; Kreuzlingen (72) 752663; **L** Langnau im Emmental (35) 24526; Laufen (53) 296152; **Lausanne** (21) 6165782; Leissigen (36) 471214; Lugano (91) 562728; **Lucerne** (41) 368800; **M** Maloja (82) 43258; Mariastein-Rotberg (61) 7311049; Meiringen (36) 711715; Melchsee-Frutt (41) 671467; **Montreux-Territet** (21) 9634934; **N** Neuchatael (38) 313190; **P** **Pontresina** (82) 67223 **R** Richterswil (1) 7862188; Romanshorn (71) 631717; **S** Saanen-Gstaad (300 41343; St.Antonien (81) 542238; St.Gallen (71) 254777; Sta Maria im Munstertal (reservations (82) 85052); Ste. Croix (24) 611810; **St. Moritz** (82) 33969; Safien-Thalkirch (81) 421107; Schaan-Vaduz (75) 2325022; Schaffhausen (53) 258800; **Sion** (27) 237470; Solothurn (65) 231706; Stein am Rhein (54) 411255; **V** Valbella-Lenzerheide (81) 341208; Vallorbe (21) 8431349; **W** Waltalingen (54) 451828; Wildhaus (74) 51270; Winterthur-Heigi (52) 2423840; **Y** Yverdon-les-Bains (24) 211233; **Z** Zermatt (28) 672320; Zofingen (62) 522316; **Zug** (42) 215354; **Zurich-Wollishofen** (1) 4823544.

Work

You must have work permit before entering the country and you must have special skills to work here, but unofficially you can look for work in ski resorts.

Babysitting

Geneva-Service de Placement de l'Universite 4, rue de Candolle tel: 329-39-70 or 705-77-02 call no later than 8:30 a.m. or Baby Call, 4, rue du Vieux-Billard tel: 781-06-66 Zurich-call Kady at 211-37-86.

Useful Addresses & Tourist Offices in U.S.

Switzerland Tourism

608 Fifth Ave., New York, NY, l0020 tel: (212) 757-5944 fax: (212) 262-6116

222 No. Sepulveda Blvd., suite 1570, El Segundo,(L. A.) CA 90245 (310) 335-5980 fax (310) 335-5982

150 N. Michigan Ave, suite 2930 Chicago, IL 60601 tel: (312) 630-5840 fax: (312) 630-5848

in Canada

926 The East Mall, Etobicoke, Ontario M9B6Kl tel: (416) 695-2090

in the U.K.

Swiss Centre, 1 New Coventry St., London W1V 8EE, tel: 0171/734-1921

in Switzerland

Bern - tourist office at Bahnhofplatz - main station - tel. 031/3116611

Luzern - city tourist office, at Frankenstrasse 1 tel. 041/517171

Zurich - Switzerland Tourist Office at 15 Bahnhofplatz - tel: 01/2114000 get the Swiss Pass or Swiss Half-Fare Card for 50% discounts on bus, rail, boat travel within the country

Swiss Student Travel Office, Leonhardstrasse 10, 8026 Zurich tel:242 30 00; in Geneva, Gare de Cornavin, main station, 022/738-5200; in Lugano, Riva Albertolli 5, downtown at the Lake Promenade, 091/24/4664/

Swiss Embassies

in U.S.

2900 Cathedral Ave. NW, Washington D.C. 20008-3499 tel: (202) 745-7900

Consulates: Atlanta, Chicago, Houston, Los Angeles, New York, San Francisco

in Canada

5 Marlborough Ave., Ottawa, Ontario KlN 8E6 tel: (613) 235-1837, Consulates in Montreal, Toronto, Vancouver

in the U.K.

16-18 Montagu Place, London, W1H 2BQ, tel: 171 723 0701

Foreign Posts in Switzerland

Geneva

Canadian Consulate, Pre-de-la-Bichette, 102 Geneva, tel: (022) 733-9000 fax (022) 734-7919

British Embassy, 37-39 Rue de Vermont, tel: 734-12-04

Bern

Canadian Consulate, Kirchenfeldstrasse 88, 3005 Bern, tel: (031) 44 6381, fax (031) 44-7315

United States Embassy, Jubilaumstrasse 93, 3005 Bern, tel: (031) 43-7011, fax (031) 43-7344

Zurich

United States Consulate, Zollikerstrasse 141, 8008 Zurich, tel: (01) 422-2566, fax (01) 383-9814

Driving Distances (in km)
From Berne to cities in Switzerland:

Basel 94	Interlaken 65	Montreux 100
Brig 112	Lausanne 94	St. Moritz 309
Davos 279	Lucerne 92	Taesch/Zermatt 149
Geneva 155	Lugano 273	

From Berne to cities in Europe:

Amsterdam 873	Milan 301	Stockholm 2,525
Berlin 982	Munich 448	Venice 581
Frankfurt 440	Paris 604	Vienna 873
Innsbruck 405	Rome 907	
Madrid 1,725	Salzburg 567	

Telephone Information: International Code 00, Country Code 41, Main City Area Codes: Basel 61, Bern 31, Geneva 22, Lausanne 21, Zurich 1; time difference (Eastern Daylight) plus 6 hours. Emergency # 117

SYRIA

A Little History

Syria was formerly part of Turkey's Ottoman Empire. Turkish forces were defeated in WWI (1914-1918) and Syria was occupied in 1920 by France. Syrian nationalists proclaimed an independent republic in 1941 and in 1949 Syria came under an army dictatorship, led by Brig. Adib Shishekly. He was elected President in 1953 and overthrown by another army coup in 1954. In 1958 Syria merged with Egypt to form the United Arab Republic, then following an army coup in Damascus, Syria seceded and formed the independent Syrian Arab Republic.

From 1977 onwards, frequent assassinations of Alawites (a minority Islamic sect to which President Assad belonged) reflected sectarian tension within Syrian society, and Assad attributed much of the opposition to the Muslim Brotherhood, a conservative Islamic group. In 1982 an uprising in Hama, from the outlawed muslim Brotherhood, was brutally suppressed.

Increasing border tension with Israel led to the Six-Day War in 1967 and the capture of the Golan Heights by Israel.

It was rumoured in 1991 that President Assad was preparing to introduce a degree of liberalization into Syria's political system, which is widely regarded as one of the most autocratic in the world. Assad did indicate in 1992 to the People's Assembly that new political parties might be established; however, he rejected the adoption of foreign deomocratic frameworks as unsuited to the country's level of economic development.

Capital - Damascus
Population - 12, 200,000
Government - Republic
Religion - Moslem
Language - Arabic, English and French
Money- Syrian pound (SL), one pound equals 100 piastres; declare your
foreign currency, you can take an unlimited amount in; you must change
US$100 into Syrian pounds at the border at a poor exchange rate.
U.S.$1 = 47 pounds, Cdn.$1 = 41pounds, British £ = 69 pounds

Public Holidays
The weekly holiday is Friday; January 1st, New Year's Day; March 8th
Revolution; March 21, Mother's Day; April 17th, Independence Day;
May 1st, Labour Day; May 6th, Martyr's Day; December 25th, Christ-
mas Day; Moveable Feasts: Easter, Id al-Fitr, Id al-Adhha, Hegira New
Year, Birthday of the Prophet Muhammad.

Visas
Canadians, Americans and U.K. citizens must get their visa at a Syrian consulate or embassy before you leave or at a Syprian post in another country; if
you plan to stay longer than 15 days report to the 'Direction de l 'Immigration des Passeports el de la Nationalite. Don't have an Israeli stamp in your
passport. Visas for Americans and U.K. citizens cost $35, $50 for multiple
entries, Canadians are charged $45, $70 for multiple entries.

Peculiar Customs and Odd Expressions
Syrians often will greet visitors with a warm embrace and will inquire
about their health. Women usually exchange kisses on either cheek.

Best Festivals
Aleppo - Cotton Festival in July
Bosra Festival in October
Damascus - International Flower Show in May, Film and Theatre Festival
in November
Sweida - annual exhibition of apples and vines during September

Night Activities and More
In Damascus, visit the Nawfara square east of the Omayyad Mosque, there
are many popular cafes, they provide the nargileh hubble bubble for
smoking

Must See Tourist Sights
Aleppo - the bazaar, the Great Mosque, Aleppo Citadel, Museum, Convent
of Semaan
Amrit - south of Tartus, unique temple carved in rock and surrounded by
water (5th century B.C.), huge stadium that holds 11,000
Bosra - 6th century Byzantine cathedral, Roman baths and Trajan's Palace,
Roman theater holds 15,000
Damascus - Grand Bazaar, Omayad Mosque, Azem Palace, National

Museum, the tomb of Saladin, Tetrapil Archway, the Wall of Damascus and its ramparts, Al-Maryamyah Cathedral, Nureddin bath-one of the most popular

Dara'a - caves and ancient dwellings, Roman amphitheater, remnants of some Roman baths and the old Oumari Mosque

Hama - huge old Roman waterwheels

Krak des Chevaliers - best crusader castle in the Middle East, worth going out of your way to visit, off the main Tartus to Homs highway, watch out for kids who throw large stones, hitching to it is ok, start early in the day

Latakia - beaches,ancient city, many ruins including a Roman trimphal arch, circa 200 A.D.Maalula - archaeologically famous for Deir Mar Tecia, Deir Mar Sarkis and the Funeral Caves. The people still speak Aramean, the language of Christ

Palmyra - wonderful ruins in the desert, ancient cemeteries, Citadel of the Ma'anites

Qala'at Salah al-Din - probably the most impregnable crusader fortress

Qala'at al-Marqab - near Banyas, enormous citadel, over 14 square and round towers

Qanawat - The Seraglio, Temple of the God of the Sun, the Temple of Zeus, the Church

Ras Shamra - important excavations, the first alphabet in the world, preserved on a clay tablet in the National Museum in Damascus

Seydnaya - convent which houses "Icon of Wonders", Church of Sophia, Deir Sherobim (convent)

Shahba - palaces, temples, arches, baths and a theatre surrounded by a huge wall

Sweida - city built of black volcanic rocks, many ruins

Yabroud - Iskafta Cave, the most ancient prehistoric cave; Yabroud Temple

Places to Avoid

Be aware that from May to Oct. there is a malaria risk, get a cholera shot and don't drink the water; avoid the Homs-Palmyra road-military movement (check with the tourist board or government office while in the country to find out if it is o.k. to travel on the road); don't tell people you were in Israel

Best Scenery

Kasab - the road leading to it from Latakia is one of the most beautiful in Syria-woods, meadows, wild flowers, groves of olive and pine leading to the beautiful forest of Frulloq

Slenfeh - 1,200 metres above sea level, spectacular scenery

Zeyzoun - several beautiful valleys, waterfalls, parks and cafes

Transportation

Buses are very cheap and overcrowded.

Hitch-Hiking

Fairly good, women should have a male companion.

Accommodation
Youth hostels are only12 pounds/night, hotels around 48 pounds.
Youth Hostel
Damascus - Damascus Youth Hostel, Saleh el Ali Street 66, Mazra'a Square,
  tel: 45 95 40 (same address for Syrian Youth Hostel Association) Other
  hostels are located in: Aleppo, Bosra, Der'a, Homs, Latakia, Zabadani
Useful Addresses & Tourist Offices
No tourist offices in North America, contact the embassies or consulates
  for information.
Damascus-Syrian Youth Hostel Association, Saleh el Ali Street 66, Mazra'a
  Square, tel:
45 95 40; Student Office at ISESTE (Syrian committee), University of
  Aleppo, Aleppo
in the U.K.
visit the embassy for tourist information
Syrian Embassies
in U.S.
2215 Wyoming Ave. N.W. Washington D.C. 20008, tel: (202) 232-6313,
  fax (202) 234- 9548
in Canada
Consulate: 1111 St. Urbain Ave. Room 109, Montreal, Quebec H2 1Y6,
  tel: (514) 397-9595, fax: (514) 397-6801
in the U.K.
Lebanese Embassy, Syrian Interest Section 8, Belgrave Square, London,
  SW1 BPH, tel: 245 9010
Foreign Posts in Syria
Damascus
US Embassy, P.O.Box 29, Abu Roumaneh, rue Al-Mansur 2, tel: 11-333-
  052, 332 557
British Embassy, P.O.Box 37, Quartier Malki, 11 rue Muhammed Kurd
  Ali, Immeuble Kotob, tel: 11-712 561/2/3
Driving Distances (in km)
From Damascus to cities in Syria:

Aleppo 355	Homs 162	Seydnaya 30
Bloudan 55	Kasab 407	Slenfeh 382
Bosra 137	Latakia 348	St. Simeon 397
Crac des Chevaliers 223	Ma 'lula 56	Sweida 106
Draykish 255	Palmyra 207	Tartus 258
Dara 'a 101	Quneitra 67	Zabadani 47
Hama 209	Safita 240	

Telephone Information:
International Code 011, Country Code 963, Main City Area Code: Damascus 11; time difference (Eastern Daylight) plus 7 hours.

A Little History

No need to travel to Rome to see the monuments the ancient Romans left. For nearly 600 years, Tunisia trembled to the tread of Roman legions. The great Colosseum at El Jem is far better preserved than the one in Rome. At Dougga or Sbeitla - only two of 250 historic sites - you wander among villas, temples and amphitheaters, with wild flowers and olive trees now growing between the ancient stones.

Long before the Romans arrived, Tunisia was the birthplace of the powerful Carthaginian Empire. From Carthage, Hannibal set out to crush the Romans, leading his 59,000 men and 40 elephants across the Alps in an epic campaign. Rome took a terrible revenge in 149 B.C., when Scipio left the city in ruins.

For 70 years before independence, Tunisia was a French protectorate, which explains why the capital, Tunis, has such a cosmopolitan and elegant air. Yet another example of the civilized Mediterranean influence that Tunisia reflects.

Capital - Tunis
Population - 8,200,000
Government - Independent republic under one-party presidential regime
Religion - majority are Moslem, religious tolerance is widespread
Language - Arabic, second language is French, English widely spoken in cities and tourist areas.
Money - Dinar (TD) One dinar equals 1,000 millimes. Coins of 5, 10, 20, 50, 100 millimes, and of 1/2, 1 dinar. Notes of 5, 10, 20 dinars.
U.S.$1 = .9 dinars, Cdn.$1 = .7 dinars, British £. = 1.7 dinars
Public Holidays
New Year, 1 January; 20-21 March; 9 April; 1 May; 25 July; 13 August; 7 November
Visas
Americans, Canadians and U.K. citizens do not need a visa.
Peculiar Customs and Odd Expressions
Tea and jasmin are symbols of welcome.
Best Festivals
Carthage International Festival - music and theater, July-August
Dougga International Festival - July - theater festival held in a Roman theater
El Jem International Festival of Symphonic Music, July-August
Hammamet International Festival, music and theater July-August
Sousse International Festival, music and theater July-August
The Oases Festival in Tozeur, bands and cultural activities in December

Night Activities and More
Hotels in major cities or tourist areas for dancing and music.
Must See Tourist Sights
Carthage - visit the magnificent Roman amphitheatre, the Antonine thermal baths, the Cathedral, the Museum
Dougga - incredible ruins, ruins of Bulla Regia nearby and the ruins of Teboursouk
Douz - Thursday morning market, sand dunes and oases
El Jem - extraordinary 3rd-century 30,000-seat Roman amphitheatre
Gabes - oasis town of 300,000 palm trees, handicraft town of Chenini nearby
Houmt - Souk-Bordj el Kebir - 15th century waterfront fort
Kairouan - holy city - one of the most important in Islam, see the Grand Mosque, the Medina
Matmata - citizens live underground in pits, 20-30 feet below the surface
Monastir - most interesting Ribat (monastery) in the country, climb the tower for the view of the Bourguiba mausoleum
Sousse - the fortified monastery - great view, Grand Mosque courtyard, the Museum
Tabarka - great coral diving, forests, and the famous Dougga archaeological sites nearby
Tozeur and Nefta in the south - beautiful oases, sand dunes, salt lake and medina
Tunis - the ancient medina, Djama ez Zitouna mosque, Bardo National Museum, visit Carthage nearby-Antonine Thermal Baths, amphitheatre
Places to Avoid
Hammamet - just a beach and tourists; Sfax - not an interesting village
Best Scenery
Sidi Bou Said - most appealing city in Tunisia
View of the two old ports of Carthage and the Gulf of Tunis from the summit of Mount Byrsa
See Tozeur, Nefta, Douz and the mountain oases: Chebika, Tamerza and Mides
Monastir and Sousse
Cap Bon peninsula
Cycling
Bicycle rental shops in Tunis: Ben Kilani: Avenue H. Bourguiba - tel: 31. 622; Ben Othmane - Avenue Habib Bourguiba; and Ben Aleya - Rue Sassi Bahri.
Transportation
Buses and trains very cheap.
Hitch-Hiking
People are friendly and curious, very good for rides, do not hitch with your thumb,wave your hand up and down.

Accommodation

Hotels range from 4-9 dinars, ranging from 1 to 5 stars.

Youth Hostels

Expect to pay in the area of 3-4 dinars per night plus linen rental if needed.

Contact: Association Tunisienne des Auberges de Jeunesse, 10 rue Ali Bach Hamba, BP 320-1015 Tunis RP, Tunisia, tel: (216) (1) 353277, fax (216) (1) 352172.

Youth Hostel Town Locations and Telephone Numbers

A Ain Draham (8) 647087; **B** Beja (8) 450621; Bizerte (2) 431608; **C** La Chebba (5) 683815; **G** Gabes (5) 270271; Gafsa (6) 220268; **H** Hammamet no tel. #; **J** Jendouba (8) 631292; Jerba (5) 650619; **K** Kairouan (7) 220309; Kasserine (7) 470053; Kebili (5) 490635; Kelibia (2) 296105; Korba (2) 289296; **M** Mahdia (3) 681559; Matmata Ancienne - mountain location, 530 km from Tunis; Mednine (5) 640338; Menzel Temime (2) 298116; Monastir (3) 461216; **N** Nabeul - 3 hostels - 1) Town Centre Hostel, tel: (2) 285547; 2) La Gazelle Hostel refer to de sejour et de vacances 'La Gazelle', Dat chaabane el fehri, tel: (2) 221366; 3) Maison des Jeunes Hostel, ask for street address, tel: (2) 286689; Nasrallah (7) 260045; **R** Ramla-Kerkenah (4) 281148; Rimel (2) 440804; **S** Seliana (8) 870871; Sfax (4) 243207; Sousse (3) 227548; **T** Teboursouk (8) 465095; Tozeur (6) 450235; Tunis - 3 hostels - 1) Jelili ez Zahra Hostel, refer to Centre d'hebergement, tel: (1) 481547; 2) Medina Hostel on 25 rue saida Ajoula-located in the old city of Medina, tel: (1) 567850; 3) Rades Hostel on Maison des Jeunes de Rades, 10 km outside Tunis, tel: (1) 483631; **Z** Zaghouan (2) 675265; Zarzis (5) 681599.

Useful Addresses & Tourist Offices

in U.S.

Tunisian Information Office, 1515 Massachusetts Ave. N.W., Washington, DC 20005. tel: (202) 466-2546, fax (202) 466-2553

in Canada

Tunisian National Tourist Office, 1253 McGill College, suite 655, Montreal, Quebec, H3B 2Y5, tel: (514) 397-1182, fax (514) 397-1647

in the U.K.

77A Wigmole St., London, W1, tel: 171 2266 98

Tunis

Tunisian National Tourist Office - 1 avenue Mohamed V , tel. 341-077

Tunisian Embassies

in U.S.

1515 Massachusetts Ave. N.W., Washington D.C. tel: (202) 862-1850, fax: (202) 862-1858

in Canada

515 O'Connor St., Ottawa, Ontario, K1S 3P8, tel: (613) 237-0330, fax: (613) 237-7939

in the U.K.
29 Brimes Gate, London, SW7 10G, tel: 584 81 17
Foreign Posts in Tunisia
Tunis
US Embassy , av. de la Liberte 144, tel: 232 566
British Embassy, place de la Victoire 5, tel: 245 100
Driving Distances (in km)
From Bizerta to cities in Tunisia:

Ain Draham 164	Monastir 228	Utique 38
Djerba 614	Sfax 334	
Dougga 158	Sousse 204	
Hammamet 126	Tabarka 138	
Kairouan 224	Tunis 64	

Telephone Information: International Code 00, Country Code 216, Main City Area Codes: Tunis 1, Sousse 3, Sfax 4, Gabes/Djerba 5, Bizette/ Nabeul 2, Tabarka 8; time difference (Eastern Daylight) plus 6 hours.

TURKEY

A Little History

Turkey has been called the "cradle of civilization" and by traveling through this historic land the tourist will discover exactly what is meant by this phrase. The world's first town, a neolithic city at Catalhoyuk, dates back to 6,500 B.C. From the days of Catalhoyuk up to the present time, Turkey boasts of a rich culture that through the centuries has made a lasting impression on modern civilization. The heir to many centuries of cultures, Turkey is a paradise of cultural wealth. Hattis, Hittites, Phrygians, Urartians, Lycians, Lydians, Ionians, Persians, Macedonians, Romans, Byzantines, Seljuks and Ottomans have all held important places in Turkey's history, and ancient sites and ruins scattered throughout the country give you proof to each civilization's unique distinction.

Turkey also has a very fascinating recent history. Upon the decline of the Ottoman Empire, a young man named Mustafa Kemal, who was a soldier by occupation but a great visionary in character, took the defeat of WWI and turned it into a shining victory by liberating Turkey of all foreign invaders. Mustafa Kemal Ataturk founded the Republic of Turkey in 1923. He led his country into peace and stability, with tremendous economic growth and complete modernization. Through decades of change and growth, Turkey still boasts of this success, living by their adopted motto of "Peace at Home, Peace in the World".

Capital - Ankara
Population - 63,000,000

Government - Republic

Religion - Muslim

Language - Turkish, some English, German, French and other European languages

Money- Turkish lira; Coins of 1,000, 2,500, 5,000, 10,000, Notes of 5,000, 10,000, 20,000 50,000, 100,000, 500,000, & 1,000,000 lira; the currency is weak, exchange money as frequently as needed, cash traveler's checks at banks-commissions charged, the best place for Visa cash advance is Turkiye Is Bank- no charge, keep currency exchange receipts so you change excess lira back to a hard currency. There are many private and legal change offices where the rates are better.

U.S.$1 = 38,762 lira, Cdn.$1 = 28,571 lira, British £ = 73,455 lira

Visas

Canadians do not need visas for stays less than 3 months. U.K. citizens and Americans need a visa- cost for U.K. citizens is $10 and Americans pay $20 - you can get a sticker visa at border gates for up to 3 months.

Peculiar Customs and Odd Expressions

Shake hands firmly when greeting or being introduced to a Turkish man, it is not customary to shake hands again upon departure; Turks may greet a close friend of either sex with a two-handed handshake and/or kiss on both cheeks. Displaying the soles of your shoes or feet to someone is insulting. Avoid blowing your nose in public, especially in a restaurant - if you must, turn away from others and blow as quietly as possible. Kissing, hugging, or even holding hands with someone of the opposite sex in public is only o.k. in cosmopolitan districts of big cities and tourist areas. "No" by wagging the head from side to side is a Turkish gesture for "I don't understand". It is considered rude to point your finger directly at someone. If you eat in someone's home, a gift will be expected such as wine, liquor, candy, pastries, roses, vase or goblet. If you stay overnight a better gift might be expected, such as records or books in English or small toys for the children. Wearing shorts is appropriate at the beach resorts and other tourist sites. Avoid taking sides in any Turkish political question or on the Turkish-Greek dispute over Cyprus. Hospitality is one of the cornerstones of the Turkish way of life; Turks are gracious and generous hosts. Hospitality is taken to such lengths that a foreigner often feels he is suffering from an overdose of it after being plied with food and drinks for hours and being unable to refuse anything, lest he hurt his host's feelings. Visit Turkish coffee-houses where men talk, sip coffee and play the national game of backgammon. In Istanbul, men can still be seen smoking their hubble bubble pipes called 'nargile'. Visitors to mosques should cover their arms and legs, and avoid prayer times. Women should dress conservatively.

In conservative circles marriages are still arranged by parents and they enforce strict rules of behavior.

Best Festivals

Ankara - International Childen's Festival - showcase of world cultures performed by children

Bursa - Karagoz folk dancing competition, July 7-12

Canakkale - Ayazma Festival - the world's oldest beauty contest, celebrating the goddesses Aphrodite, Athena, and Hera, August 17-19

Cesme-Izmir - Sea Festival & International Music contest-many famous pop singers

Edirne - 634th Annual Oil Wrestling tournament, folk dancing too

Istanbul Festival - June 20 - July 5 - international singers and concerts

Konya - demonstrations of Whirling Dervishes, Dec.10-17

Mugla - international car rally on April 4

Night Activities and More

Istanbul - Cafe Guitar, many other cafe-bars on Aptullah Sokak; best bet rooftop bar of the Orient Youth Hostel; other bars-Bebek, Orient Express, Kaktus; jazz-Hayal Kahvesi; check out the Aegean villages for camel wrestling

Oil wrestling - Turkish national sport, in July, wrestling championships are held in Kirkpinar, outside Edirne; the 'Javelin Game' - daredevil horsemanship with wooden javelins thrown at horseman of the opposing team to gain points. The game is played mainly in Eastern Turkey.

Turkish baths have been available since medieval times, get a rub-down, but they are known to be a bit uncomfortable for people who have never had one.

Must See Tourist Sights

Ankara - Museum of Anatolian Civilizations, Citadel

Antalya - Turkey's Riviera, 30 km away is the Karain Cave, dates back to 50,000 B.C., is the site of the oldest settlement in Turkey

Antakya (Antioch) - St. Peter's - oldest cave church in Christendom

Aphrodisias - city walls encircle several ancient buildings, 30,000 seat oval stadium, the museum, Temple of Aphrodite, Baths of Hadrian

Ayvalik - picturesque town, best views from Seytan Sofrasi; taxi ride to 4,000 year old hot spring in the Kosak Mountain

Bergama - Asclepion - ruins of ancient medical center

Bodrum - St.Peter castle

Dalyan - see the Caunos Rock Tombs

Dogubayazit - Ishak Pasa Palace- also gives beautiful view of the area

Edirne - Selimiye Camii - 2nd largest mosque in the world

Efes (Ephesus) - is one of the biggest Ionian harbors, many Ionian, Byzantine and Roman ruins, visit the Upper Agora - the Odeion, various baths, Temple of Domitian; walk along Marble St. built by Nero, 54-68 A.D., the beautiful theatre - seats 25,000; Library of Celsus

Istanbul - Arkeoloji Muzesi - one of the oldest ancient-art collections in the world; Blue Mosque; Hagia Sophia-beautiful church - turned into a mosque; district of Ortakoy - cafe, markets, cobblestone streets; Topkapi Palace, Yerebatan Sarayi - subterranean water reservoir; The Hippodrome; Kapali Carsi- the Grand Bazaar, Dolmabahce Palace

Izmir - bazaar; Kadifekale Castle

Kaymakli and Derinkuyu - near Nevsehir - incredible underground cities

Konya - Mevlana Muzesi-museum, Selimye Camii (Selim Mosque)

Samandag (Simon Mountain) important ruins of Sluice

Places to Avoid

Completely avoid the south-east area- armed conflict, especially in the Iraq border area; women should take the trains or buses, if you do hitch, do it with a male friend, dress conservatively. Do not deal in drugs and only change money at official locations. Do not sleep out in the open.

Best Scenery

Aegean Coast - the famous archaeological sites - Ephesus, Aphrodisias

Selcuk - Temple of Artemis (one of the seven wonders of the ancient world) St. John's Basilica

Cappadocia - this area stretches 150 km from Ihlara Gorge to the 5,000 room underground city of Derinkuyu and ancient Kayseri, this area has some of the most interesting landscape formations in the world - wind and weather have eroded the soft volcanic rock into hundreds of strangely shaped pillars, cones and "fairy chimneys", nearby is Goreme - people sleep in rock houses and Zelve - a deserted village carved into side of the hills

Pamukkale - natural wonder - petrified water falls, visit the warm thermal springs full of calcium, one of the country's best tourist attractions, the thousands tombs of Hierapolis near by

South coast of Turkey has beautiful beaches

Bus

Very efficient, cheap and reliable, and you can flag a bus down if you are stranded. Cost $1/100 km. Taxis also very cheap. Pay depending on the taximeter or approved rate; a modest tip is always welcomed.

Hitch-Hiking

No problems, people are friendly. Hitch by moving your hand up and down.

Train

Eurail only goes as far as Istanbul, InterRail can be used throughout the country. Istanbul to Ankara is only U.S.$10 for a 7 hour trip.

Camping

Cost U.S.$2, very few sites, but they are located on principal routes, near towns and tourist centres, open generally from April or May until October, contact tourist boards in major cities.

Guest Houses

Contact the tourist offices and TUREVS -Association for the Development of the Tourist Guest House, Cumhuriyet Blulvari, Elbir Ishani, No : 84/ 404, Alsancak, Izmir, tel: (232) 4257273; they can make a reservation anywhere in Turkey - reasonable prices.

Host Families

Arranging stays with host families contact: Genctur Turizm ve Seyahat Acentasi, at Yerebatan Cad., 15/3, 34410, Sultanahmet-Instanbul, tel (212) 5205274/75

Hotels

Only U.S.4-$9 a night.

Youth Hostels

U.S.1-$2 a night.

Youth Hostel Town Locations and Telephone Numbers

Istanbul - Istanbul Yucelt Interyouth Hostel on Caferiye Sok No. 6/1, Sultanahmet 34400, Istanbul, (1) 5136150

Marmaris Interyouth Hostel, Kemeralti Mah, Iyiliktas Mevkii, Marmaris, (612) 16432

Useful Addresses & Tourist Offices

in U.S.

Turkish Tourism Office, 821 United Nations Plaza, New York, NY 10017, tel: (212) 687-2194, fax (212) 599-7568

1717 Massachusetts Ave. N.W. suite 306 Washington D.C. 20036, tel: (202)-429-9844

in Canada

Turkish Tourism Office, 360 Albert St., suite 801 Ottawa, Ontario K1R 7X7 tel: (613) 230-8654 fax (613) 230-3683

in the U.K.

170-173 Piccadilly, 1st Floor, London W1V 9DD, tel: 0171/734-8681

in Turkey

Istanbul - agents locations - Sultanahmet district at Sultanahmet Meydani 3, at north tip of Hippodrome tel:1/518-18-02 Mon-Sat 9-5; also at Karakoy ferry docks., Hilton Hotel tel.212/233-0592 and at Ataturk Airport tel.212/ 663-6363

Ankara- 33 'Gazi Mustafa Kemal Bulvari, Demirtepe tel: 2301911

There are information offices at the airports in Istanbul and Ankara.

Turkish Embassies

in U.S.

1714 Massachusetts Ave. N.W., Washington D.C. 20036, tel: (202) 659-8200, fax: (202) 659-0744

in Canada

197 Wurtemburg St., Ottawa, Ontario K1N 8L9, tel: (613) 789-4044, fax: (613) 789-3442

in the U.K.

43 Belgrave Square, London, SW1X 8PA, tel: 4471 393 0202

Foreign Posts in Turkey
Istanbul
Canadian Consulate- Buyukdere Ca. 107, Gayrettepe, tel: 1/272-51-74
British Embassy - Mesrutiyet Cad. 34, Beyogulu, tel: 1/244-75-40
United States Embassy - Mesrutiyet Cad. 104-108, Tepebasi, tel: 1/251-36-02

Driving Distances (in km)
From Istanbul to cities in Turkey:

Adana 939	Izmir 565	Sivas 892
Ankara 454	Kayseri 770	Trabzon 1,079
Bursa 325	Konya 663	Usak 504
Edirne 227	Malatya 1,124	Yozgat 671
Giresun 942	Ordu 898	Zonguldak 333
Isparta 602	Samsun 733	

From Istanbul to cities in Europe:

Amsterdam 2,771	Copenhagen 2,718	Madrid 3,730	Dublin 3,634
Athens 1,205	Frankfurt 2,317	Milan 2,002	Sofia 558
Belgrade 940	Geneva 2,399	Munich 1,928	Stockholm 3,327
Berlin 2,257	Helsinki 3,005	Oslo 3,297	Venice 1,726
Brussels 2,726	Lisbon 4,374	Paris 2,759	Warsaw 2,009
Bucharest 729	London 3,100	Prague 1,909	Vienna 1,600
Budapest 1,135	Luxembourg 2,500	Rome 1,977	Zurich 2,230

Telephone Information: International Code 011 , Country Code 90, Main City Area Codes: Adana 322, Ankara 312, Bursa 224, Istanbul - 212 for European Istanbul and 216 for Asian Istanbul, Izmir 232; time difference (Eastern Daylight) plus 7 hours

UNITED KINGDOM England, Wales, Scotland, Northern Ireland

A Little History

In A.D. 43, the Roman emperor Claudius invaded Britannia, as the island was then called, and began the conquest of the Celtic tribes who inhabited it. The Romans ruled until the early 400's, when they withdrew to defend Rome from invaders. The Britons were then attacked and driven into Wales by Germanic tribes, especially the Angles, Saxons, and Jutes, who set up kingdoms throughout southern and eastern England. The Angles and Saxons soon became the most powerful tribes in England. During the 800s, the Danish Vikings attacked and conquered all the Anglo-Saxon kingdoms except Wessex. In 886, Alfred the Great, King of Wessex, drove back the Vikings and pushed them into the northeastern third of England. In 1066, Harold, the last Saxon king, was killed at the Battle of Hastings by Normans, led by William the Conqueror of France, who was crowned king of England.

England was occupied in the 1300s and 1400s against France in the Hundred Years' War (1337-1453) and the War of the Roses (1455-1485), a bitter struggle for control of the Crown. King Henry V11 emerged as England's new ruler. In 1707, Queen Ann joined England, Wales and Scotland under one Kingdom known as the Act of Union. At the end of the Seven Year's War, Britain acquired many of France's territories in North America and India. The Revolutionary War in America (1775-1783) resulted in the loss of the colonies that became the U.S. Britain grew richer than ever before through trade with the new nation. In the late 1700s, the Industrial Revolution began in Britain to make the country the richest in the world.

Britain was on the winning side of both World Wars, and after WW11 Britain's colonies demanded independence. From 1940-1980, about 40 British colonies became independent nations. Most remained associated with Britain through the Commonwealth of Nations.

The United Kingdom became a full member of the European Community in 1973. In 1987, Great Britain and France began construction of a railway tunnel under the the English Channel which has now linked Britain with mainland of Europe.

England	**Wales**
Capital - London	**Capital**-Cardiff
Population - 46,950,000	**Population -** 2,700,000
Government - Constitutional monarchy	**Government -** Constitutional monarchy
Religion - Church of England	**Religion -** Church in Wales
Language - English	**Language -** Welsh and English

Money- Pound Sterling (£) One pound equals 100 pence. Coins of 1, 2, 5, 10, 20, 50 pence and £1 . Notes of 5, 10, 20, and 50 £; Wales - same currency 1£ = U.S.$1.53, 1£ = Cdn$2.17

Public Holidays

January 1, Good Friday, Easter Monday, first Monday in May, last Monday in May or first Monday in June, last Monday in August, Christmas Day and 26 December. Most shops are closed on public holidays and bus and railway services are restricted. Also every town has one early closing day (1pm) weekly. Most shops close by 6 p.m.

Visas

Americans and Canadians do not need visas.

Peculiar Customs and Odd Expressions

Always shake the persons hand when visiting a home. When introduced, say "how do you do?; it is considered impolite to talk with one's hands in one's pockets. The British often do not look at the other person while they talk; don't point with your fingers, but instead indicate something with your head; sitting with your ankle resting on your knee may be seen as impolite; tapping your nose means confidentiality, or a secret; it is inappropriate to touch others in public; even backslapping or putting an arm around the shoulders of another can make the English uncomfortable; avoid excessive hand gestures when speaking; men give their seats to women on crowded public transportation

stiff upper lip- don't let it get you down

brill - fantastic, brilliant, great

cheers - pub toast, or thank you or goodbye

knock you up - wake up call

a ring - telephone call

Best Festivals

Contact British Tourist Authority for 'Forthcoming Events and Arts Festivals' Here's a good sample:

Bath International Arts Festival, late May

Chichester Drama Festival - 65 miles southwest of London-summer

Glastonbury Festival-huge, open-air music festival in Glastonbury, Somerset

Glyndebourne Music Festival in the county of Sussex

Henly-on-Thomas, Oxfordshire - late June-Henly Royal Regatta - premier rowing and social event

London - first week of June - Beating Retreat - military bands and marching, Whitehall, London

late August-Notting Hill Carnival-huge Caribbean carnival in London, also see the Easter Parade

Oxford/Cambridge University Boat Race, last week of March

Wales

In Llangollen - International Musical Eisteddfod, July, call 01978-860-236

Night Activities and More

London - discos - Hippodrome, Le Palais, Curzon, Gullivers, Shaftebury's, Gullivers; clubs - Wag Club, The Fridge, Gossips -all have cover charges.

Must See Tourist Sights

Aston Clinton - Buckinghamshire County Museum, Ascott House, Waddesdon Manor

Bath - Abbey Church, Roman Baths, Costume Museum

Brighton - number one seaside town

Bristol - Glass Museum, Thornbury Castle, Clifton Suspension Bridge

Cambridge - visit the Old Court, Saint Benet's Church

Canterbury - Cathedral; St.Augustines's Abbey

Carlisle - Farlam Hall-near Carlisle surrounded by 4 acres of walled gardens

Durham- cobbled streets and its cathedral

Exeter- one of the best cathedrals in England

London - such an array of sights and things to do in London, best to get organized by visiting the Tourist Information Center at Victoria Station

Covent Garden - central market and mostly boutiques; Buckingham Palace- Changing of the Guard daily at 11:30 a.m. from April to early August, every other day in winter; National Gallery; St. Paul's Cathedral; Guildhall; Tower of London; The Houses of Parliament; Westminster Abbey; Westminster Cathedral; Imperial War Museum; Tate Gallery; British Museum; Hyde Park; Kensington Palace and its gardens; Picadilly Circus, Leicester Square - great at night

Norwich - visit the Cathedral - begun in 1069 and many more churches

Salisbury - St.Mary's Cathedral, nearby famous Stonehenge

Stratford-Upon-Avon - Shakespeare's birthplace, Antique Car Museum

Warwick - one of England's best castles

Wells - probably the most beautiful cathedral in England

Winchester - Winchester Cathedral

Windsor Castle - an hour from London

York - Monk Bar - medieval gate, York Minster, York Castle Museum and much more

Wales

Cardiff - Cardiff Castle plus 150 more castles; Welsh Folk Museum, National Museum of Wales

Carmarthen - attractive old market town

Conwy - Conwy Castle - one of the grandest

Harlech - famous castle

Llandudno - two beautiful beaches and amazing limestone headland-the Great Orme

Swansea - lovely town

Wye Valley - Chepstow Castle

Best Scenery

England

Beachy Head (East Sussex), Land's End to St.Ives (Cornwall), Tintagel, Ilfracombe to Lynton/Lynmouth (Devon), St. David's to Cardigan (Dyfed, Wales), Scarborough to Saltburn (North Yorkshire), Exmoor National Park in North Devon, the Lake district, the Cotswolds

Wales

Valleys of the Usk and Wye-castles and Tintern Abbey, the Black Mountains and St. David's to Cardigan (Dyfed, Wales); and there are three National Parks -Brecon Beacons overlook some of the best scenery of Wales, wild and mountainous Snowdonia, and the beautiful Pembrokeshire Coast National Park

Bus

Much cheaper than trains, but slower.

Cycling

Many places in United Kingdom to rent bikes, approx. 15 pounds/week, can be taken on most trains, contact the Cyclists' Touring Club tel: 01483-

417211, at Cotterell House, 69 Meadrow, Godalming, Surrey GU7 3HS

Hitch-Hiking

Use entrance ramps to highways, illegal on highways, take bus or tube as far out of the city as possible to get a head start.

Train

BritRail Passes must be bought outside U.K. at travel agencies or contact BritRail Travel Information Office, l500 Broadway, New York, NY l0036 tel:1-800-677-8585. Buying individual full fare tickets is very expensive. Passes cover all of U.K., for BritRail prices see chapter 12 on train prices.

The Great British Heritage Pass offers you entrance to over 600 castles, stately homes, monuments, and gardens. Cost - 7 days Cdn $46, 15 days Cdn $62, 1 month Cdn.$90. Contact: Red Seal Tours, 170 Evans Ave. Ste. 201, Toronto, Ontario M8Z 5Y6, tel: (416) 503-2233 or 1-800-668-4224, fax (416) 503-0466

BritRail Travel International, 1500 Broadway, suite1000, New York, NY 10036 tel: 1-800-677-8585, fax: (212)-575-2542

Camping

For a listing buy Camping and Caravaning in Britain published by the Automobile Association, or contact the tourist boards.

Youth Hostels

Locations and membership information -YHA Adventure Shop, 14 Southhampton St. London WC2 7HY England near Covent Garden; tel: (44) (171) 836 1036, Fax (44) (171) 8366372; under 18 prices range from 3 to10 pounds, adults 5 to10 pounds; or contact the Youth Hostels Association for England and Wales at Trevelyan House, 8 St. Stephen's Hill, St. Albans, Hertfordshire AL1 2DY tel: (44) (1727) 855215, fax (1727) 845047. Over 240 youth hostels available, mostly in the countryside, cathedral cities and interesting towns, with many hostels serving meals.

Youth Hostel Town Locations and Telephone Numbers

A Acomb (1434)602864; Alfriston (1323) 870423; Alston (1434) 381509; **Ambleside** (15394 32304; Arnside (1524) 761781; Arundel (1903) 882204; Aysgarth Falls (1969) 663260; **B** Badby (1327) 703883; Bakewell (1629) 812313; Bala (1678) 520215; Baldersdale (1833) 650629; Bangor (1248) 353516; **Bath** (1225) 465674; Beer (1297) 20296; Bellever (1822) 88227; Bellingham (1434) 220313; Beverley (1482) 881751; Birmingham (1789) 297093; Blackboys (1825) 890607; Black Sail no #; Blaencaron (1974) 298441; Blaxhall (1728) 688206; Boggle Hole (1947) 880352; Borrowdale (17687) 77257; Borth (1970) 871498; Boscastle Harbour (1840) 250287; Boswinger (1726) 843234; Bradenham (1494) 562929; Bradwell Village (1908) 310944; Brandon (1842) 812075; Bretton (114) 2884541; Bridges Long Mynd (1588) 650656; Bridport (1308) 422655; Brighton (1273) 556196; **Bristol** (117) 9221659; Broad Haven (1437) 781688; Broadstairs (1843) 604121; Bryn Gwynant (1766) 890251; Bryn Poeth Uchaf (15505)

235; Burley (1425) 403233; Buttermere (17687) 70245; Buxton (1298) 22287; Byrness (1830) 520519; **C** Calshot (1703) 892077; **Cambridge** (1223) 35460l; **Canterbury** (1227) 462911; Capel Curig (16904) 225; Capel-y-Ffin (1873) 890650; **Cardiff** (1222) 462303; Carlisle (1228) 23934; Carrock Fell (16974) 78325; Castle Hedingham (1787) 460799; Castleton (1433) 621767; Charlbury (1608) 810202; Cheddar (1934) 742494; Chester (1244) 680056; Cleeve Hill (1242) 672065; Clun Mill (1588) 640582; Cockermouth (1900) 822561; Colchester (1206) 867982; Colwyn Bay (1492) 530627; Coniston (Holy How) (15394) 41323; Coniston Coppermines (15394) 41261; Copt Oak (1530) 242661; Corris (1654)761686; Coverack (1326) 280687; Crowcombe Heathfield (1984) 667249; Crowden-in-Longdendale (1457) 852135; Cynwyd (1490) 412814; **D** Dartington (1803) 862303; Dentdale (15396) 25251; Derwentwater (17687) 77246; Dimmingsdale (1538) 702304; Dolgoch (1222) 222122; **Dover** (1304) 201314; Dufton (17863) 51236; Duntisbourne Abbots (1285) 821682; Durham (191) 3842217; **E** Earby (1282) 842349; Eastbourne (1323) 721081; Edale (1433) 670302; Edmundbyers (1207) 55651; Ellingstring (1677) 460216; Elmscott (1237) 441367; Elterwater (15394) 37245; Elton (1629) 650394; Ely (1353) 667423; Ennerdale (Langdale) (1946) 861237; Epping Forest (181) 5085161; Eskdale (19467) 23219; Exeter (1392) 873329; Exford (164383) 288; Eyam (1433) 630335; **F** Ffestiniog (1766) 762765; **G** Glascwm (1982) 570415; Golant (1726) 833507; Gradbach Mill (1260) 227625;Grasmere - 2 hostels - 1) Butterlip Hostel on Butterlip How, tel: (15394) 35316; 2) Thorney How Hostel on Thorney How, tel: (15394) 35591; Great Yarmouth (1493) 843991; Greenhead (16977) 47401; Grinton (1748) 884206; **H** Harlow (1279) 421702; Hartington (1298) 84223; Hastings (1424) 812373; Hathersage (1433) 650493; Hawes (1969) 667368; Hawkshead (15394) 36293; Haworth (1535) 642234; Helmsley (1439) 770433; Helvellyn (17684) 82269; Hindhead (142) 8604285 Hombury St. Mary (1306) 730777; Honister Hause (17687) 77267; Hunstanton (1485) 532061; **I** Idwal Cottage (1248) 600225; Ilam (1335) 350212; Ilfracombe (1271) 865337; Ingleton (15242) 41444; Instow (1271) 860394; Ironbridge Gorge (1952) 433281; Ivinghoe (1296) 668251; **J** Jordans (1494) 873135; **K** Keld (1748)886259; Kemsing (1732) 761341; Kendal (1539) 724066; Keswick (17687) 72484; Kettlewell (1756) 760232; Kings, Dolgellau (1341) 422392; King's Lynn (1553) 772461; Kirby Stephen (17683) 71793; **L** Land's End (1736) 788437; Langdale (High Close) (15394) 37313; Langdon Beck (1833) 22228; Langsett (114) 2884541; Lincoln (1522) 522076; Linton (1756) 752400; Litton Cheney (1308) 482340; Llanbedr (1341) 241287; Llanberis (1286) 870280; Llanddeusant (15504) 634; Llangollen (1978) 860330; Lledr Valley (16906) 202; Llwyn y Celyn (1874) 624261; Llwynypia (1443) 430859; Lockton (1751) 460376; **London** - 7 hostels- 1) **City of London Hostel** on 36 Carter

Lane, tel: (171) 2364965; 2) **Earls Court Hostel** on 38 Bolton Gardens, tel: (171) 3737083; 3) **Hampstead Heath Hostel** on 4 Wellgarth Rd.,tel: (181) 4589054; 4) **Highgate Village Hostel** on 84 Highgate West Hill, tel: (181) 3401831; 5) **Holland House Hostel** very near Golders Green Tube Station, tel: (171) 9370748; 6) **Rotherhith Hostel** on Salter Rd, tel: (171) 2322114; 7) **Oxford Street Hostel** on 14 Noel St., tel: (171) 7341618; Ludlow (1584) 872472; Lulworth Cove (1929) 400640; Lynton (1598) 53237; **M** Maeshafn (1222) 396766; Malham (1729) 830321; Malton (1653) 692077; Malvern Hills (1684) 569131; **Manchester** (171) 2486547; Mankinholes (1706) 812340; Manorbier (1834) 871803; Marloes Sands (1646) 636667; Matlock (1629) 582983; Maypool (1803) 842444; Meerbrook (1629) 650394; Minehead (1643) 702595; Monmouth (1600) 715116; **N** Newport (1222) 396766; Newcastle upon Tyne (191) 2812570; Ninebanks (1434) 345 288; Norwich (1603) 627647; **O** Once Brewed (1434) 344360; Osmotherley (1609) 883575; **Oxford** (1865) 62997; **P** Patterdale (17684) 82394; Pendennis Castle (1326) 311435; Pentlepoir (1834) 812333; Penycwm (Solva) (1437) 720959; Pen-y-Pass (1286) 870428; Penzance (1736) 62666; Perranporth (1872) 573812; Plymouth (1752) 562189; Poppit Sands (1239) 612936; Port Eynon (1792) 390706; Portsmouth (1705) 375661; Pwll Deri (13485) 233; **Q** Quantock Hills (1278) 871826; **R** Ravenstor (1298) 871826; Ridgeway (12357) 60253; Rowen no tel. #; **S** Saffron Walden 91799) 523117; St. Briavels Castle (1594)530272; St. David's (1437) 720345; Salcombe (154884) 2856; Salisbury (1722) 327572; Sandown (Isle of Wight) (1983) 403565; Scarborough (1723) 361176; Sheringham (1263) 823215; Shining Cliff (1629) 650394; Shrewsbury (1743) 357423; Shiddaw House (no reservations possible, remote location, no one turned away, no access by car); Slaidburn (1629) 825850; Slimbridge (1453) 890 275; Snowdon Ranger (1286) 6500391; Stainforth (1729) 823577; Steps Bridge (1647) 252435; Stouthall (1792) 391086; Stow-on-the-Wold (1451) 830497; **Stratford-upon-Avon** (1789) 297093; Streatley-on-Thames (1491) 872278; Street (1458) 442961; Swanage (1929) 422113; **T** Tanners Hatch (1372) 452528; Tebay (15396) 24286; Telscombe (1273) 301357; Thirlmere (17687) 73224; Thixendale (1377) 288238; Thurlby (1778) 425588; Tintagel (1840) 770334; Totland Bay (Isle of Wight)(1983) 752165; Trevine (1348) 831414; Treyarnon Bay (1841) 520322; Truleigh Hill (1903) 813419; Tyncornel (1222) 222122; Ty'n-y-Caeau (1874) 665270; **W** Wastwater (19467) 26222; Welsh Bicknor (1594) 860300; Wheathill (1746) 787236; Wheeldale (1947) 896350; Whitby (1947) 602878; Wilderhope Manor (1694) 771363;Winchester (1962) 853723; Windermere (15394) 43543; **Windsor** (1753) 861710; Woody's Top (1507) 533323; Wooler (1668) 281365; **Y** **York** (1904) 653147;Youlgreave (1629) 636518;Ystradfellte (1639) 720301;Ystumtuen (197085) 693.

University Accommodation

Contact British Universities Accommodation Consortium, Box No 967, University Park, Nottingham NG7 2RD tel: 0115-950-4571 usually includes breakfast.

Work Permits

Citizens of Commonwealth countries between 17 and 27 inclusive can apply for a Working Holiday Entry Certificate that allows you to spend up to two years in the UK, you must apply before you leave your country at a UK embassy/consulate. You can't change your status as a visitor while in the UK to get employment legally. When you apply, you must prove to the authorities that you have sufficient funds or access to funds to pay for a return or onward ticket. If you are a Commonwealth citizen and have a parent born in the UK you may be eligible for a Certificate of Entitlement to the Right of Abode. This allows you to live and work in Britain free of immigration control. American students 18 or older visiting the UK can get a work permit for 6 months - apply at a cost of $125 through Council on International Educational Exchange at 205 East 42nd St, New York, NY 10017 tel: 212 661-1414. In the UK, ask at the Home Office, Immigration and Nationality Department, Lunar House, Wellesley Rd, Croydon CR2 (East Croydon BR) tel:0181-686-0688. Americans should contact the British Embassy in Washington D.C. and Canadians should contact the British High Commission in Canada (see addresses below).

Babysitting

In London call Babsitters Childminders, 9 Paddington St., W.l. tel: 071-930-8422

Useful Addresses and Tourist Offices
in U.S.

British Tourist Authority, 551 5th Ave. 7th Floor, New York, NY 101 76-0799 tel:(212) 986-2266, fax 212-986-1188 or 1-800- 462-2748, information and brochures (212) 986-2200;

or 625 North Michigan Ave., suite 1510, Chicago, IL 60611 tel: (312) 787-0490

or 350 South Figueroa St., suite 450, Los Angeles, CA 90071 tel: (213) 628-3525

in Canada

111 Avenue Road, suite 450, Toronto, Ontario M5R 3J8 tel: (416) 925-6326
in London

Tourist Info. from the British Tourist Authority in London at Victoria Station, Forecourt, 12 Regent St. off Piccadilly Circus, tel:071 730 3488; British Travel Centre at 12 Regent St. tel: 071 730 3400; London Tourist Board and Convention Bureau, 26 Grosvenor Gardens, SWl tel: 071 730 3488 or at the Heathrow Travel Center

Wales Tourist Board at 2 Fitzalan Rd., Cardiff CF2 lUY tel: 01222-499909, outside of Britain contact BTA

UK Embassies
in U.S.
British Embassy, 3l00 Massachusetts Ave. NW, Washington DC 20008 tel:(202) 462-l340
in Canada
British High Commission, 80 Elgin St. Ottawa KlP 5K7 tel: (6l3) 237-l530
Foreign Posts in England
London
Canada House, 38 Grosvenor St. tel: 0171/258-6600, Tube (Subway) stop: Bond St. M-F 8:45-3
United States Embassy 24 Grosvenor Sq., tel: 0171/499-9000 Tube stop: Marble Arch or Bond St. M & W - F 8:30-12, T 8:30-12
Driving Distances (in miles)
From London to cities in the U.K.

Aberdeen 528	Glasgow 327	Plymouth 234
Birmingham 120	Inverness 501	Southampton 80
Bristol 208	Liverpool 243	
Dover 77	Manchester 208	
Edinburgh 450	Newcastle Upon Tyne 342	

Telephone Information: International Code 011, Country Code 44, Main City Area Codes: London 71 or 81, Cardiff 222, Chester 244, York 904, Manchester 61, time difference (Eastern Daylight) plus 5 hours. Emergency # 999

SCOTLAND

Population - 5,200,000
Capital - Edinburgh
Government - Constitutional monarchy
Religion - Presbyterian
Language - English, some Gaelic
Money - £ Sterling (same as England) - Scottish notes are also accepted (in Scotland only)
Peculiar Customs and Odd Expressions
Slans-jevah-a Gaelic toast instead of saying 'cheers'; a "foursome" in golf means two balls and four players; in the 'wee sma oors'- in the early hours; face washing in dew on Arthur's Seat, Edinburgh; 'first footing' - the first person who comes into a friends' house (crosses the threshold) on New Year's Eve must bring a lump of coal or a 5 lb. bag of sugar.

Best Festivals

Contact the BTA for a complete list and exact dates.

Edinburgh Folk Festival - last week in March

Edinburgh Military Tattoo - pagaentry and military displays, runs for 3 weeks, early August; and in mid-August the International and Fringe Festivals for 3 weeks; Nov. 5 -Guy Fawkes Day - in memory of an unsuccessful Catholic coup, bonfires and fireworks around Great Britain.

Glasgow Mayfest - arts festival runs for 3 weeks, early May

Night Activities and More

golfing - Old Course at St. Andrews-open to public; contact Tours and Travel Promotions at 25 Brunstane Dr., Edinburgh EH15 2NF tel:(031) 669-5344 for places to golf , hunt, fish, ride and sail

Edinburgh - discos- The Network, Calton Studios, Red Hot Pepper Club, the Amphitheatre, Buster Brown's, Century 2000

Must See Tourist Sights

Aberdeen - St. Machars's Cathedral, Fish Market

Ballater - castles-Balmoral, Craigievar, Braemar, Crathes , Gardens, Drums

Banff - Slains Castle

Cupar - Fernie Castle - 14th century

Edinburgh - Edinburgh Castle, Parliament House, St.Giles Cathedral, Anchor Close - 16th century taverns; Royal Museum, National Gallery, Georgian House; Linlithgow Palace 1 hour outside of Edinburgh, Holyrood Palace

Glasgow - Cathedral 1197; University 1450, Croodston Castle

Loch Ness - best view of this infamous monster is from Urquhart Castle

St. Andrews - famous golf course, the Castle, town museum, 12th century Cathedral

Stirling - beautiful castle

Best Scenery

The Highlands contain mountains-including Britain's highest-Ben Nevis ; plains of the Central Lowlands, the coastline especially on the west coast; visit the forest parks of Galloway and Argyll - beautiful, unspoilt countryside

Youth Hostels

Contact: Scottish Youth Hostels Association, 7 Glebe Crescent, Stirling, FK8 2JA, Scotland, tel: (44) (786) 451181; Fax (44) (786) 450198, over 80 hostels available ranging from 3-10 pounds a night.

Youth Hostel Town Locations and Telephone Numbers

A Abbey St. Bathans (13614) 311; Aberdeen (1224) 646988; Achininver (1584) 622254; Achmelvich (1571) 844480; Ardgartan (13012) 362; Armadale (1471) 844260; Aviemore (1479) 810345; Ayr (1292) 262322; **B** Ballater (13397) 55227; Berneray - no tel. #; Braemar (13397) 41659; Broadford (14718) 22442; Broadmeadows (175076) 262; **C** Cannich (1456) 415244; **Carbisdale Castle** (1549) 421232; Carn Dearg (1445) 2219

Coldingham (18907) 71298; Craig no tel. #; Crianlarich (1838) 300260; **D** Durness (1971) 511244; **E** Eday (18572) 283; **Edinburgh** - 2 hostels - 1) **Bruntsfield Hostel** on 7 Bruntsfield, tel: (131) 4472994; 2) **Eglinton Hostel** on 18 Eglinton Crescent, tel: (131) 3371120; **F** Falkland (1337) 857710; **G** Garenin (Isle of Lewis) no tel. #; Garramore (16875) 268; **Glasgow** (141) 3323004; Glen Affric no tel#; Glenbrittle (1478) 640278; Glencoe (1855) 811219; Glendevon (1259) 781206; Glendoll (1575) 550236; Glen Nevis (1397) 702336; **H** Helmsdale (1431) 821577; Howmore no tel. #; Hoy no tel. 3; **I** Inveraray (1499) 2454; Inverey no tel. #; **Inverness** (1463) 231771; Islay (1496) 85385; **J** John o'Groats (195581) 424; **K** Kendoon no tel. #; Killin (1567) 820546; Kingussie (1540) 661506; Kirkwall (1856) 872243; Kirk Yetholm (1573) 420631; Kyleakin (1599) 4585 **L** Lerwick (1595) 2114; Loch Ard (18777) 256; Loch Lochy (18093) 501239; Loch Lomond (1389) 850226; Lochmaddy (1876) 500368; Loch Morlich (1479) 861238; Loch Ness (1320) 351274; Loch Ossian (1397) 732207; Lochranza (1770) 830631; **M** Melrose (189682) 2521; Minnigaff (1671) 402211; **N** New Lanark (1555) 666710; **O** Oban (1631) 62025; **P** Papa Westray (18574) 267; Perth (1738) 623658; Pitlochry (1796) 472308; **R** Raasay (1478) 660240; Rackwick no tel. #; Ratagan (1599) 511243; Rhenigidale no tel. #; Rowardennan (1360) 870259; **S** Snoot (145088) 259; **Stirling** (1786) 473442; Stockinish (1859) 530373; Strathpeffer (1997) 421532; Stromness (1856) 850589; **T** Tighnabruaich (1700) 811622; Tobermory (1688) 302481; Tomintoul no tel. #; Tongue (184755) 301; Torridon (1445) 791284; **U** Uig (1470) 542211; Ullapool (1854) 612254; **W** Wanlockhead (1659) 74252; Whiting Bay (17707) 00339.

Babysitters
Edinburgh - call Guardian Babysitting, 13 Eton Terrace, tel 343-3870.
Useful Addresses and Tourist Offices
Scottish Tourist Board 23 Ravelston Terrace, Edinburgh tel; 332 2433 - postal and telephone inquiries only or Scottish Tourist Board Inormation Department, P.O. Box 705, Edinburgh E4H 3EU tel: 031-332-2433
Edinburgh University Student's Association at Bristo Square tel: 667 -0214
in London, contact Scottish Tourist Board, 19 Cockspur St..London SW15BL, near Trafalgar Square tel: 0171-930-8661
Scottish Youth Hostels Assoc., 7 Glebe Crescent, Stirling FK8 2JA tel: 01786-451181
Telephone Information: International Code 011, Country Code 44, Main City Area Codes: Edinburgh 131, Glasgow 141, Inverness 1463, Stirling 1786; time difference (Eastern Daylight) plus 5 hours. Emergency # 999
100 Best Castles in the United Kingdom and Ireland
Castles seem to always evoke a romantic notion of medieval nirvana. Step back in time to meander through some castles that were built over 1,000 years ago. Often overlooked are the beautiful gardens, lawns and hedges

which provide the perfect back-drop of these masterpieces. You will never find two castles that look alike, so if you are not too far from one of these 100 castles, be sure to take the time visit one. The castles listed are in no particular order of preference.

England

1 Tower of London
2 Leeds Castle, near Maidstone, Kent
3 Deal Castle, Kent
4 Dover Castle, Kent
5 Richbrough Castle, near Sandwich, Kent
6 Hever Castle, Kent
7 Rochester Castle, Kent
8 Pevensey Castle, East Sussex
9 Bodiam Castle, East Sussex
10 Arundel Castle, West Sussex
11 Amerley Castle, West Sussex
12 Portchester Castle, Hampshire
13 Carisbrooke Castle, Isle of Wight
14 Mont Orgueil, Gorey, Jersey
15 Castle Cornet, St.Peter Port, Guernsey
16 Corfe Castle, Dorset
17 Windsor Castle, Bershire
18 Thornbury Castle, Avon
19 Darmouth Castle, Devon
20 Launceston Castle, Cornwall
21 St. Mawes Castle, near Falmouth, Cornwall
22 Tintagel Castle, Cornwall
23 Dunster Castle, Somerset
24 Berkeley Castle, Gloucestershire
25 Sudeley Castle, near Winchcombe, Gloucestershire
26 Colchester Castle, Essex
27 Hedingham Castle, Essex
28 Framlingham Castle, Suffolk
29 Orford Castle, Suffolk
30 Caister Castle, Norfolk
31 Castle Rising, Norfolk
32 Lincoln Castle, Lincolnshire
33 Tattershall Castle, Lincolnshire
34 Kenilworth Castle, Warwickshire

35 Warwick Castle, Warwick
36 Goodrich Castle, near Ross-on-Wye. Hereford & Worcester
37 Ludlow Castle, Shropshire
38 Lancaster Castle, Lancashire
39 Coisbrough Castle, South Yorkshire
40 Skipton Castle, North Yorkshire
41 Ripley Castle, North Yorkshire
42 Richmond Castle, North Yorkshire
43 Raby Castle, near Staindrop, County Durham
44 Durham Castle, Durham
45 Carlisle Castle, Cumbria
46 Housesteads, near Bardon Mill, Northumberland
47 Warkworth Castle, Northumberland
48 Alnwick Castle, Northumberland
49 Dunstanburgh Castle, near Embleton, Northumberland
50 Bamburgh Castle, Northumberland

Wales

51 Caerleon Roman Fort, Gwent
52 Chepstow Castle, Gwent
53 Raglan Castle, Gwent
54 Caerhilly Castle, Mid Glamorgan
55 Cardiff Castle, Cardiff
56 Manorbier Castle, Dyfed
57 Pembroke Castle, Dyfed
58 Carreg Cennen Catle, near Llandeilo, Dyfed
59 Cilgerran Castle, Dyfed
60 Powis Castle, near Welshpool
61 Harlech Castle, Gwynedd
62 Caernarfon Castle, Gwynedd
63 Beaumaris Castle, Gwynedd
64 Conwy Castle, Gwynedd
65 Chirk Castle, Clwyd

66 Denbigh Castle, Clwyd
67 Rhuddlan Castle, Clwyd
68 Castle Rushen, Castletown, Isle of Man

Scotland

69 Hermitage Castle, Borders
70 Caerlaverock Castle, near Bankend, Dumfries & Galloway
71 Threave Castle, near Castle Douglas, Dumfries & Galloway
72 Bothwell Castle, Strathclyde
73 Edinburgh Castle, Lothian
74 Tantallon Castle, near North Berwick, Lothian
75 Stirling Castle, Central
76 Doune Castle, Central
77 Loch Leven Castle, near Kinross, Tayside
78 Glamis Castle, Tayside
79 Edzell Castle, Tayside
80 Blair Castle, Tayside
81 Dunnottar castle, near Stonehaven, Grampian
82 Castle Fraser, near Kemnay, Grampian
83 Kildrummy Castle, Grampian
84 Fyvie Castle, Grampian

85 Delgatie Castle, near Turriff
86 Urquhart Castle, near Drumnadrochit, Highland
87 Eilean Donan Castle, Dornie, Highland
88 Cawdor Castle, Highland
89 Brodick Castle, Isle of Arran
90 Rothesay Castle, Isle of Bute
91 Dunvegan Castle, Isle of Skye

Northern Ireland

92 Carrickfergus Castle, County Antrim
93 Dunluce Castle, Portballintrae, County Antrim
94 Dundrum Castle, Newcastle, County Down
95 Enniskillen Castle, Enniskillen, County Fermanagh
96 Dublin Castle, Dublin
97 Mahahide Castle, County Dublin

Ireland

98 Bunratty Castle, County Clare Ireland
99 King John's Castle, Adare, County Limerick
100 Blarney Castle, County Cork

NORTHERN IRELAND

A Little History

The sectarian tension that has characterized Ireland's history began with the first major settlement by British Protestants, particularly Presbyterians from Scotland, in the 17th century. The main area of Protestant colonization in Ireland was the province of Ulster. Protestant supremacy over the indigenous Roman Catholics was established in a large part of the province. As a result of the Act of Union (1800), Ireland became part of the new United Kingdom. Throughout the 19th century there were frequent demands for Irish independence, strongly supported in most of the island, and an organized movement seeking Home Rule emerged. In the north, however, an Ulster Unionist Council was established in 1911, with Protestant support, to resist Irish nationalist demands and to campaign for the continuation of union with Great Britain.

The resentment of Irish nationalists came to a head in 1916 with the Easter rising in Dublin. The rebellion was suppressed, but a volunteer force, the Irish Republican Army (IRA), continued to wage a guerrilla campaign against the British administration in an attempt to force British withdrawal from Ireland. Faced with mounting popular support for independence, the British government conceded to the demand for Home Rule, but only to a limited extent, since this was strongly opposed by Protestants in Ulster, who did not wish to become part of a Catholic-dominated all-Ireland state. The Government of Ireland Act (1920) provided for two parliaments in Ireland: one in Dublin, for 26 of the 32 counties, and one in Belfast, for the remaining six counties, which collectively became known as Northern Ireland and stayed within the United Kingdom.

Population - 1,500,000
Capital - Belfast
Government - Constitutional monarchy
Religion - Prostestant and Roman Catholic
Language - English
Money - same as U.K.; British £ sterling and Ulster Bank notes look very much the same, but it is difficult to exchange the Ulster Bank notes in England, Scotland and Wales.
Public Holidays
July 12 - the day of the parades of Orangemen; in Belfast 20,000 men with bands and banners take part-the week in which this day falls is the traditional holiday week. Bank holidays are the same as in England, with the addition of March 17 (St.Patrick's Day) and July 12.
Night Activities & More
Quaint Belfast pubs- Crown Liquor Saloon, Morning Star White's Tavern, Ye Olde Eglantine Inn and Botanic Inn
Must See Tourist Sites
Armagh - historic city, the ecclesiastical center of Northern Ireland with the Roman Catholic church and Church of Ireland located here, known as the 'city of saints and scholars', visit the St.Patrick's Roman Catholic Cathedral and St.Patrick's Church of Ireland Cathedral
Belfast - City Hall, Bushmills Distillery, the clock tower, old Grand Opera House
Londonderry - 17th century Walls of Derry encircle the historic city centre and offer good views of the surrounding area
Best Scenery
Dramatic lakeland scenery in the west

Antrim Coast Road, Glens of Antrim which are beautiful small valleys-great for walking

Carrick-a-rede-rope bridge on the way to Giant's Causeway

Giant's Causeway - one of the natural wonders of the world, incredible formation of basalt rock

There are beautiful walking and cycling trails and great fishing.

Accommodation

For complete hostel listings contact Youth Hostel Association of Northern Ireland at 22 Donegall Rd, Belfast BT12 5JN tel: (01232) 324733

Youth Hostels

Youth Hostel Association of Northern Ireland, 22 Donegall Rd., Belfast, BT12 5JN, Northern Ireland, tel: (44) (1232) 324733, fax (44) (1232) 439699; prices range from 5 -8.50 pounds per night including bedlinen.

Youth Hostel Town Locations and Telephone Numbers

B Belfast (1232) 324733; **C** Castle Archdale (13656) 28118; Cushendall (12667) 71344; **L** Londonderry (1504) 372273; **N** Newcastle (13967) 22133; **O** Omagh (1662) 241973; **P** Portaferry (12477) 29598; **W** Whitepark Bay (12657) 32034.

Useful Addresses and Tourist Offices

Northern Ireland Tourist Board, 551 5th Ave. 7th floor, New York, NY 10176 tel: (212) 922-0101 or 1-800 326-0036

111 Avenue Rd., suite 450 Toronto, Ontario M5R 3J8 tel. (416) 925-6368

NITB in Dublin-16 Nassau St., tel (01) 679-1977, in Belfast, 59 North St., Belfast BT1 1NB tel: (01232) 246609

Telephone Information: International Code 00, Country Code 44, Main City Area Codes: Belfast 1232; time difference (Eastern Daylight) plus 5 hours. Emergency # 999

'Voluntary' sleep in a small town police station in Germany.

14.

General Advice: Traveler's Tips

Some Do's...

Always visit the national and city tourist offices when you arrive in a city. Pick up brochures and study them to plan your activities.

Visit embassies and consulates to get advice and information on the areas you're visiting and any neighboring countries you plan to visit. Martial law can be implemented without much warning in certain countries (not a problem in Western Europe). As well as to catch up on hometown news by reading Canadian or U.S. newspapers.

Collect something: small coins, seashells, pebbles, stamps. I collected coins and the smallest paper currency from each country, the front page of national newspapers (in Finland the first two pages are advertising!) and bottle-openers from each country.

Keep an eye open for casual jobs - check English newspapers.

Shop with a relative or friend who lives in the country to avoid paying tourist prices - shop where the locals shop.

Join the local recreation. Work out in a gym, join a pick-up soccer game, or join the locals as a spectator. Try a foreign movie. Rent a bike from a student (your l.D. will do as security) to tour a city. Attend high school/university classes and church services.

Use your camera and your tape-recorder to bring back memories later. Exchange cassette tapes.

Collect addresses and make a point of sending a card or a note later on to people who've been kind to you.

Always verify directions and intstructions from at least two or three people.

Sterilize drinking water in questionable areas, or stick to soft drinks, beer, tea, coffee, or bottled water.

Take a few small objects to barter with.

Speak your own language at customs; be pleasant and patient.

Keep your money and passport on your person.

If you are hitching, keep looking back or attach a small rear-view mirror on
your backpack so you don't miss a driver who might be waiting for you.

Peel fruit, cook meat, eat cooked vegetables, boil water.

Get your International Student Identity Card, Youth Hostel Card, International Driver's Licence.

Be familiar with the location of the door handle during your ride in case
you need to make a quick exit and put your backpack in the backseat, not
the trunk.

...And Some Don'ts

Don't wear sunglasses while hitch-hiking.

Don't arouse a driver's suspicions by making unnecessary movements in
the car.

Don't waste time hitch-hiking in a city where there are local buses. A sign
indicating you are going to a city 200 km away won't get you a ride in a
city where the drivers are all bound for the office or factory.

Avoid paying for rides unless you are going very long distances with the
same driver, then it would be nice to help out if you can afford to.

Don't leave your valuables unattended.

Avoid hitch-hiking at night.

Don't smoke in a car or someone's home unless they do.

Never try and cross a border with drugs or weapons.

In case your driver is carrying drugs or other contraband at a border, leave
the car, cross on your own, and rejoin your driver on the other side.

Never develop film on your travels, the company's chemicals may develop
blurry pictures, and costs are higher.

Be careful not to hold the hand of an Arab girl. Something as innocent as
this may get you in hot water from the father or even passer-bys.

Try and call ahead to a hotel. If you arrive late at night, they may feel you
are at their mercy and charge you the highest rate possible. Ask for a
discount.

Avoid sleeping at night on a train and if you do, keep your valuables inside
your sleeping bag, not your backpack.

Never leave your backpack out of sight at train stations. You can sometimes leave it with an honest looking shopkeeper.

When making telephone calls, be patient, sometimes there can be as much
as a minute delay of silence before the connection is made.

15.

Important Sources of Information

Work, Study, Travel Abroad, published by Council on International Educational Exchange (CIEE) is probably the best source for work and study in Europe. For information, send $1 or call to CIEE, 205 E. 42nd St., New York, NY 10017-5706, tel: (212) 661-1450. They have 47 offices around the U.S. **Council Travel** is a subsidiary of CIEE, and has 34 offices throughout the U.S., Europe and Asia, selling railpasses, guidebooks, Hostelling International (HI) cards, student identification and budget airfares. Three main offices include: 205 E. 42nd St, New York, NY 10017 tel:(212) 661-1450; 1093 Broxton Ave. #220, Los Angeles, CA 90024 tel: (310) 208-3551; and 28A Poland St.London WIV 3DB tel (071)-287-1565. **Council Charter**, part of CIEE , sells charter flights which can be bought through Council Travel offices.

Other sources to contact for studying abroad:
The American Institute for Foreign Study/American Council of International Studies, 313 E. 43rd St. New York, NY 10017 tel: 1-800-237-4636;
The Experiment in International Living/School for International Training (EIL), Kipling Rd. Box 676, Battleboro, VT 05302, tel 1-800-451-4465 offers the Semester Abroad Program;
The Institute of International Education 809 U.N. Plaza, New York , NY 10017 (212) 883-8200 publishes two comprehensive guides: Academic Year Abroad and Vacation Study Abroad.
American Institute for Foreign Study/American Council for International Studies, at 102 Greenwich Ave., Greenwich, CT 06830, tel: 1-800-727-2347, for high school students.
National Association of University Travel Agents, University Student Union, 18111 Nordhoff St., Northridge, CA 91330 tel:(818) 701-1177. It is also known as the University Student Travel Network. It is a national organization of independent travel agencies on or near college campuses

around the U.S. They offer international student fares, Eurail passes, ISIC cards, student tours, car leases and youth hostel cards.

CUTS (Canadian Universities Travel Service, Ltd.) 187 College St. Toronto, Ontario, M5T 1P7 416 979-2406 is a well-respected travel agency throughout Canada that sells discounted airline tickets to Canadian students and issues the ISIC, IYC and hostel cards. Located on or near university campuses.

Educational Travel Center 438 N. Francis St., Madison, WI 53703 608 256-5551 sells tickets to students and the public for low-cost flights within the U.S. and around the world. Many flights depart from Chicago. Ask for their free brochure 'Taking Off'-it claims they can beat student and charter fares. They also issue hostel cards.

Hostelling International (HI) - membership in your country allows you to stay at an HI-affiliated hostel at member rates ($6-$20 per night).If you do not have a membership card you can purchase a Hostelling International Card or buy individual 'welcome' stamps when you spend a night in a hostel. You can obtain your Membership Card from the YHA of the country where you live or a Hostelling International Card at any hostel outside your own country. If the hostel is full, members will have first choice. Discounts on rail and bus travel. Travelers of any age can join, for those over 26, you may have to pay a few extra dollars but you can stay in most hostels anywhere around the world. Contact-Box 37613, Washington DC 20013, tel: (202) 783-6161. A one-year membership costs $25 for adults 18-35 (renewal $20) and $10 for those under 18 (renewal $10), and $15 for those over 54 (renewal $15). Family membership for a husband and wife, and any number of children under 16, the cost is $35, renewal is $25. A lifetime membership costs $250.

Look into International Booking Network which allows you to reserve a bed up to six months in advance at more than 200 HI hostels worldwide - for reservations call (202) 783-6161 or 1-800-444-6111. For booking a bed in North America call at least one day in advance. You pay the cost of the bed upfront and overseas bookings have a $5 booking fee, for bookings within North America there is no charge. Each youth hostel can also book you a bed elsewhere if they are part of the network, you pay at that point.

Sleeping accommodation (usually bunk beds) will range from rooms sleeping two to four people up to rooms with 20 bunks, though these are becoming much rarer. Bedding is provided but you do need to bring or hire your sheets and pillowcases or a sheet sleeping bag in some hostels. Families who want the privacy of a family room and groups should always book in advance. If you book without paying a deposit, you need to arrive at the hostel and claim your reservation by 6 p.m., unless a different time is agreed. Basic food supplies will be available in the hostel or close by.

In Canada also contact Canadian Hostelling International-Canada at suite 400, 205 Catherine St. Ottawa, Ontario K2P LC3, tel: (6l3) 237-7884. Membership cards cost $25 for those 18 and over (including those 54 and older) and $35 for a two year card, renewals cost the same, students under 18, the card costs $12. Canadians must call 1-800-663-5777 to book a bed overseas. The same number, 1-800-444-4111, is valid in Canada for North American bookings.The booking fee for beds outside North America is $5.00 and no charge within North America.

INTERNATIONAL STUDENT IDENTITY CARD

This is a must if you want to save a bundle going to museums, sports events, theaters, or getting on a boat. Sometimes the operator does not always accept the card, but in most cases they do, so be sure to flash the card at every opportunity. The last place in the world I thought the card would be honoured were at the boat docks in Alexandria, Egypt. But instead of paying $l50 for the one way ticket to Athens, I paid only $75. The $16 cost for the card bought through CIEE, student travel organizations or Travel CUTS in Canada will also get you limited sickness and accident insurance, emergency medical evacuation insurance and access to a 24 hour international, toll-free hotline for assistance in medical, legal, and financial emergencies. Make sure you check with your insurance company to see if you might be duplicating any insurance coverages. This card is for people 12 or older.

The Go 25: International Youth Travel Card is for travelers under 26 has basically the same services and benefits as the ISIC. It costs $16, bring a passport-size photo and your passport to youth and student travel offices or some Youth Hostel Associations.

For $17, you can get the International Teacher Identity Card, sponsored by the International Travel Confederation, available to all teachers. The benefits and services are nearly identical to the other two cards. Contact your hostelling association

International Student Travel Confederation (ISTC)
The ISTC is made up of various associations which exist to promote youth and student travel. Amongst the services are:
• The International Student Identity Card
• The Explorer Pass - distributed by the International Student Rail Assoc. which gives young people up to 1 month unlimited, low-cost rail travel within participating rail networks in Europe.
• The Student Air Travel Assoc. (SATA) is made up of travel organizations that negotiate special fares for students with over 70 major airlines. The airline tickets, which are only issued by the various SATA organizations, are specially-priced fares for students which have very few restrictions.
• ISIS Travel Insurance is a specially-priced form of travel insurance which is associated with the International Association of Student Insurance Serv-

ices. ISIS is the world's leading low cost insurance for young people and in many countries provides direct refunds in case of accidents in many countries.

• The International Association for Educational and Work Exchange Programmes, is a group of organizations that facilitate work exchange programmes between youth, student and educational institutions worldwide.

The ISTC was founded in 1948 and works closely with organizations such as IYHF to provide a special range of travel services for the international student and youth community. If you would like to find out more about ISTC and its services please contact: ISTC, Box 9048, DK1000 Copenhagen, Denmark, tel: (45) 33939303, Fax (45) 33937377.

Hitched a ride on the bus with an Australian tour group in Venice, Italy.

16.

Trust

Our lives are built around trust, from the simple act of depositing money in a bank or flying on a airplane, from the foods we eat to the people we deal with at work on a daily basis, right down to the experience of sharing an apartment with someone who answers a newspaper ad and dividing the refrigerator food into 'yours' and 'mine'. From close family relationships to the neighbour next door, we all form different degrees of trust with the people we meet. If you are from a metropolis you lock your doors; if you live in a quiet neighborhood in a small hamlet along the coast of Rhode Island, you leave your keys in your car. Depending on where you are from and what experiences you have had until the day you decide to travel, you will have formed a certain level of trust. It's important to realize, though, that just because you were mugged or robbed three times last year in a crime-ridden city does not mean the same thing is going to happen to you in the countryside of Scotland. I urge you to leave behind any doubts or bad feelings you have about people in your own country and start your travels with an open mind. If you are preoccupied with mistrust on your travels, you will meet very few people and have very few experiences to bring home. But aren't some parts of the world just as dangerous or even more dangerous than the most crime-ridden American inner city? What about the hot spots you read about in the newspapers? You can easily plan your route to miss those places, or take some precautions if you decide to include them. Many incidents of terrorism are isolated. And it is fairly easy to determine whether your are likely to be in any real danger in a particular city or country. In many countries where there is unrest, the locals are not threatening or harming tourists, just each other. To help size up the situation you can talk to the embassy of the country involved before you leave, as well as to the External Affairs Department in Canada or the State Department in the U.S. Your own government may appear to be overcautious in the warnings it issues. You will also find that people in totalitarian countries do not feel personally responsible for their governments; they did not elect them and are powerless to change them. They are therefore not likely to hold you responsible for your government. Their government may be involved in a war of words with yours, but this will not usually mean the ordinary citizen will treat you with any hostility.

This issue of trust has to be addressed because so many people are amazed by my experiences. They can't believe I was able to travel with such spontaneity and openess.

In Belgium, I was dropped off by my driver, walked to the first restaurant-service-station establishment along the country road. I was simply seeking shelter from the cold, when the man behind the weiner-hamburger counter, introduced me to a piece of ham and to the woman working with him. Within minutes, I found myself back at her house communicating through a dictionary accompanied by strong drinks. Need I say more? The most amazing aspect of this affair was that she went home to spend the rest of the night with her parents, leaving me alone to lock up when I left in the morning!!!

At the Austrian border I was able to get a ride all the way into Vienna. The driver had plans to do some business in town, and we agreed to meet again later that day. He suggested I leave my backpack in his car (you can't be more trusting as a traveler) so I could see Vienna without the extra weight on my shoulders. Plans were to meet at 7 p.m. at a cafe he had suggested. At 7:30, I started to worry, but no sooner had I wiped the first bead of sweat off my forehead when he appeared. Apparently, I misunderstood him and I was sitting in the wrong cafe. After a few laughs about the situation over drinks, I was invited to stay in his studio for the night.

With my thumb out on a deserted stretch of highway near Guadalajara, Mexico, I was picked up by a truck driver carrying bags of flour. Again with no words spoken, he motioned for me to ride on top of the flour bags. This was a great way to see the scenery. I was prepared to thank him for the ride when we reached the next town, but he didn't stop when I expected him to. He drove through the winding streets to eventually stop at his home. He had wanted me to meet his wife and four children. I ended up eating with the family cross-legged on a dirt floor. The father and I tried to communicate to the amusement and laughter of the children who had never heard anyone speak English before. I am very glad I didn't follow my first impulse and jump off the truck in a panic.

In 1983, I planned a lecture tour of the universities in South Africa. My major dilemma was securing affordable transportation to tour from city to city. While on the flight to Johannesburg, I was able to arrange a ride into the city, right to Witwatersrand University. There I talked to the resident hall director, who not only gave me a place to stay, but found a student who was willing to 'rent' his car to me. I told the student my exact driving route - a 5,000 mile tour of the country over three weeks. The student didn't flinch. He simply handed me the keys, didn't want any money up-front or any identification. I was astonished by his enormous trust and generosity. We agreed on $125 and off I went. This experience is probably the best example of trust I have ever encountered.

...and Some of the Bad Experiences Everyone Loves to Read About...

The many kindnesses of the people I met provide some of the most memorable moments of my trip. Trusting the people you meet with will most often bring quite surprising rewards. These will far outweigh the bad experiences you have...but there will be some of those too. I don't know any traveler who doesn't have a few tales to tell of mishap or misadventure. And you will find when you get home these often make great stories. There's a touch of what the Germans call "schadenfreude" in everyone...your friends and family may enjoy your tales of sights seen and adventures that turned out right, but they'll also relish the misadventures, whether you are duped into buying a worthless watch from a Moroccan hustler, temporarily lose your luggage at an airport and get it back minus an item or two, or have your pockets picked my a swarm of gypsy children in Italy.

I certainly had a few bad experiences:

I was looking for a place to stay in Copenhagen and ended up meeting this nice Danish girl in a cafe. Here I was a complete stranger and she was willing to let me crash in her place for the night. At bedtime, she laid out a blanket on the floor next to her bed for me to sleep on. Then she proceeded to undress with her back to me. Being a young male I acted on my first impulse and mistook this act of openness as an invitation. I was in for a surprise. She was so upset she went into another room and buried herself in her book. Even though she ignored my sincere apologies she allowed me to stay. She never said another word. I thanked her and left in the morning shaking my head in disbelief about the differences that exist between cultures.

It is common in the Middle East to find cars being used as unmarked taxis. As I was walking the streets of Damascus minding my own business, a car pulled along side, waving for me to hop inside. I thought this man was being hospitable to a foreigner and this ride would also help me get to the other side of the city. When he stopped, he held out his hand for what I thought was a handshake. He shook his head and asked for money. I politely refused, got out of the car, and I was soon encircled by about ten unshaven locals. Refusing to give in since I had not solicited the ride, I stood my ground, called their bluff, strode through the crowd and kept on walking, looking back only once to see their incredulous faces.

While hitch-hiking through central Turkey I was picked up by a dump-truck driver and his friend. I ended up sitting between the two of them. Communication was very limited; even our use of hand language and facial expressions confused us both. Neither of us had the foggiest idea what the other was trying to convey. After a while the drivers' friend became increasingly frustrated and agitated over our lack of communication. Not that I was in any danger, but this was the most uncomfortable time I have had with a driver, and not taking any chances, I hopped out at our next stop.

I was walking through the countryside of former Yugoslavia trying to hitch a ride. It was probably the worst weather I had ever encountered - it was a very wet, bone-chilling driving sleet with no shelter at hand. As I kept walking I came across a car parked along the shoulder with an army official and his family simply sitting there with room to spare. I know I looked like a drowned rat, but the family never even rolled down their window, acknowledged me or made eye contact. I continued my walk feeling like a miserable lost soul and will remember the lack of hospitality the rest of my life.

While visiting the Dead Sea in Israel, I thought I would try and float on the water as suggested by the local people. What I did not know was that the water has ten times the salt content of regular sea water. As I tried to wash my hair with it, I got a few drops in my eyes. The pain was excruciating. I couldn't open my eyes and had to crawl out of the water over rocks. Practically feeling my way to my hotel room, I rinsed my eyes for at least ten minutes before the pain subsided.

On our honeymoon, a few years ago, my wife and I stopped at a deserted shopping plaza just outside Venice early on a Sunday morning. We made our bread and milk purhase in less than five minutes, came back to our rental car to discover it had been professionally broken into. The thieves had taken our prized camera, with its irreplaceable pictures and our binoculars. We were told our foreign licence plates made us a preferred target.

The craziest boat trip I ever experienced was from Alexandria to Athens. I was the only North American on the boat, so I was a curiousity. Everyone befriended me, including the ships' crewmen and captain. I was even allowed to man the wheel for awhile. Unfortunately, the weather turned really bad. Dinner plates flew everywhere, people vomited where they stood and to top it all off, the ship's postman died during the storm from a heart attack. When we're only what seemed a stone's throw from the docks of

Athens, I was told no one could leave the ship for at least two days, until the "death at sea" matter was cleared up. Still feeling very sick, not helped by the sickening smell of vomit throughout the ship I thought I'd rather burn in hell rather than endure these horrible conditions. Since it is customary to hand over your passport at the start of the voyage, I was in no position to dictate to the captain that I be allowed to go ashore. But, I took a chance and confronted the captain. One thing led to another and before I knew it, we were grabbing at each other's throats. The crew eventually broke us up, and the ship docked shortly thereafter. I received my passport and walked the plank ... onto shore.

As you can see none of these experiences were life-threatening. I have no tales to tell you about crashing into a mountainside on a bus or being held at gun-point. Some events are not under your control, but learning how to minimize your potential loss or danger is a lesson in itself. As long as you walk with confidence and become a little "street wise" you shouldn't have any reason to hurry back home.

A typical driver on my travels who gave me a ride in Spain.

17.

Traveling and Perspective

Without a doubt, the single most important aspect of traveling is how it puts life into a clearer perspective. I had quite a few vague ideas, notions and misconceptions of what life was like in different countries, simple things like the colour of peoples' hair and their skin, if they were friendly or hostile. Take the assumption, for instance, that "everyone speaks English". It is true, particularly in cities in Europe, that you will nearly always be able to find someone who speaks your language. But it would be a huge mistake to count on this being the case everywhere you go. And even if many people you meet speak English, you will find that a brave attempt to speak their language is much appreciated. Very often, as you struggle along with the unfamiliar words, the person you are addressing will interrupt you in English to save you embarrassment. The people of Paris puzzled me at first; was their legendary rudeness caused by too many tourists assuming they all spoke English? My primitive French didn' t get much of a response there, and I decided perhaps it was because Parisians had been inundated all summer long with foreign tourists, or ...who knows...perhaps they were all having a collective bad hair day. In the French countryside, however, as almost everywhere else on my travels, my efforts to speak the local language were well received.

When I was in Austria I wasn't sure if I should hitch-hike in Hungary or take the train. I had made the mistake of associating the people of the country with the communist government at the time. I had wrongly assumed the people would not be friendly. I was amazed at the great interest people had in me while in their country. I was able to get rides very quickly from people of all ages, male or female. You will find when you travel throughout certain parts of the world many people don't have the same opportunity we have to meet foreigners. In North America, we tend to take each other for granted because we are a land of immigrants, but your encounter with an Hungarian peasant will probably be his first encounter with any foreigner.

I traveled to the Scandanavian countries for many reasons. One was to see if it was true that nearly everybody had blonde hair and blue eyes. On the spur of the moment, I walked into a school in Turku, Finland and asked the teacher if she would assemble her students for a class picture. Sure enough, all the school kids at least had blonde hair. The teacher was pleased with my spontaneous request. Since I was in the area in the wintertime I was also curious about reports that alcohol consumption was particularly high in Scandinavia in winter. A few visits to bars and my own dramatically increased consumption demonstrated to me the effect that the short winter day (only two or three hours of sunshine) could have.

One of my most enlightening encounters was in Yamit, Israel which is now part of Egypt. While sitting down at the dinner table in an Israeli's home, the man told me how sick and tired he was of the fighting going on between Israelis and Palestinians. Just witnessing the anguished expression on his face told me more about the problems in his country than I had learned from all the newspaper and television reports over the years.

A Moroccan student approached me, while I was sitting on a park bench in Rabat, trying to impress me with the lingo acquired from watching American movies, invited me to stay with him and his room-mate for two nights. They were university students who had to study using candles as their main source of light! I also appreciated the small lesson of sharing food as I ate off the same plate with seven other people. I was never worried I might get sick eating this way, and didn't. This simple experience was a little lesson in trusting my own judgement and that of others.

When I stayed with a family in Mentana, just outside of Rome, I discovered how closely knit Italian families were. Three generations of the family lived in the same apartment building. The family couldn't understand why North Americans would live more than 5 or 10 miles from work.

If you keep your eyes and ears open, cultural differences will fascinate you and these tidbits of information you gather by staying with the families will be the highlights of your travels .

18.

Speaking the Language

There are so many different languages on even a short tour of Europe and the Mediterranean area that even the most accomplished linguist is bound to hit a language barrier sooner or later. Efforts to speak even a phrase or two in the local language are nearly always well received.But since it's not practical, or possible, to learn all the necessary phrases, you can save yourself a lot of frustration by showing the following written phrases for getting food, accommodation, rides, and directions.

In this chapter you'll find basic words in twenty languages. In addition, there are specific phrases used by travelers. Simply turn to the appropriate page, fill in the blank, and show the particular phrase to the person and you will find yourself saving a lot of money for transportation, accommodation and food. Directions and signs that can be used to amuse the motorist and get his/her attention are also included.
Note: the universal word in Europe for "hitch-hiking" is "auto-stop".

Specific Phrases

Getting Rides
Hello, I am a student from _____. I need a ride in the direction of _____.
Is it possible to get a ride? I would be most grateful. Thank you.

Getting Accommodation   (to only be used with farmers)
Hello, I am a student from _____. Can you please help me? I am traveling to _____ early tomorrow morning. I would be willing to work for 2-3 hours in return for a bed (point to sleeping bag), dinner and breakfast and an opportunity to learn a little bit about your culture. I would leave early in the morning. Thank you very much.
or
Hello, I am a student from _____. Can you please help me? I am traveling to _____ early tomorrow morning. I would be willing to give a gift or money in return for a bed (point to sleeping bag), dinner and breakfast and an opportunity to learn a little bit about your culture. I would leave early in the morning. Thank you very much.

Getting Food (to only be used in restaurants)
May I wash dishes in your kitchen for one or two hours in exchange for a meal?

Directions
1. Where is the highway to _____?
2. Where is the bus to get to _____?
3. Where is the train to get to _____?
4. What is the name or number of the bus that can take me close to the highway?

Hitch-Hiking Signs
City... in English or native lanuguage
The following should be in the native language: Home to Mom...I'm safe...Trees...
Please...Thank you...Anywhere...

300

Hello	Ahlan	ah-lan
How are you?	Ezayak?	keyf ha-lak
Very well	Kewaiess Khaliss	kas-a-nan
Thank you	Shukran	shu-kran
Goodbye	Ma'a el salama	ma'a sal-a-ma
Please	Men fadlek	min fad-lak
Yes	Na'ám or Ah!	na'am
No	La	lah
Give me	Iddini	a'teeni
Where is?	Fein?	feen
the station	mehatah	al- ma-ha-ta
the youth hostel	beit el shabab	bit el sha-bab
the university	el gami 'à	al-jamea'h
a restaurant	matáam	al-mat'am
the toilet	twalit	toy let
the grocery store	el bakal	al bak-a-lah
To the right	Lel Yexmeen	el-a lya-meen
To the left	Shimal	she-mal
Straight ahead	Ála tool	ala-tool
I would like	Anna awiz	ouhe-bu ann atan-a-wal
to eat	akol	a-kul
a room	owdha	oh-da
How much is it?	Be kam?	be kam
The check, please	El sheek men fadlak	al sheek min fad-lek
When?	Imta?	im-ta
Yesterday	Imberah	im-bear-ah
Today	En naharda	en na-har-da
Tomorrow	Bukra	boo-kra
Breakfast	Ftar	fo-tour
Lunch	Ghada	gha-da
Dinner	Asha	ash-a

1	wahad	wa-hed	30	talateen	thal-a-theen
2	tnein	ith-nan	40	arbeaeen	ar-ba'-een
3	talatq	tha-lath	50	khamseen	kham-seen
4	arbàa	ar-ba	60	sitteen	si-teen
5	khamsa	kham-sa	70	sab 'aeen	sab-een
6	sitta	si-ta	80	tamaneen	tham-a-neen
7	sab 'aa	sa-ba	90	tes 'aen	tes-een
8	tamania	tham-an-ya	100	mia	me-ah
9	tesaa	tes-a	500	khomsomia	khams me-ah
10	ashra	as-ra	1,000	alf	alf
20	eshreen	esh-reen			

"84 Cent" Foods

apples-tofah, bananas-mouz, beer-bera, bread-ish, cheese-gibnah, chocolate-choculata, coffee-ahwa, egg-bedh, fish-samak, fruit-fakha, meat-lahma, milk-laban, oranges-bortokan, potatoes-batatiss, salt-malh, sandwich-sandawitch, sausage-sogoq, soup-shorba, sugar-sukar, tea-shai, vegetables-khodhar, water-mayya, wine-nibeet.

Getting Rides

Ahlan, anna taleb men_____. Anna awiz arouh.

Getting Accommodation
Marhaba, anna taleb men _____. Momken tissa'adini men fadlalak? Anna messafer bokrah badri. Anna momken ashtaghal sa 'eteen_____. Talatah mokabel annam, wi _____ ghadah wa fitar. Wa hi forssah at álem shewaiah án thakafit el balad. Anna missafer badri el sobh. Shokran gazeelan.
or
Marhaba, anna taleb ela bokrah badri. Anna mayyal addi hidiah aw folouss mogabel annam wa atghaza wa after _____. Wa hi forssah at á lem shiwaiah án thagafitkom. Anna messafer badri bokrah_____. Shokran gazeehan.

Getting Food
Momken aghsil sohoun fi el matbakhak s'aah aw-itnin li aklah wahda?

Directions
1. Feen el tareek le ____?
2. Feen el bus ela _____?
3. Feen el atr elli yorouh _____?
4. Issm el bus elli yqarabnni men al ta reek el 'omomi?

Hitch-Hiking Signs
City...write it in the native language
The following should be in the native language:

Home to Mom	Arouh le ommi
I'm safe	Anna bikhare
Trees	Shaghar
Please	Men fadlek
Thank you	Shoukran
Anywhere	Ay makan

BULGARIA	**Pronunciation Guide**
Hello	zdravei
How are you?	kak ste
Very well	mnoga dobre
Thank you	blagodaria
Goodbye	dovijdane
Please	molia
Yes	da
No	ne
Give	medai mi
Where is?	kade e?
the station	garata
the youth hostel	studentiski hotel
the university	universiteta
a restaurant	restoranta
the toilet	toaletnata
the grocery store	magazin plod zelenchuk
to the right	na diasno
to the left	na liavo
straight ahead	na pravo
I would like	bih zhelal
to eat	da se hrania
a room	edna staia
How much is it?	kolko struva tova
The check, please	chekat molia
When?	koga?

302

Yesterday			vchera	
Today			dnes	
Tomorrow			utre	
Breakfast			zakuska	
Lunch			obiad	
Dinner			vecheria	
1	edno	16		shestnadeset
2	dve	17		sedemnadeset
3	tri	18		osemnadeset
4	chetiri	19		devetnadeset
5	pot	20		dvadeset
6	shest	30		trideset
7	sdem	40		thetirideset
8	osem	50		petdeset
9	devat	60		shestdeset
10	deset	70		sedemdeset
11	edinadeset	80		osemdeset
12	dvanadeset	90		devetdeset
13	trinadeset	100		sto
14	chetirinadeset	500		petstotin
15	petnadeset	1,000		hiliada

"84 Cent" Foods

apples-jabalki, bananas-banani, beer-bira, biscuits-biskviti, bread-hljab, cheese-sirene, chocolate-shokolad, coffee-kafe, egg-jaitze, fish-riba, fruit-plod, meat-meso, milk-mliako, mineral water-mineralna voda, oranges-portokali, potatoes-kartofi, salt-sol , sandwich-sandwich, sausage-kolbas or krenvirs, soup-supa, sugar-zahar, tea-tchai, vegetables-zelentchutz, water-voda, wine-vino

Getting Rides

Zdravejte, oz sam student ot _____. Nujdaia ot prevaz do _____. Mojete li da me vzemete? Ste sam vi mnoga blegodaren. Blagodaria.

Getting Accommodation

Zdravejte, oz sam student ot _____. Mojete li da mi pomogneto? Patuvam za _____ rano utre sutrinta. Bih zelalda rabotia 2-3 tchasa srestu lego, vecheria i zakuska. Bih zelal da se zapoznaia s vashia ratchin na jivot. Ste napysna utre rano sutrinta. Blagodaria mongo.

or

Zdravejte, az sam student ot _____. Mojete li da mi pomognete? Potuvam za _____rano utre sutrinta. Bih zelal da napravia podarek ili da dam pari, srestu leglo, vecheria i zakuska. Bih iskal da se zapoznaia s vashia natchin na jivot. Ste napusna utre rano sutrinta. Blagodaria mnogo.

Getting Food

Bih iskal da mia tchinii vav vashata kuhnia za edin-dvo tchasa, srestu hrana, ako e vazmojno?

Directions

1. kade e patia za _____?
2. Kade e reisa za _____?
3. Kade e vlaka za _____?
4. Kai reis maje da me zavede olizo do magistralato?

Hitch-Hiking Signs

City....write it in the native language

The following should be in the native language:

Home to Mom	Udoma pri mama
I'm safe	Bezopasen sam
Trees	Kam gorata
Please	Blagadaria
Anywhere	Kadeto i da e

CZECH   Pronunciation Guide

Hello	Dobryy den	daw-bree den
How are you?	Jake se mate	yahk seh mah-teh
Very well	Velmi dobre	vel-mee daw-brsheh
Thank you	Dekuji vam	dyek-ooee vahm
Goodbye	Na shledanou	nah skleh-dah-noh-oo
Please	Prosim	praw-seem
Yes	Ano	ah-no
No	Ne	neh
Give me	Dejte mi	deyte mee
I don't understand	Nerozumim	neh-raw-zoo-meem
Just a moment	Moment, prosim	maw-ment, praw-seem
Excuse me	Prominte	praw-min-teh
Where is?	Kde je?	gde yeh?
the station	stanice	stan-itze
the youth hostel	hostel	hostel
the university	universita	une-ver-sita
a restaurant	restaurace	rest-aur-atze
the toilet	záchod	zaa-khod
the grocery store	samoobsluha	sa-moob-sluha
To the right	Doprava	do-prava
To the left	Doleva	do-leva
Straight ahead	Rovne	rov-nee
I would like	Rád bych	raad bykh
to eat	jedl	jedl
to have a room	mel pokoj	zee-skal po-coy
How much is it?	Kolik to stojí	coleec to stoyee
The check, please	Úcet prosim	ootzet proseem
When?	Kdy?	kthya
Yesterday	Vcera	vtzer-aah
Today	Dness	dnees
Tomorrow	Zítra	zee-tra
Breakfast	Snidane	snee-danye
Lunch	Obed	obyed
Dinner	Vecere	vet-zere

1	jeden	yeh-den		14	ctrnact	chtur-nahtst
2	dva	dvah		15	patnact	paht-nahtst
3	tri	trshee		16	sestnact	shest-nahtst
4	ctyri	chtee-rshee		17	sedmnact	seh-doom-nahtst
5	pet	pyet		18	osmnact	aw-soom-nahtst
6	sest	shest		19	devatenact	deh-vah-teh-nahtst
7	sedm	seh-duhm		20	dvacet	dvah-tset
8	osm	aw-suhm		30	tricet	trshee-tset
9	devet	deh-vyet		40	ctyricetch	ti-rshee-tset
10	deset	deh-set		50	padesat	pah-deh-saht
11	jedenact	yeh-deh-nahtst		60	sedesat	she-deh-saht
12	dvanact	dvah-nahtst		70	sedmdesat	seh-duhm-deh-saht
13	trinact	trshee-nahtst		80	osmdesat	aw-suhm-deh-saht

90	devadesat	deh-vah-deh-saht	500	pet set	pyet set
100	sto	staw	1,000	tisic	tyee-seets

"84 Cent" Foods
apples-jablko, bananas-banany, beer-pivo, biscuits-susenky, bread-chleba, cheese-sýr, chocolate-cokolada, coffee- káva, egg-vejce, fish-ryba, fruit-ovoce, meat-maso, milk-mléko, mineral water-minerální voda, oranges-pomerance, potatoes-brambory, salt-sul sandwich-sendvic, sausage-klobasa, soup-polevka, sugar-cukr, vegetables-zelenina, water-voda, wine-vino.

Getting Rides
Dobry den, jsem student z_____. Potrebuji svezt do _____. Mohl byste me svezt? Budu vam velmi zavazan.

Getting Accommodation
Dobrý den, jsem student z_____. Muzete mi pomoci? Cestuji do _____ zítra brzo ráno. Rád bych Vám pomohl s prací obrátkou za ubytování (postel, veceri a snídani). (Ukazte na spaci pytel) Rad bych se dozvedel neco o Vasi kulture. Odjedu brzo rano. Dekuji Vam za Vasi pomoc.

or

Dobrý den, jsem student z_____. Muzete mi pomoci? Cestuji do _____ zítra brzo ráno. Rád Vám dám dárek nebo peníze za ubytování u Vas, veceri a snídani. Mám spací pytel. Rád bych se dozvedel neco o Vasí kulture. Odjedu brzo ráno. Dekuji Vám za Vasi pomoc.

Getting Food
Mohl bych ve Vasi restauraci umýt nádobí obrátkou za jídlo? Pracoval bych asi jednu nebo dve hodiny.

Directions
1. Kudy se jede na dálnici smerem na _____?
2. Kde staví autobous jedoucí do _____?
3. Kde staví vlask jedoucí do _____?
4. Jaké je císlo autobusu, který jede nejblíze k dálnici do _____.

Hitch-Hiking Signs
City...write it in the native language
The following should be in the native language:

Home to Mom	Domu k máme
I'm safe	Nemusíte se me bat
Trees	Stromy
Please	Prosím
Thank you	Dekuji
Anywhere	Kamkoliv

DANISH		**Pronunciation Guide**
Hello	God Dag	go da
How are you?	Hvordan har De det?	vohr-dan hahr dee det
Very well	Tak, godt	tak gaht
Thank you	Tak	tak
Goodbye	Farvel	fahr-vel
Please	Vaer saa venlig	vayr saw venlee
Yes	Ja	ya
No	Nej	nai

English	Danish	Pronunciation
Give me	Giv mig	gee-mai
Where is?	Hvor er det?	vohr ayr det
the station	jernbanestationen	yayrn-ban-uh-sta-sh-onun
the youth hostel	vandre hjem	von drayh yeh
the university	universitet	oona-ver-see-tee
a restaurant	en restaurant	in rest-oh-rahng
the toilet	toilettet	twah-let-tud
the grocery store	købman	kerp-man
To the right	Til hojre	til hoi-ruh
To the left	Til venstre	till ven -struh
Straight ahead	Lige ud	lee-ood
I would like	Jeg vilde gerne have	yai-vil-luh- gayr-nuh ha
to eat	noget at spise	noh-ud ah spee-suh
a room	et Vaerelse	it vay-rul-suh
How much is it?	Hvor meget?	vohr ma-yud
When?	Hvornaar?	vohr-nawr
Yesterday	i Gaar	ee gawr
Today	i Dag	ee dag
Tomorrow	i Morgen	ee mawrn

#	Danish	Pronunciation	#	Danish	Pronunciation
1	en	ayn	16	seksten	saiss-tun
2	to	toh	17	sytten	ser-tun
3	tre	tray	18	atten	a-tun
4	fire	fee-rah	19	nitten	ni-tun
5	fem	fem	20	tyve	tee-vuh
6	seks	sex	30	tredive	tred-vuh
7	syv	syee	40	fyrre	fer-raw
8	otte	oh-tuh	50	halvtreds	hal-tress
9	ni	nee	60	tres	tress
10	ti	tee	70	halvfjerds	half-yayrss
11	elve	el-vuh	80	firs	feerss
12	tolv	tahll	90	halvems	halfemss
13	tretten	tret-un	100	hundrede	hoon-rud-uh
14	fjorten	fyawr-tun	500	fem hundrede	fem hoon-rud-uh
15	femten	fem-tun	1,000	tusind	too-sin

"84 Cent" Foods

apples-aebler, bananas-bananer, beer-ol, biscuits-kiks,bread-brod, cheese-ost, choco-late- chokolade, coffee- kaffe, egg-eg, fish-fisk, fruit-frugt, meat-kød, milk-maelk, mineral water-mineral vand, oranges-appelsiner, potatoes-kartoffel, salt-salt, sand-wich-smørre-brod, sausage-polser, soup-suppe, sugar-sukker, tea-te, vegetables-grøntsager, water-vand, wine-vin.

Getting Rides

Goddag, jeg er en student fra _____. Jeg søger en køretur til _____. Er det muligt at få en køretur? Jeg vil vaere meget taknemmelig for det. Mange tak.

Getting Accommodation

Goddag, jeg er en student fra _____. Kan du hjaelpe mig? Jeg er på vej til _____ tidlig i morgen. Jeg er villig til at arbejde for 2-3 timer huis jeg kan få en seng, middagsmad og morgenmad. (point to sleeping bag). Og en chance til at laere lidt om jeres kultur. Jeg vil gá tidlig i morgen. Mange tak.

or

Goddag, jeg er en student fra _____. Kan due hjaelp mig? Jeg er pa vej til _____ tidlig i morgen. Jeg er villig til at give en gave eller penge huis jeg kan fa en seng, middagsmad og maorgenmad (point to sleeping bag). Og en chance til at laere lidt om jeres kultur. Jeg vil gå tidlig i morgen. Mange tak.

Getting Food
Ma jeg gore upvasken for em time eller to i bytte for et måltid.

Directions
1. Hvor er hovedvejen til _____?
2. Hvor kan jeg få bussen til _____?
3. Hvor kan jeg på toget til _____?
4. Hviken bus vil tage mig naermest til hovedvejen?

Hitch-Hiking Signs
City...write it in the native language
The following should be in the native language:

Home to Mom	Hjem til mor
I'm safe	Jeg er sikker
Trees	Traeer
Please	Vaer venlig
Thank you	Mange tak
Anywhere	Alle vegne

DUTCH — Pronunciation Guide

Hello	Hallo	ha-loh
How are you?	Hoe gaat het met U?	hoo-haht-ut met-oo
Very well	Uitstekend	out-stayk-end
Thank you	Dank U	dahnk-ew
Goodbye	Goeden dag	hoo-dun dahk
Please	Alstublieft	ah-stoo-bleeft
Yes	Ja	yah
No	Neen	nay
Give me	Geeft U mij	hayft oo may
Where is?	Waar is?	vahr iz
the station	het station	het stah-ssyonh
the youth hostel	de jeugdherberg	der yugd-hair-berk
the university	universiteit	uni-ver-see-tide
a restaurant	een restaurant	uhn res-to-rahng
the toilet	het toilet	het twah-let
the grocery store	supermarket	super market
To the right	Rechts	rekhts
To the left	Links	links
Straight ahead	Rechtdoor	rekht-dour
I would like	Ik zou graag	ik zow hrah
to eat	eten	ay-ten
a room	een kamer	uhn kah-mer
How much is it?	Hoeveel kost het?	hoo fayl kawst het
The check, please	De rekening	duh ray-ken-ing
When?	Wanneer?	vah-neer
Yesterday	Gisteren	his-ter-en
Today	Vandaag	van-dahkh
Tomorrow	Morgen	mor-hen
Breakfast	Ontbijt	ohnt-bayt
Lunch	Lunch	lunch
Dinner	Diner	dee-nay
1	een	ayn	5	vijf	vayf
2	twee	tway	6	zes	zes
3	drie	dree	7	zeven	zay-vun
4	vier	veer	8	acht	akht

9	negen	nay-hen	20	twintig	tvintihk
10	tien	teen	30	dertig	dare-tihk
11	elf	aylf	40	veertig	fare-tihk
12	twaalf	twahlf	50	vijftig	fife-tihk
13	dertien	dehr-teen	60	zestig	zess-tihk
14	veertien	feer-teen	70	zeventig	zeh-ven-tihk
15	vijftien	fife-teen	80	tachtig	tahk-tihk
16	zestien	zess-teen	90	negentig	neh-khen-tihk
17	zeventien	zeh-ven-teen	100	honderd	hohn-dert
18	achttien	ahkht-teen	500	vijf honderd	five hon-derd
19	negentien	neh-khen-teen	1,000	duizend	doy-zent

"84 Cent" Foods

apples- appels, bananas-bananen, beer-bier,biscuits-koekjes, bread-brood, cheese-kaas, chocolate-chocolate, coffee-koffie, egg-ei, fish-vis, fruit-fruit, meat-vlees, milk-melk, mineral water- mineraal water, oranges-sinaasappelen, potatoes-aardappelen, salt-zout, sandwich-belegd broodje, sausage-worst, soup-soep, sugar-suiker, tea- thee, vegetables-groenten, water-water, wine-wijn.

Getting Rides

Hallo ik ben een studentvan _____. Ik wil graag naar de richting van _____ als u die richting uit gaat zau u my dan een lift willen geven, alvast heel harrelyk bendankt.

Getting Accommodation

Hallo ik ben een student van _____ Zou umekunnen helpen? Ik ben op weg naar _____. Ik hoop vraeg indemorgen te vertrekken. In ruil voor een slapplaats en ontbyt of eenwarme maaltÿd (wÿs maar slaapzak) zau ik wel 2 à 3 uur voon u willen werken, en help dan gelÿk gelegenheid om wat van de kultuur te zien ente leren. Ik hoop vroeg in de morgen te vertrekken alvast heel hartelyk bedankt.

or

Hall ik ben een student van _____. Zou ume kunnen helpen? Ik ben op weg naar _____. Ik hoop vroeg in de morgen te vertrekken. In ruil voor een slaapplaats en ontbyt of een warme maaltyd (wys naar een slaapzak) Zou ik u graag wat willen betalen of een kado willen geven, en heb dan gelyk gelegenheid om wat van de kultuur te zien en te leren. Ik hoop vroeg in de morgen te vertrekken alvast heel hartelyk bedankt.

Getting Food

Zou ik in ruil voor een maaltyd een paar uur in de keuken kunnen werken o. a. af wassen.

Directions

1. Waar is de snelweg naar _____?
2. Waar is de bus naar _____?
3. Waar is de trein naar _____?
4. Wat is het bus mummer dat my naar de grote weg brengt?

Hitch-Hiking Signs

City...in English or native language
The following should be in the native language:

Home to Mom	Tervg naar huis
I'm safe	Ik ben veilig
Trees	Bomen
Please	Alstublieft
Thank you	Dank U
Anywhere	Overal

Hello	Hei	hey
How are you?	Kuinkavoit?	coo-enka voyt
Very well	Hyvin	hue-vin
Thank you	Kiitos	kee-tos
Goodbye	Näkemiin	na-ke-meen
Please	Ole Hyrä	oley-hue-va
Yes	Kyllä	coo-la
No	Ei	eh
Give me	Anna	anna
Where is?	Msisa?	mee-sa
the station	asema	a-sa-ma
the youth hostel	retkeilymaja	ret-kai-ly-ma-ya
the university	yliopistoo	u-lee-opees -to
a restaurant	ravintola	rav-in-to-la
the toilet	vessa	ves-sa
To the right	Oikealle	oy-ke-ah-le
To the left	Vasemalle	vas-em-al-le
Straight ahead	Eteenpäin	ee-teen-pain
I would like	Mina haluan	mina hal- wan
to eat	syoda	sooa-da
a room	huone	hoo-a-na
How much is it?	Kuinka paljon?	ku-enka paly-on
The check, please	Lasku, ole hyva	las-koo, oley hoo-va
When?	Koska?	kos-ka
Yesterday	Eilen	ay-len
Today	Tänään	ta-nan
Tomorrow	Huomenn a	hu-o-men-na
Breakfast	Aamiainen	i-ma-nen
Lunch	Lounas	loo-nas
Dinner	Illallinen	ill-al-li-nen

1	yksi	vek-si	16	kuusitoista	koo-see-tois-ta
2	kaksi	cock-si	17	seitsemäntoista	sate-se-tois-ta
3	kolme	kol-may	18	kahdeksantoista	kah-dek-san- tois-ta
4	nelja	nell-ya	19	yhdeksäntoista	veh-dek-saen-tois-ta
5	viisi	vee-se	20	kaksikymmentä	kak-si-kuem-men-ta
6	kuusi	ko-si	30	kolmekymmentä	coal-me-kuem-men-ta
7	seitsemän	sait-se-man	40	neljäkymmentä	nel-eea-kuem-men-ta
8	kahdeksan	ka-dek-san	50	viisikymmentä	vee-see-kuem-men-ta
9	yhdeksan	veh-dek-san	60	kuusikymmentä	coo-see-kuem-men-ta
10	kymmenen	coo-em-me-nen	70	seitsemänkymmentä	sait-se-man-kuem-men-ta
11	yksitoista	vek-si-tois-ta	80	kahdeksankymmentä	kah-dek-sank-kuem-men-ta
12	kaksitoista	kak-si-tois-ta	90	yhdeksänkymmentä	u-deck-san-kuem-men-ta
13	kolmetoista	coal-me-toista	100	sata	sa-ta
14	neljatoista	nel-ia-tois-ta	500	viisisataa	vee-se-sa-ta
15	viisitoista	vee-see-tois-ta	1,000	tuhat	tu-hat

"84 Cent" Foods

apples-omenoita, bananas-banaanit, beer-olut, biscuits-keksejat, bread-leipä, cheese-juusto, chocolate-suklaa, coffee-kahvi, egg-muna, fish-kala, fruit-hedelma, meat-liha, milk-maito, mineral water-kivenais vesi, oranges-upelssiini, potatoes-perunat, salt-suola, sausage-makkara, soup-keitto, sugar-sokeri, tea-tee, vegetables-vihannekset, water-vesi, wine-viini.

Getting Rides

Päivää, olen opiskelija_____. Tarvitsisin kyytiä _____ päin. Saisinko sinulta kyytiä? Olisin kiitollinen. Kiitos.

Getting Accommodation

Päivää, olen opiskkelija _____sta. Voisitteko auttaa minua? Matkustan _____ aikaisin huomenna. Aamiaisesta, lounaasta ja illallisesta ja nukkumapaikasta olisin valmis tekemään par-kolme tuntia työtä. Haluaisin samalla vähän teidän kulttuuriinne. Lähtisin pois aikaisin aamulla. Kiitos paljon.

or

Päivää, olen opiskelija _____sta. Voistteko auttaa minua? Matkustan _____ aikaisin huomenna. Olisiko mahdollista maksaa tai antaa teille pieni lahja nukkumapaikasta, aamiaisesta, lounaasta ja illallisesta? Haluaisin samalla vähän teidän kulttuuriinne. Lahtisin pois aikaisin aamulla. Kiitos paljon.

Getting Food

Olisiko mahdollista tiskata keittiössänne ateriaa vastaan?

Directions

1. Missä on valtatie_____iin?
2. Missä on bussi milla paasisin_____iin?
3. Missä on juna milla paasisin_____iin?
4. Mikä olisi bussin tai junan, nimi tai numero millä pääsisin_____iin?

Hitch-Hiking Signs

Please Note: Finns are traditionally conservative. Many Finns may think your signs are too unusual.... use them at your discretion. Just hitch-hiking or writing the city name may be best.

City... write it in English or native language
The following should be in the native language:

Home to Mom	Kotiin Aidin luo
I'm safe	Olen Vaaraton
Trees	Metsää
Please	Ole hyvä
Thank you	Kiitos
Anywhere	Minne vain

Hello	Bonjour	bohn-zhoor
How are you?	Comment allez-vous?	koh-mawh-tah-lay-voo
Very well	Très bien	tray-byanh
Thank you	Merci	mayr-see
Goodbye	Au revoir	aw-ruh-vwahr
Please	S'il vous plait	sill-voo-play
Yes	Oui	wee
No	Non	nawh
Give me	Donnez-moi	duh-nay-mwah
Where is?	Où est?	oo-ay
the station	la gare	lah-gar
the youth hostel	l'auberge de jeunesse	l'owberge de jerness
the university	l'université	le une-i-ver-si-tay
a restaurant	un restaurant	uh-res-tow-rawh
a grocery store	une épicerie	oon eh-pee-sir-ee
the toilet	les toilettes	les twa-let
To the right	A droite	ah-drwaht
To the left	A gauche	ah-gohsh
Straight ahead	tout droit	too dwar
I would like	Je voudrais	zhuh-voo-dray
to eat	manger	mawh-zhay

water	eau			oh		
a room	une chambre			ewn-shawm-bruh		
How much is it?	Combien ça coûte			kawm-byanh-sah-koot		
The check, please	Láddition, s.v.p.			ah-dee-syohnh		
When?	Quand?			kawnh		
Yesterday	Hier			yayr		
Today	Aujourd'hui			oh-zhoor-dwee		
Tomorrow	Demain			duh-manh		
Breakfast	Le petit déjeuner			luh puh-tee day-zhuh-nay		
Lunch	Déjeuner			day-zhuh-nay		
Dinner	Diner			dee-nay		

1	un	uhnh	16	seize	seyz	
2	deux	duh	17	dix-sept	dees-set	
3	trois	trwa	18	dix-huit	dees-weet	
4	quatre	kahtr	19	dix-neuf	dees-nerf	
5	cinq	sank	20	vingt	van	
6	six	seess	30	trente	trent	
7	sept	set	40	quarante	kar-rarnt	
8	huit	weet	50	cinquante	san-karnt	
9	neuf	nerff	60	soixante	swah-sant	
10	dix	deess	70	soixante-dix	swah-sant dees	
11	onze	onz	80	quatre-vingts	catre van	
12	douze	dooz	90	quatre-vingt-dix	catre van dees	
13	treize	traiz	100	cent	sonn	
14	quatorze	ka-torz	1,000	mille	meel	
15	quinze	kanze				

"84 Cent" Foods

apples-pommes, bananas-bananes, beer-bière, bread-pain, cheese-fromage, chocolate-chocolat, coffee-café, egg-oeuf, fish-poisson, fruit-fruit, meat-viande, milk-lait, mineral water-eau minérale, oranges-oranges, potatoes-pommes de terre, salt-sel, sandwich-sandwich, sausage-saucisse, soup-soupe or potage, sugar-sucre, tea-thé, vegetables- legumes, water-eau, wine-vin.

Getting Rides

Bonjour, je suis un(e) étudiant(e) de _____ Je voudrais aller dans la direction de _____. Pourriez-vous m'emmener s'il vous plait? Je vous en serais très reconnaissant. Merci.

Getting Accommodation

Bonjour, je suis un étudiant de _____. Pourriez-vous m'aider s'il vous plait? Je pars demain matin pour _____. Je serais prêt à travailler 2-3 (deux-trois) heures en échange d'un diner et d'un lit pour la nuit. Et je pourrais apprendre un peu du mode de vie français. Merci beaucoup.
or
Bonjour, je suis un étudiant de _____. Pourriez-vous m'aider s'il vous plait? Je pars demain matin pour _____. Je serais prêt à vous donner un cadeau ou un peu d'argent en échange d'un diner et d'un lit pour la nuit. Et je pourrais découvrir un peu le mode de vie français. Merci beaucoup

Getting Food

Me laisseriez-vous faire la vaisselle chez vous en échange d'un repas?

Directions

1. Où se trouve l'autoroute pour _____?
2. Où prend-on le bus pour aller à _____?

3. Où prend-on le train pour aller à _____?
4. Quel est le numero ou le nom du bus qui peut m'emmener près de l'autoroute?

Hitch-Hiking Signs
City... write it in English or native language
The following should be in the native language:

Home to Mom	Chez Maman
I'm safe	Je ne mords pas
Tree	Arbres
Please	S'il vous plait
Thank you	Merci
Anywhere	N'importe où

GERMAN — Pronunciation Guide

Hello	Guten Tag	goo-ten-tahk
How are you?	Wie geht es Ihnen?	vee gayt ess ee-nen
Very well	Sehr gut	zayr goot
Thank you	Danke schön	dahn-keh-shen
Goodbye	Auf Wiedersehen	owf vee dayr-zayn
Please	Bitte	bit-tuh
Yes	Ja	yah
No	Nein	nine
Give me	Geben Sie mir	gay-ben zee meer
Where is?	Wo ist?	voh eest
the station	der Bahnhof	dayr bahn-hohf
the youth hostel	die Jugendherberge	dee you gend-er-berga
the university	die Universität	dee uni-vayr-zee-tait
a restaurant	ein Restaurant	ain res-tow-rahng
the toilet	die Toilette	dee twah-let-tuh
the grocery store	lebensmittelgeschaft	layy-ben-smeetel-day-scheft
To the right	Nach rechts	nakh reshts
To the left	Nach links	nakh-leenks
Straight ahead	Geradeaus	gay-ray-day-ous
I would like	Ich möchte	ikh mersh-ta
to eat	essen	ess-en
a room	ein Zimmer	ain tzim-mer
How much is it?	Wieviel kostet es?	vee-feelkaw-stetees
The check, please	Zahlen, bitte	tzah-len bit-tuh
When?	Wann?	vahn
Yesterday	Gestern	geh-stern
Today	Heute	hoy-tuh
Tomorrow	Morgen	more-gen
Breakfast	Frühstück	free-shteck
Lunch	Mittagessen	mi-tahg-ess-en
Dinner	Abendessen	ah-bend-ess-en

1	eins	aintz	11	elf	elf
2	zwei	tzwai	12	zwölft	zwuhlf
3	drei	dry	13	dreizehn	drytzain
4	vier	feer	14	vierzehn	feertzain
5	fünf	fewnf	15	fünfzehn	funfzain
6	sechs	zex	16	sechzehn	zextzain
7	sieben	zee-ben	17	siebzehn	seebtzain
8	acht	ahkht	18	achtzehn	arktzain
9	neun	noyn	19	neunzehn	noyntzain
10	zehn	tzayn	20	zwanzig	tzvahntzig

30	dreissig	dry-zig	80	achtzig	ark-tzig
40	vierzig	feer-tzig	90	neunzig	noyn-tzig
50	fünfzig	funf-tzig	100	hundert	hoon-dert
60	sechzig	zex-tzig	1,000	tausend	tow-sent
70	siebzig	zeeb-tzig			

"84 Cent" Foods

apples-äpfel, bananas-bananen, beer-bier, bread-brot, cheese-käse, chocolate-schokolade, coffee-kaffee, egg-ei, fish-fisch, fruit-obst, meat-fleisch, milk-milch, mineral water-mineralwassen, oranges-apfelsinen, potatoes-kartoffeln, salt-salz, sandwich-belegtes brötchen, sausage-wurst, soup-suppe, sugar-zucker, tea-tee, vegetables-gemüse, water-wasser, wine-wein.

Getting Rides
Austrian German
Guten Tag, ich bin ein Student aus _____. Ich brauche eine Mitfahrgelegenheit nach _____. Ist es möglich, mit Ihnen mitzufahren? Ich ware Ihnen sehr dankbar. Vielen Dank.
or
Swiss German
Hallo, ich bin ein Student von _____. Ich würde Ihnen sehr dankbar sein, wenn Sie mir ins Auto mitnehmen könnten? Ich muss nach_____ fahren. Vielen Dank.

Getting Accommodation
Austrian German
Guten Tag, ich bin ein Student aus _____. Können Sie mir bitte helfen? Ich mochte frühmorgens nach _____ fahren. Ich wäre bereit, 2-3 Stunden für ein Bett, Abendessen und Frühstück zu arbeiten und diese Möglichkeit zu nutzen, Ihre Kultur etwas naher kennenzulernen. Ich würde sehr früh weiterreisen. Vielen Dank.
or
Guten Tag, ich bin ein Student aus _____. Können Sie mir bitte helfen? Ich möchte frühmorgens nach _____ fahren. Ich wäre bereit, Ihnen ein Geschenk oder Geld im Austausch für ein Bett, Abendessen und Frühstück zu geben und somit die Möglichkeit zu nutzen, Ihre Kultur etwas näher kennenzulernen. Ich würde sehr früh weiterreisen. Vielen Dank.
Swiss German
Hallo, ich bin ein Student von_____. Können Sie mir bitte helfen? Ich werde morgen früh nach _____ fahren und würde bereit sein, 2-3 Stunden zu arbeiten, um dann freies Abendessen, Uebernachtung und Frühstück zu bekommen. Es würde für mich eine gute Gelegenheit sein, Ihre Kultur näher kennenzulernen. Ich werde morgen früh weggehen. Vielen Dank.
or
Hall, ich bin ein Student von_____. Können Sie mir bitte helfen? Ich werde morgen früh nach _____ fahren. Als Gegenleistung für Abendessen, Uebernachtung, Frühstück und die Gelegenheit ein bisschen Ihre Kultur kennenzulernen, wäre ich bereit zu bezahlen oder Ihnen ein Geschenk zu geben. Ich werde morgen früh weggehen. Vielen Dank.

Getting Food
Austrian German
Darf ich im Austausch fur eine Mahlzeit in Ihrer Küche ein paar Studen Geschirr abwaschen?
Swiss German
Darf ich für 1-2 Stunden Teller waschen als Gegenleistung für eine Gratismahlzeit?

Directions
Swiss German

1. Wo ist die Autobahn nach_____?
2. Wo ist der Bus nach _____?
3. Wo ist der Zug nach _____?
4. Welcher ist der Busname oder-nummer, der mich am nächsten zur Autobahn bringt?

Hitch-Hiking Signs
City....write it in the native language
The following should be in the native language:

Home to Mom	Heim zur Mutter
I'm safe	Ich bin sicher
Trees	Pflanzen or Bäume
Please	Bitte
Thank you	Danke
Anywhere	Irgendwo

GREEK — Pronunciation Guide

English	Greek	Pronunciation
Hello	Yia sou	yeea-sou
How are you?	Tee kanees	tee ka-nees
Very well	Polee kala	polee ka-la
Thank you	Efhaceesto	ef-kah-ree-stoh
Goodbye	Anteeo	an-tee-o
Please	parakalo	pah-rah-kah-lo
Yes	Ne	neh
No	Ohi	o-hee
Give me	Dose mou	do-se mou
Where is?	Pou enai	poo-ee-neh?
the station	o stathmos	oh stath-mose
the youth hostel	pansion gia neous	pan-sion giaa neous
the university	panepistimio	panepis-tee-meeo
a restaurant	estiatorio	estia-torio
the toilet	tovaleta	tova-le-ta
the grocery store	padopolio	pan-tu-po-leeo
To the right	Dexia	dex-ee-ah
To the left	Aristera	ari-ste-raa
I would like	Tha ethela	tha-ee-the-la
to eat	na fao	na fa-o
a room	ena domatio	e-na do-ma-tio
How much is it?	Poso kani?	po-so ka-nee
The check, please	Ton logariasmo parakalo	ton lo-ga-ria-smo para-kaloo
When?	Pote?	po-tee
Yesterday	Ehthes	eh-thees
Today	Simera	see-mer-ah
Tomorrow	Avrio	ah-vree-oh
Breakfast	Proino	pro-ee-no
Lunch	Masimeriano	me-si-me-ria-no
Dinner	Vradino	vra-di-no

#	Greek	Pronunciation	#	Greek	Pronunciation
1	ena	mee-den	9	enneea	e-nay-a
2	dyo	thee-oh	10	deka	de-ka
3	treea	tree-ah	11	edeka	e-de-ka
4	tessera	tes-sera	12	dodeca	do-de-ka
5	pente	pend-eh	13	decatria	deca-tree-a
6	exee	ek-see	14	decatesera	dec-a te-sse-re
7	epta	ef-tah	15	decapende	de-ca pen-te
8	okto	oc-to	16	decaexi	de-ca e-xee

17	decaefta	de-ca e-pta	60	exida	ek-seen-dah
18	decaohto	de-ca octo	70	evdomida	ev-doh-meen-dah
19	decaenia	de-ca-eneea	80	ogdoda	oc-don-dah
20	ekosi	ee-koh-see	90	enenida	e-ne-neen-dah
30	triada	tree-an-dah	100	ekato	e-ka-toh
40	sarada	sa-ran-dah	500	pentakosia	pen-da-ko-sya
50	penida	pe-neen-dah	1,000	hilia	hi-lia

"84 Cent" Foods

apples-meela, bananas-bananes, beer-bira, biscuits, bread-psomi, cheese-tiri, chocolate-sokolata, coffee-kafe, egg-avga, fish-psari, fruit-fruta, meat-kreas, milk-gala, oranges-portocalia, potatoes-patates, salt-alati, sandwich-santouits, sausage-loukaneeko, soup-soupa, sugar-zaharee, tea-tsaee, vegetables-chortarika, water-nero, wine-krasi.

Getting Rides

Yia sas, eeme enas mathetees apo_____. Hreeazome na pao pros _____. Eéne deenaton na me parete? Tha eeme eepohreos. Efhareesto.

Getting Accommodation

Yia sa, eeme enas mathetees apo _____. Boreete na me voeetheesete? Taxidevo pros _____ noris avreeo proee. Tha borousa na doulepso (2) deeo, (3) trees ores yia man mou dosete eena krevatee, fayeeto ke proinó ke meea efkereea na matho yia teen kultura sas tha feego noris to proee. Efhareesto para polee.

or

Yia sas, eeme enas mathetees apo _____. Boreete na me voeetheesete? Taxidevo pros _____noris avreeo proee. Tha borousa na sas dóso éna dóro eé hreémata yia na mou dosete eena krevatee, fayeeto ke proinó ke meea efkereea na matho yia teen kultura sas tha feego noris to proee. Efhareesto para polee.

Getting Food

Boró na pleéno peeáta steen kouzeéna sas yia (1) meea ee (2) deeo ores yiá eena peeato fageeto?

Directions

1. Pou eene o ethneekos _____?
2. Pou eene to leoforeeo na pao sto _____?
3. Pou eene to tréno na pao sto _____?
4. Peeo eene to onoma ee arithmos too leo foreeou pou boree na mee paee kontaa ston kentreeko dromo.

Hitch-Hiking Signs

City...write it in the native language
The following should be in the native language:

Home to Mom	Spiti me teen mama
I'm safe	Eéme asfalees
Trees	Dentra
Please	Parakalo
Thank you	Efha rifto
Anywhere	Opoudipote

HEBREW

Since people from all over the world have brought with them a slightly different variation of the written Hebrew language, I have provided the pronunciation of each word only. For all words and especially the 'Specific Phrases', you should read the necessary phrase verbally to the person you meet. The Israeli may not know what the 'pronunciation' word means, but he/she will once they hear it spoken.

Pronunciation Guide

Hello	Shalom
How are you?	Ma shlom cha?
Very well	Beseder gamour
Thank you	Tohah
Goodbye	Shalom
Please	Bevakash
Yes	Ken
No	Lo
Give me	Ten lee
Where is?	Efo?
the station	ha tachana merkazeet
the youth hostel	achsania
the university	hauneversita
a restaurant	namisake
the toilet	haseroteem
the grocery store	hamakolet
To the right	Leyamin
To the left	Lesmol
I would like	Efshar, anee ritze
to eat	leechol
a room	cheder
How much is it?	Kahmah zeh?
The check, please	Hacheshbon bevakasha
When?	Matai?
Yesterday	Etmol
Today	Hayon
Tomorrow	Machar
Breakfast	Arucha boker
Lunch	Arucha tzoriem
Dinner	Arucha erev

1	echad	30	shlosheem
2	shtaim	40	arbaeem
3	shalosh	50	chameesheem
4	arba	60	shisheem
5	chamesh	70	sheveem
6	shesh	80	shmoneem
7	shevah	90	teasheem
8	shmonah	100	maya
9	teshah	500	chamesh mayot
10	eser	1,000	elef
20	ereem		

"84 Cent" Foods

apples-tapucheej, bananas-bananot, beer-beerah, biscuits-biscuitem, bread-leachm, cheese-gvenah, chocolate-chocola, coffee-cafe, egg-betza, fish-dag, fruit-payrot, meat-basar, milk-chalav, mineral water-mayeem minerali, oranges-tapuzeem, potatoes-tapuchee adamah, salt-melach, sandwich-sandwich, soup-marak, sugar-sukar, tea-tay, vegetables-yerakot, water-mayeem, wine-yaeen.

Getting Rides

Shalom, anee student me _____. Anee tzarech tramp bekevon le _____. Efsnar lekabel tramp? Todah raban.

316

Getting Accommodation
Shalom, anee student me _____. Efshar laazor otee? Anee hoseah le _____
mukdam machar baboker. Anee yacol laavod le camah shaot eem anee yokol
lekabel metah, aruchat erev vearuchat boker vegam ze moten lee epsharut leelmod
kesat al hatarbut. Anee aazov mukdam baboker. Todah rabah.
or
Shalom, anee student me _____. Efshar laazor otee? Anee noseah le _____
mukdam machar baboker. Anee efshar latet kesef o mutannah velekabel meetah,
aruchat erev. Vearuchat boker vegam ze noten lee epsharut leelmod kesat al
hatarbut. Anee aazov mukdam baboker. Todah rabah.

Getting Food
Efshar lenakot et hakelim lesha vemekabel arucha?

Directions
1. Epho harehov le _____?
2. Epho haautobus lehagid le _____?
3. Epho harakevet lehagia le _____?
4. Ezo mispar autobus yachol lehavee lee hachee karov le _____?

Hitch-Hiking Signs
City...write it in the native language
The following should be in the native language:

Home to Mom	Habatai le ima
I'm safe	Anee beseder
Trees	Efseem
Please	Bevakasha
Thank you	Tova
Anywhere	Le ezehu makom

HUGARIAN   Pronunciation Guide

Hello	Jo napot	yoh naw-poht
How are you?	Hogy van?	hoj vawn
Very well	Nagyo jol	naw-jon yohl
Thank you	Koszonom	kur-sur-nurm
Goodbye	Viszontlatasra	vee-sont-lah-tahsh-raw
Please	Legyen szives	leh-jen see-vesh
Yes	Igen	ee-gen
No	Nem	nem
Give me	Adjon	aad joon
Where is?	Hol van?	hohl-vawn
the station	a vasútállomás	vaashooth-aalawmaaash
the youth hostel	ifjusagl szalla's	eefyoosh-aaghee saa-laash
the university	az egyetem	oz aed-lae-taem
a restaurant	az etterem	oz aut-taeraem
the toilet	a WC	vaytsay
the grocery store	az êlelmiszerbolt	aylael-meesaer-bawlt
I would like	Szeretnêk	saerae-tnayk
to eat	enni	oennee
a room	egy szobat	oed sawbaa
How much is it?	Mennyibe Keral?	maen'ee bee kaereul
The check, please	Fizetek	feezoe-toek
When?	Mikor?	meekawr
Yesterday	Tegnap	taeg-nop

317

Today	Ma		mo	
Tomorrow	Holnap		hawl-nop	
Breakfast	Reggeli		rae-gaelee	
Lunch	Ebéd		aebayd	
Dinner	Vacsora		vocha-wro	
1	egy	ej	16 tizenhat	teez-en-hawt
2	kettö	ket-tur	17 tizenhét	teez-en-hayt
3	három	hah-rohm	18 tizennyolc	teez-en-nyohlts
4	négy	nayj	19 tizenkilenc	teez-en-kee-lents
5	öt	urt	20 húsz	hoos
6	hat	hawt	30 harminc	hawr-meents
7	hét	hayt	40 negyven	nej-ven
8	nyolc	nyohits	50 ötven	urt-ven
9	kilenc	keelents	60 hatvan	hawt-vawn
10	tiz	teez	70 hetven	het-ven
11	tizenegy	teez-en-ej	80 nyolcvan	nyohlts-vawn
12	tizenkettö	teez-en-ket-tur	90 kilencven	kee-lents-ven
13	tizenhárom	teez-en-hah-rohm	100 szaz	sahz
14	tizennégy	teez-en-nayj	500 ötszaz	urt-sahz
15	tizenot	teez-en-urt	1,000 ezer	e-zewr

"84 Cent" Foods
apples-alma, bananas-banan, beer-sor, biscuits-pogacsa, bread-kenyer, cheese-sajt, chocolate-csokolade, coffee-kave, egg-tojas, fish-halak fruit-gyunolcs, meat-hus, milk-tej, mineral water-asvanyviz, oranges-narancs, potatoes-burgonya, salt-so, sausage-kolbasz, soup-leves, sugar-cukor, tea-tea, vegetables-zoldseg, water-viz, wine-bor.

Getting Rides
Hello _____ (amerikai -America, or Kanadia- Canada) diak vagyok _____
-be szeretnek menni. Elvinne? Nagyon halas volnek. Koszonom.

Getting Accommodation
Hello _____ (America, Canada) diak vagyok. Nem tudna segiteni? Holnap koran reggel _____ -be kell utaznom. Szivesen dolgoznek ket-harom orat cserebe egy agyert, vacsoraert es reggeliert. Es szivesen megismerkednek a maguk eletevel. Koran reggel mar el is mennek. Koszonom szepen.
or
Hello _____ (America, Canada) diak vagyok. Nem tudna segiteni? Holnap koran reggel _____-be utazom. Szivesen fizetnek erte vagy ajandekot adnek, ha itt aludhatnek es vacsorat meg reggelit kapnek es megismerkedhetnek a maguk eletevel. Koran reggel mar el is mennek. Koszonom szepen.

Getting Food
Mosogathatnek egy-ket orat a konyhaban egy tal etelert cserebe?

Directions
1. Merre van a _____-i ut?
2. Honnan indul a _____-i busz?
3. Honnan indul a _____-i vonat?
4. Melyik busszal mehetnek ki az autosztradara?

Hitch-Hiking Signs
City....write it in the native language
The following should be in the native language:
Home to Mom   Haza anyamhoz

I'm safe	Rendes gyerek vagyok	
Trees	Fák	
Please	Kerem	
Thank you	Koszonom	
Anywhere	Bárhová	

ITALIAN — Pronunciation Guide

English	Italian	Pronunciation
Hello	Buon giorno	bwohn djor-noh
How are you?	Come sta?	koh-may-stah
Very well	Molto bene	mohl-toh bay-nay
Thank you	Grazie	grah-tzyeh
Goodbye	Arrivederci	ah ree-vay-dehr chee
Please	Per favore	payr fah-voy-ray
Yes	Si	see
No	No	non
Give me	Mi dia	mee dee-ah
Where is?	Dov'è?	doh-vay
the station	la stazione	la stah-tzyonay
the youth hostel	l'albergo per giovani	al bairgo per joh-vah-nee
the university	l'universita	l'oonay-ver-see-ta
a restaurant	un ristorante	oon rees-to-rahn-tay
a grocery store	un negozio alimentare	oon ney-go-tzo a-la-men-tar-a
the toilet	il gabinetto	eel ga-bee-naytoh
To the right	A destra	ah dess-trah
To the left	A sinistra	ah see-nee-strah
Straight ahead	Diritto	dee-ret-toh
I would like	Vorrei	vohr-ray
to eat	mangiare	mahn-djah-ray
a room	una camera	oona kah-may-rah
How much is it?	Quanto costa?	kwan-toh kaw-stah
The check, please	Il conto, per favore	eel kohn-toh
When?	Quando?	kwahn-doh
Yesterday	Ieri	ee-yay-ree
Today	Oggi	aw-djee
Tomorrow	Domani	doh-mah-nee
Breakfast	Colazione	koh-lah-tzyoh-nay
Lunch	Pranzo	prahn-tzoh
Dinner	Cena	chay-nah

1	uno	oo-noh	16	sedici	say-dee-chee
2	due	doo-ay	17	deciassette	deeh-cheeah-set-tay
3	tre	tray	18	diciotto	dee-chiot-toh
4	quattro	kwah-troh	19	diciannove	dee-cheeah-noh-vay
5	cinque	cheen-kway	20	venti	vayn-tee
6	sei	say	30	trenta	trayn-ta
7	sette	set-tay	40	quaranta	kwah-rahn-ta
8	otto	aw-toh	50	cinquanta	cheen-kwahn-ta
9	nove	noh-vay	60	sessanta	sais-sarn-ta
10	dieci	dee-ah-chee	70	settanta	set-tan-ta
11	undici	dee-ay-chee	80	ottanta	ot-tan-ta
12	dodici	doh-dee-chee	90	novanta	no-van-ta
13	tredici	tray-dee-chee	100	cento	chayn-to
14	quattordici	kwat-torr-dee-chee	1,000	mille	mee-lay
15	quindici	kween-dee-chee			

"84 Cent" Foods

apples-mele, bananas-banane, beer-birra, bread-pane, cheese-formaggio, chocolate-cioccolata, coffee-caffè, egg-uovo, fish-pesce, fruit-frutta, meat-carne, milk-latte, mineral water-acqua minerale, oranges-aranci, potatoes-patate, salt-sale, sandwich-panino, sausage-salsiccia, soup-minestra, sugar-zucchero, tea-te, vegetable-legumi water-acqua, wine-vino.

Getting Rides

Salve, sono studente e vengo da _____. Mi puo' dare un passaggio verso _____. Per cortesia, è possibile farmi dare un passagio? Le saro molto grato/a . Grazie.

Getting Accommodation

Salve, sono studente e vengo da _____. Puo'aiutarmi per favore? Vado a _____ domani mattina presto. Sarei pronto a lavorare 2 0 3 ore in scambio di un letto e da mangiare e la possibilità di imparare un po'della cultura Italiana. Partiro' presto la mattina. Grazie tante.

or

Salve, sono studente e vengo da _____. Puo' aiutarmi per favore? Vado a _____ domani mattina presto. Mi puo'dare l'ospitalità per questa motte sono pronto a pagare o a offrire un regalo in scambio di un letto e da mangiare e la possibilità di imparare un po'della cultura Italian. Partiro'presto la mattina. Grazie tante.

Getting Food

Posso lavorare in cucina per un'ora o due a lavare i piatti in scambio di un pasto.

Directions

1. Dov 'è l' autostrada per _____?
2. Dove si prende l 'autobus per _____?
3. Dov 'è il treno che va a _____?
4. Che nome o che numero ha l'autobus che mi porta il più vicino all 'autostrada?

Hitch-Hiking Signs

City.... write it in the native language
The following should be in the native language:

Home to Mom	A casa, da mamma
I'm safe	Non sono pericoloso
Trees	Alberi
Please	Per favore
Thank you	Grazie
Anywhere	Qualsiasi posto or Dovunque

NORWEGIAN		**Pronunciation Guide**
Good morning	God morgen	goo maw-ern
Good afternoon	God dag	goo kvehil
Good night	God natt	goo knot
Hello	Hallo	halloo
How are you?	Hvordan står det til	vorden store day till
Very well	Takk, bare bra	tack, bara braa
Thank you	Takk	tack
Goodbye	Adjo	adieu (Fr.)
Please	Vaer sa god	vayayrer ser goo
Yes	Ja	yaa
No	Nei	nay

Give me	Kan du gi meg	kan du yi may
Where is?	Hvor er?	vor er
the station	buss stasjonen	buss stashonen
the youth hostel	vardrehjemmet	hairbearge
the university	universitetet	univaishitait
a restaurant	en restaurant	on raistewrahngg
the toilet	toilettet	toilettet
the grocery store	dagligvarebutikken	daalivahrebouteecken
To the right	Til hoyre	til hayre
To the left	Til venstre	til vainstrer
Straight ahead	Rett frem	rett frame
I would like	Jeg vil svaert gjerne	yeg vil svart jerne
to eat	spise	speeser
a room	ha et rom	haa et roomm
How much is it?	Hvor mye koster det?	vor may coster day
The check, please	Kan jeg fa regningen	can yay for rayningen
When?	Når?	nor
Yesterday	I går	igor
Today	I dag	i daag
Tomorrow	I morgen	i mawern
Breakfast	Frokost	froocost
Lunch	Lunsi	lernsh
Dinner	Middag	middaah

1	en	enn	16	seksten	saystern
2	to	too	17	sytten	certern
3	tre	tray	18	atten	ahtern
4	fire	fira	19	nitten	nittern
5	fem	fame	20	tjue	shoer
6	seks	saix	30	tretti	trayti
7	sju	shoe	40	forti	ferti
8	atte	otte	50	femti	fame-ti
9	nik	nee	60	seksti	saix-ti
10	ti	tee	70	sytti	certi
11	elleve	ailver	80	atti	otti
12	tolv	toll	90	nitti	nitty
13	tretten	traitern	100	hundre	hewndrer
14	fjorten	fyootern	500	fem hundre	fame hewndrer
15	femten	fame-ten	1,000	tussen	toosern

"84 Cent" Foods

apples-epler, bananas-bananer, beer-øl, biscuits-kjeks, bread-brod, cheese-ost, choco-late--sjokolade, coffee-kaffe, egg-egg, fish-fisle, fruit-frukt, meat-kjøtt, milk-melk, mineral water-mineralvann, oranges-appelsiner, potatoes-poteter, salt-salt, sandwich-smørbrød, sausage-pølse, soup-suppe, sugar-sukker, tea-te, vegetables-grønnsaker, water-vann, wine-vin.

Getting Rides
Hallo, jeg er en student fra _____. Jeg skulle gjerne hatt skyss i retning _____. Jeg ville vaere svaert takknemlig hvis jeg kunne jeg få sitte på med deg?

Getting Acommodation
Hallo, jeg er en student fra _____. Kan du muligens hjelpe meg? Jeg skal dra videre til _____ imorgen tidlig. Jeg kan gjerne arbeide i 2-3 timer hvis jeg kan få lov til å overnatte, og kanskje få litt mat, og få laere litt om norks kultur. Jeg vil dra videre tidlig om morgenen.

or

Hallo, Jeg er en student fra _____. Kan du muligens hjelpe meg? Jeg skal dra videre til _____ imorgen tidlig. Jeg kan gjerne betale litt, eller gi en presang fra mitt hjemland, hvis jeg kan få bo hos dere en natt, og kanskje fa litt mat og Ire litt om norsk kultur. Jeg vil dra videre tidlig om morgenen.

Getting Food
Kan jeg hjelpe til på kjøkkenet mot å få et måltid mat?

Directions
1. Hvor er veien til _____?
2. Hvor finner jeg bussen til _____?
3. Hvor finner jeg toget til _____?
4. Hva er navnet eller nummeret på bussen som kan ta meg til narmeste hovedvei?

Hitch-Hiking Signs
City... write it in the native language
The following should be in the native language:

Home to Mom	Hjem til mor
I'm safe	Jeg er ikke farlig
Trees	Traer
Please	Vaer så snill
Thank you	Takk
Anywhere	Hvor som helst

POLISH		Pronunciation Guide
Hello	Czesc	tsheshch
How are you?	Jak sie masz	yak-sye-mash
Very well	Bardzo dobrze	bard-so dob-zheh
Thank you	Dziekuje	dzhehn-koo-yeh
Goodbye	Do widzenia	doh vid-sen-yeh
Please	Prosze	pro-sheh
Yes	Tak	tak
No	Nie	nyeh
Give me	Daj mi	dahy me
Where is?	Gdzie jest?	gdzheh yehst
the station	stacja	staht-syah
the youth hostel	schronisko miodziezowe	skhron-is-koh mwodzh-ez-hov-eh
the university	uniwersytet	uh-nee-ver-si-teht
a restaurant	restauracja	rehst-ah-wraht-sy-ah
the toilet	toaleta	twah-leh-tah
the grocery store	skelp spozywczy	sklehp spoh-zhiwt-shih
To the right	Na prawo	nah prah-voh
To the left	Na lewo	nah leh-voh
I would like	Chcialbym	khtsh-aw-bim
to eat	jesc	yeh-shch
a room	pokoj	poh-kooy
How much is it?	Ile to kosztuje?	eel-eh toh kosht-ooy-eh
The check, please	Prosze o rchunek	pro-sheh oh rahk-hoon-ehk
When?	Kiedy?	kyeh-dih
Yesterday	Wczoraj	fchor-igh
Today	Dzisiaj	dzhees-yigh
Tomorrow	Jutro	yoo-troh
Breakfast	Sniadanie	syn-ah-dah-nyeh
Lunch	no translation	
Dinner	Obiad	o-by-ahd

1	jeden	yeh-dehn	16	szesnascie	shehs-nahsy-tsheh
2	dwa	dvah	17	siedemnascie	syehdehm-nahsy-tsheh
3	trzy	chshi	18	osiemnascie	osyehm-nahsy-tsheh
4	cztery	chte-hri	19	dziewietnascie	dzheh-vyeht-nahsy- tsheh
5	piec	pyehntsh	20	dwadziescia	dvah-dzhehsy-tshah
6	szesc	shehsytsh	30	trzydziesci	chshi-dzhehsy-tshee
7	siedem	sye-dehm	40	czterdziesci	chtehr-dzhehsy-tshee
8	osiem	o-syehm	50	piecdziesiat	pyehn-dzhehs-yont
9	dziewiec	dzheh-syehntsh	60	szescdziesiat	shehsy-dzhehs-yont
10	dziesiec	dzheh-syehntsh	70	siedemdziesiat	syehdehm-dzhehs-yont
11	jedenascie	yeh-deh-nah-sy-tsheh	80	osiemdziesiat	osyehm-dzhehs-yont
12	dwanascie	dvah-nahsy-tsheh	90	dziewiecdziesiat	dzhehvyehn-dzhehs-yont
13	trzynascie	chshi-nahsy-tsheh	100	sto	sto
14	czternascie	chtehr-nahsy-tsheh	500	piecset	pyehn-tseht
15	pietnascie	pyeht-nahsy-tsheh	1,000	tysiac	tis-yonts

"84 Cent" Foods

apples-jablka , bananas-banany, beer-piwo, biscuits-ciastka, bread-chleb, cheese-ser, chocolate-czekolada, coffee-kawa, egg-jajko, fish-ryba, fruit-owoce, meat-mieso, milk-mleko, mineral water-woda mineralna, oranges-pomarancze, potatoes-ziemniaki, salt-sol, sandwich-kanapka, sausage-kielbasa, soup-zupa, sugar-cukier, tea-herbata, vegetables-warzywa, water-woda, wine-wino.

Getting Rides

Dzien dobry. Jestem studentem z _____. Jade w kierunku _____. Czy moze Pan/Pani mnie podwiezc. Bede bardzo wdzieczny. Dziekuje.

Getting Accommodation

Dzien dobry. Jestem studentem z _____. Czy moze mi Pan/Pani pomoc. Jutro rano wyjezdzam do _____. Chetnie popracuje przez dwietrzy godziny w zamian za nocleg, posilek i mozliwosc poznania waszych tradycji. Wyjade wczesnie jutro rano. Dziekuje bardzo.

or

Dzien dobry. Jestem studentem z _____. Dzien dobry. Jestem studentem z _____. Czy przyjma panstwo poderek lub pieniadze w zamian za nocleg, posilek i mozliwosc poznania waszych tradycji. Wyjade wczesnie jutro rano. Dziekuje bardzo.

Getting Food

Czy moge pozmywac naczynia przez jedna lub dwie godziny w zamian za posilek?

Directions

1. Gdzie jest droga do _____?
2. Gdzie jest autobus do _____?
3. Gdzie jest pociag do _____?
4. Ktory autobus dowiezie mnie do glownej drogi?

Hitch-Hiking Signs

City.... write it in the native language
The following should be in the native language:

Home to Mom	Ide dodomu mamy
I'm safe	Ja jestem bezpieczn(y) (for females hitching, substitute the 'y' for 'a')
Trees	Drzewo
Please	Procze
Thank you	Dziekvje
Anywhere	Wczedzie

English	Portuguese	Pronunciation
Hello	Olá	oh-lah
How are you?	Como está?	ko-mo esh-tah
Very well	Muito bem	muy-toh bym
Thank you	Muito obrigado	muy-toh ob-ree-gah-doo
Goodbye	Adeus	ah-day-ush
Please	Por favor	Por fah-vohr
Yes	Sim	sem
No	Não	naion
Give me	Dê-me	deh-meh
Where is?	Onde fica?	on-deh fee-kah
the station	a estação	o aish-tah-ssaion
the youth hostel	a pousada da juventude	a poosad da juve-n-tude
the university	a universidade	ah uh-nee-ver-see-dah-deh
a restaurant	um restaurante	om rash-tah-ran-teh
the toilet	a casa de banho	ah kah-zah de bahn-yoo
the grocery store	a supermercado	o suh-er-mer-cah-doh
To the right	À direitaa	ah dee-rai-tah
To the left	À esquerda	aah ask-ker-dah
Straight ahead	Em frente	ym frain-tah
I would like	Gostaria de	goosh-tah-ree-ah de
to eat	comer	koh-mehr
a room	um quarto	oom kwar-toh
How much is it?	Quanto custa?	kwahn-to koosh-tah
The check, please	A conta por, favor	ah kohn-tah por, fah-vohor
When?	À Quando?	kwahn-doe
Yesterday	Ontem	ohn-tym
Today	Hoje	hoyh-je
Tomorrow	Amanha	ah-mai-nyayh
Breakfast	Café da manha	cah-fey dah ma-nyaha
Lunch	Almoco	al-moh-sso
Dinner	Jantar	jhan-tar

1	um	oom	16	dezasseis	deh-zai-ssaish
2	dois	doysh	17	dezassete	deh-zai-ssai-teh
3	três	traish	18	dezoito	deh-zoy-toh
4	quatro	kwah-troh	19	dezanove	deh-za-noh-veh
5	cinco	sseen-koh	20	vinte	veen-teh
6	seis	ssaish	30	trinta	treehn-tah
7	sete	ssai-teh	40	quarenta	kwah-rain-tah
8	oito	oy-toh	50	cinquenta	sseen-kwain-tah
9	nove	noh-veh	60	sessenta	ssai-ssaihn-tah
10	dez	daish	70	setenta	ssai-tain-tah
11	onze	on-zeh	80	oitenta	oy-tain-tah
12	doze	doh-zeh	90	noventa	noh-vain-tah
13	treze	trai-zeh	100	cem	sym
14	catorze	kah-tohr-zeh	500	qinhentos	ki-nyen-tos
15	quinze	keen-zeh	1,000	mil	mill

"84 Cent" Foods

apples-macas, bananas-bananas, beer-cerveja, biscuits-biscoites, bread- pao, cheese-queijo, chocolate-chocolate, coffee-cafe, egg-ovos, fish-peixe, fruit-frutas, meat-carne, milk-leite, mineral water-agua mineral, oranges-laranjas, potatoes-batatas, salt-sal, sandwich-sandviche, sausage-linguiça, soup- sopa, sugar-acucar, tea-chá, vegetables-verduras, water-agua, wine-vinho.

Getting Rides
Olá, sou estudante em_____. Precisava de uma boleia em direcção a _____.
Será possivel levar-me? Ficaria muito agradecido. Obrigado (a).

Getting Accommodation
Olá, sou estudante em _____. Pode-me ajudar? Parto para _____àmanhã de
manhã. Estou disposto (a) a dar-lhe um presente ou dinheiro em troco de dormida,
jantar e almoço (point to sleeping bag) e pela oportunidade de aprender alguma
coisa sobre a sua cultura. Vou-me embora àmanhã cedo. Muito obridado (a).
or
Olá, sou estudante em _____. Pode-me ajudar? Parto para _____àmanhã de
manhã. Eu estaria disposto a trabalhar, por 2 ou 3 horas em troco de dormida,
jantar e almoço (point to sleeping bag) e pela oportuniade de aprender alguma
coisa sobre a sua cultura. Vou-me embora amanha cedo. Muito obridado (a).

Getting Food
Deixa-me lavar louça na sua cozinha por uma ou duas horas, em troco de uma
refeição?

Directions
1. Onde é a auto-estrada para _____?
2. Onde se apanha o autocarro para _____?
3. Onde se apanha o comboio para _____?
4. Qual é o nome ou o número do autocarro que me pode levar perto da autoestrada?

Hitch-Hiking Signs
City....write it in the native language
The following should be in the native language:

Home to Mom	Para casa
I'm safe	Sou seguro
Trees	Árvores
Please	Faz favor
Thank you	Obrigado (a)
Anywhere	Para qualquer sítio

ROMANIAN — Pronunciation Guide

Hello	Salut	sah-loot

(it is more polite to use the next three salutations instead of Salut)

Good morning	Buna dimineata	boona deemeeneeatsa
Good afternoon	Buna ziua	boona zeeooa
Good evening	Buna seara	boona seara
How are you?	Ce mai faceti	che my fachetsi
Very well	Foarte bine	foarte beene
Thank you	Multumesc	mooltsoomesk
Goodbye	La revedere	la revedere
Please	Và rog	va rohg
Yes	Da	dah
No	Nu	noo
Give me	Dati-mi	datseme
Where is?	Unde este?	oonde ehste
the station	Gara	gahrah
the youth hostel	Hotelul	hotelool
the university	Universitatea	ooniverseetatea
the restaurant	restaurantul	restaurantool

the toilet	toaleta				tohaleta
the grocery store	magatin alimentar				mahgahzeen aleementar
To the right	La dreapta				lah dreapta
To the left	La stanga				lah stengah
Straight ahead	Inainte				enaeente
I would like	Asi dori				ahsh doree
to eat	sa manàne				sa menenk
a room	o camerà				o kahmehra
How much is it?	Cat costà?				ket kostah
The check, please	Nota de platà				notah deh plahtah
When?	Cand				kend
Yesterday	Ieri				ee-ehre
Today	Astazi				ahstaze
Breakfast	Mic dejun				meek dehjoon
Lunch	Dejun				dehjoon
Dinner	Cina				cheena

1	unu	oonoo	16	saisprezece	saischeprehzecheh
2	doi	doi	17	saptesprezece	shaphptehprehzecheh
3	trei	tree	18	optsprezece	optprehzecheh
4	patru	pahtroo	19	nouasprezece	noh-ooaprehzecheh
5	cinci	cheenche	20	douazeci	dohooazeche
6	sase	shahseh	30	treizeci	treizeche
7	sapte	shaphpteh	40	patruzeci	pahtroozeche
8	opt	opt	50	cincizzci	chenchezehche
9	noua	nohooa	60	saizeci	shaheezehehe
10	zece	zeheheh	70	saptezeci	shaptehzehehe
11	unsprezece	oonsprehzehcheh	80	optzeci	optzehehe
12	doisprezece	doisprehzecheh	90	nouafeci	noh-ooa zehehe
13	treisprezece	treisprehzecheh	100	o suta	o soota
14	patrusprefece	pahtrooprehzecheh	500	cinci sute	chenche sooteh
15	cincisprezece	cheencheprehzecheh	1,000	o mieo	mee-eh

"84 Cent" Foods

apples-mere, bananas-banane, beer-bere, biscuits-biscuiti, bread-branza, cheese-cioco, chocolate-ciocolata, coffee-cafea, egg-oua, fish-peste, fruit-fructe, meat-carne, milk-lapte, mineral water-apa minerala, oranges-portocale, potatoes-cartofi, salt-sare, sandwich-sanvici, sausage-carnati, soup-supa, suger-zahar, tea-ceai, vegetables-legumes, water-apa, wine-vin.

Getting Rides

Sunt un student din _____. Doresc sa ajung (sa calatoresc) la _____. Ma puteti lua cu Dumneavoastra. Asi fi foatre recunoscator. Multumesc.

Getting Accommodation

Sunt un student din _____. M-ati putea ajuta? Voi pleca maine dimineata, devreme, la _____. Sunt dispus sa muncesc cateva ore pentru a putea ptrece o seara cu Dumneavoastra sa invat din cultura Romaniei. Asi avea nevoie de o cazare, cina si mic dejun.

or

Sunt un student din _____. M-ati putea ajuta? Voi pleca maine dimineata, devreme, la _____. Asi putea sa va recompensez daca voi avea posibilitatea sa petrec o seara in familia Dumneavoastra pentru a invata putin din cultura Romaniei.

Getting Food

Asi putea sa spal vasele o ora pentru o portie de mancare?

326

Directions
1. Care este drumul spre _____?
2. Care este autobuzul spre _____?
3. Care este trenul spre _____?
4. Ce autobuz merge spre soseaua catre _____?

Hitch-Hiking Signs
City... write it in the native language
The following should be in the native language:

Home to Mom	Ma intorc acasa lamma
I'm safe	Sunt bine
Trees	Copaci
Please	Va rog
Thank you	Multumesc
Anywhere	Oriunde

SLOVAK   Pronunciation Guide

Hello	Ahoj (ahoy) or Cau (csau) very informal	
Hello	Dobrý den (dobri : dyen) formal	
How are you?	Ako sá mas?	akoh sah ma :sh
Very well	Dakujem, dobre	dyakuyem, dobra
Thank you	Daku jem	dyakuyem
Goodbye	Zbohom	zbohom
Please	Prosím	prohsi : m
Yes	Áno	a : noh
No	Nie	nyah
Give me	Prosím si	prohsi : m see
Where is?	Kde je?	gdye yeah
the train station	zeleznicná stanica	zhalazneecsna : stanitsa
the bus station	autobusová stanica	autoboosohva : stanitsa
the youth hostel	studentský hostel	shtoodentski : hostel
the university	univerzita	uhneeverzitah
a restaurant	restaurácia	reshtaura : tsya
the toilet	WC (ve: -tse:) or zachod (za : khod)	
the grocery store	drogéria	droge : rya
To the right	Doprava	doprahva
To the left	Dol'ava	dolyava
Straight ahead	Rovno	rovnoh
I would like	Chcel by som	khtsel bee som
to eat	nieco jest	nyacso yast
a room	izbu	eezbuh
How much is it?	Kol'ko to sto ji:	kolkoh toh stoi
The check, please	Prosím si úcet	prosi : m sih u : cset
When?	Kedy?	kehdee
Yesterday	Vcera	fcsyerah
Today	Dnes	dnyes
Tomorrow	Aajtra	zaytrah
Breakfast	Rana jky	rahnyaykee
Lunch	Obed	obead
Dinner	Vecera	vecsera

1	jeden	veden	6	sest	shast
2	dva	dvaj	7	sedem	sadyem
3	tro	tree	8	osem	ohsem
4	styri	shteeree	9	devat	dvesat
5	pat	pät	10	desat	dyesat

11	jedenást	yedena : st	30	tridsat	treetsat
12	dvanást	dvama : st	40	styridsat	shteeritsat
13	trinást	treena : st	50	pätdesiat	peadvesvat
14	strnást	shtrna : st	60	sestdesiat	shesdvesvat
15	pätnást	peatna : st	70	sedemdesiat	sedyemdesyat
16	sestnást	shesna : st	80	osemdesiat	osemdvesvat
17	sedemnást	sedvyemna : st	90	devätdesiat	dyevadyesyat
18	osemnást	ohsemna : st	100	sto	stoh
19	devätnást	dyevatna : st	500	pätsto	patstoh
20	dvadsat	dvatsat	1,000	tisic	tveesi : ts

"84 Cent" Foods

apples-jablká, bananas-banány, beer-pivo, bisucits-keksy, bread-chleba, cheese-syr, chocolate-cokoláda, coffee-káva, egg-vajce, fish-ryba, fruit-ovocie, meat-mäso, milk-mlieko, mineral water-minerálka, oranges-pomarance, potatoes-zemiaky, salt-sol, sandwich-sendvic, sausage-párok/klobása, soup-polievka, sugar-cukor, tea-caj, vegetables-zelenina, water-voda, wine-vino, butter-maslo, lemonade-malinovka.

Getting Rides

Dobrý den, som študent z _____. Idete smerom do _____. Zveziete ma kúsok? Budem vám velmi vdacný. Dakujem.

Getting Accommodation

Dobrý den, som študent z_____. Potrebujem pomoc. Skoro ráno cestujem do _____. Za noclah, ranajky v veceru odpracujem 2-3 hodiny (point to sleeping bag). Odidem skoro ráno. Velmi pekne dajujem.

or

Dobry den, som študent z_____. Potrebujem pomoc. Skoro ráno cestujem do _____. Za noclah, ranajky a veceru (point to sleeping bag) moznost spoznat vašu kulturu vam dám peniaze alebo darcek. Odidem skoro ráno. Velmi pekne daju jem.

Getting Food

Za jedlo budem hoinu az dve unyvat riad.

Directions

1. Kde je dialnica do _____?
2. Odkial ide autobus do _____?
3. Odkial ide vlak do _____?
4. Ktory autobus ide najblizsie ka dialnici?

Hitch-Hiking Signs

City... write it in the native language
The following should be in the native language:

Home to Mom	Domov k mame
I'm safe	Nie som nebezpecný
Trees	Stromy
Please	Prosím
Thank you	Daku jem
Anywhere	Kamkolvek

SPANISH		Pronunciation Guide
Hello	Hola!	ho-la
How are you?	Cómo está usted?	koh-moh ess-tah oo-steth

English	Spanish	Pronunciation
Very well	Muy bien	mwee byen
Thank you	Gracias	grah-thee-ahss
Goodbye	Adios	ah-dyohss
Please	Por favor	pohr fah-bohr
Yes	Sí	see
No	No	noh
Give me	Déme	day-may
Where is?	Dónde está?	dohn-day ess-tah
the station	la estación	la ess-tah-thyohn
the youth hostel	el albergue juvenil	el al-ber-goh hoovay-nee
the university	la universidad	unee-ver-see-dad
a restaurant	un restaurante	oon-res-tow-rahn-tay
the toilet	el bano	el ba-no
the grocery store	supermercado	soo-pair-mer-ca-doe
To the right	A la derecha	ah lay day-ray-chuh
To the left	A la izquierda	ah lah eeth-kyayr-duh
Straight ahead	Derecho	day-ray-choh
I would like	Quiero	kyehr-oh
to eat	comer	koh-mayr
a room	una habitación	oo-nah ah-bee-tah-thyon
How much is it?	Cuánto es?	kwahn-toh ess
The check, please	La cuenta por favorlah	kwen-tah pohr fah-bohr
When?	Cuándo?	kwan-doh
Yesterday	Ayer	ah-yayr
Today	Hoy	oy
Tomorrow	Manana	mahn-yah-nah
Breakfast	Desayuno	deh-sai-yoo-noh
Lunch	Almuerzo	ahl-mwayr-thoh
Dinner	Comida	coe-mid-da

1	uno	oo-noh	16	dieciseis	dee-eth-ee-see-ay-tay
2	dos	dose	17	diecisiete	dee-eth-ee-see-ay-tay
3	tres	trayss	18	dieciocho	dee-eth-ee-o-choh
4	cuatro	kwah-troh	19	diecinueve	dee-eth-ee-nooay-vay
5	cinco	theen-koh	20	veinte	vain-tay
6	seis	sayss	30	treinta	train-ta
7	siete	syeh-tay	40	cuarenta	kwa-renta
8	ocho	oh-choh	50	cincuenta	thin-kwenta
9	nueve	nway-bay	60	sesenta	say-senta
10	diez	dyeth	70	setenta	say-tenta
11	once	on-thay	80	ochenta	o-chenta
12	doce	do-thay	90	noventa	no-venta
13	trece	tray-thay	100	cien	thee-en
14	catorce	ca-tor-thay	500	quinientos	keen-nee-entos
15	quince	keen-thay	1,000	mil	meel

"84 Cent" Foods

apples-manzanas, bananas-plátanos, beer-cerveza, bread-pan, cheese-queso, chocolate-chocolate, coffee-café, egg-huevo, fish-pescado, fruit-fruta, meat-carne, milk-leche, mineral water-agua mineral, oranges-naranjas, potatoes-patatas, salt-sal, sandwich-bocadillo, sausage-salchicha, soup- sopa, sugar-azúcar, tea-te, vegetables-verduras, water-aqua, wine-vino.

Getting Rides

Hola! Soy un estudiante de _____. Necesito un aventon en la direccion de. Puede usted darmelo? Muchas gracias.

Getting Accommodation

Hola! Soy un estudiante de _____. Puede usted ayudarme? Viajo para

_____ mañana por la mañana. Estoy dispuesto a trabayar 2-3 horas en pago por alojamiento (cama), comida y desayuno (point to sleeping bag) y la oportunidad de aprender un poco de su cultura. Yo saldré muy temprano en la mañana. Muchas gracias.

or

Hola! Soy un estudiante de _____. Puede usted ayudarme? Viajo para _____ mañana par la mañana. Estoy dispuesto a dar un regalo o dinero par alojamiento (cama), comida y desayuno (point to sleeping bag) y la oportunidad de aprender un poco de su cultura. Yo saldré muy temprano en la mañana. Muchas gracias.

Getting Food

Puedo lavar platos en su cocina por una o dos horas en cambio de una comida?

Directions

1. Dónde está la carretera para _____?
2. Dónde puedo tomar el autobús para _____?
3. Dónde puedo tomar el tren para _____?
4. Cuál es el nombre ao número del autobús que puede llevarme cerca de la carrefera?

Hitch-Hiking Signs

City...write it in the native language
The following should be in the native language:

Home to Mom	Vuelvo a casa
I'm safe	Soy responsable
Trees	Árboles
Please	Por favor
Thank you	Gracias
Anywhere	Adondesea

SWEDISH   Pronunciation Guide

English	Swedish	Pronunciation
Hello	God dag	goo dah
How are you?	Hur star det till?	hoor store det till
Very well	Tack, bra	tahk brah
Thank you	Tack	tahk
Goodbye	Adjo	ah-yer
Please	Var snall och	wahr snell oh
Yes	Ja	yah
No	Nej	nay
Give me	Ge mig	yay may
Where is?	Var finns?	vahr finss
the station	stationen	stah-shoo-nen
the youth hostel	vandrarhem	vahn-drar-hem
the university	universitetet	unee-vasee-tay-tet
the restaurant	en restaurang	en rest-oh-rahng
the toilet	toaletten	twah-let-ten
the grocery store	matvaruattären	mowt-varer-a-faren
To the right	At höger	oht her-ger
To the left	At vänster	oht yen-ster
Straight ahead	Rakt tram	rot from
I would like	Jag vill ha	ya vill hah
to eat	mat	maht
a room	ett rum	et ruhm
How much is it?	Vad kostar det?	vahd kaw-stahr dayt

When?	Nar?			nayr	
Yesterday	I gar			ee gore	
Today	I dag			ee dah	
Tomorrow	I morgon			ee mawr-rawn	
1	ett	et	16	sexton	sex-ton
2	tva	tvoh	17	sjutton	shew-ton
3	tre	tray	18	arton	air-ton
4	fyra	fee-rah	19	nitton	nit-ton
5	fem	fem	20	tjugo	tshu-goh
6	sex	sex	30	trettio	treht-tyee
7	sju	shew	40	fyrtio	fur-tyee
8	atta	awt-tah	50	femtio	fem-tyee
9	nio	nee-joh	60	sextio	sex-tyee
10	tio	tee-yoo	70	sjuttio	shew-tyee
11	elva	ehl-vah	80	attio	oht-tyee
12	tolv	tohlv	90	nittio	nit-tyee
13	tretton	treht-ton	100	ett hundra	et hun-dra
14	fjorton	fyohr-ton	500	tem hundra	fem hun-dra
15	femton	fem-ton	1,000	ett tusen	et too-sen

"84 Cent" Foods
apples-applen, bananas-bananer, beer-ol, biscuits-kex, bread-brod, cheese- ost, chocolate-chokolad, coffee-kaffe, egg-agg, fish-fisk, fruit-frukt, meat-kott, milk-mjolk, mineral water-mineralvatten, oranges-apelsiner, potatoes-potatis, salt-salt, sandwich-smorgas, sausage-korv, soup-soppa, sugar-socker, tea-te, vegetables-gronsaker, water-vatten, wine-vi.

Getting Rides
Goddag, jag är student och kommer från_____. Jag är på väg till _____.
Skulle jag kunna få lift? Jag vore mycket tacksam. Tack.

Getting Accommodation
Goddag, jag är student och kommer från _____. Skulle ni kunna hjälpa mig. Jag reser till _____ tidigt imorgon. Jag skulle gärna arbeta 2-3 timmar för sovplats, middag och frukost, och en möjlighet att lära mig litet om er kultur. Jag skulle resa min väg pa morgonen. Tack så mycket.
or
Goddag, jag är student och kommer från _____. Skulle ni kunna hjälpa mig. Jag reser till_____ tidigt imorgon. Jag skulle gärna ge er en gåva eller pengar för en sovplats, middag och frukost och en möjlighet att lära mig litet om er kultur. Jag skulle resa min väg tidigt på morgonen. Tack så mycket.

Getting Food
Skulle ni möjligtvis låta mig diska i ett par timmar för ett mål mat?

Directions
1. Var är motorvägen till _____?
2. Var är bussen som går till _____?
3. Var är tåget som går till _____?
4. Vilket nummer har bussen som tar mig till närheten av motorvägen?

Hitch-Hiking Signs
City...write it in English or native language
The following should be in the native language:

Home to Mom	Hem till mamma
I'm Safe	Jar är ofarlig
Trees	Träd

Please	Snälla
Thank you	Tack
Anywhere	Vart som helst

Hello	Merhaba	mare-hah-bah
How are you?	Nasilsiniz?	nah-sill-sin-iz
Very well	Çok iyi	choke-e-yee
Thank you	Tesekkür ederim (or mersi)	tesh-eck-ker eh-dehr-im
Goodbye	Allaha ismarladik	ah-lah-hah iss-marr-lah-duk
Please	Lütfen	loot-fen
Yes	Evet	eh-vet
No	Hayir	higher
Give me	Bana veriniz	bah-nah ver-in-iz
Where is?	Nerede?	nair-eh-deh
the station	istasyon (nerede)	iss-stass-e-own
the youth hostel	gencler yurdu (nerede)	gench-ler yur-do
university	üniversite (nerede)	oon-e-ver-sea-tay
a restaurant	bir lokanta (nerede)	beer low-con-tah
the toilet	tuvalet (nerede)	too-vah-let
the grocery store	bakkal (nerde)	bok-call
To the right	Saga	saw-ah
To the left	Sola	so-lah
Straight ahead	Dogru	dough-roo
I would like	Istiyorum	iss-tea-your-room
to eat	yemek (istiyorum)	mem-meck
a room	bir oda (istiyorum)	beer ode-ah
How much is it?	Ne kadar? or Kaç para?	nay ka-dar or kotch par-ah
The check, please	Hesap lutfen	hes-sop loot-fen
When?	Ne zaman?	nay zah-mon
Yesterday	Dün	doon
Today	Bugün	boo-goon
Tomorrow	Yarin	yar-un
Breakfast	Kahvalti	kah-fault-tay
Lunch	Öglen yemegi	ooh-len yem-may-yee
Dinner	Aksam yemegi	ahk-shom yem-may-yee

1	bir	beer		16	onalti	own-alt-teh
2	iki	icki		17	onyedi	own-yed-dee
3	üc	ooch		18	onsekiz	own-seck-kiz
4	dört	dirt		19	ondokuz	own-dough-kooz
5	bes	besh		20	yirmi	year-meh
6	alti	alt-teh		30	otuz	oh-tooz
7	yedi	yed-dee		40	kirk	kirk
8	sekiz	seck-kiz		50	elli	ell-lee
9	dokuz	dough-kooz		60	altmis	alt-mish
10	on	own		70	yet mis	yet-mish
11	onbir	own-beer		80	seksen	seck-sen
12	oniki	own-icki		90	doksan	doughk-son
13	onüc	own-ooch		100	yuz	yooz
14	ondört	own-dirt		500	besyüz	besh-yooz
15	onbes	own-besh		1,000	bin	been

to the words "hos geldiniz" (welcome), you reply "hos bulduk" which means, literally "we find it pleasant" or "I'm glad to see you are well".

"84 Cent" Foods
apples-elma, bananas-muz, beer-bira, biscuits-biskuit, bread-ekmek, cheese-peynir; chocolate-cukulata, coffee-kahve, egg-yumurta, fish-balik, fruit-meyva, meatet, milk-süt , mineral water-maden suyu, oranges-portakal, potatoes-patates, salt-tuz, sandwich-sanduvic, sausage-sosis, soup-corba, sugar-seker, tea-cay, vegetables-sebze, water-su, wine-sarap.

Getting Rides
Merhaba, örgrenicyim. _____hyim. Bu tarafa gidecek bir araca ihitiyacim var. Mümkün mü? Çok memnun olurum. Tesekkür ederim.

Getting Accommodation
Merhaba, ögrenciyim _____den(dan). Lütfen bana yardim eder misiniz? Yarin sabah erkenden _____ ye (ya) seyahat ediyorum. Yatacak bir yer, aksam yemegi, kahvalti ve sizen adetlerinizi ögrenmek icin gunde iki üç saat çalismaya raziyim. Sabah erkenden ayrilacagim. Çok tesekkür ederim.
or
Merhab ögrenciyim _____ den (dan). Lütfen bana yardim edermisinz? Yarin sabah erkenden _____ ye (ya) seyahat ediyorum. Yatacak bir yer, aksam yemegi, kahvalti ve sizin adetlerinizi ögrenmek için size bir hediye yada para vermeye raziyim. Sabah erken-den ayrilacagim. Çok tesekkür ederim.

Getting Food
Yemek karsiligi, bir iki saatligine mutfaginizda ki bulasiklari yikayabilirmiyim?

Directions
1. _____ yolu nerede?
2. _____ ya (ye) gidecek otobüs nerede?
3. _____ya (ye) gidecek tren nerede?
4. Beni ana yola götürecek otobusun adi yada numarasi nedir?

Hitch-Hiking Signs
City....write it in the native language.
The following should be in the native language:

Home to Mom	Eve dönüyorum
I'm safe	Ben iyiyim
Trees	Agaçlar
Please	Lütfen
Thank you	Tesekkür ederim
Anywhere	Nereye olursa olsun

19. APPENDICES

Weights & Measures

Miles/Kilometres

A kilometer is roughly 6/10ths of a mile. Multiply the number of kilometres by 6 and move the decimal point one place to the left - 159 kilometres x 6 = 954. Insert the decimal point one place to the left = 95.4 miles).

km	miles/km	miles
1.609	1	0.621
16.093	10	6.214
160.930	100	62.136
804.650	500	310.680
1609.300	1,000	621.360

Metres to Feet

Heights are measured in metres. One metre is 39.4 inches or 3.28 feet.

Metres	Feet
100	328
200	656
300	984
400	1,312
500	1,640
1,000	3,280

2,000	6,560
3,000	9,840

Kilograms/Pounds

10 grams = 1/3 oz.
100 grams = 31/2 oz
500 grams = 1/2 kilo=just over 1 lb.
1,000 grams = 1 kilo = 21/5 lb.
There are 2.2 pounds to a kilogram.

kg	lb/kg	lb
0.453	1	2.205
0.907	2	4.409
1.360	3	6.614
1.814	4	8.818
2.268	5	11.023

Litres/Gallons

The American gallon is slightly less than 4 litres.
1 litre = 1 3/4 pints

litres	gallons/litres	gallons
4.55	1	0.22
22.73	5	1.10
45.46	10	2.20

Equivalent Sizes
Women's clothing sizes

British	36	38	40	42	44	46
NorthAmerican	34	36	38	40	42	44
Europe	42	44	46	48	50	52

Men's Suits and Coats

British and North American	36	38	40	42	44	46
Europe		46	48	50	52	54	56

Shirts

British and American	14	141/2	15	151/2	16	161/2	17
Europe		36	37	38	39	41	42	43

Shoes

British and American	3	4	5	6	7	8	9	10
Europe		36	37	38	39	41	42	43	44

City Name Translations

The following translations of place names are provided for two reasons:
1. Your request for directions will be better understood by the local person if you ask for a city in his language, not yours.
2. Your hitch-hiking sign will be better understood if the motorist read it in his native language.

On my first trip to Europe, trying to find "Vienna" on a map, I almost came to the conclusion there was no such place and I had somehow confused it with Venice or Verona. It was on my map, of course, in its Austrian version: "Wien".

English Spelling	Local Spelling	English Spelling	Local Spelling
Helsinki	Helsingfors	Warsaw	Warszawa
Turku	Abo	Lisbon	Lisboa
Geneva	Geneve	Florence	Firenze
Danzig	Gdansk	Genoa	Genova
Gothenburg	Goteburg	Naples	Napoli
Copenhagen	Kobenhavn	Rome	Roma
Milan	Milano	Athens	Athinai
Munich	Munchen	Belgrade	Beograd
Prague	Praha	Bucharest	Bucuresti
Venice	Venezia	Sofia	Sofiya
Vienna	Wien	Salonica	Thessaloniki

The following is a list of official country abbreviations that you will find on vehicle licence plates in Europe.

A	Austria	AL	Albania	AND	Andorra	AUS	Australia
B	Belgium	BG	Bulgaria	BR	Brazil	CC	Consular Corps
CDN	Canada	CH	Switzerland	CY	Cyprus	CZ	Czech Republic
D	Germany	DK	Denmark	DZ	Algeria	E	Spain
EST	Estonia	ET	Egypt	F	France	FL	Liechtenstein

FR	Faroe Islands	GB	Great Britain	GBA	Alderney	GBG	Guernsey
GBJ	Jersey	GBM	Isle of Man	GBZ	Gibraltar	GR	Greece
H	Hungary	HKJ	Jordan	HR	Croatia	I	Italy
IL	Israel	IND	India	IRL	Ireland	IRQ	Iraq
IS	Iceland	J	Japan	KWT	Kuwait	L	Luxembourg
LAR	Libya	LT	Lithuania	LV	Latvia	M	Malta
MA	Morocco	MC	Monaco	MEX	Mexico	N	Norway
NA	Netherlands	NZ	New Zealand	P	Portugal	PAK	Pakistan
PL	Poland	RIM	Mauritania	RL	Lebanon	RO	Romania
SM	San Marino	RUS	Russia	S	Sweden	SF	Finland
SK	Slovak Rep.	SLO	Slovenia	SME	Surinam	SN	Senegal
SYR	Syria	TN	Tunisia	TR	Turkey	USA	United States of America
V	Vatican City	VN	Vietnam	WAM	Nigeria	ZA	South Africa

Weather Facts of United Kingdom, Europe, The Middle East & North Africa

The information given below details temperature and precipitation at important cities throughout these regions.

Temperature- Average daily maximum and minimum temperatures are shade temperatures. Maximum temperatures usually occur in early afternoon, and minimum temperatures just before sunrise.

Precipitation- Includes all forms of moisture falling on the earth, mainly rain and snow.

Average monthly

Farenheit = (Celsius x 1.8) + 32

Celsius = (Fahrenheit - 32) x .55

			J	F	M	A	M	J	J	A	S	O	N	D
Amsterdam														
Temperature	F	Max	40	42	49	56	64	70	72	71	67	57	48	42
		Min	31	31	34	40	46	51	55	55	50	44	38	33
Temperature	C	Max	4	5	10	13	18	21	22	22	19	14	9	5
		Min	-1	-1	1	4	8	11	13	13	10	7	3	1
Precipitation		mm	68	53	44	49	52	58	77	87	72	72	70	64
Athens														
Temperature	F	Max	55	57	60	68	77	86	92	92	84	75	66	58
		Min	44	44	46	52	61	68	73	73	67	60	53	47
Temperature	C	Max	13	14	16	20	25	30	33	33	29	24	19	15
		Min	6	7	8	11	16	20	23	23	19	15	12	8
Precipitation		mm	62	37	37	23	23	14	6	7	15	51	56	71

		J	**F**	**M**	**A**	**M**	**J**	**J**	**A**	**S**	**O**	**N**	**D**

Berlin

Temperature	F	Max	35	37	46	56	66	72	75	74	68	56	45	38
		Min	26	26	31	39	47	53	57	56	50	42	36	29
Temperature	C	Max	2	3	8	13	19	22	24	23	20	13	7	3
		Min	-3	-3	0	4	8	12	14	13	10	6	2	-1
Precipitation		mm	46	40	33	42	49	65	73	69	48	49	46	43

Brussels

Temperature	F	Max	40	44	51	58	65	72	73	72	69	60	48	42
		Min	30	32	36	41	46	52	54	54	51	45	38	32
Temperature	C	Max	4	7	10	14	18	22	23	22	21	15	9	6
		Min	-1	0	2	5	8	11	12	12	11	7	3	0
Precipitation		mm	66	61	53	60	55	76	95	80	63	83	75	88

Bucharest

Temperature	F	Max	34	38	50	64	74	81	86	85	78	65	49	39
		Min	19	23	30	41	51	57	60	59	52	43	35	26
Temperature	C	Max	1	4	10	18	23	27	30	30	25	18	10	4
		Min	-7	-5	-1	5	10	14	16	15	11	6	2	-3
Precipitation		mm	59	43	66	62	66	98	148	90	70	59	62	74

Budapest

Temperature	F	Max	34	39	50	63	72	79	82	81	73	61	46	39
		Min	25	28	36	45	52	59	61	61	54	45	37	30
Temperature	C	Max	1	4	10	17	22	26	28	27	23	16	8	4
		Min	-4	-12	2	7	11	15	16	16	12	7	3	1
Precipitation		mm	59	59	66	78	105	101	78	74	70	82	64	52

Cairo

Temperature	F	Max	65	69	75	83	91	95	96	95	90	86	78	68
		Min	47	48	52	57	63	68	70	71	68	65	58	50
Temperature	C	Max	18	21	24	28	33	35	36	35	32	30	26	20
		Min	8	9	11	14	17	20	20	22	20	18	14	10
Precipitation		mm	5	5	5	3	3	0	0	0	0	0	3	5

Copenhagen

Temperature	F	Max	36	36	41	51	61	67	71	70	64	54	45	40
		Min	28	28	31	38	46	52	57	56	51	44	38	34
Temperature	C	Max	2	2	5	10	16	19	22	21	18	12	7	4
		Min	-2	-3	-1	3	8	11	14	14	11	7	3	1
Precipitation		mm	49	39	32	38	43	47	71	66	62	59	48	49

		J	F	M	A	M	J	J	A	S	O	N	D

Dead Sea, Israel

Temperature F	Max	68	72	78	85	93	99	102	101	96	90	80	71
	Min	53	56	61	68	75	80	83	83	81	75	65	56
Temperature C	Max	20	22	25	29	33	37	39	38	36	32	27	22
	Min	11	13	16	20	24	27	28	29	27	24	18	13

Precipitation N/A

Dublin

Temperature F	Max	47	47	51	54	59	65	67	67	63	57	51	47
	Min	35	35	36	38	42	48	51	51	47	43	38	36
Temperature C	Max	8	8	11	13	15	18	19	19	17	14	11	8
	Min	1	2	3	4	6	9	11	11	9	6	4	3
Precipitation	mm	105	86	78	74	90	78	109	117	109	105	105	101

Frankfurt

Temperature F	Max	38	41	51	60	69	74	77	76	69	58	47	39
	Min	29	30	35	42	49	55	58	57	52	44	38	32
Temperature C	Max	3	5	11	16	20	23	25	24	21	14	8	4
	Min	-1	-2	2	6	9	13	15	14	11	7	3	0
Precipitation	mm	58	44	38	44	55	73	70	76	57	52	55	54

Helsinki

Temperature F	Max	27	26	32	43	55	63	71	66	57	45	37	31
	Min	17	15	22	31	41	49	58	55	46	37	30	22
Temperature C	Max	-3	-3	0	6	13	19	20	19	13	8	3	0
	Min	-8	-8	-5	0	6	11	13	12	8	4	0	-5
Precipitation	mm	86	66	66	66	74	78	90	129	109	113	105	94

Istanbul

Temperature F	Max	46	47	51	60	69	77	82	82	76	68	59	51
	Min	37	36	38	45	53	60	65	66	61	55	48	41
Temperature C	Max	8	9	11	16	21	25	28	28	24	20	15	11
	Min	3	2	3	7	12	16	18	19	16	13	9	5
Precipitation	mm	109	92	72	46	38	34	34	30	58	81	103	119

Lisbon

Temperature F	Max	57	59	63	67	71	77	81	82	79	72	63	58
	Min	46	47	50	53	55	60	63	63	62	58	52	47
Temperature C	Max	14	15	17	20	21	25	27	28	26	22	17	15
	Min	8	8	10	12	13	15	17	17	17	14	11	9
Precipitation	mm	111	76	109	54	44	16	3	4	33	62	93	103

			J	**F**	**M**	**A**	**M**	**J**	**J**	**A**	**S**	**O**	**N**	**D**

London

Temperature	F	Max	43	44	50	56	62	69	71	71	65	58	50	45
		Min	36	36	38	42	47	53	56	56	52	46	42	38
Temperature	C	Max	6	7	10	13	17	20	22	21	19	14	10	7
		Min	2	2	3	6	8	12	14	13	11	8	5	2
Precipitation		mm	54	40	37	37	46	45	57	59	49	57	64	48

Luxembourg

Temperature	F	Max	37	40	49	57	65	70	73	71	66	56	44	39
		Min	29	31	35	40	46	52	55	54	50	43	37	32
Temperature	C	Max	3	4	10	14	18	21	23	22	19	13	7	4
		Min	-1	-1	1	4	8	11	13	12	10	6	3	0
Precipitation		mm	90	78	74	82	94	98	109	101	94	105	105	109

Luxor

Temperature	F	Max	74	79	86	95	104	106	107	106	103	98	87	78
		Min	42	44	50	59	69	70	73	73	71	65	54	45
Temperature	C	Max	24	27	29	33	40	41	42	41	39	33	29	24
		Min	5	9	11	14	20	22	23	24	21	17	10	8

Precipitation N/A

Madrid

Temperature	F	Max	47	52	59	65	70	80	87	85	77	65	55	48
		Min	35	36	41	45	50	58	63	63	57	48	42	36
Temperature	C	Max	9	11	15	18	21	27	31	30	25	19	13	9
		Min	2	2	5	7	10	15	17	17	14	10	5	2
Precipitation		mm	39	34	43	48	47	27	11	15	32	53	47	42

Marrakesh

Temperature	F	Max	65	68	74	79	84	92	101	100	92	83	73	66
		Min	40	43	48	52	57	62	67	68	63	57	49	42
Temperature	C	Max	18	20	23	26	29	34	37	35	34	29	23	19
		Min	4	6	9	11	14	17	20	19	17	14	10	5
Precipitation		mm	39	43	51	47	23	11	4	4	15	34	47	47

Oslo

Temperature	F	Max	28	30	39	50	61	68	72	70	60	48	38	32
		Min	19	19	25	34	43	50	55	53	46	38	31	25
Temperature	C	Max	-2	-1	4	10	16	20	22	21	16	9	3	0
		Min	-7	-7	-4	1	6	10	13	12	8	3	-1	-4
Precipitation		mm	49	35	26	43	44	70	82	95	81	74	68	63

			J	**F**	**M**	**A**	**M**	**J**	**J**	**A**	**S**	**O**	**N**	**D**
Paris														
Temperature	F	Max	42	45	55	61	69	75	80	79	73	61	50	43
		Min	30	31	37	42	49	55	59	58	53	45	38	33
Temperature	C	Max	10	11	18	23	28	31	33	32	29	22	14	10
		Min	-1	0	3	6	9	13	15	14	12	7	4	0
Precipitation		mm	52	46	53	56	69	85	56	89	93	77	80	57
Prague														
Temperature	F	Max	49	53	64	73	82	88	91	89	84	71	57	50
		Min	7	10	18	29	36	44	49	47	38	29	24	14
Temperature	C	Max	10	11	18	23	28	31	33	32	29	22	14	10
		Min	73	67	55	47	45	46	49	48	51	60	73	78
Precipitation		mm	18	18	18	27	48	54	68	55	31	33	20	21
Rome														
Temperature	F	Max	52	55	59	66	74	82	87	86	79	71	61	55
		Min	40	42	45	50	56	63	67	67	62	55	49	44
Temperature	C	Max	11	13	15	19	23	28	30	30	26	22	16	13
		Min	5	5	7	10	13	17	20	20	17	13	9	6
Precipitation		mm	71	62	57	51	46	37	15	21	63	99	129	93
Stockholm														
Temperature	F	Max	30	30	37	47	58	67	71	68	60	49	40	35
		Min	23	22	26	34	43	51	57	56	49	41	34	29
Temperature	C	Max	-1	-1	3	8	14	19	22	20	15	9	5	2
		Min	15	15	14	1	6	11	14	13	9	5	1	-2
Precipitation		mm	43	30	25	31	34	45	61	76	60	48	53	48
Tel Aviv														
Temperature	F	Max	65	67	72	80	89	95	98	99	95	89	78	68
		Min	49	48	51	54	63	67	70	72	69	59	54	47
Temperature	C	Max	18	19	20	22	25	28	30	30	31	28	25	19
		Min	9	9	10	12	17	19	21	22	20	15	12	9
Precipitation N/A														
Vienna														
Temperature	F	Max	34	38	47	58	67	73	76	75	68	56	45	37
		Min	25	28	30	42	50	56	60	59	53	44	37	30
Temperature	C	Max	1	3	8	15	19	23	25	24	20	14	7	3
		Min	-4	-3	-1	6	10	14	15	15	11	7	3	-1
Precipitation		mm	39	44	44	45	70	67	84	72	42	56	52	45

		J	F	M	A	M	J	J	A	S	O	N	D
Warsaw													
Temperature F	Max	32	32	42	53	67	73	75	73	66	55	42	35
	Min	22	21	28	37	48	54	58	56	49	41	33	28
Temperature C	Max	0	1	6	13	19	23	24	23	19	14	6	3
	Min	-7	-6	-2	3	8	12	14	13	9	5	1	-2
Precipitation	mm	39	44	44	45	70	67	84	72	42	56	52	45

		J	F	M	A	M	J	J	A	S	O	N	D
Zurich													
Temperature F	Max	36	41	51	59	67	73	76	75	69	57	45	37
	Min	26	28	34	40	47	53	56	56	51	43	35	29
Temperature C	Max	2	5	10	15	19	23	25	24	20	14	7	3
	Min	-3	-2	1	4	8	12	14	13	11	6	2	-2
Precipitation	mm	74	69	64	76	101	129	136	124	102	77	73	64

Inside the Colosseum, Rome, Italy.

20.

Your "84 Cent" Diary

Date ....
Name ....
Address ....
Gift given or work performed ....
Method used to cut costs ....
Best experience that day ....

Date ....
Name ....
Address ....
Gift given or work performed ....
Method used to cut costs ....
Best experience that day ....

Date ....
Name ....
Address ....
Gift given or work performed ....
Method used to cut costs ....
Best experience that day ....

Date ....
Name ....
Address ....
Gift given or work performed ....
Method used to cut costs ....
Best experience that day ....

Date ....
Name ....
Address ....
Gift given or work performed ....
Method used to cut costs ....
Best experience that day ....

Date ....
Name ....
Address ....
Gift given or work performed ....
Method used to cut costs ....
Best experience that day ....

Date ....
Name ....
Address ....
Gift given or work performed ....
Method used to cut costs ....
Best experience that day ....

Date ....
Name ....
Address ....
Gift given or work performed ....
Method used to cut costs ....
Best experience that day ....

Homes built under a rock near Malaga, Spain.

Date..
Name..
Address ....
Gift given or work performed ....
Method used to cut costs ....
Best experience that day ....

Date..
Name..
Address ....
Gift given or work performed ....
Method used to cut costs ....
Best experience that day ....

Date..
Name..
Address ....
Gift given or work performed ....
Method used to cut costs ....
Best experience that day ....

Date..
Name..
Address ....
Gift given or work performed ....
Method used to cut costs ....
Best experience that day ....

Date..
Name..
Address ....
Gift given or work performed ....
Method used to cut costs ....
Best experience that day ....

Date..
Name..
Address ....
Gift given or work performed ....
Method used to cut costs ....
Best experience that day ....

Date...
Name..
Address ....
Gift given or work performed ....
Method used to cut costs ....
Best experience that day...

Date...
Name..
Address ....
Gift given or work performed ....
Method used to cut costs ....
Best experience that day...

Date...
Name..
Address ....
·Gift given or work performed ....
Method used to cut costs ....
Best experience that day...

Date...
Name..
Address ....
Gift given or work performed ....
Method used to cut costs ....
Best experience that day...

Date...
Name..
Address ....
Gift given or work performed ....
Method used to cut costs ....
Best experience that day...

Date...
Name..
Address ....
Gift given or work performed ....
Method used to cut costs ....
Best experience that day...

Date ....
Name ....
Address ....
Gift given or work performed ....
Method used to cut costs ....
Best experience that day ....

Date ....
Name ....
Address ....
Gift given or work performed ....
Method used to cut costs ....
Best experience that day ....

Date ....
Name ....
Address ....
Gift given or work performed ....
Method used to cut costs ....
Best experience that day ....

Date ....
Name ....
Address ....
Gift given or work performed ....
Method used to cut costs ....
Best experience that day ....

Date ....
Name ....
Address ....
Gift given or work performed ....
Method used to cut costs ....
Best experience that day ....

Date ....
Name ....
Address ....
Gift given or work performed ....
Method used to cut costs ....
Best experience that day ....

Date ....
Name ....
Address ....
Gift given or work performed ....
Method used to cut costs ....
Best experience that day ....

Date ....
Name ....
Address ....
Gift given or work performed ....
Method used to cut costs ....
Best experience that day ....

Date ....
Name ....
Address ....
Gift given or work performed ....
Method used to cut costs ....
Best experience that day ....

Blissful relaxation in Pamukkale's thermal waters, in Turkey.

Date ....
Name ....
Address ....
Gift given or work performed ....
Method used to cut costs ....
Best experience that day ....

Date ....
Name ....
Address ....
Gift given or work performed ....
Method used to cut costs ....
Best experience that day ....

Date ....
Name ....
Address ....
Gift given or work performed ....
Method used to cut costs ....
Best experience that day ....

Date ....
Name ....
Address ....
Gift given or work performed ....
Method used to cut costs ....
Best experience that day ....

Date ....
Name ....
Address ....
Gift given or work performed ....
Method used to cut costs ....
Best experience that day ....

Date ....
Name ....
Address ....
Gift given or work performed ....
Method used to cut costs ....
Best experience that day ....

Date...
Name...
Address ....
Gift given or work performed ....
Method used to cut costs ....
Best experience that day ....

Date...
Name...
Address ....
Gift given or work performed ....
Method used to cut costs ....
Best experience that day ....

Date...
Name...
Address ....
Gift given or work performed ....
Method used to cut costs ....
Best experience that day ....

Date...
Name...
Address ....
Gift given or work performed ....
Method used to cut costs ....
Best experience that day ....

Date...
Name...
Address ....
Gift given or work performed ....
Method used to cut costs ....
Best experience that day ....

Date...
Name...
Address ....
Gift given or work performed ....
Method used to cut costs ....
Best experience that day ....

Date ....
Name ....
Address ....
Gift given or work performed ....
Method used to cut costs ....
Best experience that day ....

Date ....
Name ....
Address ....
Gift given or work performed ....
Method used to cut costs ....
Best experience that day ....

Tea-time in Cappadocia, Turkey.

21.

Traveler's Turn to Tell Tales

I would like to know if you use any of my methods, how successful they were for you and if you discover any additional cost-saving methods on your travels. Please let me know of any exciting experiences with the people and even any unfortunate ones. I would like to include your response with your name in a future edition but will withold your name if you prefer. Please send a postcard or write to:

Gil White R.R. #1 St.Anns, Ontario
L0R 1Y0   Canada

Travel slowly stranger and enjoy,
Stop now and then, meet and make a friend
Love but only shortly, form no new ties to bind you down,
For you are a continual traveler, your journey is not yet done.
When daybreak calls go on, only to rest when dusk and silence prevail,
Then rise again at dawn and travel on
For life is a traveler like you and visits only shortly,
Then travels on leaving you behind to your journey's end.

Kim Fair
St.Catharines, Ontario
Canada

Author's Disclaimer
Please Note: Please understand information can change at a moment's notice, such as visa costs and requirements, telephone numbers and addresses, hours of operation, rental, transportation and accommodation prices. Europe on 84¢ a Day cannot be responsible for any inconvenience the changes may cause on your travels. I would be most grateful if you could send a postcard notifying me of these changes.

Thank you
Yours truly,

Gil White

351

EUROPE

Be sure to supplement the maps in this book with Michelin maps - the best maps in the world. They contain the most accurate information required by a traveller who wants to stray from the major highways. Always refer to your Michelin maps to locate your youth hostel.

NORWAY
Bergen
NORTHERN IRELAND
SCOTLAND
Edinburgh
NORTH SEA
IRELAND
Belfast
Dublin
Cork
WALES ENGLAND
Cardiff
London
HOLLAND
Amsterdam
GERM
ATLANTIC OCEAN
English Channel
Brussels
Bonn
BELGIUM
Frankfurt
Paris
LUXEMBOURG
FRANCE
Munich
Lyon
Bern
SWITZERLAND
LIECH STE
Milan
Ven
Marseille
ITALY
Nice
Monte Carlo
PORTUGAL
Madrid
Barcelona
Corsica
Rom
Lisbon
SPAIN
Granada
Balearic Islands
Sardinia
Gibraltar
Tangier
MEDITERRANEAN SEA
Palerm
Rabat
Algiers
Tunis
Sici
Fés
MAL
MOROCCO
ALGERIA
TUNISIA
Tripol

0   200   400mi.

0   200   400   600Km.

352

EUROPEAN
DRIVING DISTANCES

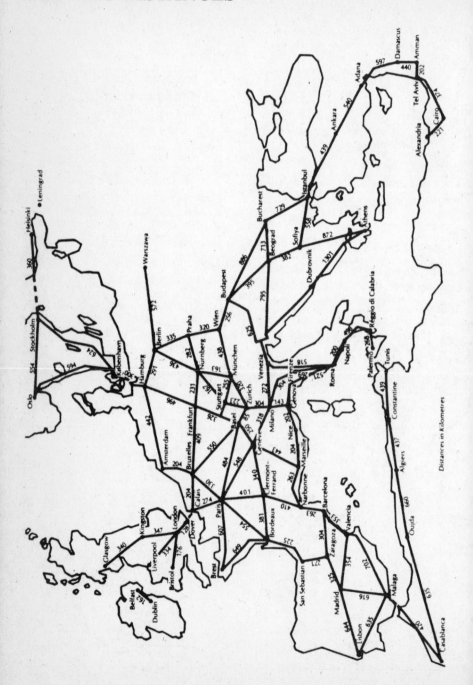

YOUTH HOSTEL LOCATION MAPS

ALGERIA

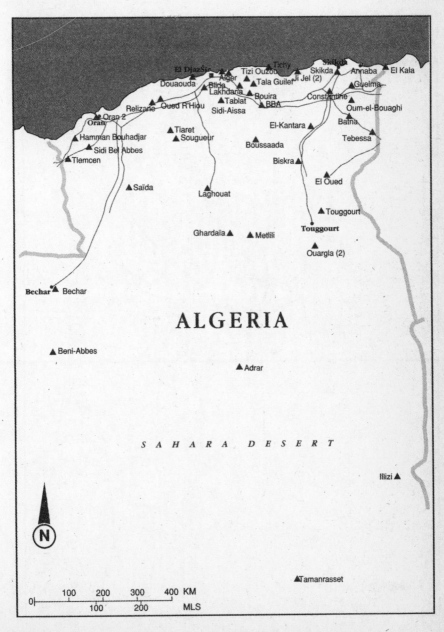

AUSTRIA

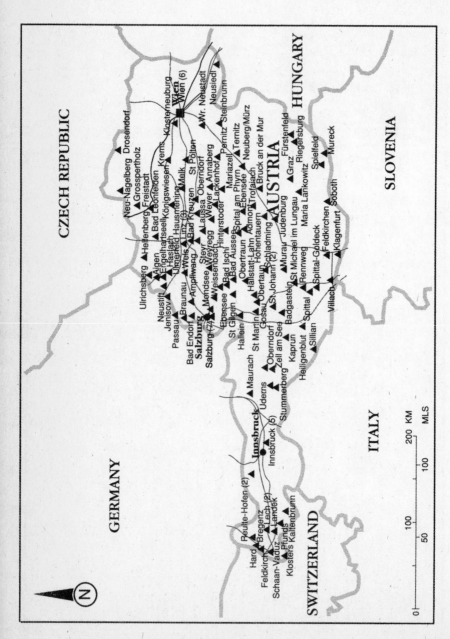

BELGIUM

CYPRUS

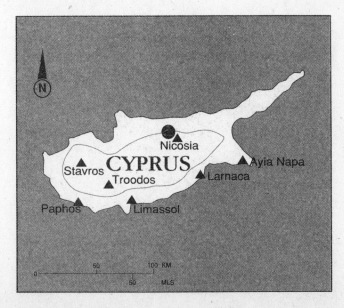

357

BULGARIA

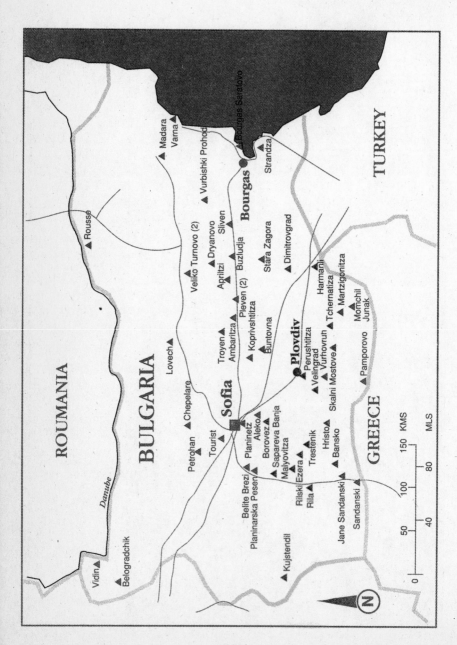

CZECH REPUBLIC

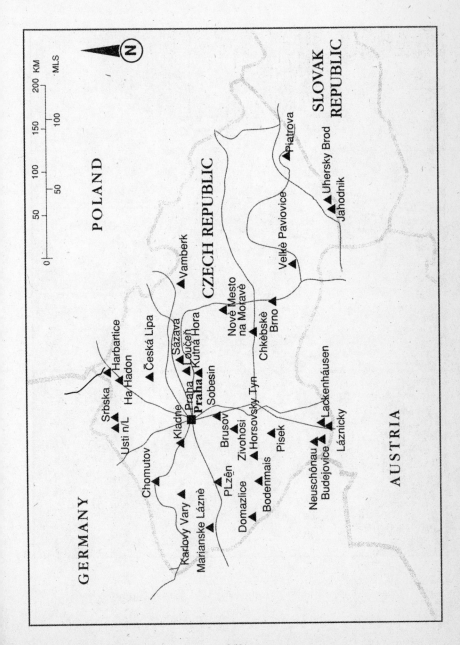

DENMARK

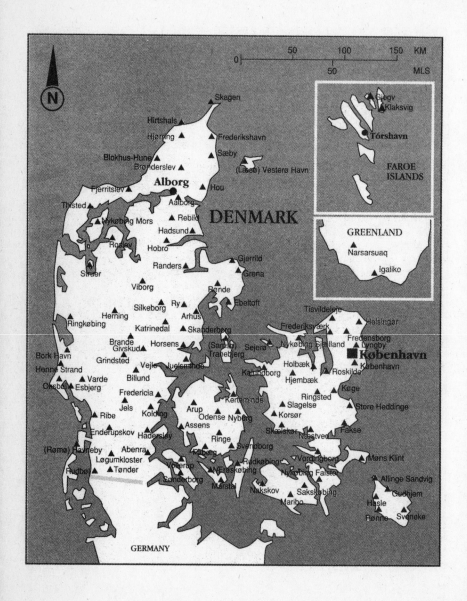

EGYPT

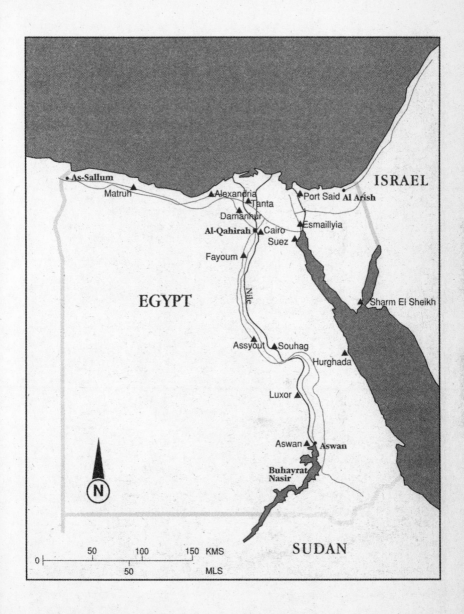

ENGLAND & WALES

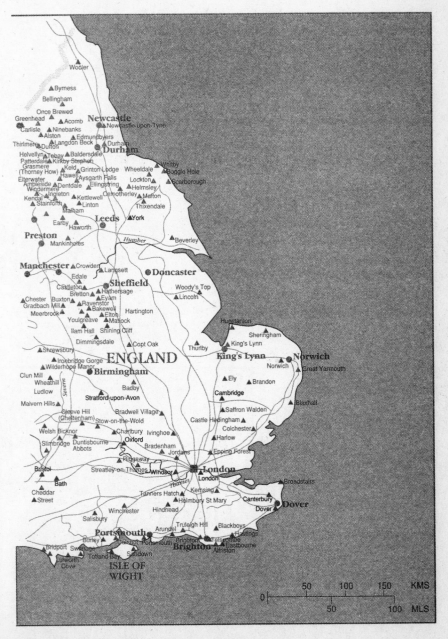

Wooler

▲Byrness

Bellingham

Once Brewed

Greenhead ▲ **Newcastle**

Carlisle ▲ Ninebanks ▲Acomb ▲Newcastle-upon-Tyne

Thirlmere▲Dufton ▲Alston ▲Edmundbyers

Helvellyn▲ ▲Langdon Beck **Durham**

Patterdale▲ ▲Tebay ▲Baldersdale ▲Durham

Grasmere ▲ ▲Kirkby Stephen

(Thorney How) ▲Keld ▲Grinton Lodge Wheeldale ▲Whitby

Elterwater ▲ ▲Hawes ▲Aysgarth Falls Lockton ▲Boggle Hole

Ambleside▲ ▲Dentdale Ellingstring ▲Helmsley ▲Scarborough

Windermere▲ ▲Ingleton ▲Osmotherley ▲Malton

Kendal▲ ▲Kettlewell ▲Thixendale

▲Stainforth ▲Linton

Malham ▲York

Earby ▲ **Leeds** ●York

●Preston Haworth

▲Crowden Mankinholes ▲Beverley

Humber

Manchester ▲Crowden ▲Langsett

Edale ●**Doncaster**

Castleton ▲ ▲**Sheffield** Woody's Top

Chester▲ Buxton▲ ▲Bretton ▲Hathersage ▲Lincoln

Gradbach Mill▲ ▲Ravenstor

Meerbrook ▲ ▲Bakewell Hartington

▲Youlgreave ▲Elton Hunstanton

Ilam Hall ▲Matlock ▲Sheringham

Dimmingdale Shining Cliff ▲King's Lynn

▲Copt Oak Thurlby ▲**King's Lynn** ●**Norwich**

▲Shrewsbury **ENGLAND** Norwich ▲Great Yarmouth

▲Ironbridge Gorge

▲Wilderhope Manor ▲Ely ▲Brandon

Clun Mill▲ ●**Birmingham**

Wheathill▲ **Cambridge**

Ludlow Badby ▲Saffron Walden

Malvern Hills▲ Stratford-upon-Avon ▲Blaxhall

Cleeve Hill▲ Bradwell Village Castle Hedingham▲

(Cheltenham) Stow-on-the-Wold ▲Colchester

Welsh Bicknor ▲Charlbury Ivinghoe ▲Harlow

Slimbridge▲ Duntisbourne Oxford

Abbots Bradenham Epping Forest

▲Ridgeway ▲Jordans

Bristol▲ Streatley-on-Thames Windsor ▣**London**

Bath Thames ▲London ▲Broadstairs

Cheddar▲ Tanners Hatch Kemsing ▲Canterbury

Street▲ ▲Holmbury St Mary **Canterbury** ●**Dover**

Winchester Hindhead Dover

Salisbury Truleigh Hill Blackboys

Arundel ▲Hastings

Portsmouth ▲Telscombe

Bridport Burley▲ ▲Portsmouth Brighton ▲Eastbourne

Swanage **Brighton** Alfriston

Lulworth Totland Bay Sandown

Cove **ISLE OF**

WIGHT

	50	100	150	**KMS**
0				
	50		100	**MLS**

FINLAND

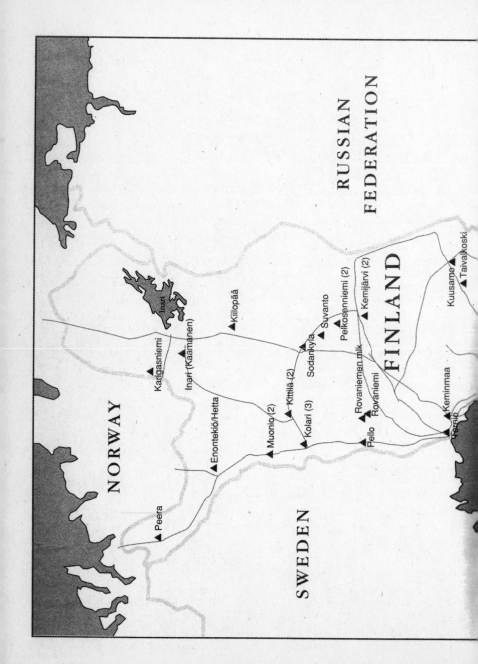

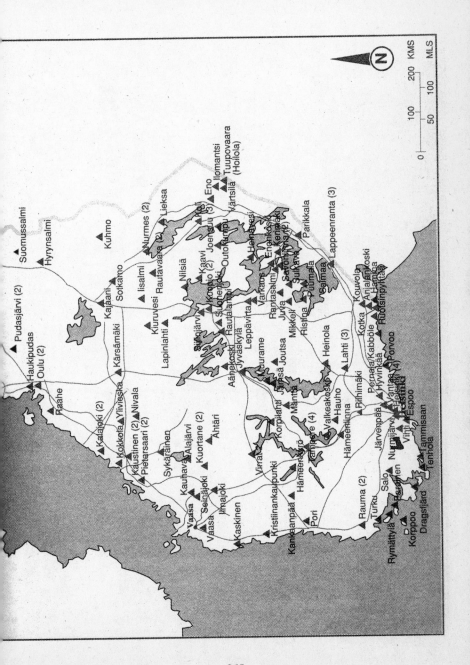

FRANCE

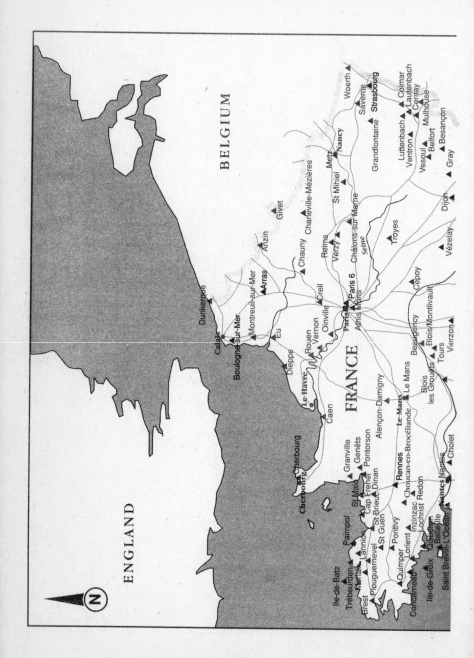

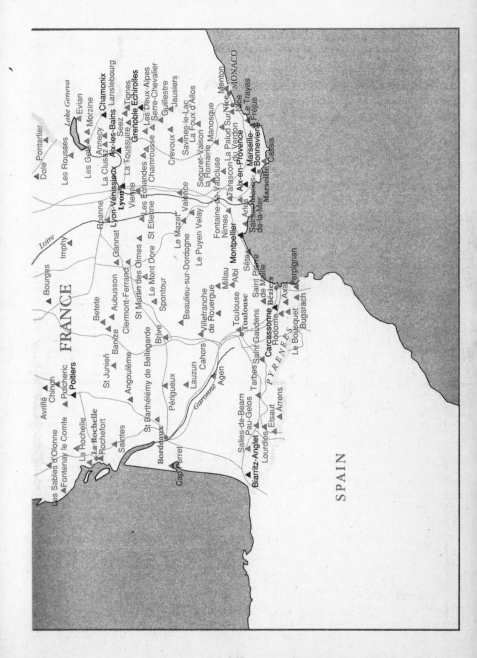

SPAIN

FRANCE

MONACO

Lake Geneva

Loire

Garonne

PYRENEES

Dole
Pontarlier
Les Rousses
Les Gets
Morzine
Evian
Annecy
La Clusaz
Chamonix
Lansiebourg
Tignes
Seez
Aix-les-Bains
Les Deux-Alpes
Serre-Chevalier
Guillestre
Jausiers
Grenoble Echirolles
La Toussuire
Chamrousse
La Foux d'Allos
Crévoux
Savines-le-Lac
Menton
Nice
Le Travas
Fréjus
Bonnevène
Cassis
La Palud Sur Nice
Manosque
Seguret-Vaison
la Romaine
Tarascon
Fontaine-de-Vaucluse
Aix-en-Provence
Marseille
Marseille
Roanne
Lyon-Vénissieux
Lyon
Vienne
Les Echandes
Valence
Arles
Saintes Maries-
de-la-Mer
Imphy
Bourges
Gannat
St Etienne
Le Mont Dore
Le Mazet
Le Puyen Velay
Nimes
Montpellier
Sète
St Martin des Olmes
Clermont-Ferrand
Spontour
Beaulieu-sur-Dordogne
Millau
Albi
Saint Pierre
de Mille
Perpignan
Bétele
Aubusson
Villefranche
de Rouergue
Béziers
Arles
Banze
Brive
Toulouse
Toulouse
Rodome
Carcassonne
St Junien
St Barthélémy de Bellegarde
Cahors
Lauzun
Saint Gaudens
Le Bousquet
Bugarach
Angoulême
Périgueux
Agen
Avrillé
Chinon
Pulcheric
Poitiers
Bordeaux
Tarbes
Les Sables d'Olonne
Fontenay le Comte
La Rochelle
Rochefort
Saintes
Cap Ferret
Salles-de-Bearn
Pau-Gelos
Biarritz-Anglet
Lourdios
Etsaut
Arrens

GERMANY - NORTH WEST

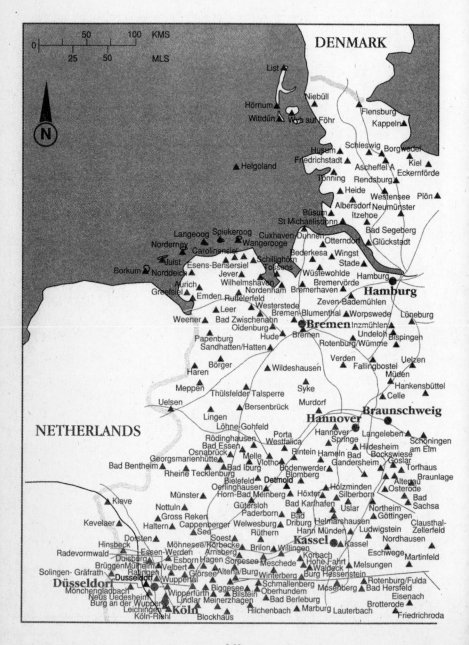

DENMARK

NETHERLANDS

50   100   KMS
0
25   50   MLS

List

Hörnum   Niebüll
Wittdün   Wyk auf Föhr   Flensburg
                                    Kappeln
                         Schleswig Borgwedel
                  Husum
              Fredrichstadt   Ascheffel A   Kiel
Helgoland   Rendsburg   Eckernförde
                  Tönning
                              Heide   Westensee   Plön
                        Albersdorf Neumünster
                  Büsum   Itzehoe
              St Michaelisdonn   Bad Segeberg
Langeoog Spiekeroog Cuxhaven-Duhnen Otterndorf Glückstadt
Norderney   Wangerooge   Bederkesa Wingst
        Carolinensiel   Schillighörn   Stade
Borkum Juist   Esens-Bensersiel Tossens Wüstewohlde Hamburg
        Norddeich Jever   Bremervörde
        Aurich Wilhelmshaven Nordenham Bremerhaven Hamburg
Greetsiel Emden Ruttelfeld   Zeven-Bademühlen
        Leer   Westerstede Bremen-Blumenthal Worpswede Lüneburg
Weener Bad Zwischenahn   Inzmühlen
              Oldenburg   Bremen   Undeloh Bispingen
        Papenburg   Hude   Rotenburg/Wümme
        Sandhatten/Hatten   Verden   Fallingbostel Uelzen
        Börger   Wildeshausen   Müden
Haren   Hankensbüttel
Meppen   Thülsfelder Talsperre   Syke   Murdorf   Celle
Uelsen   Bersenbrück   Braunschweig
        Lingen   Hannover
        Löhne-Gohfeld   Porta   Hannover   Langeleben Schöningen
        Rödinghausen   Westfalica Springe Hildesheim   am Elm
        Bad Essen   Rinteln Hameln Bad Bockswiese
Bad Bentheim Osnabrück   Melle   Vlotho   Gandersheim Goslar
        Georgsmarienhütte   Bad Iburg Bodenwerder   Torfhaus
        Rheine Tecklenburg Bielefeld Blomberg   Altenau Braunlage
                Oerlinghausen Detmold   Holzminden Osterode
        Münster   Horn-Bad Meinberg Höxter Silberborn   Bad
                Gütersloh   Uslar Northeim Sachsa
Kleve   Nottuln   Paderborn Bad Karlshafen   Göttingen
        Gross Reken   Bad   Clausthal-
Kevelaer Haltern Cappenberger Welwesburg Driburg Helmarshausen Ludwigstein Zellerfeld
        Dorsten   See   Soest   Rüthern Hann Münden   Nordhausen
Hinsbeck Möhnesee-Korbecke Brilon Willingen Kassel   Kassel Eschwege
Radevormwald Essen-Werden Arnsberg   Korbach Hohe Fahrt Martinfeld
        Duisburg Esborn Hagen Sorpesee Meschede Waldeck Melsungen
Solingen- Gräfrath Brüggen Velbert Glörsee Altena/Burg Winterberg Burg Hessenstein
        Mülheim Ratingen   Schmallenberg Mosenberg Rotenburg/Fulda
Düsseldorf Wuppertal Biggesee   Oberhundem   Bad Hersfeld
Mönchengladbach Wipperfürth Bilstein   Bad Berleburg   Eisenach
Neus Uedesheim Lindlar Meinerzhagen   Brotterode
Burg an der Wupper Leichingen Köln Hilchenbach Marburg Lauterbach Friedrichroda
        Köln-Riehl Blockhaus

368

GERMANY - NORTH EAST

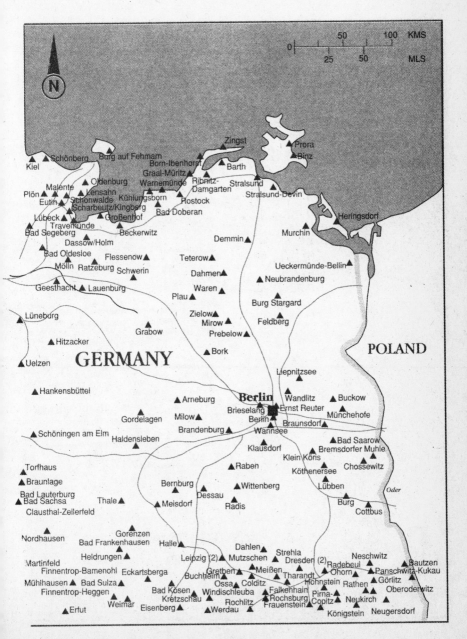

50 100 KMS

0 25 50 MLS

N

Zingst
Prora
Binz
Schönberg Burg auf Fehmarn
Kiel Born-Ibenhorst Barth
Graal-Müritz
Oldenburg Warnemünde Ribnitz- Stralsund
Malente Damgarten
Plön Lensahn Kühlungsborn Stralsund-Devin
Eutin Schönwalde
/Scharbeutz/Kingsberg Rostock
Lübeck Großenhof Bad Doberan Heringsdorf
Travemünde
Bad Segeberg Beckerwitz Murchin
Dassow/Holm Demmin
Bad Oldesloe Flessenow Teterow
Mölln Ratzeburg Schwerin Ueckermünde-Bellin
Dahmen Neubrandenburg
Geesthacht Lauenburg Waren
Plau Burg Stargard
Lüneburg Zielow Feldberg
Mirow
Grabow Prebelow
Hitzacker Bork
Uelzen GERMANY POLAND
Liepnitzsee
Hankensbüttel
Berlin Wandlitz Buckow
Arneburg Brieselang Ernst Reuter
Gordelagen Milow Berlin Münchehofe
Schöningen am Elm Brandenburg Braunsdorf
Haldensleben Wannsee
Klausdorf Bad Saarow
Bremsdorfer Muhle
Klein Köris
Torfhaus Raben Köthenersee Chossewitz
Braunlage Bernburg Wittenberg Lübben Oder
Bad Lauterburg Dessau
Bad Sachsa Thale Meisdorf Radis Burg
Clausthal-Zellerfeld Cottbus
Gorenzen
Nordhausen Bad Frankenhausen Halle
Dahlen Neschwitz
Heldrungen Strehla Radebeul
Martinfeld Leipzig (2) Mutzschen Dresden (2) Bautzen
Finnentrop-Bamenohl Eckartsberga Gretben Meißen Ohorn Panschwitz-Kukau
Mühlhausen Bad Sulza Buchheim Tharandt Hohnstein Görlitz
Finnentrop-Heggen Ossa Colditz Rathen Oberoderwitz
Bad Kösen Windischleuba Falkenhain Pirna-
Kretzschau Rochsburg Copitz Neukirch
Erfut Weimar Eisenberg Rochlitz Frauenstein Neugersdorf
Werdau Königstein

369

GERMANY - SOUTH WEST

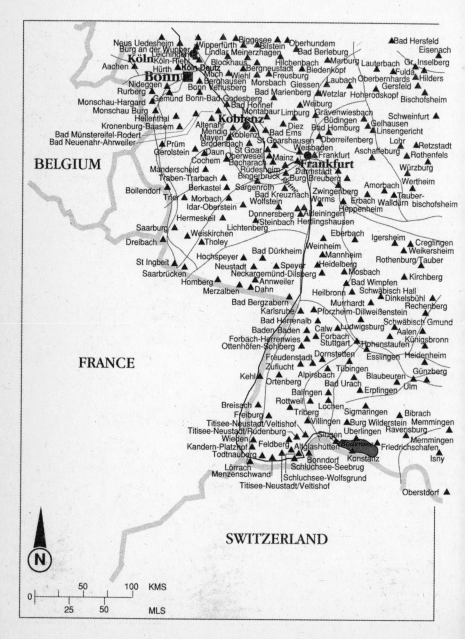

BELGIUM

FRANCE

SWITZERLAND

Neus Uedesheim
Burg an der Wupper
Eichholtz
Aachen
Hürth
Köln Köln-Rieth
Köln-Deutz
Wipperfürth
Lindlar
Blockhaus
Bergneustadt
Much
Wiehl
Berghausen
Nideggen
Rurberg
Bonn Venusberg
Gemünd Bonn-Bad Godesberg
Monschau-Hargard
Monschau Burg
Hellenthal
Kronenburg-Baasem
Bad Münstereifel-Rodert
Bad Neuenahr-Ahrweiler
Prüm
Gerolstein
Manderscheid
Traben-Trarbach
Bollendorf
Trier
Saarburg
Dreibach
St Ingbeit
Saarbrücken
Homberg
Merzalben
Bad Bergzabern
Karlsruhe
Bad Herrenalb
Baden-Baden
Forbach-Herrenwies
Ottenhöfen-Sohlberg
Kehl
Breisach
Freiburg
Titisee-Neustadt/Veltishof
Titisee-Neustadt/Rüdenburg
Wieden
Kandern-Platzhof
Todtnauberg
Lörrach
Menzenschwand
Titisee-Neustadt/Veltishof

Biggesee
Bilstein
Meinerzhagen
Hilchenbach
Morsbach
Bad Honnef
Altenahr
Mayen
Brodenbach
Daun
Cochem
Berkastel
Morbach
Idar-Oberstein
Hermeskeil
Weiskirchen
Tholey
Hochspeyer
Neustadt
Annweiler
Dahn
Calw
Freudenstadt
Zuflucht
Ortenberg
Rottweil
Triberg
Villingen
Feldberg
Altglashütten
Bonndorf
Schluchsee-Seebrug
Schluchsee-Wolfsgrund

Oberhundem
Bad Berleburg
Biedenkopf
Freusburg
Giessen
Bad Marienberg
Montabaur
Koblenz
Diez
Koblenz
St Goar
Oberwesel
Bacharach
Rüdesheim
Bingerbruck
Sargenroth
Bad Kreuznach
Wolfstein
Donnersberg
Steinbach
Lichtenberg
Bad Dürkheim
Speyer
Neckargemünd-Dilsberg
Pforzheim-Dillweißenstein
Ludwigsburg
Dornstetten
Alpirsbach
Balingen
Lochen
Sigmaringen
Stingen
Überlingen

Köln
Bonn
Koblenz

Bad Hersfeld
Eisenach
Marburg Lauterbach Gr. Inselberg
Fulda
Laubach Oberbernhards Hilders
Wetzlar Hoheroodskopf
Weiburg
Limburg Grävenwiesbach
Büdingen
Bad Ems
Oberreifenberg
Weisbaden
Mainz
Darmstadt
Burg Breuberg
Bad Homburg
Frankfurt
Frankfurt
Aschaffeburg
Gelhausen
Linsengericht
Lohr
Würzburg
Wertheim
Amorbach
Tauber-
Walldürn bischofsheim
Heppenheim
Eberbach
Igersheim
Weinheim
Mannheim
Heidelberg
Mosbach
Bad Wimpfen
Heilbronn
Schwäbisch Hall
Murrhardt
Stuttgart
Hohenstaufen
Esslingen
Tübingen
Blaubeuren
Bad Urach
Erpfingen
Ulm
Schwäbisch Gmund
Aalen
Künigsbronn
Heidenheim
Günzberg
Creglingen
Weikersheim
Rothenburg/Tauber
Kirchberg
Dinkelsbühl
Rechenberg
Bad Wilderstein
Ravensburg
Friedrichshafen
Isny
Bibrach
Memmingen
Memmingen
Bodensee
Konstanz

Oberstdorf

N

0   50   100   KMS

25   50   MLS

370

GERMANY - SOUTH EAST

Eisenach Finnentrop-Heggen Bad Kösen Windischleuba Falkenhain Neukirch Neugers-
Kretschau Rochsburg Pirna-Copitz Hohnstein dorf
Weimar Eisenberg Werdau Rochlitz Rathen Oberoderwitz
Friedrichroda Erfut Greiz Chemnitz Augustusburg Königstein Waltersdorf
Hilders Tambach-Dietharz Lichtenstein Frauenstein Sayda Königstein Bad Jonsdorf
Gräfenroda Bad Blankenburg Plolthen Ehrenfriedersdorf Pockau Schellerhau Schandau
Bischofsheim Ilmenau Coburg Leuchtenburg Fröbers Hormersdorf Altenberg Geising Reinhardtsdorf-
Schweinfurt Katzhütte Schwarzburg-Neidenbergagrün Affalter Warmbad Holzhau Zinnwald Schöna
Königsberg Neuhaus Plauen Geyer Neudorf Zinnwald-
Lausoha Bamberg Kulmbach Taltitz Sosa Rittersgrün Georgen-
Schöneck Johanngeorgenstadt feld
Retzstadt Ebrach Kronach Bad Brambach Klingenthal Zöblitz
Rothenfels Grumbach
Würzburg Kitzingen Wirsberg Marktredwitz
Wertheim Ochsenfurt Hohenberg **CZECH**
Lichtenfels Kulmbach **REPUBLIC**
Warmensteinach Wunsiedel
Wiesenttal Windischeschenbach
Bayreuth
Gössweinstein Pottenstein
Erlangen Hartenstein
Creglingen **Nürnberg** Leinburg Waldmünchen
Nürnberg Amberg Furth i. W Bayerisch-Eisenstein
Kirchberg Spalt Lam Zwiesel
Dinkelsbühl **BAYERN** St Englmar Frauenau
Rechenberg Regensburg Mauth Neuschönau
Straubing Oberbreitnau Haidmühle
Nördlingen Eichstätt Neureichenau
Künigsbronn Ihrlerstein Saldenburg
Donauwörth Ingolstadt Bischofsmais Passau
Heidenheim
Günzberg Landshut
Ulm Mühldorf
Augsburg **München** Burghausen
München Ebersberg Bad Endorf
Memmingen Pullach Benediktbeuern
Ravensburg Wörthsee Schliersee Prien Traunstein
Ottobeüren Bergen
Kempten Kochel Bayrischezell
Isny Walchensee Lenggries
Oberammergau Kreuth Strub
Garmisch-Partenkirchen Mittenwald
Oberstdorf Füssen

AUSTRIA

N

50 100 KMS
0
25 50 MLS

GREECE

HUNGARY

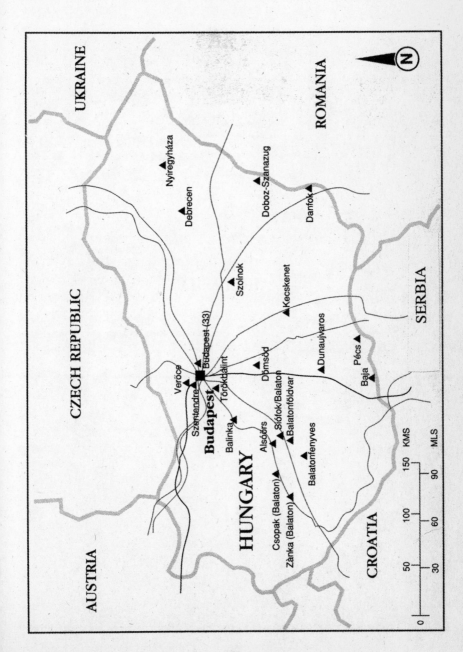

IRELAND (Republic of)

N

Trá na Rosann
Errigal
Crohy Head
Aranmore Island

NORTHERN
IRELAND

Ball Hill

Lough
Neagh

Belfast

Pollatomish
Killala
Sligo

REPUBLIC OF
IRELAND

Omeath

Traenlaur
Westport

Killary Harbour
Ben Lettery
Cong

Indreabhan
Galway
Galway
Doorus

Dublin
Dublin International
Dublin Harcourt Street
Baltyboys
Ballinclea
Glenmalure

Glencree
Knockree
Tiglin
Glendaloch

Aghavannagh

Limerick

Ballydavid Wood
Mountain Lodge

Foulksrath
Castle

Dún Chaoin
Killarney
Loo Bridge

Arthurstown
Rosslare

Valentia Island
Ballinskelligs
Black Valley

Glanmore Lake
Cork
Cork

Allihies

Cape Clear Island

50   100   150   KM
0
        50   MLS

IRELAND (Northern)

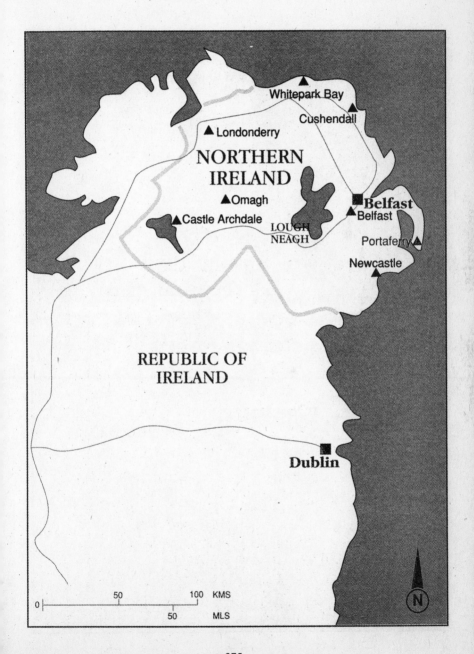

Whitepark Bay ▲

Cushendall ▲

▲ Londonderry

NORTHERN IRELAND

▲ Omagh

▲ Castle Archdale

LOUGH NEAGH

■ **Belfast**
▲ Belfast

Portaferry ▲

Newcastle ▲

REPUBLIC OF IRELAND

■ **Dublin**

50   100   KMS
0
        50   MLS

N

ISRAEL

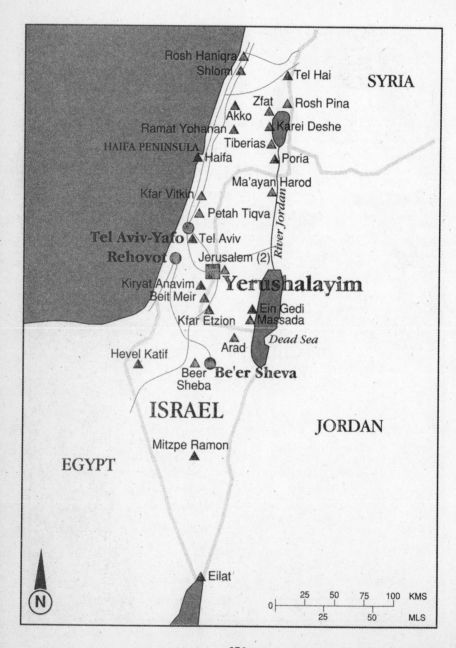

376

ITALY

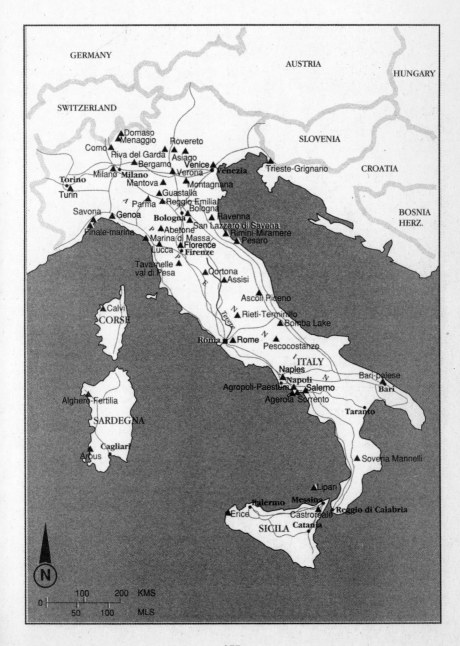

GERMANY

AUSTRIA

HUNGARY

SWITZERLAND

SLOVENIA

CROATIA

BOSNIA
HERZ.

Domaso
Menaggio
Como
Riva del Garda
Bergamo
Milano **Milano**
Mantova
Torino
Turin
Savona
Genoa
Finale-marina
Parma
Bologna
Abetone
Marina di Massa
Lucca
Tavarnelle
val di Pesa
Rovereto
Asiago
Venice
Verona
Guastalla
Reggio Emilia
Bologna
Venezia
Trieste-Grignano
Montagnana
Ravenna
San Lazzaro di Savena
Rimini-Miramere
Pesaro
Florence
Firenze
Cortona
Assisi
Ascoli Piceno
Rieti-Terminillo
Bomba Lake
Roma Rome
Pescocostanzo
ITALY
Naples
Napoli
Agropoli-Paestum
Agerola Sorrento
Salerno
Bari-palese
Bari
Taranto

Calvi
CORSE

Alghero-Fertilia
SARDEGNA
Cagliari
Arbus

Soveria Mannelli

Lipari
Palermo
Erice
Messina
Castroteale
Catania
SICILA
Reggio di Calabria

N

100   200 KMS
0
50   100   MLS

377

JORDAN

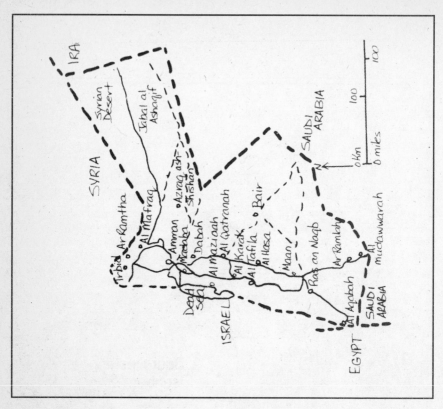

LIECHTENSTEIN

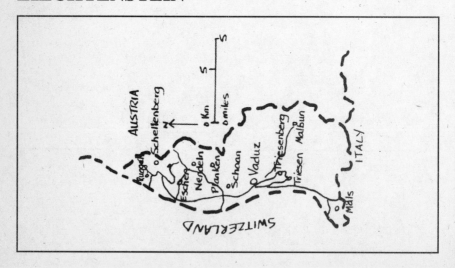

LUXEMBOURG

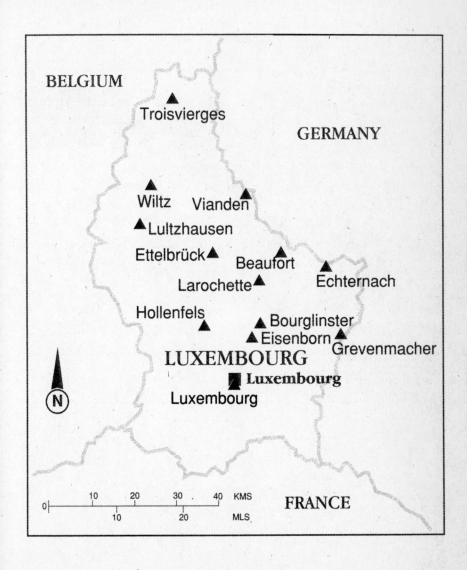

BELGIUM

GERMANY

Troisvierges

Wiltz   Vianden

Lultzhausen

Ettelbrück

Beaufort

Larochette

Echternach

Hollenfels

Bourglinster

Eisenborn

Grevenmacher

LUXEMBOURG

Luxembourg

Luxembourg

N

FRANCE

MOROCCO

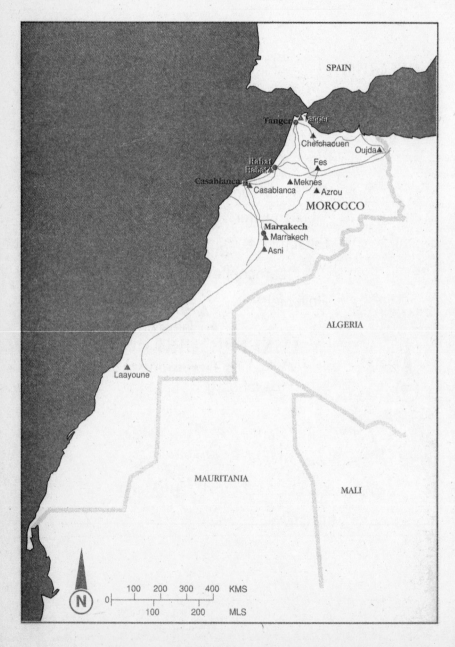

NETHERLANDS

NETHERLANDS

Schiermonnikoog
Ameland ▲
Terschelling ▲

▲ Texel
Den Oever

Sneek ▲ Grou
Scheemda
▲ Roderesch
Heeg ▲

Egmond ▲
Bakkum ▲
Heemskerk ▲
Haarlem ▲
Hoorn ▲
Amsterdam
Amsterdam ▲
Meppel ▲
Oldebroek ▲

Noordwijk ▲
Soest ▲
Nijverdal ▲
Gorssel ▲

Den Haag ▲
Bunnik ▲
Elst ▲
Apeldoorn ▲
Rotterdam ▲
Dordrecht ▲
Doorwerth ▲ Arnhem

GERMANY

Bruinisse ▲
Bergen op Zoom
Domburg ▲
Chaam ▲
Valkenswaard ▲

BELGIUM

Maastricht ▲

N

| 50 | 100 | 150 | KMS |

0

50

MLS

NORWAY

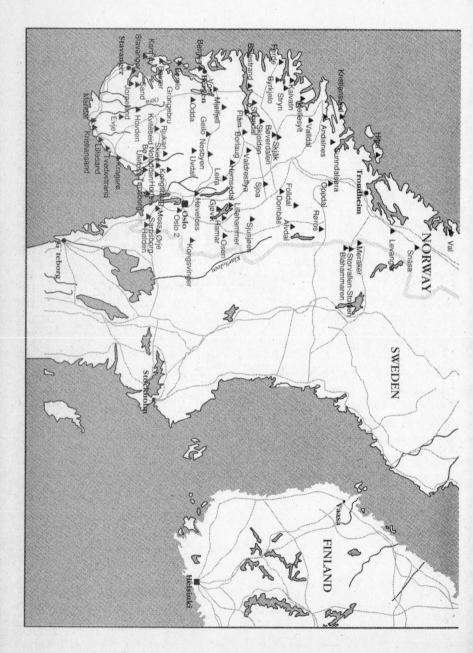

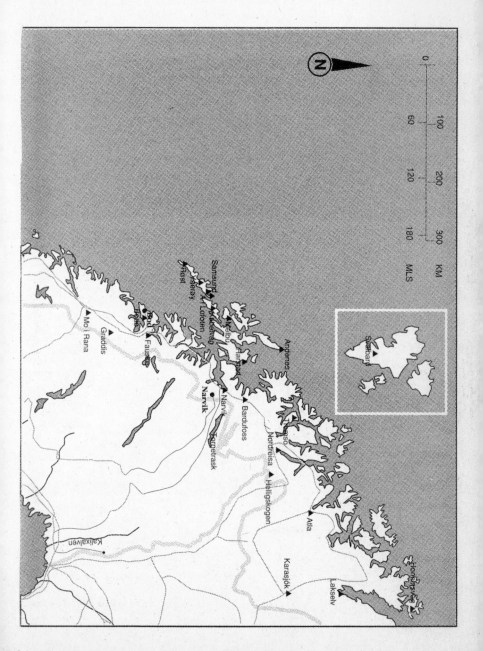

POLAND

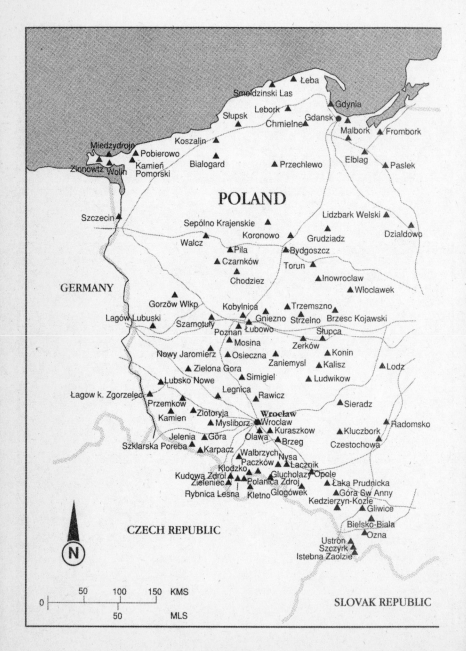

POLAND

GERMANY

Łeba
Smołdzinski Las
Lebork
Słupsk
Chmielne
Gdansk
Gdynia
Malbork
Frombork
Koszalin
Pobierowo
Miedzydroje
Kamień
Pomorski
Bialogard
Przechlewo
Elblag
Paslek
Zinnowtz
Wolin
Szczecin
Sepólno Krajenskie
Lidzbark Welski
Działdowo
Walcz
Koronowo
Grudziadz
Pila
Bydgoszcz
Czarnków
Torun
Inowroclaw
Chodziez
Wloclawek
Gorzöw Wlkp.
Kobylnica
Trzemszno
Lagów Lubuski
Szamotuły
Gniezno Strzelno Brzesc Kojawski
Poznan Łubowo
Słupca
Mosina
Zerków
Nowy Jaromierz
Osieczna
Konin
Zielona Gora
Zaniemysl
Kalisz
Lodz
Lubsko Nowe
Simigiel
Ludwikow
Łagow k. Zgorzelec
Legnica
Rawicz
Przemkow
Sieradz
Kamien
Zlotoryja
Radomsko
Mysliborz
Wroclaw
Wrocław
Jelenia
Göra
Kuraszkow
Kluczbork
Szklarska Poreba
Karpacz
Olawa
Brzeg
Czestochowa
Walbrzych
Nysa
Paczków
Lacznik
Klodzko
Glucholazy
Opole
Kudowa Zdrol
Polanica Zdroj
Zieleniec
Łaka Prudnicka
Rybnica Lesna
Kletno
Glogówek
Góra Sw Anny
Kedzierzyn-Kozle
Gliwice
Bielsko-Biala
CZECH REPUBLIC
Ozna
Ustron
Szczyrk
Istebna Zaolzie

N

50   100   150   KMS
0
        50   MLS

SLOVAK REPUBLIC

384

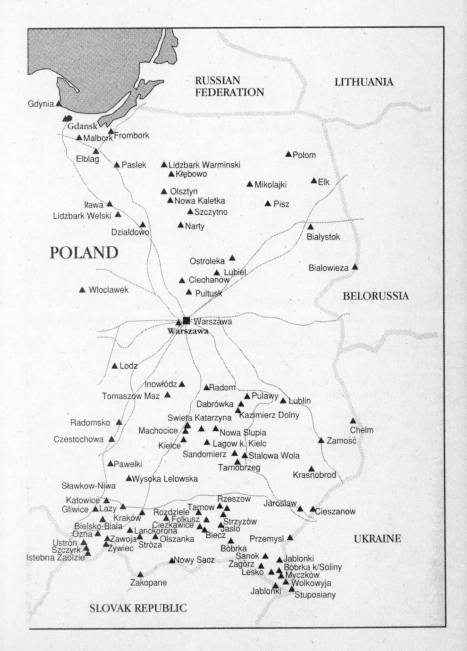

RUSSIAN
FEDERATION

LITHUANIA

Gdynia ▲

Gdansk
Malbork Frombork

Elblag
Paslek ▲ Lidzbark Warminski
▲ Kłębowo

Polom ▲

Iława ▲
Lidzbark Welski ▲

Olsztyn ▲
Nowa Kaletka ▲
▲ Szczytno

Mikolajki ▲
Pisz ▲

Elk ▲

POLAND

Dzialdowo

Narty ▲

Bialystok ▲

Ostroleka ▲
▲ Lubiel
▲ Ciechanow

Bialowieza ▲

▲ Wloclawek

▲ Pultusk

BELORUSSIA

▲ Warszawa
Warszawa

▲ Lodz

Inowłódz ▲
Tomaszow Maz ▲

Radom ▲
Dabrówka ▲
Pulawy ▲ Lublin

Radomsko ▲

Swieta Katarzyna
Machocice ▲
Kielce

Kazimierz Dolny
Nowa Slupia
▲ Lagow k. Kielc

Chelm ▲
▲ Zamość

Czestochowa ▲

▲ Pawelki
▲ Wysoka Lelowska

Sandomierz ▲
▲ Stalowa Wola
Tarnobrzeg

Krasnobrod

Sławkow-Niwa
Katowice ▲
Gliwice ▲ Lazy
Kraków
Bielsko-Biala
Ozna ▲
Ustron ▲ Zawoja
Szczyrk ▲ Zywiec Stroza
Istebna Zaolzie

Rozdziele
Folkusz
Ciezkawice
Lanckorona
▲ Olszanka Biecz

Rzeszow
Tarnow ▲
Strzyzów
Jaslo
Bóbrka
Nowy Sacz

Jaroslaw
Cieszanow ▲

Przemysl ▲

UKRAINE

Zakopane ▲

Sanok ▲ Jablonki
Zagórz ▲ Bóbrka k/Soliny
Lesko ▲ Myczkow
Wolkowyja
Jablonki Stuposiany

SLOVAK REPUBLIC

PORTUGAL

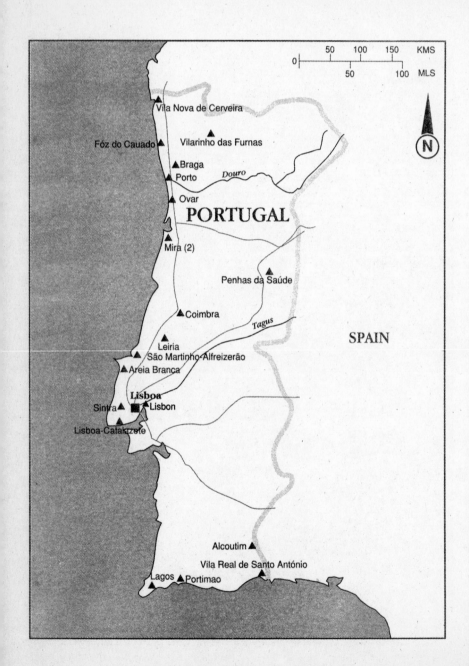

Vila Nova de Cerveira

Fóz do Cauado ▲ ▲ Vilarinho das Furnas

▲ Braga
▲ Porto   *Douro*

▲ Ovar

PORTUGAL

Mira (2) ▲

▲ Penhas da Saúde

▲ Coimbra

Tagus

▲ Leiria   **SPAIN**
▲ São Martinho ▲ Alfreizerão
▲ Areia Branca

Lisboa
Sintra ▲ ■■ ▲ Lisbon

Lisboa-Catakizeie

50   100   150   KMS
0
50   100   MLS

N

Alcoutim ▲
Vila Real de Santo António
Lagos ▲ ▲ Portimao

ROMANIA (No accredited youth hostels)

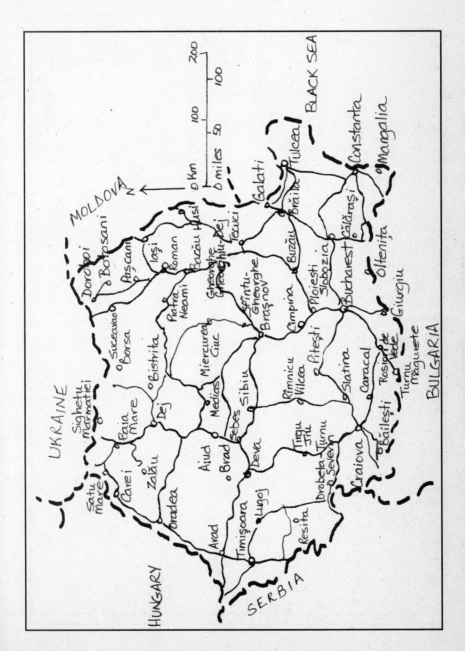

SLOVAK REPUBLIC

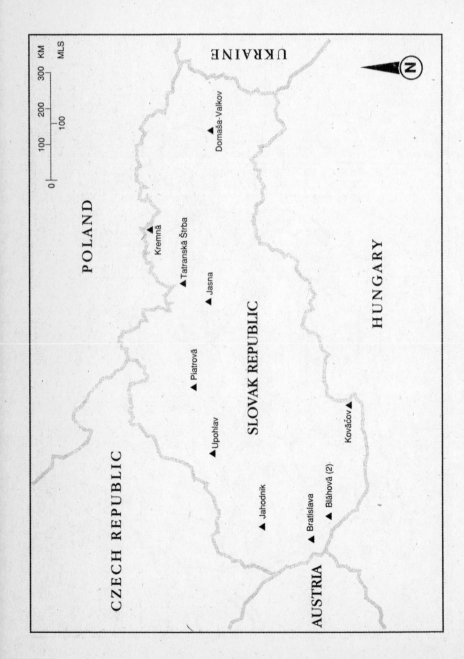

SPAIN

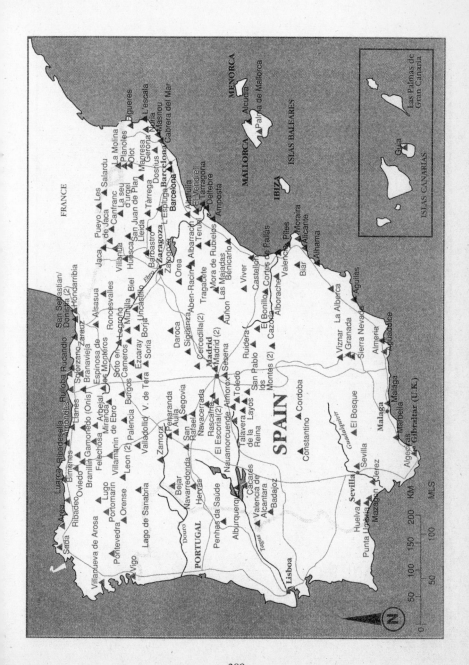

SCOTLAND

SWEDEN - NORTH

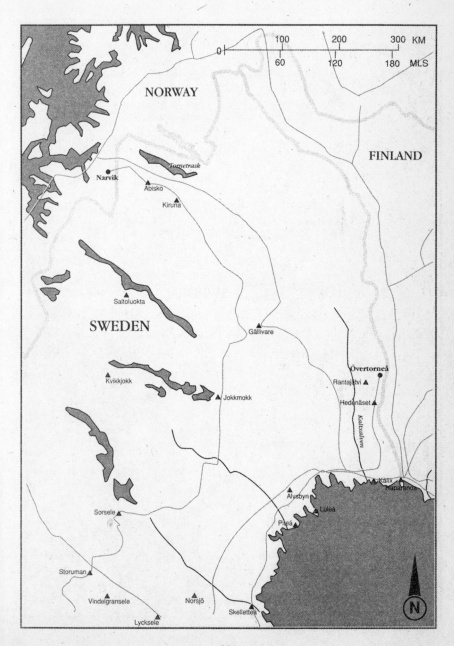

SWEDEN - CENTRAL

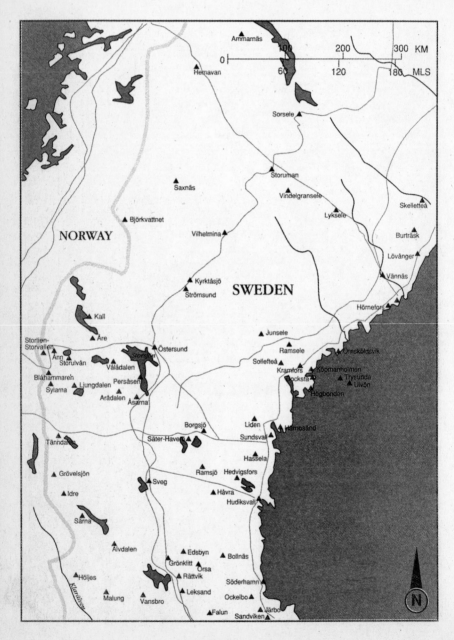

Ammarnäs

0 100 200 300 KM

Hemavan 60 120 180 MLS

Sorsele

Storuman

Saxnäs

Vindelgransele

Skellefteå

Björkvattnet

Lyksele

NORWAY

Vilhelmina

Burträsk

Lövånger

Vännäs

Kyrktåsjö

SWEDEN

Strömsund

Hörnefors

Kall

Junsele

Storlien-Storvallen

Åre

Östersund

Ramsele

Örnsköldsvik

Ann

Storulvån

Storsjön

Sollefteå

Blåhammaren

Våladalen

Kramfors

Köpmanholmen

Sylarna

Ljungdalen

Persåsen

Docksta

Trysunda

Ulvön

Arådalen

Åsarna

Högbonden

Borgsjö

Liden

Härnosánd

Tänndalen

Säter-Havern

Sundsvall

Hassela

Grövelsjön

Ramsjö

Hedvigsfors

Sveg

Idre

Håvra

Hudiksvall

Sårna

Älvdalen

Edsbyn

Bollnäs

Grönklitt

Höljes

Orsa

Rättvik

Söderhamn

Malung

Vansbro

Leksand

Ockelbo

Falun

Järbo

Sandviken

N

SWEDEN - SOUTH

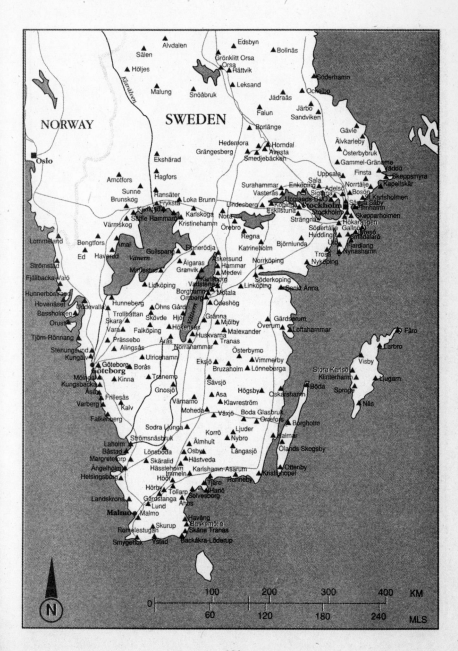

NORWAY

SWEDEN

Oslo

Álvdalen
Sälen
Höljes
Malung
Snöåbruk

Edsbyn
Grönklitt Orsa
Orsa
Rättvik
Leksand
Jädraås

Bollnäs
Söderhamn
Ochelbo

Falun
Borlänge

Hedemora
Grängesberg
Ekshärad
Hagfors
Amotfors
Sunne
Brunskog
Ransäter
Loka Brunn
Fryksta
Karlstad
Säffle Hammarö
Värmskog

Horndal
Avesta
Smedjebäcken

Järbo
Sandviken

Gävle
Älvkarleby
Österbybruk
Gammel-Gränome
Uppsala
Sala
Finsta
Surahammar
Västerås
Enköping
Lindesberg
Nota
Kristinehamm
Örebro

Adelsö
Sigtuna
Upplands-B.
Köping
Eskilstuna
Stockholm
Strängnäs

Skeppsmyra
Norrtälje
Kapellskär
Bosön
Karlsholmen
Sätra Säby
Finnhamn
Skepparholmen
Hökarängen

Lommeland
Bengtfors
Ed Haverud
Strömstad
Fjällbacka-Valö
Hunnerbostrand
Hovenäset
Bassholmen
Orust
Tjörn-Rönnang
Stenungsund
Kungäv
Mölnge
Kungsbacka
Äsa
Frillesås
Varberg
Kalv
Falkenberg

Amal
Vänern
Gullspang
Mariestad
Lidköping
Hunneberg
Öhns Gård
Trollhättan
Skara
Vara
Falköping
Prässebo
Alingsås
Ulricehamn
Göteborg
Borås
Kinna
Tranemo
Gnosjö
Värnamo
Moheda
Sodra Ljunga

Finnerödja
Älgaras
Granvik
Karlsborg
Vadstena
Borghamn
Omberg
Ödeshög
Hjo
Hökensås
Gränna
Mjölby
Malexander
Huskvarna
Tranas
Norrahammar
Eksjö
Bruzaholm
Sävsjö
Asa
Klavreström
Växjö
Boda Glasbruk
Örefors

Askersund
Hammar
Medevi
Motala
Linköping
Sankt Anna
Söderköping

Regna
Katrineholm
Björnlunda
Norrköping
Nyköping
Trosa

Södertälje
Huddinge
Lidö

Gallnö
Ljusterö
Smadalarö
Hjardlang
Nynashamn

Gärdserum
Överum
Loftahammar
Vimmerby
Lönneberga
Högsby
Oskarshamn

Stora Karlsö
Klinterhamn
Böda
Sproge

Fårö
Larbro
Visby
Ljugarn
Näs

Ljuder
Korrö
Älmhult
Lönsboda
Osby
Margretetorp
Hässleholm
Ängelholm
Helsingborg
Hörby
Landskrona
Gärdstanga
Lund
Malmö Malmo
Romelestugan
Smygehuk
Ystad

Ljuder
Nybro
Långasjö
Hästveda
Immeln
Höör
Tollarp
Solvesborg
Ahus
Havång
Baskemölla
Skåne Tranas
Backåkra-Löderup

Kalmar
Ölands Skogsby
Ottenby
Kristanopel
Ronneby
Tjäro
Hanö

Borgholm

| 0 | 100 | 200 | 300 | 400 | KM |
| 60 | 120 | 180 | 240 | MLS |

N

393

SWITZERLAND

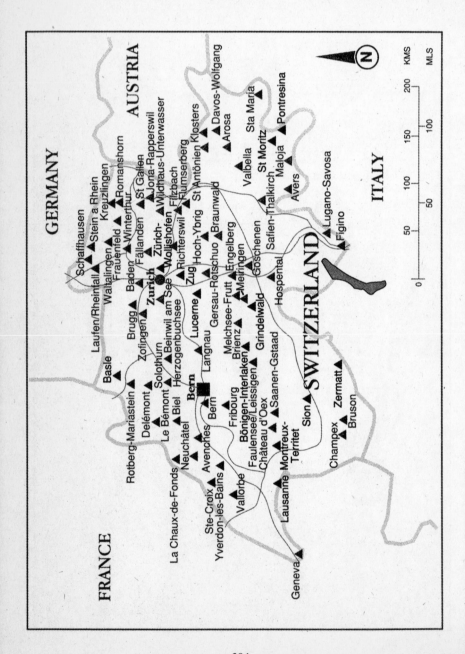

GERMANY

AUSTRIA

FRANCE

ITALY

SWITZERLAND

N

KMS

MLS

0 50 100 150 200

0 50 100

Schaffhausen
Laufen/Rheinfall
Stein a Rhein
Kreuzlingen
Romanshorn
Frauenfeld
Waltalingen
Winterthur
St Gallen
Jona-Rapperswil
Wildhaus-Unterwasser
Fällanden
Filzbach
Baden
Zürich
Zurich
Flumserberg
Richterswil
Wollishofen
St Antönien Klosters
Klosters
Davos-Wolfgang
Arosa
Sta Maria
Pontresina
Valbella
St Moritz
Maloja
Hoch-Ybrig
Gersau-Rotschuo
Braunwald
Zug
Lucerne
Engelberg
Safien-Thalkirch
Avers
Göschenen
Schenen
Lugano-Savosa
Figino
Hospental
Brugg
Zofingen
Beinwil am See
Herzogenbuchsee
Langnau
Melchsee-Frutt
Meiringen
Brienz
Grindelwald
Solothurn
Le Bémont
Biel
Bern
Bern
Basle
Delémont
Rotberg-Mariastein
Neuchâtel
Fribourg
Bönigen-Interlaken
Faulensee/Leissigen
Saanen-Gstaad
Sion
Zermatt
Champex
Bruson
Château d'Oex
La Chaux-de-Fonds
Ste-Croix
Yverdon-les-Bains
Vallorbe
Avenches
Lausanne
Montreux-Territet
Geneva

SYRIA (No accredited youth hostels)

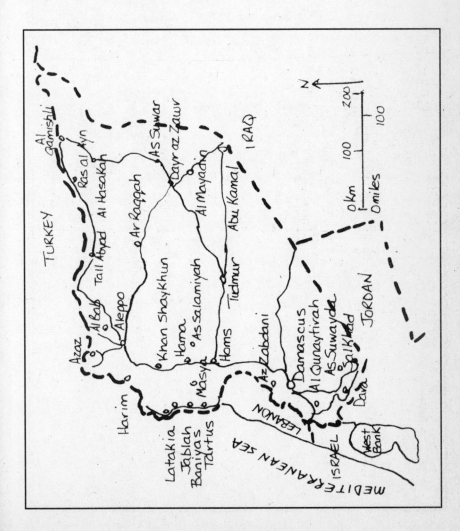

TUNISIA

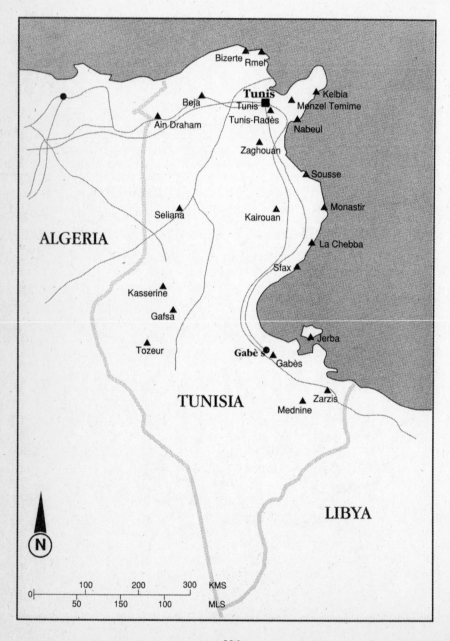

- Bizerte
- Rmel
- Beja
- **Tunis**
- Kelbia
- Tunis
- Menzel Temime
- Ain Draham
- Tunis-Radès
- Nabeul
- Zaghouan
- Sousse
- Seliana
- Kairouan
- Monastir
- La Chebba
- ALGERIA
- Sfax
- Kasserine
- Gafsa
- Jerba
- Tozeur
- **Gabès**
- Gabès
- TUNISIA
- Zarzis
- Mednine
- LIBYA

N

| 100 | 200 | 300 | KMS |
| 50 | 150 | 100 | MLS |

0

TURKEY (3 accredited youth hostels in Istanbul)

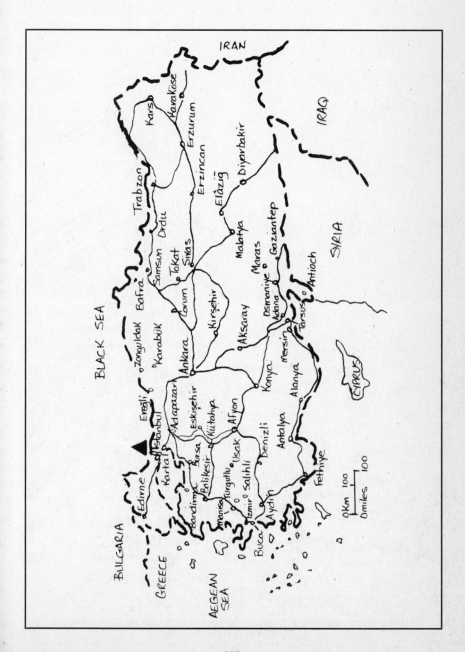

▲ The triangles indicate the location of the youth hostels

AUSTRIA

SALZBURG - Jugendgastehaus

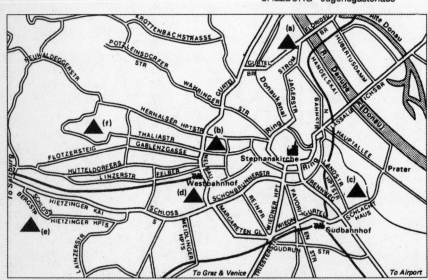

VIENNA - (a) Jugendgastehaus, (b) Myrthengasse, (c) Lechnerstrasse, (d) Ruthensteiner,
(e) Stadt Wien, (f) Wilhelminenberg

BELGIUM

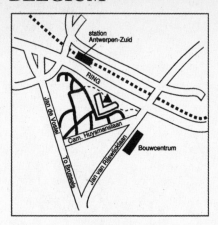

ANTWERPEN

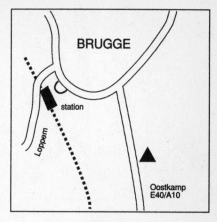

BRUGGE

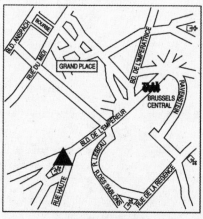

BRUSSELS - Bruegel

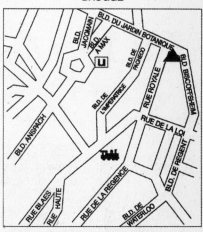

BRUSSELS - Jacques Brel

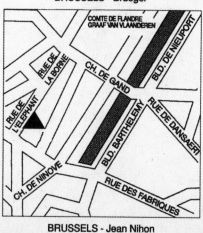

BRUSSELS - Jean Nihon

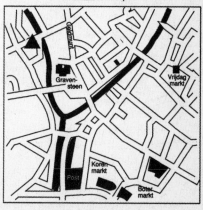

GENT

BULGARIA

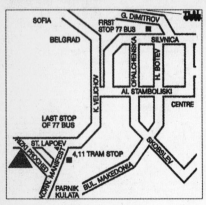

SOFIA - "Tourist"

CYPRUS

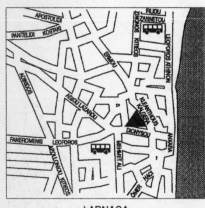

LARNACA

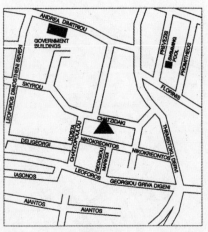

NICOSIA

400

CZECH REPUBLIC

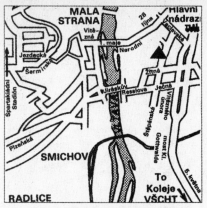

PRAHA - CKM Juniorhotel

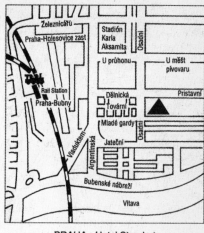

PRAHA - Hotel Standart

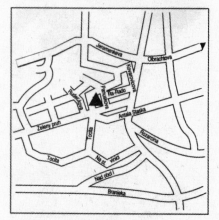

PRAHA -Hotel Beta

DENMARK

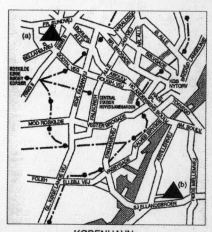

KØBENHAVN -
(a) "Bellahøj", (b) Amager

EGYPT

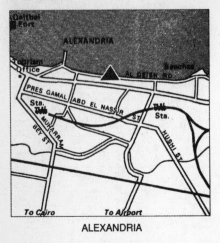

ALEXANDRIA

CAIRO

ENGLAND

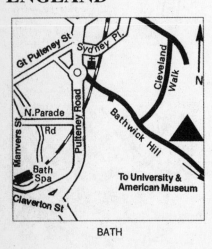

BATH

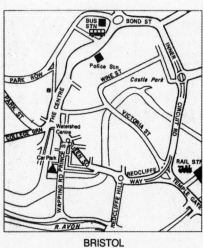

BRISTOL

ENGLAND

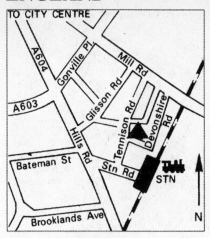

CAMBRIDGE

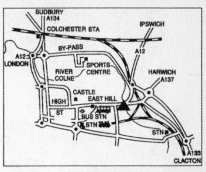

COLCHESTER

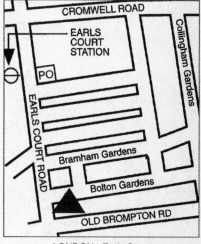

LONDON - Earls Court

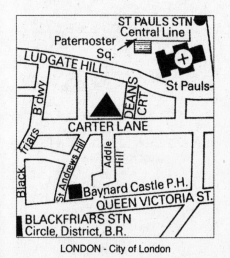

LONDON - City of London

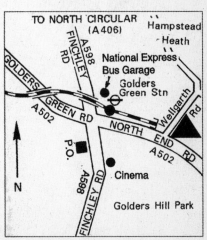

LONDON - Hampstead Heath

ENGLAND

LONDON - Highgate

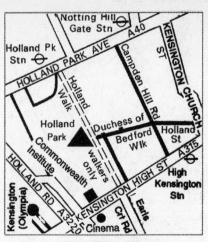

LONDON - Holland House

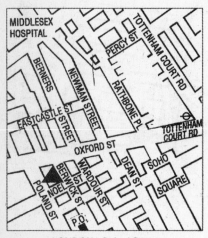

LONDON - Oxford Street

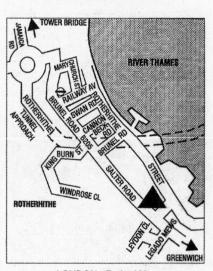

LONDON - Rotherhithe

ENGLAND

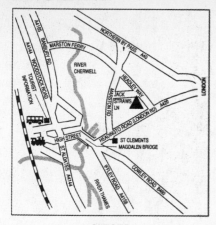

OXFORD

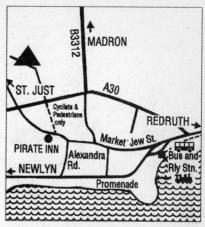

PENZANCE

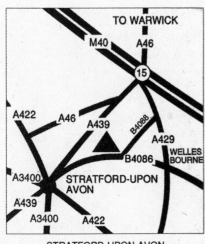

STRATFORD-UPON-AVON

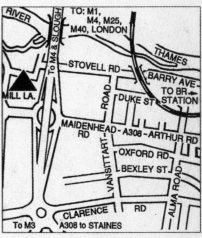

WINDSOR

405

ENGLAND

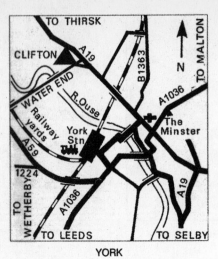

YORK

FINLAND

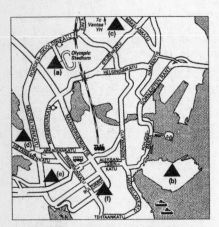

HELSINKI - (a) Stadium, (b) Eurohostel,
(c) Vantaa, (d) Academica,
(e) Satakuntatalo, (f) Erottajanpuisto

406

FRANCE

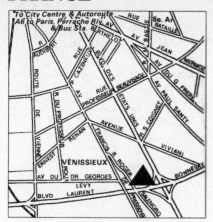

LYON - Vénissieux

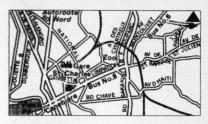

MARSEILLE - Château de Bois-Luzy

MARSEILLE - Bonneveine

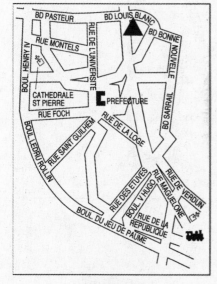

MONTPELLIER

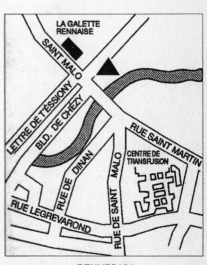

RENNES YH

FRANCE

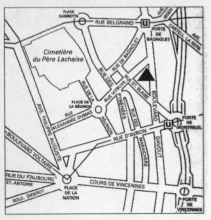

PARIS - Le D'Artagnan

PARIS - Jules Ferry

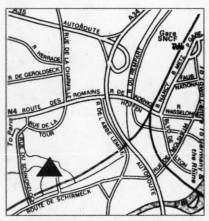

STRASBOURG - René Cassin

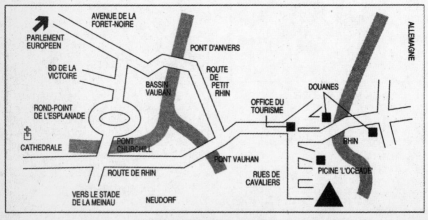

STRASBOURG - Parc du Rhin

408

GERMANY

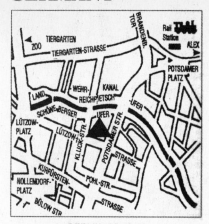

BERLIN - Kluckstr

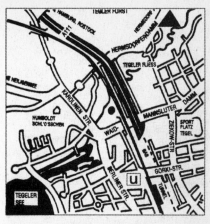

BERLIN - Ernst Reuter

BERLIN - YGH am Wannsee

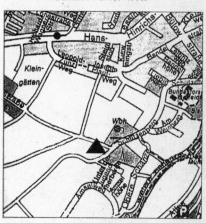

DETMOLD

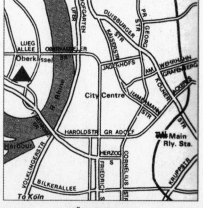

DÜSSELDORF

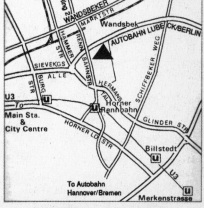

HAMBURG - Horner Rennbahn

GERMANY

HAMBURG - Auf dem Stintfang

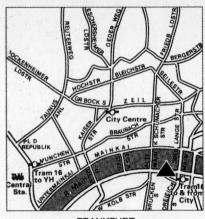

FRANKFURT

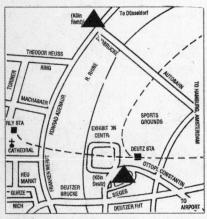

KÖLN - DEUTZ & KÖLN - RIEHL (COLOGNE)

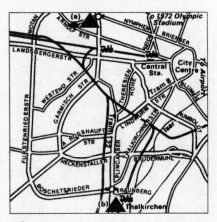

MÜNCHEN - (a) Neuhausen JH, (b) Thalkirchen

HUNGARY

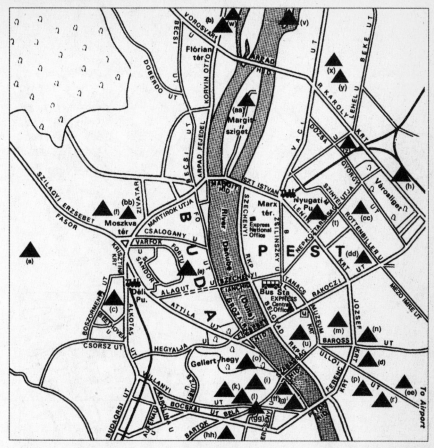

BUDAPEST -
(a) Csillebérc Gyermek, (b) Lidó, (c) Express, (d) Bakfark, (e) Donáti, (f) Felvinci, (g) Universitas,
(h) Zugló, (k) Rózsa, (l) Landler, (m) Kinizsi, (n) Ráday, (o) KEK, (p) Sote Balassa, (r) Selye,
(u) Ottó z Viktor, (v) River Club, (w) Touring, (x) Flandria, (y) Ében, (z) Diáksport, (aa) Sirály,
(bb) Bakfark, (cc) Bárczy, (dd) Elm, (ee) Platánus, (ff) Vásárhelyi, (gg) Schönherz, (hh) Góliát

IRELAND (REPUBLIC)

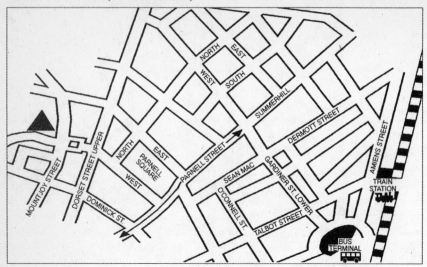

DUBLIN - International YH

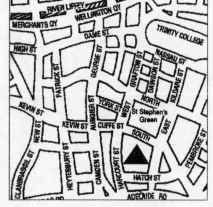

DUBLIN - Harcourt St

IRELAND (NORTHERN)

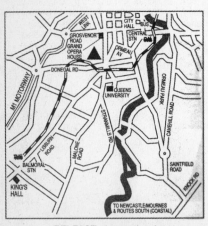

BELFAST - International

412

ITALY

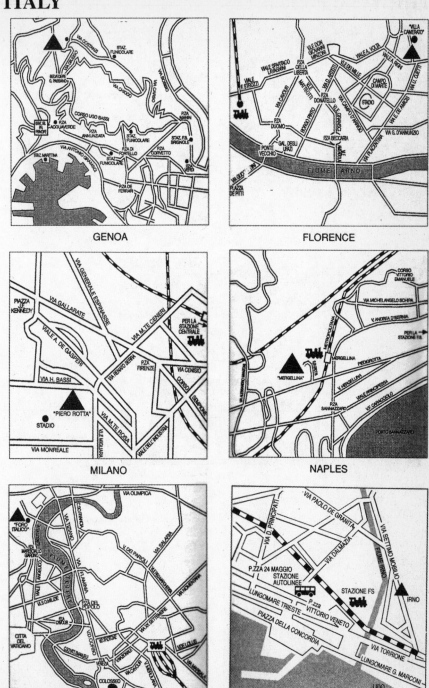

GENOA

FLORENCE

MILANO

NAPLES

ROME

SALERNO

413

ITALY

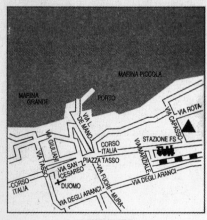

SORRENTO

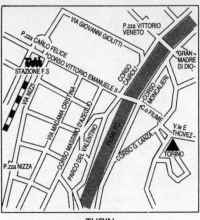

TURIN

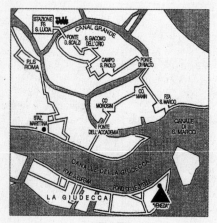

VENICE

414

ISRAEL

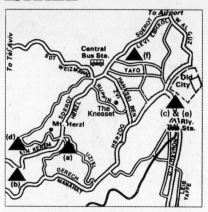

JERUSALEM -
(a) Louise Waterman Wise, (b) Ein Karem,
(c) Bet Bernstein, (d) Jerusalem Forest,
(e) Old City, (f) Hadavidka

TEL AVIV

LUXEMBOURG

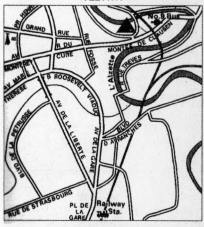

LUXEMBOURG - City

MOROCCO

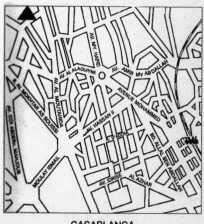

CASABLANCA

415

NETHERLANDS

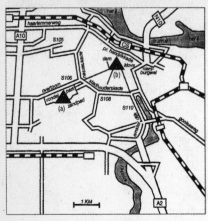

AMSTERDAM -
(a) Vondelpark, (b) Stadsdolen

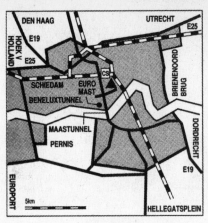

Rotterdam

NORWAY

BERGEN

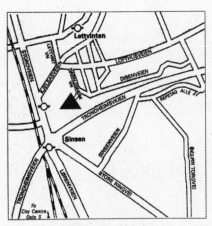

OSLO - Haraldsheim

416

POLAND

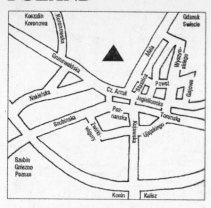

BYDGOSZCZ

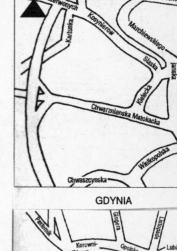

GDYNIA

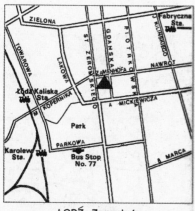

ŁODŹ - Zamenhofa

KRAKÓW - Oleandry, Kosciuszki, Szablowskiego

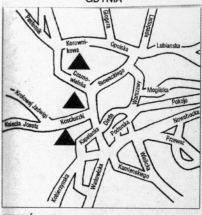

POZNAN - Berwinskiego

Warszawa -
(a) Karolkowa, (b) Smolna, (c) Reytana

417

PORTUGAL

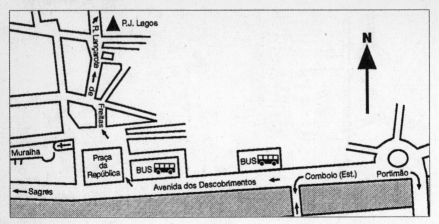

LAGOS

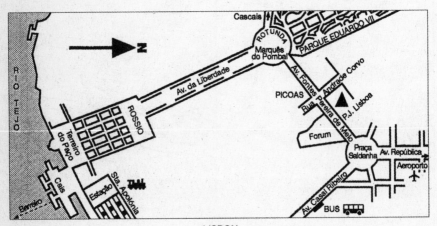

LISBON

SCOTLAND

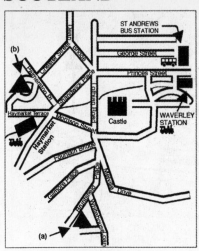

EDINBURGH -
(a) Bruntsfield, (b) Eglington

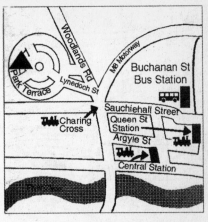

GLASGOW

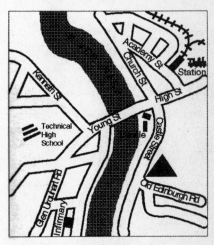

INVERNESS

SPAIN

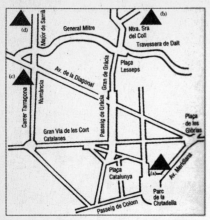

BARCELONA - (a) Hostal de Joves,
(b) Montserrat, (c) Pere Tarrés, (d) Studio

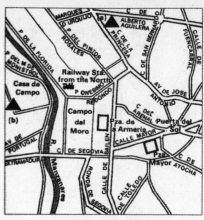

MADRID - (a) Marcenado,
(b) Richard Schirrmann

SWEDEN

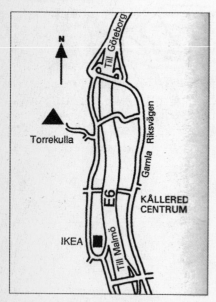

GÖTEBORG - Mölndal

STOCKHOLM - Långholmen

SWEDEN

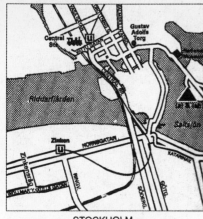

STOCKHOLM -
(a) af Chapman, (b) Skeppsholmen"

STOCKHOLM - Zinken

SWITZERLAND

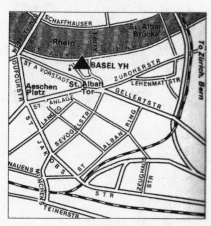

BASLE

BERN

SWITZERLAND

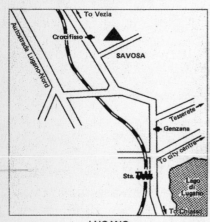

GENÈVE

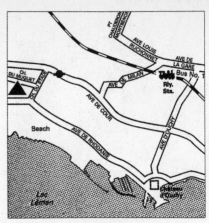

LAUSANNE

LUGANO

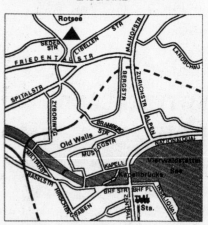

LUCERNE

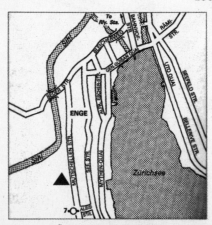

ZÜRICH - WOLLISHOFEN

TUNISIA

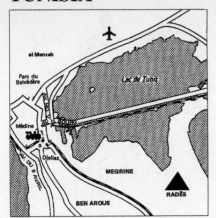

TUNIS - Radès